MACHIAVELLI'S VIRTUE

MACH

HARVEY C.
MANSFIELD

AVELLI'S
VIRTUE

THE UNIVERSITY OF CHICAGO PRESS
CHICAGO & LONDON

HARVEY C. MANSFIELD is the William R. Kenan Jr. Professor of Government at Harvard University.

The University of Chicago Press, Chicago 60637
The University of Chicago Press, Ltd., London
© 1996 by The University of Chicago
All rights reserved. Published 1996
Printed in the United States of America
05 04 03 02 01 00 99 98 97 96    1 2 3 4 5

ISBN: 0-226-50368-2 (cloth)

Library of Congress Cataloging-in-Publication Data

Mansfield, Harvey Claflin, 1932–
Machiavelli's virtue / Harvey C. Mansfield.
p.    cm.
Includes bibliographical references and index.
1. Machiavelli, Niccolò, 1469–1527—Contributions in political
science.  2. Machiavelli, Niccolò, 1469–1527—Ethics.  I. Title.
JC143.M4M355  1995
320.1′092—dc20                                        95-24115
                                                          CIP

CONTENTS

In both my documentation and parenthetical text references, page numbers citing the works of Niccolò Machiavelli (NM) refer to his *Tutte le opere,* ed. Mario Casella and Guido Mazzoni (Florence: G. Barbera, 1969). His works are abbreviated as follows:

*AW*   *Art of War*

  *D*   *Discourses on Livy*

*FH*   *Florentine Histories*

  *P*   *The Prince*

All translations are my own.

M achiavelli as the principal character in his own thought: that is the theme of this collection of articles and essays. The articles are presented in formal dress, supported by footnotes, and the essays were written for occasions when the textual proof of one's statements is not expected or desired, and when arguing with authority is otiose. All begin from or come to Machiavelli's "strange suggestion that he was a prince." In describing princes, which he does in all his writings and not only in his most famous book, called *The Prince,* Machiavelli was explaining himself and his undertaking.

That "strange suggestion" is distinctive, but it is not original with me. It can be found in Leo Strauss's *Thoughts on Machiavelli,* published in 1958, a work whose reception is related in chapter 9. I have followed out Strauss's general suggestion and some of the many, many specific points contained in that marvelous book.

Strauss combined two opposite reactions to Machiavelli's work. The anti-Machiavellians, who after the publication of Machiavelli's major works (posthumously, in 1531) sprang up angrily to defend morality and religion in politics, saw well enough that Machiavelli was the first philosopher not merely to lack respect for the just, the noble, and the sacred or even to *show* his lack of respect—but actually to *advise* all others to act without respect. Modern philosophers following Machiavelli, such as Bacon, Spinoza, Montesquieu, and Rousseau, showing regard like Machiavelli himself for the power of moral outrage, cautiously took notice of his responsibility for initiating the escape of philosophy, and thereafter society, from the superintendence of Christianity. But Strauss was the first to argue the point in detail while never losing sight of the question raised by Machiavelli's immoralities and blasphemies.

Strauss's book is open to the excitement of modernity at its origin and to the indignation of those who defend the tradition. It does justice to both. Most Machiavelli scholars of our time care for neither: they are not sufficiently impressed by Machiavelli's innovation, and they excuse him for his immorality. They do not appreciate his innovation because, following him unconsciously, they excuse his immorality; and they excuse that because they do not see how far his innovation extends. They do not think that Machiavelli poses a question for us today. In this book I have tried to keep both sides of the coin in view—not an easy task, since indignation blinds understanding and understanding tends to dissipate indignation.

When I say that Machiavelli is the principal character in his own thought, I do not mean to give him a postmodern gloss or a deconstruction. I do not mind if some are attracted to the self-referential character of his thought because it is fashionable to treat great thinkers as betraying themselves. But they should understand that Machiavelli will reveal himself only to those willing to listen to him, that is, to read his books attentively and even submissively. If they wish to find Machiavelli the prince, they must consider his *intention*. When Machiavelli speaks of his undertaking as an enterprise (*la mia impresa*), he does not refer to the horizon that marks the daily limits of his conventional thoughts or to a self-created Nietzschean perspective that he means to impose on us. His undertaking refers to what, in view of the truth about his situation, he means to *do*. His situation is the weakness of modern times, for which he has a political, not an aesthetic, remedy. The remedy is a great revolution in thought, to be followed by great changes in society. Since Machiavelli is mortal and cannot be everywhere even while he is alive, he will act through his books. He will rule from afar, although in a sense he will live as prince in the countries he conquers. He is not interested in, let alone preoccupied by, a job for himself. He is not primarily interested in saving Florence or in unifying Italy. He wants to defend "the world" against those who have caused it to become weak. Since he cannot rule directly, he will be the mastermind behind the operation, mastering future generations through his mind.

Machiavelli is a philosopher but not merely a contemplative one. He does not stop at observing, nor is he satisfied to indulge himself in wishing. It is true that he writes as an observer of ancient and modern "examples," frequently introduced or concluded with savory judgments from the observer—the Machiavellisms for which he is famous. But at another level he is telling the reader how he, Machiavelli, will manage his campaigns, conquer his enemies, or treat his captains. For he is at war like the princes he describes, except that he does not hold arms; he is "unarmed." Or is he? Machiavelli has before his eyes the war always being fought by the soldiers of the cross and their army, the Church. Perhaps he can learn something from them of the method of propaganda, of conquering men's minds without capturing their cities. Perhaps he can learn from the ministers of modern weakness, who are, after all, not entirely weak. Perhaps the unarmed prophet whom he condemns can be, not just in a sense but ultimately and truly, armed and potent. Machiavelli cites the example of Savonarola, who, like all unarmed prophets, came to ruin (*P* 6). But did not Savonarola speak in his sermons of "Captain Christ" at the head of his armies?[1]

All of Machiavelli's writings, and every paragraph of them, have to be examined for their application to his own enterprise. In one instance, a chapter in *The Prince* (*P* 22) on "those whom princes have as secretaries," the convergence between Machiavelli's observations and his own state becomes almost obvious. (The way I used *state* in the previous sentence, as a realm of which some person or persons hold mastery, is explained in chapter 12.) In the body of the chapter, the former Florentine secretary discusses the relationship between a prince and his "minister," not secretary; and he gives just one example—that of a minister with more brain than the prince. How can a prince in this delicate situation trust his minister? How can he avoid being deceived? Machiavelli supplies an infallible rule for deciding whom to trust that is in fact very deceptive. He says that a prince should take care that a minister thinks more of him than of himself, and that he should do this by loading him with honors, wealth, and burdens so that he does not desire change.

Machiavelli's advice both denies and presupposes that the minister thinks of himself. It makes sense only when applied to Machiavelli, who is both minister and prince. As minister he advises princes and works on their behalf, but since he has the kind of brain that "understands by itself," without others' aid, he also directs them when he helps them. As minister, he thinks more of what is useful to princes than they do; as prince, he allows them, as his ministers, to be loaded with the world's honors, wealth, and burdens. The ordinary princes accept Machiavelli's advice because they can see it is to their advantage. They have no idea that they are in fact ministers to Machiavelli and that he rules them as their extraordinary prince.

In entering the text so briefly, I have only begun to explore the intricate ironies of one of Machiavelli's chapters. Machiavelli believed that he had found a way to get around the stupidity of the powerful, that his books would, so to speak, force themselves on princes and would be read and received by resisting minds. Princes would learn to welcome a message that accords with their instincts and frees them from their inhibitions. To have written a book that is in the reader's interest, whatever the level of his brain, is to have written a book that has to be read, that is an instrument of rule: every author's dream of glory, Machiavelli would say. Only Machiavelli has achieved such glory, and only he can ever achieve it. The philosophers who follow him can only imitate him; he is the sole new prince above all others—*il maestro di color che fanno*—smiling over the deeds of those whom he has made his ministers. His glory will not be generally recognized either by princes or peoples. Only the most competent will see him for what he was—to which we may add the greater number in our day who have been taught by Machiavelli's successors to practice a rather easier liberation from morality than the one recommended by the master.

I do not claim for this book any part of Machiavelli's irresistibility. I have to make my way on my knees. I can offer as further inducement these subsidiary themes to the main point, which are not to be found in other books on Machiavelli: the importance of the sect; the character of Machiavelli's political science; and a critique of the classical republican interpretation of Machiavelli.

In the *Discourses on Livy,* Machiavelli says that the men most praised are those who have been founders, "heads and orderers," of religions; they are put ahead of those who have founded republics or kingdoms (*D* I 10). But religion considered politically, as does Machiavelli, is a sect (*setta*), a party of followers. Founders of sects are praised more than founders of states because religion makes claims to men's loyalties that go above and across political boundaries. This is true especially of the modern, universal religions. To understand them as sects, however, is to cut them down to size as worldly powers that transcend particular states but do not succeed in becoming universal. This is *Machiavelli's* deconstruction.

If Machiavelli as prince wants to reform particular states, he needs to change the climate of opinion in which they operate; he needs to become the founder of a new sect in order to reform or replace the Christian sect. He cannot become a new prince, making everything anew—for the essential prince is a new prince—without gaining control over religion. So Machiavelli does not confine his attention to the self-sufficient politics of the classical regime but turns also to the broader religious-political community of the sect. That is the meaning of the distinction he introduces at the beginning of the *Discourses on Livy* and the *Florentine Histories* between domestic and foreign affairs; the modern regime is sustained, and threatened, by the influence of a universal opinion that is "foreign" to it. Its domestic and foreign affairs are inevitably, inextricably, entangled with each other.

Here, in Machiavelli's reaction to his situation, is the origin of modern "ideological politics," the politics of human rights that lays a claim of universal justice, rather than salvation, against all regimes. But of course Machiavelli does not go so far. Anxious to revive the virtue that brings success in politics, he wants to keep states in conflict, both domestic and foreign, so as to sustain the demand for virtue. For the sake of virtue as he understands it, he stops short of universal political solutions and retains the exclusivity, if not the self-sufficiency, of the classical regime. But with his concern for the sect, he takes a step toward the more modern politics that is infused with universal and moral political opinion addressing the good of men as human beings rather than subjects or citizens.

I consider Machiavelli to have been the master of politics, when politics is understood as aiming to win with no reference to a standard above politics. To *master* means to dominate, and as I have intimated, Machiavelli intended to become a kind of tyrant over mankind by imposing a remedy that only the wisest of men—if they—would consent to. But a master is also a teacher, and so is Machiavelli. He has a new political science that deserves to be taken seriously as an attempt at the true political science, as the best understanding of the nature of politics. In this book I do not adopt the historicist view that Machiavelli's thought was useful only in its time or for what it prepared (much as it did prepare). Those who take that view do not have a sufficient motive to study Machiavelli's political science, since they believe it to be inadequate before they begin.

I have tried to bring to light what historicism ignores and to present Machiavelli's political science on its merits. To see its merits requires some reference to history, not so much to events as to the history of political science. The peculiar character of Machiavelli's political science emerges only by contrast to Aristotle's, which was, with humanist and scholastic variations, the dominant political science of Machiavelli's time. And so (in chapters 1, 3, 4, 10, 11, 12, and 13) I keep coming back to Aristotle, taking little notice of the intermediaries between him and Machiavelli. In the great dispute between Machiavelli and Aristotle, two philosophers who sought, in Machiavelli's phrase, "to acquire the world," I make out a distinction between direct and indirect government. Direct government, that of Aristotle's regime, is essentially as it appears, and it publicly tells the world who rules. In Machiavelli's indirect government the rulers do not appear but try to hide themselves; and since princes of some kind always rule, it is defined not by *who* rules but by *how* they rule. That distinction is necessary to the understanding of liberal, constitutional government, which borrows from both, but especially, and surreptitiously, from Machiavelli. Again, we must not assume the superiority of our way, but the special character of constitutionalism, combining Aristotle's formalism with Machiavelli's realism, comes into view in the comparison. To us, Machiavelli contributes a clear view of politics unobstructed by abstract claims of equality and unreasonable demands for justice.

Since I believe that Machiavelli's political science presents a contrast to Aristotle's, I do not think much of the scholarly current that sees Machiavelli as a "classical republican" not much different from Aristotle. Aristotle's republic lived by partisan belief, defining itself against the alternatives even if it was a mixed regime. He hoped to instruct partisan belief by getting each party to take the other's claims seriously and to reject extremism on both sides. Machiavelli's republic incorporates princes, as we know from his frequent phrase, "the princes of a republic," and Machiavelli mocks the partisan beliefs of princes who do not wish to depend on the people and of republics who reject the name of *king* while accepting the reality.

Machiavelli's political science is in principle hostile to partisan claims, which make inflated professions of good that mislead any politician or observer who takes them seriously. Machiavelli's republic owes nothing to republicanism as an *ism;* since it is not generated or protected by belief, it is not based on education. It has no "ideology" but survives rather by ignoring self-righteous assertions in favor of concealed or unavowed motives.

This is not to say that Machiavelli believed in the efficacy of self-interest as do the bourgeois liberals of our day. He put forward virtue, his own virtue. The often unconcealed motive of the classical republican interpretation in our day is to find a way simultaneously to maintain liberal sentiments and to despise the bourgeoisie, without falling into Marxism. Its proponents understand Machiavelli's virtue admiringly as self-sacrifice for the common good of the republic. That it is not. The best one could say on behalf of their interpretation is that, for Machiavelli, virtuous princes must learn to take account, and take advantage, of those who *believe* that virtue is self-sacrifice. By doing so they will gain greater glory, which is not a self-sacrifice even though it does not come to the lazy.

Glory is a reward of bold ambition, prudence, and artfulness, the reverse of bourgeois honesty. But it shares the loneliness, if not the regularity, of bourgeois calculation. Machiavelli was no bourgeois, but after he was regularized by modern science—with the possible assistance of that strange construction called the "Protestant Ethic" —his individualism became acceptable in a commercial package. For Machiavelli, the sum of man is not a republican citizen but a prince, and the highest reach of a prince is "to be alone" (*essere solo*), even if that means murder. That Machiavelli is somehow nonetheless favorable to republics is a problem—for him and for us—that cannot be solved by wishful thinking. What we find appealing in his thought is bound to what we find appalling.

A word needs to be said about the references to Machiavelli's numerology that occasionally appear in the text and notes. I have tried to keep such references discreet for two reasons. First, some scholars are simply not open to the possibility that Machiavelli contrived the frequency of his word usage or the numbering of chapters or other things to indicate his meaning. They are upset by the very idea of such a practice, and they regard any mention of it as sectarian and unsound, to be treated with embarrassed silence or, if necessary,

ridicule. In part they are shocked that a great author such as Machiavelli might be insincere, and that he might undemocratically reserve
his choicest thought for a few of his readers. In part, too, these
scholars are uncomfortable with the notion that great authors might
practice reserve, because it suggests that the ideas they hold might
be theirs rather than the product of their time.

To such doubts I reply mildly that the regularities do exist, and
I await an alternative explanation. Some other students may try
too eagerly to build everything on Machiavelli's numerology. Their
enthusiasm needs to be dampened, and this is the second reason for
discretion. Machiavelli's numerology should be used only to support
or confirm an interpretation, not to construct one. Its principal value
is to convey suggestions. As a whole, it shows that something funny
is going on: that Machiavelli is speaking on two levels and that he
has something to reveal that he also wants to conceal. Those who
deny that fact have to deny every instance of it, because just one
example of hidden communication—as of life on another planet—is
enough to show that it's there.

I should add that, besides numerology, Machiavelli uses partial
and deliberately inaccurate quotation, as well as other deliberate
errors (see *D* III 48), to say something extra. For Machiavelli himself,
hidden communication is a practice one would expect. If he is himself a prince, but a minister or mastermind behind the scenes, then
he must exercise his indirect government by speaking indirectly. His
princes—the political men he advises—must not suspect that they
are his ministers and must continue to believe that he is their minister. His struggle to control their minds and to establish his own new
sect must be carried on outside their cognizance, lest they misunder-
stand him as another Savonarola trying to change the world and
cramp their liberty.

Since the chapters of this book were written for separate occasions, some repetitions occur. I have left most of them as they were
because it seems to me that the same example can be instructive in
different contexts. Each chapter is in its way about all of Machiavelli, and Machiavelli, even in what he ignores, is a teacher of the
whole human situation.

ONE

# MACHIAVELLI
# THE
# PRINCE

How can an author be a prince? How can the author of *The Prince* be considered one among the many princes he describes? An author and a prince seem quite distinct. The one leads a soft, retired life thinking of intangibles and invisibles—as sheltered an existence as he can make it; the other lives through heat and cold, luxury and privation, dealing with facts, appearance, and realities. As a result, the author, self-detached, thinks of the whole beyond himself; the prince thinks of himself and in doing so makes everything else pertain to his advantage.

In the philosophical tradition the distinction is between the philosophical or contemplative life and the practical life. Plato put it most starkly in the image of the cave in the *Republic,* in which those in society, including rulers and ruled, are contrasted with the philosophers who have access to the sun outside. Aristotle made the same point more soberly with his distinction between moral and intellectual virtue. Machiavelli dismisses that distinction. The philosopher's virtue is not in thought or speech apart from deeds and more perfect or more self-sufficient. His truth is the *effectual truth,* the truth shown in the outcome of his thought. The truth of words is in the result they produce or, more likely, fail to produce. Deeds are sovereign: when confronted by a necessity, Machiavelli advises, do not worry about justice, but act and the words to justify your action will come to you afterward.

The effectual truth of effectual truth thus seems to eliminate the power of ideas; words respond to deeds, not deeds to words. With such a notion of virtue, Machiavelli seems to accommodate the evil deeds of Renaissance princes. Far from being a prince himself, he seems to efface himself from politics and to leave the field to its practitioners. In accordance with this impression, Machiavelli offers his "homage" (*servitù*) to Lorenzo de' Medici in the dedicatory letter of *The Prince,* and gives the impression that he composed that work, the most famous book on politics ever written, to gain employment with a third-rate prince ruling in the city of Urbino.

Against that impression we have the unforgettable scene described in Machiavelli's letter of December 10, 1513, in which he enters "the ancient courts of ancient men" and feeds "on the food that is mine alone." Here he proudly asserts the distinction between the philosophers and "the vulgar" and maintains the continuity of the tradition of philosophy from ancients to moderns. Nonetheless, in following the effectual truth, he says he departs "from the orders of others" who construct imaginary principalities and republics (*P* 15)—surely the very ancient authors with whom he converses. His own writing, moreover, is as far as can be from the stale practice of rationalization. He does not serve princes by supplying platitudes for their speeches, like speechwriters in our day. How can it be that Machiavelli's ideas escape his apparent dismissal of the power of ideas? How, again, given his understanding of an author's virtue, can this author consider himself a prince?

Machiavelli says that armed prophets have always conquered and unarmed ones have come to ruin (*P* 6). His example of the latter, Savonarola, makes us think of the counterexample of Christ, who did not come to ruin but in a sense conquered a large portion of the world. To solve the puzzle, we have to consider what it means to be *armed*. In discussing the art of war, Machiavelli says, apparently with some exaggeration, that this is "the only art which is of concern to one who commands" (*P* 14). But he explains the exaggeration by adding that without the art, princes will lose their states, but with it, you can acquire one.

So, to be *armed* means to have the art of war, a feat of study and intellect rather than of arms. In this view Christ was armed with a doctrine and with the means of propaganda (in the original sense). Christ is also, of course, an unarmed prophet, in contrast to Moses and Mohammed, because neither He nor His Church carries weapons. They depend on others to wield the instruments of earthly conquest and punishment. Machiavelli is in a similar position to that of his main enemy. He, too, depends on princes to acquire states and to govern them. He is the prince of a principality. But since the principality is composed of princes who rival one another, his principality can be understood as a republic consisting of many states, like the Christian republic. His domain is the only state that is neither principality nor republic but both (*P* 1).

Machiavelli's art of war is supported by a new anti-Christian presumption against anything above politics, whether divine or secular, that might deflect politics from earthly acquisition. Neither the city of God of Christianity nor the best regime of the classical tradition will be allowed to interfere. To formulate and to propagate the new presumption, Machiavelli must be prophet and sect-maker as well as prince and founder of a republic. All his distinctions and dichotomies, having been made by him, refer back to him and are brought together in him.

Machiavelli's virtue is in him before it is distributed to the princes he advises and the peoples he describes. His virtue is broader than anyone else's because it shows how everyone's virtue makes sense in his scheme. In a sense a prince must make his own virtue, but the formal and final causes of his virtue, if not the efficient cause, are in Machiavelli. Machiavelli is sufficiently with his beloved ancients, and against his Christian enemy, to want the attributes of God for himself.

ONE

# MACHIAVELLI'S VIRTUE

Everyone knows that there is something remarkable about Machiavelli's use of the word *virtù*. Almost every book on Machiavelli
discusses *virtù*, and a number of scholarly studies are devoted to
explaining the Machiavellian meaning of that word.[1] It needs explanation because Machiavelli's usage is at first blush both shocking
and inconsistent.

A quick look at the best-known instance of *virtù* in Machiavelli
will introduce the problem that commentators seek to explain. In
the eighth chapter of *The Prince,* Machiavelli considers "those who
have attained a principality through crimes." From his account it
appears not only that the wicked prosper but also that their success
may be, at the least, "accompanied" by *virtù*, or at the most, caused
by *virtù*. Machiavelli's example from ancient times is "Agathocles
the Sicilian," who became "king" of Syracuse (Machiavelli does not
call him "tyrant") while always keeping to a life of crime at every
stage of his career. In considering this criminal Machiavelli says that
"one cannot call it virtue to kill one's citizens, betray one's friends,
to be without faith, without mercy, without religion"—all of which
Agathocles was or did. Yet in the very next sentence Machiavelli,
doing what he said one cannot do, proceeds to speak of the "virtue
of Agathocles."[2] Later he says generally, stating the principle behind
the attribution of virtue to a particular criminal, that a prince must
"not depart from good, when possible, but know how to enter into
evil, when forced by necessity" (*P* 18).

What is one to make of this? Machiavelli seems to deplore the
need for a prince to be evil, and in the next breath to relish the fact.
He alternately shocks his readers and provides relief from the very
shocks he administers: Agathocles has *virtù* but cannot be said to

6

have *virtù*. It is not enough to say that he uses the word in several "senses"[3]; he uses it in two contradictory senses as to whether it includes or excludes evil deeds. What could be more clear, more essential, and more inconsistent than that?

It is no wonder that Machiavelli's translators have difficulty in rendering *virtù*. Sometimes they simply leave it untranslated, as if to isolate it in the sixteenth century, where it cannot affect us today. More often, skirting the question of evil, they use several words referring to amoral qualities, such as *vigor, ingenuity,* or *boldness,* which treat *virtù* technically, as the means to an end. Both ways of translating the word betray unease with the question of evil: one can treat it historically as a concern of the Renaissance or scientifically as a description of behavior on which the observer passes no judgment. But these are evasions unauthorized by Machiavelli. He does not confine his view to his own time, nor does he respect the conventional opinions of that time; and he frequently speaks of *virtù* transhistorically, as pertaining to the nature of man.[4] He also passes judgment himself on the necessity of evil for *virtù,* though he does so inconsistently. And he seems aware, as many today are not, that to speak amorally in a moral context is to give a moral lesson nonetheless, and not one favorable to morality. For when Machiavelli advises a tyrant on how best to proceed—first become friendly to the people so as to bring down the nobles, then betray the people (*D* I 40)—he encourages tyranny and does not merely describe it. This is all the more true if some men have a natural inclination to tyranny, as seems to be the case according to him; and it is nonetheless true if all government, not merely that traditionally or conventionally called "tyranny," can be understood as oppressive or tyrannical, as he also seems to believe.[5]

Thus the difficulty of translators in rendering *virtù* reflects a more general squeamishness not confined to them, a reluctance to face the problem of evil. After all, the translators translate for us, and in any case their attitude can be found among those who read Machiavelli in the original. We do not want to join the pack of hounds—the anti-Machiavellians—who chased the fox when he first appeared; that seems too simple and unsophisticated, as well as futile, in our time. Yet we are also uneasily aware that Machiavelli was, to say the least, present at the origin of a revolution in morality, which can be defined loosely in our terms as a change from virtue protected by religion to self-interest justified by secularism. The revolution is known to us, again using our word, as "modernity." Our involvement in modernity makes us skeptical of claims of virtue at the same time that it stirs a certain guilt in us for trying to live without virtue. So we would rather not use the word, and Machiavelli's use of it makes us uncomfortable.

To get to the bottom of our discomfort—I do not promise to allay it—it is necessary to face this question squarely: Do human necessities require us to compromise with evil? That is the question of Machiavelli's *virtù*. To facilitate the inquiry, I shall speak of Machiavelli's virtue because the literal translation helps to preserve our sense of shock that someone might use that word to describe the misdeeds of Agathocles, for example. Moral shock does not often provide a motive for calm investigation, rather the reverse; but in our situation the danger that we might regenerate the uncomprehending moral indignation of the early anti-Machiavellians is minimal. We moderns are all too cool, and we need a spark to sustain our interest in a question that used to stir serious passion.

There is another reason for speaking of Machiavelli's virtue, and that is to think about *his* virtue, not merely his *notion* of virtue. If Machiavelli was present at the origin of modernity, in what capacity was he there—as reporter, participant, leader, or perhaps even founder? To investigate these possibilities one must begin with the last one, the most ambitious and the one that accords with his promise at the beginning of the *Discourses on Livy* to work things he believes will bring "common benefit to each" (*D* I pr). It is hard to imagine a broader ambition for a human being, as a human being, than this. But how could a new notion of virtue cooperating or compromising with evil benefit everyone? How could a new readiness to do evil bring good? How could the teacher of such virtue in a new sense be virtuous himself in an old sense? With these questions we have already glimpsed a reason for Machiavelli's inconsistent declarations on virtue. Machiavelli's own virtue, we shall see, is the key to the puzzle of his notion of virtue.

## MAN OF THE RENAISSANCE

We may appropriately begin our inquiry from Machiavelli's beginning: Machiavelli presents his notion of virtue as a revival of ancient virtue (*antica virtù*). He notes at the start of the *Discourses on Livy* that much honor is attributed in his time to antiquity, especially to the arts, and he complains that the "most virtuous works" of the ancients in politics are rather admired than imitated, and "of that ancient virtue no sign has remained with us" (*D* I pr). And again at the start of Book II, he speaks of the virtue that ruled at the time of the ancient Romans[6] by contrast to the vice that rules now (*D* II pr). The revival of ancient virtue has been said to be the theme of the *Discourses*.[7] But it also appears in the *Florentine Histories* as a standard with which Machiavelli condemns his contemporaries, when he speaks disparagingly of the admiration Italy offers to "every mediocre captain in whom any shadow of ancient virtue might be reborn" (*FH* I 39; see IV 12, V 1). In the *Art of War* (III 312b) and in Machiavelli's comedy *Mandragola* (Prol., 694a), "ancient virtue" is used as a spur to his contemporaries. Of his major works only *The Prince* does not contain the phrase.[8]

Who are the "ancients" whose virtue is to be revived? Twice, in the *Discourses*, Machiavelli uses the phrase in a general sense, once speaking of the intent of King Agis of Sparta to return that city to its ancient virtue (*D* I 9), another time referring to the ancient virtue to be found at the beginning of any republic (*D* III 22). All other times, however, he seems to have in mind the particular ancestors of the modern world, *our* ancients. And of these he means the Romans rather than the Greeks. In *The Prince* he refers to the "virtue and prudence" of the Romans as opposed to the "wise men of our times" (*P* 3); and in the *Discourses* he uses the phrase "Roman virtue" four times (*D* I 15, II 2, 8, 19), and "virtue of the Roman people" once (in the negative, *D* II 1). He never says "Greek virtue," or "Christian virtue."[9] The ancients he means are the Romans, they who had "countless most virtuous princes" (*D* I 20).

On the basis of his desire for a revival of ancient virtue, Machiavelli is commonly regarded as a man of the Renaissance. It would not be too much to say, indeed, that he is considered *the* man of the Renaissance. Jacob Burckhardt's classic interpretation, featuring the state as a work of art and a morality of individualism, would be lost without Machiavelli.[10] But does Machiavelli truly belong to the Renaissance?

Evil Machiavellian characters abound in the Renaissance, but Machiavelli, it appears, is the only writer who excuses them, nay urges them on. He is the one who says of Cesare Borgia: "I do not know what better teaching I could give to a new prince than the example of his actions" (P 7). Macaulay and Lord Acton sought to excuse Machiavelli's teaching by referring to the criminality and corruption of his time, as if Machiavelli had learned his immorality by living in a bad neighborhood.[11] But other authors of his time are not in need of such an excuse, which in any case does him little honor. Indeed, it is Machiavelli who deserves the honor of having invented that excuse. He was the first to teach openly and without apology that morality should be interpreted "according to the times" so that if the times are corrupt, one is compelled to live and behave corruptly and therefore morally excused for doing so. Machiavelli's reaction to his own time is mostly hostile and only partly approving. He condemns the princes of his day for the weakness that is manifest to all in the power and corruption of the Church and the division of Italy (P 11, 12, 26; FH I 39; D I pr, II 2, III 1). But he is willing to use the immorality of his contemporaries as a resource to remedy their weakness: do not despair! You too can sink as low as a Borgia.[12] Insofar, then, as Renaissance Italy represents excusable immorality to us, we should begin to weigh the possibility that the Renaissance belongs to Machiavelli more than he to it. The one who excuses evil is above those who commit it (D I 9).

Renaissance means "rebirth," an event both old and new. The rebirth of ancient virtue will change the thoughts and habits of the age. This combination of old and new was understood by all thoughtful participants in the movement now called "Renaissance." But Machiavelli differs in this regard too. For him, the novelty of a rebirth is not only accepted but even welcomed. In the very place where he complains that no sign of ancient virtue remains with us (D I pr) he compares himself to the explorers of "unknown waters and lands" in his time and announces a perilous discovery of his own of "new modes and orders." These new modes and orders, we learn (D III 1, 22), will need themselves to be renewed periodically. Similarly, in The Prince the hereditary prince who rules in customary ways (P 2) is soon removed from the scene by Machiavelli and replaced by the "new prince" whose virtue is to make a principality altogether new. Newness, for Machiavelli, has a value of its own that makes even the best institution dubious if it has become routine.[13] The excellence of the Roman political system ("constitution" gives it a sense too fixed to capture Machiavelli's meaning) was that it was always able to promote new men and reward innovation (*D* I 1, 60). Machiavelli gives a new positive charge to newness itself in which we can recognize the favor that goes today, or used to go yesterday, to anything "modern." How to make "ancient virtue" consistent with periodic novelty will be a problem for Machiavelli's notion of virtue.

Machiavelli differs further from others in the Renaissance by the emphasis he gives, as we have seen, to *Roman* virtue over Greek. As opposed to "the wise men of our times," we have seen, he calls attention to the "virtue and prudence" of the Romans (*P* 3). Roman virtue is in politics and war; it is not the intellectual or contemplative virtue of philosophy or religion. To revive the virtue of the ancients, for Machiavelli, is to imitate their deeds and works, not to admire beautiful creations or think high thoughts except as a necessary means to the end of imitation. Machiavelli does not suffer from nostalgia for a classic golden age. Those who do prefer Greece to Rome; he prefers Rome for its power to inspire virtuous deeds. He initiates a modern interpretation of Rome that frees it from subordination to Greece. He even tries to cure Rome of the inferiority complex by which its own writers, especially Cicero but also Livy, judge it by standards inherited from Greek philosophy. Machiavelli wants to give Renaissance humanism a hard face: to deflate its esteem for classical rhetoric, to attack its adherence to philosophical tradition, to unsettle its accommodation with Christianity, to refute its belief in the virtues of the classical gentleman, and to remind it of the value and glory of the military.

ANCIENT VIRTUE

One could give a longer account of Machiavelli's selective Renaissance and of the grave difference between his contemporaries' respectful view of ancient virtue and Machiavelli's less deferential version, or better to say, impudent appropriation of the name. Suffice it to say that none of Machiavelli's contemporaries gave the welcome to evil (or anything like it) that we have seen in him. But to understand why Machiavelli should have made this change, and to see his notion of virtue better by contrast, it is necessary to go to the source of ancient virtue. This can be none other than Aristotle. Machiavelli makes just one reference to Aristotle in the *Discourses* (*D* III 26) and none in *The Prince*. Xenophon appears to be his favorite ancient authority in morals, for a reason that will appear (Xenophon suits Machiavelli's design of politicized virtue).[14] But there is no sound reason to doubt Machiavelli's thorough familiarity with Aristotle, and in any case the full extent of Machiavelli's departure from the notion of virtue in the tradition of moral philosophy will become apparent only in comparison with its classic presentation in Aristotle's *Nicomachean Ethics*.

Here, then, is a summary of the *Ethics* as it must have looked to Machiavelli, because these are the salient features that he challenged and refashioned. Aristotle distinguished between moral virtue and intellectual virtue (*NE* 1103a6, 1178a9–10). Moral virtue is a habit, and is not given by nature; intellectual virtue requires a virtuous nature (*NE* 1103a14–26, 1143b6–10, 1144b4). Moral virtue depends on intellectual virtue in several ways but is unaware of this dependence. To persons with moral virtue, moral virtue is "in itself": it is not for the sake of anything outside or beyond itself. A virtuous deed is done for its own sake, for the sake of being virtuous; and such a deed is praised when done for a virtuous reason as opposed to personal advantage (*NE* 1099a7–22, 1115b19–24; cf. Cicero, *De Finibus* II 14.45). Moral virtue is therefore voluntary (*NE* 1109b30–35). From the standpoint of moral virtue, men appear to be the cause of their own actions (*NE* 1112b32–33, 1113b19–22, 1139b4–5). How does one acquire moral virtue? One becomes morally virtuous by being so—by habituation in which one first does the actions and then learns the reasons. Thus there is a "virtuous circle"; the morally virtuous learn from the morally virtuous (*NE* 1105a18–b12). Moral virtue is not inherited, but it is passed on as if it had no beginning.

Then one might ask of what is moral virtue the virtue? Moral virtue is a habit, but the habit of what natural thing or faculty? Aristotle indicates that it is perhaps better not to ask that question. To the morally virtuous, moral virtue appears in the plural as several cardinal virtues, each of which is complete in itself. To be courageous, for example, one does not need any other virtue; like the other virtues, courage stands on its own. A sign of the independence of the virtues is that each is flanked by a vice that is either too much or too little (*NE* 1108b11–1109b27). The virtue is just right; it is a mean and can be identified as such (courage between rashness and timidity). But some explanation is needed, despite the reluctance of the morally virtuous, of how one can choose to do a virtuous act for a virtuous reason. It is needed especially for the use of statesmen and legislators, who aim at making good citizens. The soul is the explanation; so the virtues can be understood as virtues of the soul (*NE* 1102a5–29, 1138b35–1139a3).

Another difficulty arises when it becomes necessary to order the virtues, for example when courage and moderation appear to conflict. Here prudence is needed to order the virtues, thus to guide them. Yet prudence must also be distinguished from an amoral or immoral cleverness that would manipulate the virtues; prudence must be moral (*NE* 1144a6–b24). Thus, it would appear, prudence is both the guide of morality and guided by morality. This difficulty is aggravated in the relationship between moral virtue and politics. Supposing that the legislator can be regarded as an embodiment of prudence, virtue appears in Aristotle's *Politics* first as the *means* to the best (or mixed) regime in Books 4 and 5—guided by prudence— and then as the *end* of the best regime in Books 7 and 8—the guide of prudence. The "in itself" character of moral virtue reasserts itself when moral virtue becomes the end of politics. We humans live, and live together, in order to be virtuous; we do not maintain the virtues merely to live.

## ACQUISITION AND INHERITANCE

For Machiavelli, Aristotle's authoritative statement is wrong on all counts and as a whole. It could not describe ancient virtue because it does not describe virtue. When Aristotle supposes that virtue is for its own sake, he takes human praise of virtue for its reality and essence. For virtue in itself is never seen in deed but only heard in praise. When we praise other human beings, we take aspiration as fact and flatter humanity; praise of others amounts to self-praise. Virtue is never in itself; it must be for the sake of something else; its end is acquisition.

Aristotle had spoken in the *Nicomachean Ethics* of the necessary "equipment" of virtue (*NE* 1099a31–35). To practice the virtues one must have a certain surplus of property so that one's necessities are not always foremost in one's mind. And in the first book of the

*Politics,* he says that the acquisitions of property must be limited by the requirements of virtue both in manner and amount (*Pol* 1257b38–1258a10, 1323b7–10). Neither the sharp practices of acquisition nor the luxury of great wealth favor the virtuous life, and acquisition must be kept in its place as a means to an end precisely because it has a dangerous tendency to become the end. Machiavelli, however, allows that tendency to go as far as it can. At the beginnings of both *The Prince* and the *Discourses on Livy,* he takes up the same question as Aristotle and answers it to the contrary. One can never know how much "equipment" one may need; anyone so foolish as to limit his acquisition in the name of virtue cannot count on sufficient provision by nature or God, as Aristotle does, when his virtue threatens his life or well-being. The distinction that Aristotle drew between mere life and the good life cannot be sustained because the first necessities of human life before civilization continue with undiminished or even increased force into civilized life.[15] What primitive men must do to scratch an existence from nature civilized men must do to keep ahead of their rivals.

A state will go very far wrong if it thinks that a "civil way of living" (*vivere civile*) enables it to escape from necessity into leisure (*ozio*). Leisure, or the alternate translation of laziness, is the corruption, not the condition or situation, of virtue.[16] When speaking of the cyclical change of worldly provinces, Machiavelli says that "virtue gives birth to quiet, quiet to leisure, leisure to disorder, disorder to ruin" (*FH* V l). So much for the goodness of Aristotle's *scholē!* (*NE* 1177b4–27). Machiavelli puts necessity over leisure as the concern of the legislator (*D* I l); asserts that if you aim at peace, leisure will make the republic either effeminate or divided, or both (*D* I 6; II 20, 25); includes the leisurely among the enemies of the human race (*D* I 10); and calls the gentlemen whom he denounces and Aristotle praises "leisurely" (*D* I 55). Christianity is now so enfeebling, Machiavelli judges, because it is being interpreted according to "leisure" and not virtue (*D* II 2), here direct contraries.

In moral terms, one could say that our necessary preoccupation with the conditions of virtue crowds out the possibility of virtue as an end in itself unconcerned with its own conditions. Virtue must become aware of the need for acquiring the equipment it presupposes. Aristotle's moral virtue is blind to its conditions; that is why acquisition is discussed in the *Politics,* not the *Nicomachean Ethics.*

Machiavelli's notion of virtue, more self-aware than Aristotle's, replaces confidence in the kindness of nature or God with a more secure base in necessity. It is necessary for humans to trust in necessity; necessity is the only trust that fully reflects one's inability to trust. Necessity means the necessity to acquire; so men cognizant of necessity must devote themselves to acquisition. The new, solid base beneath virtue does not leave virtue as it was but transforms it. The most obvious sign of change is Machiavelli's treatment of liberality, the first of the moral virtues discussed in *The Prince* (*P* 16). Liberality—the most congenial of virtues and the opposite of acquisition—misleads a prince so that he becomes both contemptible and hated.[17] Machiavelli is not embarrassed to speak of a "virtuous tyrant who by his spirit and his virtue of arms expands his dominion" (*D* II 2). And he betrays his aversion to the classical virtue most prized in politics—moderation—by speaking of "extraordinary" or "excessive" or "rare and extreme" virtue (*D* I 33; II 2; III 19, 21, 22, 34), by remaining silent about moderation as a virtue (see "every middle virtue" [*ogni mezzana virtù*], *D* II 16), by his rejection of kindness (*comità*) in favor of harshness (*D* III 19–23) and by condemning the "middle way"(*D* I 6, 26; II 23; III 2, 21, 40; cf. I 27). Machiavelli's moderation is expressed in the command to "measure one's forces," a military form of prudence.

In the *Discourses,* Machiavelli presents the relationship between virtue and necessity in a crescendo. In the first chapter, discussing the legislator's choice of a site for his intended city, he remarks that greater virtue is seen where choice has less authority (*D* I 1). Soon he says that men never operate well at all except through necessity, this being "what I said above" (*D* I 3), though in fact it goes well beyond. Later he says that "necessity makes virtue, as we have said many times" (*D* II 12)—but actually he says it only this one time. And, in his last explicit statement on the relationship, the only chapter in the *Discourses* where he speaks approvingly of "some moral philosophers" (*D* III 12), he mentions "the virtue of such [i.e., human] necessity." Machiavelli never says the same thing twice; and when he says he does, he challenges the reader to find the difference. In this case necessity goes from being a support of virtue, to a condition of virtue, to a producer of virtue, and finally to a virtue itself. We shall seek later for a reason why necessity appears as both independent of virtue[18] and identical to it. Here we note that Machiavelli, following "some moral philosophers" and distinctly opposing Aristotle and his tradition, abandons choice as the basis of moral virtue (*NE* 1111b4–7). And when virtue is sustained by necessity rather than choice, it is no longer clearly moral. Machiavelli says that a prince must "learn to be able to be not good, and to use this and not use it according to necessity" (*P* 15); and as an example, he discusses the necessity of ingratitude for a republic, while admitting that ingratitude is a vice (*D* I 29–30). Necessity means being compelled to do evil for the sake of acquisition.

In political terms, the necessity of acquisition compels one not to rely on an inheritance of any kind from one's ancestors or predecessors, or in general from the past. Machiavelli makes the point in *The Prince* by first calling the hereditary prince a "natural prince" (*P* 2) and soon after, canceling the equation of the natural and the inherited, by pronouncing that "it is a very natural and ordinary thing to desire to acquire" (*P* 3). Similarly, at the beginning of the *Discourses,* Machiavelli shifts from an apparent preference for a stable republic like Sparta or Venice to a definite conclusion in favor of the expansive Roman republic, the republic that became an empire. In drawing his conclusion he says that all human things are in motion, and that they move in accordance with necessity not reason (*D* I 6). Reason cannot find in nature any way of limiting the necessity of human acquisition. Not relying on inheritance to supply the equipment of morality extends not merely to property in the usual sense but most radically to nature, which men regard as their property.

### VIRTUE AS IMPRESSIVE

The reasoning (not relying on the reasonable does not compel one to forsake reasoning) by which Machiavelli proceeds to the most outstanding feature of his notion of virtue can be quickly summarized as follows. Since the prince cannot rely on inheritance, he must acquire. But how? Machiavelli's answer, almost a slogan, is through "one's own arms," not depending on others. Yet surely the prince needs assistance from others; how can he get it without depending on others? He cannot get help through the gratitude of those whom he benefits, because beneficiaries already believe or soon convince themselves that they are *entitled* to their benefits, hence that the prince is *obligated* to provide them.[19] If the prince follows a policy of favoritism, giving out favors where they are not deserved, the result is the same as if he benefited justly because the beneficiaries soon come to expect what they first got through an unprompted favor. Neither justice nor favoritism produces gratitude in beneficiaries, rather the contrary when the prince runs out of benefits to give, or even before that since some will think they are entitled to more than they get. Gratitude presupposes that enough goods have been acquired, that is, that our problem has been resolved.

What is the remedy for the impotence of justice and gratitude, or of moral virtue as the ancients understood it, in assisting acquisition? For every difficulty Machiavelli brings up, he has a *rimedio,* and the cure for ingratitude is fear. The prince can prevent self-satisfaction in beneficiaries by putting them in fear. Let them be unrewarded, or better, punished when they deserve benefits; then they will be "grateful" to receive them. Such gratitude—truly a kind of relief—can be manufactured if a prince mixes some deliberate but unexpected actions of injustice with his justice. He need not, and should not, be regularly unjust, but a few sensational, shocking executions, especially if they are "extraordinary" and hence of doubtful legality, or even blatant illegality, will cause his beneficiaries to keep their eye on him and come to his side when he needs their help, not merely when they want to give it.

The justice of the prince is thus more impressive when contrasted with his injustice. Generalizing from the case of justice, one must conclude that virtue as a whole must be impressive. Virtue must show and must be recognized. The virtuous prince must appear virtuous and so his very virtue tells him that he cannot afford to be unconcerned with his reputation. Though for Aristotle, moral virtue is subject to praise and blame, its submission is limited by the fact that people mean to praise the true virtue that is not mere appearance (*NE* 1101b10–28, 1113a23–1113b2). In any case Aristotle does not simply accept the authority of the many or the vulgar (*NE* 1095b14–22, 1105b12–17, 1179b10–16). But for Machiavelli, the virtue a prince is reputed for, whether truly or not, is the virtue he needs: virtue is reputed virtue, and the vulgar decide what is reputed. "For the vulgar are taken in by the appearance and the outcome of a thing, and in the world there is no one but the vulgar" (*P* 18).

Thus virtue is not in itself, not its own reward, not self-sufficient.

Virtue is in need of its contrary; it does not shine, or not sufficiently, on its own; it needs the added brightness that comes from contrast with vice. Virtue needs vice as a constant possibility, and in order to keep vice possible, virtue must practice vice occasionally. Virtue is therefore not a mean between two vices, as Aristotle said, but rather an extreme; so in the momentous fifteenth chapter of *The Prince,* where Machiavelli sounds the clarion call of one who "departs from the orders of others," the virtues and vices are listed in pairs as if they go together. In the *Discourses* Machiavelli sets himself against "the middle way" (*via del mezzo*) of classical virtue, unless one could call the alternation between virtue and vice a middle way.[20]

Since virtue must be impressive, it works by example and not by "profession of good" (*P* 15); and Machiavelli, reflecting this truth, writes accordingly with myriad telling and shocking examples illustrating his generalities rather than with the argumentation of a treatise. One of the most notorious examples is Cesare Borgia's use of a cruel minister, Remirro de Orco, to pacify the Romagna, followed by his spectacular disposal in two pieces in the piazza of Cesena to show that the cruelty was not Borgia's (*P* 7). But of course it was; and the question arises whether the cruelty was merely *necessary* to his virtue or actually *part* of it. In the latter case, a new definition of virtue would be required. Machiavelli speaks here of "so much ferocity and so much virtue" in Borgia as if the two were together but distinct. Later in *The Prince* he seems to answer the question when he praises the "inhuman cruelty" of Hannibal (*P* 17). Hannibal's good fortune, he says, arose from his cruelty "together with his infinite virtues." Then, elaborating, he says that without cruelty "his other virtues" would not have been enough to produce "the effect" of making him venerated and terrible in the sight of his soldiers. So in the same sentence cruelty has gone from being an accompaniment of virtue to a virtue. We recall Machiavelli's similar equivocation about the behavior of Agathocles, which can and cannot be called virtue (*P* 8).

Perhaps one could provisionally resolve the difficulty in this way. The truth of virtue is shown in, or rather *is,* its effect, for example on Hannibal's soldiers. Machiavelli promises to "go directly to the effectual truth of the thing rather than to its imagination" (*P* 15).

The well-known phrase *verità effettuale*, announcing what is loosely
called Machiavelli's realism, occurs just this once in all of Machiavelli's writings and nowhere else, so far as I know, in any other
writings of the Renaissance.[21] Applied to virtue, it says that virtue
is what it gets you. But virtue gets you "ruin rather than preservation" unless you "learn how to be able not to be good" (*P* 15).
When Machiavelli praises virtue, it would seem necessary to make
the ability to do evil a *part* of virtue. At the same time, however,
such vicious virtue achieves its effect only in contrast with what
people usually expect from virtue, that it not include vice. Thus
Machiavelli's notion of virtue, which welcomes the vices, must continue to coexist with the old notion, which is repelled by them. The
truth about virtue includes the fact that most people cannot accept
the truth about virtue.

After proclaiming his intention to go to the effectual truth,
Machiavelli discusses the moral virtues in the eight chapters following (*P* 16–23). These are not about the perfection of the prince or
of his soul but about a prince "with subjects and friends" (*P* 15).
Virtue is not for its own sake and not for the sake of self-
improvement but for the use of others—subjects and friends—in
self-aggrandizement. For this purpose the prince must always keep
in view not so much the virtues themselves as the qualities that are
held good (*tenute buone, P* 15). So in discussing the virtues of liberality, Machiavelli considers how the prince may be "held" liberal and
whether it is to his advantage to "use" that virtue "virtuously" or
not (*P* 16). At the end of Machiavelli's argument it turns out that
the prince will be held liberal only if he does not mind being held
stingy. His use of liberality transforms its meaning from giving much
into taxing little when people expect him to tax more. The prince
must get the people to expect the worst; then, as we have seen, the
virtue will appear as bringing relief in the contrast.[22] Thus the prince
is liberal because he is not cruel, faithful because not betraying, and
so forth. To create the contrast between virtue and vice, the prince
must practice both; this is what it means to *use* virtue. In using
virtue, the prince steps back from it and regards it from the outside.
The outside view of virtue redefines it, making vice a part of virtue;
but virtue as viewed remains the same, distinct from the vice with
which it is coupled.[23]

## VIRTUE POLITICIZED

Machiavelli's discussion of the moral virtues in *The Prince* deals with the prince's relationships with others, not with his own perfection. It would be a "very laudable thing" to find a prince with all the qualities that are held good, but human conditions do not permit it. For Aristotle, the moral virtues aim at individual perfection if they aim at anything outside themselves; and one of them, magnanimity, is the pride of an individual when he knows he has all the virtues. Intellectual virtue makes an individual more self-sufficient than any or all of the moral virtues (*NE* 1177b1). But for Machiavelli, the virtues are social without qualification or exception; they are about how the prince appears to and deals with "subjects and friends." Machiavelli reminds us with the reference to the *government* of a prince that the prince's relationships are political. Virtue made impressive is virtue politicized, virtue understood by its political effects.[24]

It follows from the necessity of acquisition that all social relationships are political. In an outline for a dialogue between Xenophon and Machiavelli, Leopardi put the point in Machiavelli's mouth: "The art of knowing how to live or of knowing how to rule . . . is all one, since the end of man in society is to rule over others in whatever mode, and the most cunning always rules."[25] Everyone who is not a prince depends on one, and to the extent that he understands his own necessities, he wants to become a prince so that he can depend on "his own arms" instead of someone else. That is why Machiavelli, though beginning this fundamental chapter by speaking of "a prince," goes on to say that his "intent is to write something useful to whoever understands it" (*P* 15). Many live under the delusion, of course, that it is possible to live privately in society without involvement in politics, but they do not understand the necessity of their situation.[26] The basis of their security is the accomplishment of a prince who must always look out for himself and cannot therefore be trusted to take care of them should a conflict arise between the two goals. Relying on others is the same as relying on a "profession of good," and it brings ruin. For those who understand—and, as we shall see, *only* for them—society is radically politicized, leaving no refuge for those who would rather not be involved. Everyone who understands is either a prince or a potential prince who deserves to be one. (*D* let ded)

Since politicized virtue is cut loose from individual perfection, virtues in the plural are no longer parts of virtue; they become *qualities*[27] (and Machiavelli refers to "the qualities that bring . . . either blame or praise" in *P* 15). These qualities have no natural ordering, no hierarchy, which the end of perfection would give them; they are on a level, or to speak politically as Machiavelli always invites us to do, democratized. As such, they are open to manipulation, because none of them must be preferred to others, not even those "held good" over those held bad. The ninth of the eleven pairs of virtues (in *P* 15) is *duro e facile,* hard and agreeable or easy. This pair can readily be identified as the qualities of qualities: every quality is "hard" so as to contrast with its opposite, and "easy" so as to accommodate the use of its opposite, as we have seen. Machiavelli says that a prince must learn to use the natures of both man and beast: "the one without the other is not lasting [*durabile*]" (*P* 18). Nature is not composed, he implies, of self-subsisting natures, but rather the "natures" we know depend on our manipulation for their definition and articulation.

Machiavelli adumbrates the modern scientific understanding of nature that, with Bacon, abandons natural beings and begins the search for natural laws, but he does no more than adumbrate. Since he approaches the question of the nature of nature from the standpoint of what is good for human beings, he remains faithful to the fact that in morals and politics, different natures appear distinct to us, above all the difference between good and evil. He himself promises to bring good to us (*D* I pr), and though removed from ordinary politics, he never claims the neutral status of the scientific observer. He does not oppose and attempt to replace Aristotelian physics as he did Aristotelian political science, but neither can it be said that he was unaware of the problem, had nothing to offer, or was sunk in the old orthodoxy.

Aristotle too had a politicized virtue, justice. As magnanimity contains all the virtues in an individual, so justice collects them with a view to the good of the community as seen by the legislator (whoever or however many he might be). But for Aristotle the possibility of a natural ordering in the best regime exists, based on the perfection of the individual; that regime is best which produces the best men. Thus the best man constitutes a standard of natural justice by which to judge the various regimes, though with difficulties Aristotle indicates by stating that natural justice is changeable (NE 1134b29–30). But it is clear that for him the politicized virtue is anchored in, even while it envelops, virtue that is not politicized. Machiavelli holds, however, that there is no other way to look at virtue than politically, that is, for what it gets you. In Aristotle, virtue is *shown* in politics; in Machiavelli it is *defined* there. The consequence is that he is forced to abandon justice as a virtue, for when virtue is political, the only political virtue, the one that would restrain politics, disappears. (Its replacement, we shall see, is religion.) Although Machiavelli infrequently speaks of "justice" in the sense of necessity, he never refers in any of his writings to natural justice or natural law, which were the currency of philosophical discourse on politics in his time and in the tradition. On this major point, not sufficiently remarked, he was not a man of his times but an innovator against both the Renaissance and the ancients.

REPUBLICAN VIRTUE

In a sense Aristotle's *Nicomachean Ethics* and his *Politics* are one book, the latter as he says a continuation of the former because in politics the virtuous person finds a larger arena in which to exercise his virtue (NE 1178b33–1179a4). But also, of course, they are two books, and for good reason. The "in-itself" character of moral virtue that keeps it aloof from the effects of moral actions requires an abstraction from politics. It particularly needs insulation from the regime, the organizing form that gives the virtues a partisan bent as they appear in politics; and it also needs abstraction from politically relevant but nonmoral factors, such as differences of temperament, sex, or circumstance. To state the presumption of moral virtues, Aristotle says that every human being appears to be the cause of his own actions (NE 1112b32–33). This half-Kantian (but only half!) premise means that no one is to be excused from the moral virtues because any of them is politically embarrassing or difficult for someone of his temper, sex, or hardship. This stern requirement is not the whole story for Aristotle, of course, but it is the part of moral virtue.

Machiavelli did not write separate books on ethics and politics but rather one book mainly on princes and another mainly on republics. Since he begins the first chapter of *The Prince* by asserting that "all states . . . have been and are either republics or principalities," it appears that the distinction, which is Roman rather than Greek in origin, is important to him. But on examination, one sees that it is not important to him in the way that it matters to the partisans of those regimes. He is not, as is often said, a partisan of "republican virtue," though he does appreciate the advantage of republics over principalities.[28] "The common good," he says carefully, "is not observed if not in republics" (D II 2). But the common good of one state is incompatible with that of another, and republics especially are threats to the freedom of their neighbors; moreover, within republics the common good means in effect the good only of the majority, since justice to all is impossible.

To survive, republics must be acquisitive just like principalities, and their acquisitive part consists of the princes within them who behave with as little moral virtue as princes in principalities. Machiavelli's appreciation of republics in the *Discourses on Livy* is balanced by his admiration of the new prince in *The Prince,* who makes over everything in his own interest. As Machiavelli indicates in his phrase "the princes of a republic," republics are in need of such types, and so their ambition must be made compatible with the common good, difficult as the task will be. Machiavelli never speaks of "republican virtue"; indeed, he mocks the follies of republican partisanship. Republics, he remarks, hate the name of *king,* but they willingly accept the reality of one-man rule; and the Roman republic depended for its success on resort to the dictator in emergency situations when ordinary republican institutions were too slow and too limited to act effectively. Partisan republican virtue opposes the rule of one, but Machiavelli finds it indispensable in all political organizations and situations. The excellence of a republic lies not in denying princely virtue but precisely in releasing it and then checking it, and even this not by the virtue of a multitude but again by the virtue of one whose ambition is rival to the first: "a multitude without a head is useless" (D I 44).

That is as much to say that moral virtue without selfish ambition is useless. But together in a common good that includes both, and as contraries, they are useful. In that common good moral virtue is a means making for a stronger republic that survives longer because it expands more vigorously. In Aristotle republican virtue appears both as a city's means of survival and as its end.[29] The latter, which is true classical republican virtue, the virtue that republican partisans believe in, is the claim that republics produce more virtuous citizens than do other regimes. Machiavelli does not sustain that claim.[30] He makes much of the difference between corrupt and uncorrupt peoples in republics since it marks the extent of a capacity for self-sacrifice in the citizenry—but for what? A self-sacrificing people makes for a strong republic that is also noble because it will not surrender to its enemies. But virtue such as this, though real, remains instrumental; and it must be supplemented by the selfish virtue of princely types for whom "noble" means a refusal to surrender the prizes of their ambition.

Thus for Machiavelli, more fundamental than the distinction between principalities and republics is that between princes (or "the great") and peoples, the two natural "humors" to be found in every state, regardless of its form of regime (*P* 9; *D* I 4–6; *FH* II 12, III 1). "The people desire neither to be commanded nor oppressed by the great, and the great desire to command and oppress the people" (*P* 9). What the princes desire to do is precisely what peoples desire to avoid: here is a massive political problem—*the* political problem for Machiavelli—which is also a tremendous moral difficulty since it implies a totally opposed outlook on morality. Contrary to Aristotle, morality is not essentially voluntary. It is controlled by natural temperament, by the two humors that divide all mankind and underlie all moral behavior and opinion. By speaking of *humors* Machiavelli indicates that they are not habits of the mind nor mental in origin but prerational dispositions. Not being rational in nature, they cannot be reconciled by speech or argument. These are two human types who do not understand each other—the one preferring security and comfort, suspicious of anyone who desires more, the other seeking risk and demanding honor, unbelieving that anyone could be satisfied with less.

### VIRTUE AND GOODNESS

In one place Machiavelli indicates that the moral difference in the two humors could be developed as that between virtue (*virtù*) and goodness (*bontà*). But he himself does not develop that distinction.[31] He uses both *virtue* and *goodness* frequently and in that usage seems to follow an inexplicit distinction between the ambitious virtue of a prince and the modest goodness of peoples without feeling the need

for definitions. In the one place referred to (*D* I 17), he says that a
city will remain corrupt "unless the goodness of one individual, together with virtue, keeps it free." Then he speaks of the "virtue" of
princes who might accomplish the feat, saying nothing of their goodness but asserting that in a corrupt city, "one individual" (*uno*) with
extreme force might be able to cause the material to become "good."
Here virtue in a prince seems to produce goodness in the people, as
form is imposed on material; but Machiavelli is willing nonetheless
to speak of the "virtue of the generality" (*la virtù dello universale*)
as sustaining "good orders." So when virtue is in the people, it has
been implanted there by a virtuous prince.[32] Such popular virtue is
equivalent to goodness, but in the very chapter where Machiavelli
indicates a distinction between virtue and goodness, he blurs it by
speaking of goodness as virtue.

Clearly Machiavelli wants to maintain the ambiguity in virtue
we have discussed between accepting and rejecting evil. From the
standpoint of the virtue of Machiavelli's princes, virtue is distinct
from goodness because it is willing, or eager, to do evil: "goodness
is not enough" (*la bontà non basta! D* III 30), as Machiavelli says
in reproach of his former employer Piero Soderini. But from the
standpoint of goodness, goodness is enough and so it must be part
of or identical to virtue. But why does Machiavelli care about the
standpoint of goodness, which on noteworthy occasions already
cited he seems simply to dismiss as illusion? The answer is that
goodness is needed for the impressiveness of virtue; the virtue of
princes can be impressive only if it can shock the goodness of good
people. Precisely the illusion of morality is its reality. In our day the
makers of modern art have abandoned beauty for revolutionary
shock as the goal of their art, but they do not have so clear a recognition as Machiavelli of their dependence on the philistine morality of
the bourgeois they need to shock. They do not see that they will
lose their audience if they try to win it over to their point of view.
Machiavelli, however, was content with a world in which the majority would necessarily remain anti-Machiavellians.

If virtue is to shock, it needs something to shock, the conscience.[33] Conscience for Machiavelli is an awareness of God's
awareness of one's thoughts, intents, and actions. It is a Christian
conception, but merely develops the fear of punishment and hope
of reward that characterizes the religion of any sect. Religion can be

considered a virtue, or better, an accompaniment of virtue understood as goodness.[34] Religion represents a dim and uneasy awareness
on the part of good people that goodness is not enough to secure
their future, that they need God's help and must fear his anger.
Goodness *becomes* enough through religion, or so good people believe. Machiavelli understands religion not as a yearning for impossible perfection in the goodness of God but rather as an attempt to
control chance and the unforeseeable future in the power and providence of God. Conscience or religion is reverence in the presence of
a prince (because *prince,* for Machiavelli, can refer to a superhuman
prince) who frightens you and inhibits you in a way and for a reason
you do not understand. Machiavelli appears to identify conscience
with "confusion of the brain" (*D* III 6), with the wretched foolish-
ness that would permit a man to kill his enemy but not in a church.
Such a person has some understanding of his necessities but is unable
to summon the spirit to confront them and so trembles with a sense
of his weakness that he feels as "reverence" and calls "conscience."

Religion is a weakness that can give strength, but only when it
is well used by princes. If it is not well used, it will promote the
interest of a sect, or of religion itself (since Machiavelli speaks of
religion in the sense of sect, *D* II 5) rather than the common good.
The choice, in fact, is not *whether* to use religion, since it will be
used, but *who* will use it to show that the gods support their rule, the
secular princes or the sectarian ones called priests. In a principality,
religion can be replaced by fear of the prince, but in a republic it is
indispensable for the spirit of sacrifice that keeps the republic from
becoming corrupted by the private interests of wealthy nobles. Yet
the republican spirit of sacrifice has its price in the necessity of subjecting virtue to a standard that, however invigorating, is outside
itself—the common good.

The common good compels republics to be harsh on their own
citizens and to hate foreigners; in both necessities religion and piety
are instruments or willing allies. The necessity of using religion reveals the necessity of politicizing virtue, which means reducing and
distorting it for the sake of its political consequences. It is in the
context of his praise of the utility of religion that Machiavelli makes
his deepest criticism of traditional moral virtue. Nothing is more
necessary for a prince to *appear* to have, he says, than the quality
of religion (*P* 18). Since the vulgar are taken in by the appearance

and the outcome of a thing, when a prince wins and maintains his state, "the means will always be judged honorable, and will be praised by everyone." Here, when speaking of religion, is Machiavelli at his most Machiavellian, as he explains how success comes to succeed.[35]

The reason is that religion, which is for Machiavelli essentially a doctrine of providence, explains why what has happened deserved to happen—why, in view of the outcome, the suffering of the good and the prosperity of the wicked were God's will, and thus "honorable means" to it. Politicized virtue is virtue that brings success, the virtue that must have been, that was willed by God. Precisely the morally good, who believe that goodness is enough, are guilty of Machiavellism! For to make goodness suffice, they must accept the outcome as good and thus also the means necessary to the outcome. It is sometimes claimed in extenuation of Machiavelli that he never said, "the end justifies the means." No, but he said worse: that the end makes the means honorable, and that moral men believe this.[36]

Machiavelli's notion of virtue provides the good with the success they desire and do not know how to achieve. Goodness is subject to the same necessity to acquire as is virtue, but characteristically goodness refuses to accept that necessity and takes refuge in religion, where it uncomprehendingly comes to terms with necessity. Good people do this out of their own necessity, that of the weak, which is to seek the mercy of the strong while denying that they need such mercy. That we are subject to necessity does not mean that we will willingly and knowingly submit to it, and Machiavelli allows for such recalcitrance on the part of peoples. He does not try to convince them of the necessity of princes; he only incites those of the people who have the nature of princes to rise and become what they must.

It is an unnamed plebeian prince who delivers Machiavelli's most shameless attack on conscience in a speech to the plebs, saying that your conscience ought not "dismay you, because those who win, in whatever mode they win, never receive shame from it. For faithful servants are always servants and good men are always poor" (*FH* III 13). Yet soon after, in praising Michele di Lando, perhaps the same man as the conscienceless speaker but not said to be, Machiavelli indicates that Michele's virtue is composed of spirit, goodness, and prudence. His spirit kept him faithful to the republic, "his goodness never allowed a thought to enter his mind that might be con-

trary to the universal good," and his prudence enabled him to convince and subdue those opposed to his party (*FH* III 17).

In this complicated appraisal Michele's goodness and prudence
are clearly at odds unless it can be shown that the "universal good"
requires partisan prudence.[37] The unnamed plebeian gives a carica-
ture of Machiavelli's doctrine, shamelessly right on the main point
but also exaggerated as Machiavelli shows in his praise of Michele.
Good men are always poor but Machiavelli will save their goodness
for them in an economy of virtue and goodness in which virtue
makes up for the innocence of goodness and goodness gives an excuse to the rascality of virtue.[38] Machiavelli tells us for sure that
virtue and goodness are opposed, but in him—that is, in his thought
and spirit (*animo*)—they are united. Machiavelli's virtue makes
room for goodness as its necessary and useful opponent, and so for
him, if not for Piero Soderini, goodness when corrected and no
longer too trusting is enough.


## THE MANAGEMENT OF GOODNESS

The mutual incomprehension between princes and peoples in regard
to virtue makes it impossible for Machiavelli to redefine conscience
so as to satisfy both. He does not attempt to make conscience compatible with acquisition in a new morality deriving from the universal principle of self-preservation in the manner of John Locke. Machiavelli may have prepared bourgeois morality, but he stops definitely
short of it. His utilitarianism leaves a place for the noble or, rather,
risk-seeking character of princes; he asks them to be prudent but
not to calculate. His endorsement of honesty is accompanied, not to
say strictly chaperoned, by incitement to dishonesty so that no one
could think that a steady life is the best. *Industria* for him means
astute inventiveness, not industriousness, not the "work ethic."
Whatever legacy he may have left to bourgeois liberalism—and it is
considerable—he may also be said to have anticipated the critiques
of the bourgeois that were to come from Rousseau, Nietzsche, and
their followers on the left and the right. If modern man were defined
as Machiavellian, he could not so easily be accused of a dull life, a
flat soul, and a lack of patriotism. Machiavelli enlightens princes
and those who want to become princes but leaves good people in
the dark they want and make for themselves. The latter are shown

the seamy side of moral virtue and offered instruction in scheming evil, but Machiavelli knows his teaching will not take, for it is the good, not the evil, who are incorrigible. The evil can be brought to see that their glory requires action for the common benefit, but the good are self-sufficient and ineducable because they think goodness is enough.

If the good cannot be educated, however, they can be manipulated. This is not the place to study Machiavelli's political science, but suffice it to say, with a brief discussion of three "modes of proceeding," that its purpose is to reveal the interplay of virtue and goodness. One mode is the use of "executions" (*esecuzioni*) to purge the anger of the people against the oppressions of their princes. The people, believing that goodness is its own reward or that it will be rewarded do not see why they, the good, should suffer exactions of taxation and conscription from the government. They think that justice is possible and become angry at the oppressions they wrongly consider unnecessary. That anger can be satisfied or purged only by the punishment of a scapegoat whose execution focuses their hatred on one prince while distracting it from the government as a whole.[39] Thus they consent to the necessity of some government at the same time that they vent their frustration upon one of their governors in the futility of moralism, which, according to Machiavelli, always attends moral virtue.

For a second mode of manipulation, one may carry the first a step further. When one prince has been punished with a salutary and sensational—but not necessarily deserved—execution, the rest are left untouched; or is it not more? They are excused because if they were guilty they would have been punished; to purge the guilty is to cleanse the community. Then could not that cleansing be understood as a positive consent, indeed as an *election* of those not punished? Machiavelli develops the suggestion that the meaning of electing a prince to office is failing to punish him, so much stronger is hatred than love. He illustrates the point with a beautiful discourse on what might be called the quintessential election, in which a Capuan magistrate saves the senate from the hatred of the people by giving the people an opportunity it would not accept to kill the senate (*D I 47*).

Thus the virtuous must work behind the backs of the good. They cannot persuade the good of the necessities that compel them to depart from goodness, necessities deriving from the fundamental necessity to acquire, which precedes all goodness and overrides it on occasion but never abolishes it. Since the good cannot be persuaded, they must be surprised or astonished, especially by a sensational execution or other unexpected initiative that puts them in fear and thus in a mood to obey. Virtue does not always work in the open, but it must come out in the open. To be impressive, virtue must create a visual effect. The *effectual* truth (*P* 15) of governing requires that a prince *get* an effect by *creating* an effect; in the two meanings of *effect,* it is not only efficient but also showy.

Machiavelli is fully aware that display is necessary to the efficiency of government, but the display he recommends is not so much ceremony as the rude interruption of ceremony, for example by an assassination. To achieve the requisite surprise, government itself, and not merely plotters against the government, must engage in conspiracy, a third mode of manipulation (*D* III 6; *P* 19). Virtuous princes must conspire to surprise the good so that the benefits of their rule may not be taken for granted and the obligations of allegiance do not lose their hold. When in the routine of life in "quiet times" the good become confident that goodness is enough and that they have no need of princely virtue, they relax, become unwilling to sacrifice and turn corrupt. The task of the virtuous is to shake their confidence and make them fear.

Underlying goodness is fear—the fear of the good that goodness is not enough, and that they are too weak to supply the defect. Although the good cannot be made to *understand* their necessity, they can be made to *feel* it. A virtuous prince must make the good feel exposed so that they will turn in gratitude to the one who provides security. Being exposed is the human condition at the beginnings—the beginning of life, of one's family, of one's state, of one's country, of civilization. That is why Machiavelli describes the correct policy of any government as "return to the beginnings." The life of a human institution is not in movement toward its end or in the form that directs such motion, as Aristotle thought, but in movement that anticipates necessities to come by means of occasional reminders of the fear that has been left behind. With such reminders the virtuous replace the routine confidence of the good, which thinks goodness is self-sufficient, with a manufactured security directed to a prince and sensible of dependence on him.

Everyone knows that Machiavelli ends *The Prince* by quoting a verse
from Petrarch promising a return of virtue to Italy:

> Virtue will take up arms against fury
> and make the battle short,
> because the ancient valor in Italian hearts
> is not yet dead.

But what is the virtue that Machiavelli appropriates from Petrarch to give the "exhortation" of his closing chapter (*P* 26) such
a flourish? It has been said to be based on the "Ciceronian concept
of *virtus*" a virtue of manliness derived from the marriage of philosophy and rhetoric that Petrarch adopted from Cicero.[40] The manliness
appears to be an unyielding, stouthearted patriotism that would inspire Italians to take up the just enterprise of a redeemer and free
Italy of dominating barbarians.

Certain it is that Machiavelli makes painfully evident the contrast between virtue as he sees it and effeminacy. An effeminate
people is one that is used to slavery and hence corrupt (*D* I 17,
21); it does not defend itself, that is, defend its freedom. Through
Christianity such peoples have become, as it were, universal: "the
world has been made effeminate and Heaven disarmed" (*D* II 2).
Whatever may be the case with femininity, effeminacy is taught,
since whole cities and even families within cities may be educated in
effeminacy (*D* III 46). Effeminacy is what virtue is seen to be not;
and a prudent prince like the Roman King Ancus will avoid being
judged effeminate (*D* I 19). However useful the arts or art of peace
may be (*D* I 11, 19), virtue appears as warlike and thus the contrary
of effeminate. "Lazy princes or effeminate republics" try to keep
their captains in the field from fighting (*D* III 10).

Yet in fact, manliness is not the meaning of Machiavelli's virtue,
and his use of Petrarch's verse does not signify agreement with,
much less surrender to, either Petrarch or Cicero. This is one of two
quotations of Petrarch by Machiavelli in his major prose works. His
familiarity with Petrarch (which could in any case be assumed) appears in two quotations in his letters and in his disclosure, by the
famous letter of December 10, 1513, that he would begin a typical
day of his exile by walking in the woods with a copy of Dante or

Petrarch in hand.[41] In his *Discourse or Dialogue concerning Our Language,* he lists Petrarch with Dante and Boccaccio as Florentines who "hold the first place" (772b), and so high that nobody hopes to match them, among writers of Italy; but, he says, Petrarch did not say anything about using the popular Florentine tongue and is therefore not discussed in that brief work. Yet popularity, or ability to reach the people, is one main issue in Machiavelli's judgment of the Renaissance. In *The Prince,* we have seen, he claims to depart from others in going directly to the effectual truth (*P* 15); in the *Discourses on Livy,* he says he disagrees with "all writers" in ascribing wisdom and constancy to the multitude (*D* I 58). How are these two disagreements with the classical tradition connected? And is the constancy of the multitude (for Machiavelli soon forsakes his praise of its wisdom) a consequence of manly virtue?

Petrarch is the first and foremost of the Renaissance humanists because he puts humane studies ahead of the study of nature. Seeking to loosen the grip of Aristotelian scholasticism on the learned world, he proposed a revival of the style of Cicero, whom he praises for eloquence. In his *On His Own and Many Others' Ignorance* (*De sui ipsius et multorum ignorantia,* 1367), he proclaims himself a Ciceronian not because he objects to Aristotle but because he cannot abide the "stupid Aristotelians" (*stultos aristotelicos*) who consult no one but Aristotle and relentlessly invoke the five syllables of his name in support of their own vanity.[42] As to Aristotle himself, anyone who reads his *Ethics,* says Petrarch, will know more when he finishes than when he began, but he will not be moved to love virtue more than before, if anything the contrary as he appreciates how difficult is virtue and how easy is vice. Hence one sees the use of Cicero's rhetoric when united with philosophy, particularly in motivating the unlettered virtue of nonphilosophers; and Petrarch confesses to admiring Cicero before all those who have ever written "for any people whatever" (*qualibet in gente*[43]). Thus attention to rhetoric introduces an attempt to address the people (in the sense of nonphilosophers) and therefore at least in some writings of Petrarch and of others recourse to the vernacular language on which Machiavelli comments. Although the Renaissance humanists studied many ancient authors, "the ancient writer who earned their highest admiration was Cicero."[44]

To understand the use of Cicero, let us consider the man himself for a moment. When Cicero explained what he expected from the conjunction of philosophy and rhetoric, he brought up a conception of manly virtue that was not new to the Greek philosophers but was intended for a new situation. Martial Rome was stony soil for the planting and cultivation of philosophy. Cicero does not call his fatherland brutish, but he remarks on the late appearance of poetry in Rome in comparison with the Greeks; the poets were not available to him, as they were in Greece, to serve as both lantern and foil for philosophy.[45] Moreover, Cato the Censor had railed against the softness and refinement of Greek philosophy, and his voice was echoed in Cicero's time. Cicero's problem was that he wanted to bring philosophy to a Rome disdainful of this foreign corruption and simultaneously to revive, if he could, the hard republican virtues whose decline already concerned Cato. His solution was to promote philosophy as manliness, hence preternaturally Roman, even if accidentally Greek in origin, and to accomplish this feat of salesmanship by means of an alliance between philosophy and rhetoric. Rhetoric was in fact an art in which the Romans, who excelled in politics as well as war, were not inferior to the Greeks.[46] When tamed, rhetoric could do the same useful service to philosophy as poetry and without the political disadvantages of quaintness and daintiness. Like poetry, it could help philosophy defend itself, and its disputatious habit, which is not in poetry, might keep philosophy from hardening in dogmatism.

So Cicero, in his *Tusculan Disputations,* brings out the fortitude of philosophy in its contempt for death and pain, rather than its erotic yearning to know the whole: here philosophy is medicine not love.[47] Fortitude is the virtue proper to man, and virtue (*virtus*) is so called from man (*vir*).[48] That a man is in truth all that he ought to be was, to repeat, not Cicero's discovery; and he himself yields the claim to popular insight. The idea can be found in Socrates' agreement with the rhetorician Thrasymachos that the artisan, precisely speaking, always knows what he is doing.[49] Its use by Cicero in regard to manliness does not constitute a final definition by him but is rather a product of the alliance he announces between philosophy and rhetoric. It is also an instance of the principle that a thing should be defined by its excellence, the very principle that Machiavelli rejects in demanding the "effectual truth," in which a thing is defined by its upshot or outcome.

Returning to Petrarch, we find the same alliance of philosophy and rhetoric but, as we have seen, not in the same circumstances or for the same reason. It was not necessary for the humanists to introduce philosophy where it was unknown or despised, for that had been done by their scholastic opponents; but it was perhaps necessary to bring more diversity into philosophy and so to add rhetoric and dialogue in which different opinions have equal standing to the method of the treatise in which the disputed question receives definite answers. Cicero was prized more for his stance, which was accidentally useful to the humanists, than for truths available only from him. In Petrarch's canzone, *Italia mia,* from which Machiavelli quotes to end *The Prince,* the "virtue" called for is not Cicero's manliness in the *Tusculan Disputations.* It is "virtue against fury" (*vertù contra furore*), against the anger of Italian lords (*signori*) who by squabbling among themselves open the door to foreign invasion.[50] The poem begins with a prayer to God to open hearts that have been closed by Mars, and it ends by recommending "the serene life" and calling for "peace, peace, peace." The "ancient valor in Italian hearts" that Petrarch wants to revive has nothing of Machiavelli's venomous patriotism attacking the "barbarian domination" that "stinks to everyone" but is rather a pious, moderate patriotism close to magnanimity and denouncing rather than appealing to base instinct.[51] Whereas Petrarch opposes virtue to fury, Machiavelli, while keeping them distinct, proposes an alliance between them under an "ordered virtue" that *uses* fury (*virtù ordinata,* D III 36). His use of Petrarch's virtue to end *The Prince* is a wrenching appropriation to his own quite different, less generous purpose.

Machiavelli's other quotation of Petrarch shows him inspiring a ridiculous failed conspiracy against the pope, and thus invites, or requires, a comparison between Petrarch and Machiavelli as inspirers of political action. Stefano Porcari, a noble Roman citizen, took hope from the canzone of Petrarch addressed to "Gentle spirit" (*Spirito gentil*) that appeals to a knight, Machiavelli quotes, "more thoughtful of others than himself" (*FH* VI 29). But Porcari believed himself superior to every other Roman and was unable to conduct himself in a mode that would conceal his high opinion of himself. He became suspect to the pope, who first curtailed him, then killed him. His intention was praiseworthy, we are told, but his judgment was poor. His design to seize his fatherland from the hands of the priests and to become the new founder and second father to Rome failed, we can infer, because it was filled with the "divine and prophetic spirit [*spirito*]" of a poet, which did not accord with his own excellent spirit (*animo*).[52] *Spirito* prompts one to think of others, *animo* of oneself; but in practice *spirito* makes a prince think of himself as divinely inspired. With this high thought expelling all lesser considerations, he becomes careless of the *animo* of others as well as blind to his own. When Machiavelli for his part speaks of the "virtue of an Italian spirit (*spirito*)" in the last chapter of *The Prince*, he calls for divine redemption in his way, with "military virtue," through one's own arms in alliance with fury and with an ungentle spirit. His quotation of Petrarch in the *Florentine Histories* helps one to interpret the closing of *The Prince*. In the canzone *Spirito gentil* Petrarch too laments the loss of virtue in Italy and he too wants "spirited deeds" (*animosi fatti*). But Petrarch's way to such deeds is through Rome, "our head," and the papacy, "the greatest father"; and so he supposes that *spirito* and *animo* are consistent. For Machiavelli, they are at odds. Italy is to be seized rather than served, possibly by the house of the Medici and so possibly through the papacy—yet without respect for the spirit that informs it. Politics is not to be inspired by anything higher than itself or nobler than human mastery. That is why Machiavelli did not put his politics, and his virtue, into poems of love.

If Machiavelli departs from and abuses Petrarch, he directly attacks Cicero.[53] Perhaps he discloses his opinion of the humanists in his criticism of their hero. Cicero appears in three of the *Discourses on Livy*. In the first of them he is brought out by Machiavelli to reassure those who might doubt the value of popular tumults in a free city, advising them that a man worthy of faith can easily quell a riot by speaking truth to the people (*D* I 4; cf. I 54). Next he is adduced, again to support Machiavelli's judgment, in criticism of Pompey, who opposed Caesar too late and brought on the ruin of the Roman republic. Here is Cicero speaking the truth but being too late himself (*D* I 33). Then comes a devastating reproof of Cicero's foresight when after Caesar's death he urged support for Octavian against Antony because Octavian, who was using Caesar's name, would attract Antony's soldiers from him. Instead, Octavian joined

Antony and the two destroyed the party of the Senate. Cicero should
have known that he could never rely on Caesar's name to produce
any result in accordance with the "name of liberty" (D I 52).

Cicero's rhetoric failed to take into account the power of a name
that continues to be favored by the people even after the man has
died. Searching for the parallel to this phenomenon in Machiavelli's
time and dissatisfied with his example of Cosimo de' Medici (since
the Medici had not died out), we quickly come to rest on the fact
that Machiavelli's rhetoric was not explicitly Christian and humanist
rhetoric was.[54] That fact is connected to the further fact that Machiavelli's rhetoric was, to say the least, not explicitly favorable to philosophy and humanist rhetoric was.[55]

In Machiavelli's view, the philosophical tradition—classical,
medieval, and humanist—is based on a "profession of good" rather
than the effectual truth and therefore inflates virtue from what is
attainable by princes and peoples to an unattainable image of the
best man (P 8, 18; D III 38). When that virtue is carried to the
people as philosophy descends to rhetoric, the image is personified
and deified, since the people simultaneously want virtue to be attainable (hence actual) and revered (hence divine). Christianity, in which
the best man becomes actual as God, is the effectual truth of traditional moral philosophy. The humanists may have been as much
partial to Christianity as Cicero was to Caesar, but their acceptance
of the Christian name, coupled with their promotion of philosophy,
left their rhetoric as useless as Cicero's. Machiavelli, bold as he was,
could not quite say this in so many words, but with a little speculation we can draw out the implication or the suggestion from what
he does say.


### VIRTUE MADE FLEXIBLE

Machiavelli's virtue is not ancient or Roman manliness.[56] For Cicero, as we have seen, manliness was a simplification undertaken
for a specific political purpose, one that included the protection of
philosophy, in specific circumstances. Cicero's master Plato was
quite capable of disparaging manliness together with rhetoric, and
distinguishing them both from philosophy in the spirited discussion
between Socrates and Callicles in the Gorgias (485c, 491b–c, 500c).
In general one may suggest that in drawing virtue from man (vir),

manliness takes for granted that "man" is something definite. The manly man is self-confident and calmly assured of what he knows and who he is. But in Aristotle's famous statement, man is a rational animal (*Pol.* 1253a10; 1332b3–5), a rational being sharing animality with subrational beings. Having both a higher and a lower nature, man has a double nature rather than a single definition. From this standpoint (here much abridged) manliness is but a version of ancient virtue, and one regarded with suspicion by the ancients because *human nature* is not easy to fix. On reflection, our self-assurance is shamed by our ignorance and our susceptibility.

Machiavelli too doubts the worth of manliness, but not because manly men are too confident but because they are too proud, hence too scrupulous. In the passage everyone knows, Machiavelli says that it is "necessary for a prince to know well how to use the beast and the man," and that the ancients taught this role covertly when they imagined Chiron the centaur as teacher (*P* 18). As Leo Strauss has pointed out, Machiavelli here agrees with the ancients and with Christianity that man's nature is composite, but he replaces the Christian combination of God-man with that of beast-man. He represents the latter image as ancient, except that the ancients used it *covertly;* but exposing that fact, and by speaking next of using the fox and the lion, he makes open the teaching that the ancients kept hidden. But, as Strauss also pointed out, when a hidden teaching is brought out into the light of day, it is no longer the same.[57] The ancients indicated the beastliness of man covertly so as not to encourage it, or so as not to give offense: such is man's nature that in politics especially he will and must play the beast. But to say that openly is no longer merely to indicate; it is to recommend. It is to *politicize* a teaching that began as nonpolitical.

Machiavelli takes the deprecatory posture of the pre-Socratic and anti-Socratic traditions toward politics and changes it into a method for success in politics. He fuses the Socratic tradition with that of its opponents, adopting the moral and political concern of the former and the observations of the latter. Here in this passage is the origin of what is called the "reductionism" of modernity: the reducing of high (man) to low (beast), not to reveal the truth but to improve the high by making it more effectual. When the ancients reduced man to his ugly truth in politics, they remained superior and thus also revealed the beauty of the truth about man; but the reduction becomes reductionism when Machiavelli tries to make it productive.

Machiavelli suppresses the fact that in the ancient stories Chiron was the son of Saturn, who begat him while in the shape of a horse. In Machiavelli's version human beings will take the shape of animals instead of gods.[58] By omitting the gods, Machiavelli directs our attention away from the similarity between the ancient view of man as a rational animal, in which the rationality is something divine, and the Christian view in which the divine is made incarnate. Again he *uses* ancient virtue rather than following it, and the use is to cast doubt on Christian virtue. In repeating his point he drops the "half-beast" and says that the prince must use the beast. Using the beast means using beasts, for example the fox and the lion. The man-beast is replaced by the combination of beast and beast. So evanescent is our humanity that if the divine is removed, almost nothing human remains. The only thing left is flexibility, for while beasts are confined to their single natures, man is the all-around beast who because of his rationality is free to take on the nature of any convenient beast. His rationality does not elevate him but on the contrary warns him against relying on dignity—that is, on the lion, alone.[59] Dignity has its use for Machiavelli, which is boldness; he does not share the usual understanding of Machiavellism that reduces it to foxiness.[60] But bold princes must learn how to stoop to conquer from a teacher bold enough to expose the prejudice against stooping. When Machiavelli says that the prince must use both natures (of the lion and fox), he adds that "the one without the other is not lasting [*durabile*]" (*P* 18, 19).[61] Like the two qualities of qualities, *duro* and *facile,* that are necessary to each other, the two natures are correlates not independent beings: no stable lion without a fox, no fox without a lion. Flexibility is necessary to durability— but durability as what? As man?

VIRTUE AND PRUDENCE

The "rationality" of the human beast is prudence; he must know when to adopt which nature. Prudence accompanies virtue in those whom Machiavelli holds up as models: Cesare Borgia (*P* 7), Scipio (*D* I 29), and especially the Romans (*P* 3; II 1, 19). They are together in a founder, who looks ahead (*P* 26; *D* I 9), for the office of pru-

dence is not merely to consider present circumstances but to anticipate the future by being acquainted with necessities to come (D I
11, 18, 51; III 12). Such necessities have the character of chance
particulars; one knows *that* they will come but not *when* or *in what
form*. They cannot be predicted by laws of nature, using scientific
method, in the manner of later modern philosophers like Descartes,
Hobbes, Spinoza, and Locke. Anticipating necessity cannot be done
automatically with rules, laws, or institutions (useful as they can be).
Since prudence cannot do away with risk, prudence needs to be
accompanied by virtue to deal with the chance emergencies that can,
and cannot, be seen ahead. Prudence can thus be understood as a
virtue itself (D I 29). Yet for Machiavelli, prudence is also a critic
of virtue, reminding it of necessity, as well as a guide; prudence has
something of the superiority of intellectual virtue to moral virtue.
Just once in *The Prince* and in the *Discourses on Livy* does Machiavelli speak of "science," and there he connects it to the use of images
(D III 39). Prudence uses images (for example, lion and fox), but in
science, which one can suppose is the resource of teachers such as
the ancients and Machiavelli, images are thematic and are used self-
consciously not only to convey but also to advance knowledge.

In comparison with Aristotle, Machiavelli much expands the
realm of prudence.[62] He brings theory and practice together, as did
Plato, but whereas for Plato theory (philosophy) invades practice,
for Machiavelli it is the reverse. Aristotle wished to keep prudence
separate from intellectual virtue so that moral virtue could have the
guidance of reason without falling subservient to it; the "in-itself"
character of moral virtue requires protection from intellectual virtue
outside or above. Prudence, as we have seen, therefore finds itself in
a somewhat compromised position: the guide of virtue that is im-
bued with virtue, thus itself guided by virtue. From that virtuous
circle Aristotle gains the advantage of being able to distinguish between prudence, guided by virtue, and cleverness or cunning, which
is not (NE 1144a6–b33). Machiavelli, by admitting necessity as sovereign in the realm of moral virtue carefully constructed and protected by Aristotle, foregoes—or rather, sweeps away—a distinction
between *prudenza* and *astuzia*.[63] His virtue is to be guided by a
prudence that no longer calculates in the interest of virtue. In the
passage on the lion and fox, we are told that a "prudent lord . . .
cannot observe faith, nor should he" (P 18).

Necessity, however, does not determine human actions; it does not crowd out human virtue. Here again is Machiavelli's difference with his scientific successors. Since prudence sees ahead of necessity, its counsel is not strictly *necessitated*, though Machiavelli does use that expression in a loose, unscientific sense as what one finds necessary to do. To act on prudence one must have *animo*, an animated spirit.[64] *Animo* is Machiavelli's version of the Greek *thymos*, the spirit of self-defense that paradoxically can lead to the risking of one's life for the sake of saving one's life. Cool reason will not suffice to carry out a prudent action on its own but needs the—rationally dubious—assistance of a fiery temperament. That temperament exacts a price of unreason that Machiavelli is willing to pay. Unlike his successors he does not use the concept of necessity to dampen conflict and bring peace, because he sees the connection between *animo* and virtue. Hobbes, with his right of self-preservation, cannot show why a soldier in the field should not run from danger. But for Machiavelli, *animo* is the raw material of virtue. *Animo* is brutish and uncultivated; it is subhuman and below manliness. If those who look for Machiavelli's virtue in manliness would pay attention to *animo*, they could preserve the spiritedness they rightly discern in Machiavelli's recommendations.

*Animo* is indispensable in conspiracies, the central events of Machiavellian politics, in which it is required for overcoming inhibitions, for steeling oneself to the performance of actions one can see are necessary but may not have the nerve for. In the great chapter on conspiracies in the *Discourses* (III 6), *animo* almost takes over from *virtù*,[65] and in another chapter Machiavelli scolds his former employer Piero Soderini for lacking the *animo* (not the virtue) to do a necessary thing that "his prudence" had recognized (D III 3). Besides being the basis of virtue, *animo* can be a virtue in certain great cases; Machiavelli describes the *virtù del animo suo* of Savonarola (D I 45), and of some Roman emperor (P 19), and even the *virtù di animo e di corpo* of Agathocles (P 8), and of Manlius Capitolinus (D III 8), and of Baldaccio di Anghiari (FH VI 6)—not to omit the *virtù di animo e di corpo grandissima* of Castruccio Castracani (749a). The phrase "virtue of the spirit and of the body" reminds us that *animo* is essentially spiritedness in defense of one's body, as what most belongs to oneself. It is not soul (*anima*), a word, Strauss informs us, that does not occur in *The Prince* and the *Discourses on*

*Livy.*[66] Machiavelli's virtue, we see again, is not the perfection of the soul; it is the cultivation through prudence and experience of an emanation of the body.

The animus in question is surely male, representing aggressiveness. Though Machiavelli has his feminine favorites, above all Madonna Caterina, the Countess of Forlì, it is the impetuous young male whom he incites to beat down Lady Fortune in the notorious, vivid scene at the end of the twenty-fifth chapter of *The Prince*. And Madonna Caterina is featured for having put revenge ahead, far ahead, of the care and love of her children (*P* 20; *D* III 6; *FH* VIII 34).[67]

Machiavelli's revulsion at the weakness of the world into which Christianity has delivered us causes him to revise the Aristotelian teaching on the soul that he regards as in some degree responsible for its Christian perversion. Any detachment of the soul from the body leads to promotion of the interest of the other world against this world, or to tell the effectual truth, promotion of the this-worldly interest of those who successfully claim to know the interest of the other world.

Prudence can be said to differ from virtue in not necessarily being visible: prudence is shy but virtue must show itself so as to be impressive. Junius Brutus is called prudent for pretending to be stupid (*D* III 2), but Machiavelli speaks emphatically of Theseus's showing his virtue (*P* 6), of new princes known to be virtuous (*P* 24), of the difficulty modern men have in showing or demonstrating their virtue (*D* III 10), of virtue that makes one reputed or venerated (*D* III 21; *P* 19), and above all of "rare and virtuous examples" of sensational executions that revive states by bringing them back toward their beginnings (*D* III 1). Yet Machiavelli also makes an express distinction between using and showing one's virtue (*D* II 17), and he refers to using the virtue of liberality (*P* 16; cf. *P* 21). What can it mean to use virtue as distinct from showing it? Since virtue is not an end in itself, it can surely be used as an instrument. Any virtuous person uses his virtue to gain glory, and a prince or republic uses the virtue of its subjects or citizens (a republic has the advantage in this because it does not have to fear domestic rivals, *D* III 9). But can one use virtue so that it does not show? Here we get a glimpse of Machiavelli and his own virtue.

Virtue, we have seen, must be flexible to be lasting; if it is flexible it can be formed, habituated, cultivated. But the main truth is that individuals have inflexible natures that define their virtues and limit them to flourishing in times in which those virtues are appropriate. Pope Julius II with his impetuous nature succeeded beyond what "all human prudence" could have achieved in stormy times, but he never could have turned cautious in quiet times and therefore would have failed had he lived longer (*P* 25). Machiavelli suggests that Appius Claudius, who tried unsuccessfully to conceal his harsh and arrogant nature, might have done so if he had been able to change "by due degrees" (*D* I 40–42). But in fact Appius proved inflexible and the suggestion is wasted on him. Perhaps it would not be wasted on a noble youth of "extraordinary virtue" such as Cosimo de' Medici or Julius Caesar (*D* I 33). If not a youth, it could be someone with the spirit of youth who makes himself the head of an innovation and who has "extraordinary virtue" (*D* III 21; cf. I 60), or has his "own virtue" involved "with some extraordinary operation" (*D* III 34).

Machiavelli sometimes uses *virtù* to refer to the power or excellence of something that is not a human being, as in "the virtue of a bow" (*P* 6), "virtue of arms" (*FH* pr; III 1; *D* II 2, 30; III 11), the "virtue of fortresses" (*D* II 24), the "virtue" in a tree trunk (*D* II 3), the "virtue" of the world (*D* II pr), the "natural virtues" of airy spirits that watch over men (*aere, D* I 56), and in the phrase "by virtue of . . ."[68] Such usage is not to be wondered at since it continues the practice of Greek and Latin authors and sounds strange only to us post-Kantian moderns for whom virtue has been separated from nature. But we note that when "virtue" does not describe a human being it pertains to human beings.[69] Although necessity is what makes men virtuous, Machiavelli does not want us either to lose heart for politics in the manner of Lucretius or to try to transcend necessity à la Kant. Nature must be considered harsh, but also must be recognized as the source of virtue. The highest virtue, that of "a prudent individual" (*uno prudente, D* I 18), which is expressed in Machiavelli's phrase "virtue of the body and spirit," is a gift of nature.[70] Lesser virtue is habituated according to the modes and orders of the virtue that is not the product of habit. Such virtue is prudence inspired by glory and thus combined with the kind of manliness that is comfortable with ferocity and capable of acquisitiveness. Aristotle, too, spoke of natural virtue above moral virtue, but not as a challenge to moral virtue (*NE* 1179b20–1180a19). Machiavelli imposes on human prudence the task of using and abusing moral virtue and thereby exposes to view the variability and inconsistency of nature as it denies and yet satisfies our desire that things come out right.

Machiavelli believes that prudence and virtue are confined to a very few; he does not share in the democratized prudence of Descartes and Hobbes made possible by scientific method and the theory of natural rights. His morality remains close to and depends on the great deeds of politics that are left out of account by the social-contract theorists. Great men are his theme and greatness is his aim. And yet he inaugurates the mainly democratic politics that we are accustomed to trace to the mediocre, universalized virtue of self-preservation conceived by his successors. Machiavelli's princes are still extraordinary, but they are advised to ally with the people (*P* 9); and he himself promised to work for the common benefit of everyone (*D* I pr).

In the third book of the *Discourses on Livy*, Machiavelli considers the virtue of a captain and that of an army, and he remarks on the rare "double virtue" shown when a captain not only conquers the enemy but also is constrained, before encountering the enemy, to "instruct" his army (*D* III 13). Somewhat later he adverts to the dangerous case of one who "makes himself the head of a new thing" (*D* III 35). This is a matter too long and too high to discuss, Machiavelli says reverently, but he consents to discuss the dangers of someone who makes himself the head in *advising* an enterprise. But suppose the enterprise takes the form of a war against the old regime so as to replace it with "new modes and orders" (*D* I pr), of which the adviser who is also an instructor is the true head?

To *mastermind* an operation is an apt expression for the guiding intelligence that allows others to claim the glory (and take the blame). It describes the activity and virtue of the prince behind the princes that the public sees, the prince of princes. Such a prince uses the virtue of other princes; his project, which because he does not rule directly, he might call his *republic,* gives them opportunity and promises them reward. In respect to him their virtue becomes the "ordered virtue" of soldiers in an army (*D* III 36). Their virtue is infused with his spirit (*spirito,* *D* III 31) so that republican virtue can be understood as the virtue in the captain's soldiers. Machiavelli has a "hidden virtue" resembling that of Aratus of Sicyon, who was a coward in daylight operations but excelled in "fraudulent and nocturnal expeditions" in which he captured cities (*D* II 32). And Machiavelli's virtue is like the "hidden virtue" of the people that foresees its own evil and good (*D* I 58): both the end and the means of his enterprise are hidden.[71] *His* virtue does not show.[72] Nonetheless he will be judged by the results that appear to all in broad daylight. Although his virtue *uses* others' virtue, it also *shows* in their virtue; their virtue is the effectual truth of his. His *animo*, in the sense of "mind" and "intent" as well as "spirit," is behind theirs animating them to think and act in, if not under, his direction. Machiavelli's *animo* replaces the impersonal Aristotelian *anima* (soul)—not to mention the personal God of Christianity—as the ground of human nature. Our rationality is not divine but has been reclaimed as human.

To be humanly inspired, human reason must be inspired by one human being, Machiavelli himself. Any broader inspiration in the name of humanity as a whole would have to be higher than the individual humans whom Machiavelli promises to benefit. The whole good of the species would have to transcend the species unless it were ruled—*masterminded*—by the one in the many who is "without any respect" for higher considerations. In this regard we reverse the point: Machiavelli is the effectual truth of those whom he advises and thus benefits. His inspiration amounts, or can be reduced, to his rule. To be sure of being free from the good and from God, men must submit to the prince who first secured and continues to maintain their freedom.

Because of the ferocious character of Machiavelli's notion, virtue cannot be exercised without conflict and war; he cannot benefit humanity without urging it to war. Despite his Italian or Florentine patriotism, or because of it, he is the captain of an army divided against itself. For all that Machiavelli says against the trustworthiness of mercenaries, he is in the position of a mercenary captain willing to sell his advice (it has a price!) to whoever is prudent enough to buy it. So in the midst of a denunciation of mercenaries, he takes care to praise the virtue of two mercenary captains in the superlative (*P* 12). His virtue shows itself, as we have seen, in the quotation from Petrarch praising "Italian virtue" with which he closes *The Prince*. But behind that virtue is his own, more impartial than others' and available, more or less, to "whoever understands" (*P* 15).

For Machiavelli, virtue does not consist in having a virtuous charac-ter, as for Aristotle. Virtue is alert, on the make; it is not a habit. One must of course get used to the exacting requirements of loose morals and to some extent learn by doing or at least pretending; the main need, however, is not habituation but new and better opinions, or the replacement of inadequate by adequate presumptions. The many bad men who have lived before and after Machiavelli are not Machiavellians unless they can shed the inhibitions that afflict even them; he says they do not know how to be "altogether bad" (*D* I 27). That knowledge is represented in the "art of war," to which Machiavelli gives the broadest possible meaning only once in his writings as "the only art which is of concern to one who commands" (*P* 14). "It is of such virtue," he says, "that not only does it maintain those who have been born princes but many times it enables men of private fortune to rise to that rank."[73] In this statement the art of war does not depend on propitious circumstances for its exercise, as shoemaking awaits a supply of leather, because its virtue supplies the political art of acquiring a state and an army.

"Virtue" here is the quality of a human art that makes it useful to its actual possessor, not merely abstractly and conditionally like the other arts (which in Socrates' famous argument serve the good of the customer; Plato, *Republic* 342c). The art of war would include all other arts because it is the art of acquiring everything those arts need in order to be exercised; it is the art of energizing human rationality. As such, it takes over from the liberal arts of peace, quiet, and contemplation, which were the essence of ancient virtue according to the ancient philosophers. For Machiavelli, the "arts of peace" are those of nonviolent war by fraud (*D* I 11). And far from being the home of the higher, cultivated virtues, leisure, as we have seen, is the breeding-ground of softness and vice. "Ambitious lei-sure" is his name for the condition of modern Italy, where there is no opportunity for war, hence none for virtue (*D* I pr).

Probably Machiavelli is playing with the idea of so comprehen-sive an art. He makes no such claim for it in the dialogue he entitled the *Art of War*. Such an art would have to make prudence available where it does not exist, a methodization characteristic of Machiavelli's scientific successors. In this expansive mood he pretends that everything necessary to glory and prosperity can be taught, that virtue can be reduced to an art that has a virtue. He does so, perhaps, in order to raise the following problem and offer the accompanying remedy. Virtue for Machiavelli is individual because virtue is acquiring and acquisition is for oneself alone. But art is teachable and therefore universal and to the benefit of everyone. The office of a "good man" (*uomo buono*, D II pr) is teaching others.

Yet Machiavelli's art of war says acquire for yourself: can we not reasonably suspect, then, that his teaching brings benefit to him rather than us? He says in *The Prince* and in the *Discourses on Livy* that each book contains everything he knows (which is how we know that these are his major works); but can we not suppose that this pretended gift actually serves his own glory? The captain with the double virtue of instructing and leading has a double glory that lasts, or even begins, beyond his own lifetime (*D* III 13). If Machiavelli is a prince (since all one needs to be a prince is to know the art of war, *P* 14), and princes use fraud (*P* 18; *D* II 13; III 40), does not Machiavelli use fraud, perhaps in the form of the art he teaches? In following his teaching, in allowing him to use our virtue to show his, do we not thereby accept his tyranny over us even if for our own benefit? One may doubt that Machiavelli's followers, above all the philosophers—those princes who accept and adapt his teaching that man is alone—can ever surpass him in glory. He admits, of course, that someone of them might surpass him in virtue (*D* I pr). The achievements of the scientific successors I have mentioned may cover over Machiavelli's since it is in the nature of a methodical beginning—for example, men equal in the state of nature—to forget the Machiavellian observations on the naked individual that make that beginning reasonable. But to a discerning eye not dazzled by science and unclouded by the scholars' Renaissance, Machiavelli was first. His virtue appears greater, therefore, than his art. That is why Machiavelli's own virtue cannot be separated from his notion or doctrine of virtue. He had the opportunity, the good *fortune,* to make his revolution; and this he could not share with us in his teaching.

VIRTUE AND FORTUNE

Only Machiavelli among the modern philosophers can rightly complain of "a great and continuous malignity of fortune" (D let ded). He alone had no one to inspire him toward his revolution into an unknown new world (D I pr). All the others depend on the beginning he made and thus depend on him. Despite all the many succeeding claims of novelty by his successors, he is the *uno solo*, the only new prince in modern times. Even the postmodernism of our day, which is *ipso nomine* entangled in the modern, is to say the least not freed of Machiavellism. Doubtful of modern progress, the postmoderns are bored with their leisure and eager for new experiences, though of an undemanding sort.

We see thus that Machiavelli's bad fortune in having no great man in whose path to tread (P 6) was his good fortune in having no one who preceded him on the same path. Of course he had predecessors; he inherited the whole classical tradition (and he is to this extent a hereditary prince, P 2) that was available to him in his time, the Renaissance, as in no other time since that of Cicero or Marcus Aurelius. In his letter of December 10, 1513, he tells us that he converses with the ancients. But his situation or fortune, living in the "weakness into which the present religion has led the world" (D I pr), compelled him to depart from their orders, "the orders of others" (P 15). In the *Discourses on Livy*, he represents his own rebellion in a story of the disobedience of Fabius, a Roman captain in the field who disregarded orders from the Senate when confronted with the necessity of passing through an unknown forest. The Senate excused him because it followed a wise policy of giving a "free commission" to captains in the field (D II 33). So Machiavelli too claims to be forgiven, or rather approved and praised on the ground that the ancients too would have made a departure under these extraordinary conditions from their ordinary modes. Here is his implied judgment on the Renaissance: a rebirth too faithful to succeed, which in its concessions to Christianity merely imitates the submission of the ancient world to that debilitating force.

We have come at last to the second theme of Machiavelli's doctrine of virtue, its opposition to fortune;[74] the necessity of acquisition was the first. Indeed, they are together or the same. Why does one need to acquire without limit? So as to assure oneself of enough against the turns of fortune. Why does one need to overcome fortune? So as not to depend on it, so as to be free to acquire without limit. Both points are consequences of regarding oneself as alone, as *uno solo*—Machiavelli's foundation, which now appears as a defiant beginning rather than a reluctant conclusion. In his view, the only practical alternative to depending on oneself is depending on God, which means the pope and the Church. He does not produce a proof but rather makes a decision that one should not depend on God. All his criticisms of Christianity presuppose, and do not establish, the standpoint of man alone. One could agree to them and still call for Reformation (or Counter-Reformation) as the remedy for corruption. And if those failed, as Machiavelli is confident they would (*D* III 1), then one could seek in divine grace the only recourse against worldly corruption. Machiavelli simply rebels against that possibility and offers his virtue, that is, his rebellion, as the guarantee of success. Trusting in his virtue is reasonable insofar as his design, his "new modes and orders," are visible to his followers in his books.

If Machiavelli's enterprise is the only alternative to corrupt Christianity, it must be that Aristotle's ethics, a rival thisworldly virtue, is no longer feasible. Aristotle had been forced to admit against his wish that happiness is in need of good fortune. Virtue is the core of happiness, but not the whole of it. One would like to believe that virtue is enough to secure happiness, but a virtuous man in misery can only keep his dignity, not be happy. Fortune must smile on virtue to bring happiness; so the happy man, as is indicated by *eudaimonia,* the name for happiness, is blessed (*NE* 1099b11–13). That blessing can only come from gods or God; so Aristotle admits, through the human propensity to transform chance into a willing being, that his thisworldly ethics depends in effect on the other world.

Machiavelli's virtue seeks a true thisworldly ethics not in need of a blessing. The blessing always comes from others; so depending on fortune's blessing is depending on others. In the first chapter of *The Prince,* Machiavelli analyzes the kinds of principalities and concludes his division by equating three alternatives: those used to living under a prince or used to being free; those acquired either with the arms of others or one's own; those acquired either by fortune or by virtue. Thus he tells us that freedom requires the use of one's own arms, which is virtue as opposed to fortune. But virtue in Machiavelli's day was exposed to a particular fortune, and so the general possibility of overcoming fortune must be tested by that case.

Machiavelli began, we have seen, by identifying virtue as ancient virtue. Ancient virtue was thought not only difficult but impossible to imitate in his time because it had been replaced by Christian virtue (*D* I pr); this was its bad fortune. That moral debacle had its political counterpart in the subversion and overthrow of the Roman empire, the highest achievement of ancient virtue, and its replacement by the Church of the Catholic sect (as Machiavelli impudently calls it, *FH* I 5). Somehow strong ancient virtue was defeated by weak modern (Christian) virtue. So to prove that ancient virtue can be recovered, to overcome the malignity of fortune into which he was born, Machiavelli must show how the defeat of ancient virtue occurred, and in such a mode that we see how it could have been avoided or could be prevented. In the course of the proof, the inherent weaknesses of ancient virtue come into view, as we have seen at length; its predicament in the modern world is inevitable and necessary and not bad luck. Thus the virtue first proposed to be imitated needs to be revised. Machiavelli's virtue emerges from an historical analysis to reveal a prescription for the future, "new modes and orders," which also constitute a personal triumph of secure glory for himself. Having the power with his books to create a new sect replacing Christianity, the new prince makes it possible for the virtue of many new princes to flourish.

The historical analysis is given in the second book of the *Discourses on Livy,* which is apparently devoted to the foreign policy of the Roman republic. Actually, with amazing ingenuity, it considers the "foreign policy," in the sense of the religion, of Rome—for in Machiavelli's presentation God is a power foreign to man—in order to establish the causes of Rome's subjection in the very midst of an account of its success. The key to his presentation is the parallel he uses between the warfare of the ancient Romans and the spiritual warfare of the Christian Romans. Since he too carries on a spiritual war against the Christians, the parallel extends to the difference between the ordinary princes whom he teaches and the extraordinary princes like himself who found and maintain spiritual, or rather spirited, principalities. For example—and one example will have to suffice—Machiavelli is able to discuss humility as a feature of the Romans' war with the Latins (*D* II 14).

Humility is the modern virtue; it is the virtue of weakness, the virtue that makes a virtue of weakness. To Machiavelli it is the outstanding example of the fraud he recommends to one and all in the preceding chapter; with humility, one can rise to the top like Christian priests while pretending disinterest in worldly glory. Machiavelli with his hidden virtue appropriates the Christian virtue that won the victory over ancient virtue, and he uses it against the Christians, thus reversing their good fortune and taking it for himself. At the beginning of the second book he says that Rome's great success was due to virtue, not fortune (*D* II 1). But toward the end we learn that the Romans made signal errors and that their spirits were blinded by a personified Fortune. But Fortune is such a goddess as teaches men, and as she teaches, loses her power over them (*D* II 29). So too does Machiavelli: he teaches men to anticipate fortune, and as he teaches he shares his power, his glory, and his virtue. But out of necessity or justice, he keeps the founder's share for himself.

Virtue seeks to overcome fortune, but how far can it succeed? In Machiavelli's best known discussion, he judges it "might be true" that fortune governs half of human actions, leaving the rest to human virtue (*P* 25). But his argument builds to the notorious climax that fortune is a woman who "lets herself be won" by those who command her. Machiavelli appears to encourage princes to try their luck, to take a risk; he backs the young and the young at heart. He says that "our Italian princes fear the virtue in others that is not in themselves" (*FH* VII 8), but Machiavelli, having it in himself, does not fear it in others. After all, if they should fail, defeated perhaps by another Machiavellian acting under the same encouragement, Machiavelli does not suffer. He knows that virtue is not virtue without risk; a scientific ethics attempting to guarantee virtuous behavior by overcoming the chances against it would in fact assure the death of virtue. His works are a useful antidote to the fearful pursuit of riskless happiness characteristic of our time.

Machiavelli may have personal favorites—Italy and Florence— but his thought provides no more support for them than for their enemies. His humanity is at odds with his patriotism—but not with patriotism in general. He himself can see the necessity of fortune to virtue, and at that elevation fortune is overcome by being made to serve virtue. But the princes and peoples he advises do not share in a consolation that means nothing to them. They are enlivened by the thought that their fate is not determined and that it depends, for all they know, on the use of their own arms. Machiavelli does not promote a vulgar success ethic that says that winners deserve to win; winners may win by chance rather than virtue. Yet from his elevated standpoint virtue always wins because it is given, through his advice, the widest scope it can use without consuming itself.

Virtue wins over fortune by being flexible, by changing "according to the times." A prince must be ready to be impetuous in stormy times and cautious in quiet times (P 25). But what inhibits his flexibility? It is his *nature,* for example the impetuous nature of Pope Julius II that would have prevented him from succeeding in quiet times if only he had lived that long. If princes could change their natures, they could conquer their fortunes.[75] Machiavelli does not exploit his own suggestion for the reason given: he keeps his princes' natures fixed so that he can sustain their virtue. But he shows the way to Thomas Hobbes and his successors, who set aside the diverse natures of men in order to formulate the laws of nature to which they are commonly subject.

Machiavelli himself changes his nature as he uses the diverse natures of those who follow his advice. (And clearly one does not have to be aware of Machiavelli to be Machiavellian). Still, because he uses those natures for a purpose, for his enterprise of working for the common benefit of each, he remains the same throughout. His spirit (*animo*) remains firm and retains its equanimity. He can, perhaps, even change his sex. As "the friend of the young," Machiavelli puts himself in the position of Lady Fortune, having allowed himself to be "beaten down" (P 25).[76] He, too, uses those princes to whom he appears to resign himself, and he is always there, ready for the next generation, when the youths of the preceding generation have exhausted themselves. Machiavelli obviously encourages manly impetuosity, but for that very reason it has only a share in his own virtue, which must also have room for womanly endurance, irony, and passivity. He is both quick in the use of his executive princes and steady as the mastermind behind them, and he combines these opposites not merely in philosophy, as Plato supposed, but in the actualization of philosophy (see *Republic* 503b–d).

It is with regard to Machiavelli himself, therefore, that one must understand the chapter in the third book of the *Discourses on Livy,* titled "Strong republics and excellent men retain the same spirit and their same dignity in every fortune" (*D* III 31). That title might appear to introduce a lesson on the Stoic virtue of equanimity. But nothing could be farther from the truth.[77] Stoicism, even its eclectic, Ciceronian version, is a doctrine of virtue's overcoming fortune internally (in the *soul*, that is) with the aid of Providence. Contrary to Aristotle, the man in a state of misery can be free if he is virtuous. Stoic virtue depends on the unchanging Stoic character so that *Stoic* is a byword for inflexibility. Hence in politics, a Stoic is more than willing to lose since in truth he loses nothing, and he finds it difficult to win because he will not compromise. Such is the character of the Stoic Brutus in Shakespeare's *Julius Caesar*. Stoicism in politics is always in doubt, like Brutus, between the need to prevail and the desire to remain noble. That is not Machiavelli's attitude. In this chapter he understands Roman dignity in defeat as being based on confidence in sound political and military orders that will eventually produce victory; and he recommends an education that will make you "a better knower of the world"—not of God's providence (*D* III 31). This is not Stoicism, but a substituted hardness of calculation in place of the noble, enduring qualities of the soul.

On our behalf as well as for his own glory, Machiavelli shuns the noble and closes down the soul in the belief that these uplifting notions are sources of slavery. He keeps virtue, partly as a sop to virtuous fools, mostly to provide the energy of liberty. What is Machiavelli's virtue the virtue of? That is a question not often asked by scholars who are more indebted to him than they know. It is not the virtue of the soul but of the body and the spirit—the virtue of the body and that which defends the body and is never detached from it. What makes bodies worth defending is left unspecified. Glory? But the glory of what?

TWO

# MACHIAVELLI'S BEGINNINGS

For Machiavelli there is just one beginning—necessity. Every human institution begins without an inheritance from God or nature. God did not give us a perfect beginning, as the Bible says, and nature did not provide us with a potentiality for politics, as Aristotle says. We began bare, unprotected, insecure, and justly fearful. Having nothing to remind us of the good from which we have fallen, or to which we might aspire, we must set our sights on what is necessary to us.

"Necessity" refers to what is humanly necessary, as opposed to what is necessary to the fulfillment of human nature. Necessity thereby becomes an abstraction floating free from what man is and what he is for; it becomes an excuse for the acquisition of necessities regardless of morality. Necessity is what seems necessary to human survival, without much thought about what in humanity deserves to survive. Because we need the help of princes in acquiring, necessity includes the glory necessary to inspire and reward their acquisitiveness. Apparently unnecessary glory, the desire for which is so incomprehensible to peoples because it seems so excessive, gets a cool recommendation from necessity. Here necessity does correspond to certain human natures, the princely types, but only because they embody an indefinite desire. The people, too, have an unlimited desire for security. Instead of having natures, both are under an unlimited abstract necessity.

Yet necessity abstractly understood seems irresistible; it would put human freedom in as much danger as came from Christian divinity. So Machiavelli conceives of many beginnings, not just one. A state must periodically return toward its beginning; its first beginning does not simply determine its course of life. Necessity is not so powerful as to be impossible to forget. Having faced the necessity of its beginning and found a solution, a state easily becomes complacent in the routine made possible by past success. Necessity requires more than obedience to its direction; it requires renewal by the rediscovery of necessity. That renewal shapes the role of Machiavelli himself.

Machiavelli cannot simply announce the laws of necessity in politics and then sit back to watch the inexorable results. That course would leave nothing for his princes to do, and nothing for him either. Necessity does not itself operate by necessity; men must be persuaded to follow it, or even to seek its counsel. Machiavelli must reason about necessity to persuade the princes he advises; he must use rhetoric. *His* beginning is before an audience suspicious of him and resistant to his advice. He must let the princes know that he understands their necessity to seek glory. Each of them, whether in a principality or a republic, must be allowed to have his own beginning, to be a new prince. Their beginnings are actually the completion of his enterprise, which he begins in such a way as to leave something for others to finish.

Chapter 2 is a leisurely comment on the first chapter of Machiavelli's *Discourses on Livy*. He begins that work with a discourse on Rome's beginnings in which he willfully ignores, yet by that very act denies, the divinity in the "beginnings of any city whatever." In chapter 3 I try to make precise the difference between Edmund Burke and Machiavelli, two writers altogether diverse in tone and advice. But I find that their divergence can only be described from their common view of beginnings. Machiavelli's relation to Burke is a good example of his influence on his opponents. Every modern philosopher has fought Machiavelli, more or less; but all have fought him on his ground. In chapter 4 I show how Machiavelli's beginning enables him to set in motion progress toward the "perpetual republic" he envisages. Although he is not known as a *progressive*—and with good reason—he was the first philosopher to escape the cyclical conception of politics of the classical tradition. Today's progressives could learn a home truth from him: progress needs a frequent reminder of the harsh necessity that progressives want to leave behind.

TWO

# NECESSITY IN THE
# BEGINNINGS OF CITIES

In the first chapter or discourse of his *Discourses on Livy,* Machiavelli considers "what have universally been the beginnings of any
city whatever." He brings up questions of choice and necessity: How
much can men live by their own choice in a regime constructed to
produce a certain way of life? How much must they be ruled by the
necessity of the site of their cities? "Virtue," he says, "is seen to be
greater where choice has less authority" (*D* I 1). But he says nothing
of God or religion, even though they are connected to the beginnings
of cities; for men who believe they are ruled by God or gods always
trace their connection to divinity through their beginnings or the
beginnings of their cities.

Thus Machiavelli discusses choice and necessity rather than religion, and *this* choice we need to understand. To do so, we must
suppose it no accident that Machiavelli begins the *Discourses* with
a discourse on beginnings. The difficulties he faces in persuading his
readers to adopt his "new modes and orders" reflect and reveal the
problem faced by the founder of a city: Machiavelli's literary problem is the same as the fundamental political problem. He, too, must
make a new beginning with a view to the primacy of necessity over
choice.

## MACHIAVELLI'S RHETORIC

For some scholars of Machiavelli, the literary problem of the *Discourses* is to answer the question of when it was written. Nobody

This chapter was originally published as "Necessity in the Beginning of Cities," in
*The Political Calculus: Essays in Machiavelli's Philosophy,* ed. A. Parel (Toronto:
University of Toronto Press, 1972), 101–26.

57

knows for sure, since Machiavelli did not say when he wrote the *Discourses:* the posthumous date of first publication, 1531, gives no clue to an exact dating of the writing. *The Prince,* which seems to have been completed in 1513, contains an allusion that seems to refer to the *Discourses* as if it were completed (*P* 2),[1] yet the *Discourses* contains comments upon events that occurred as late as 1517.[2] There is no manuscript evidence on this matter to hinder conjecture, and even the letter that explicitly refers to *The Prince* as if it were complete, is ambiguous.[3] Moreover, Machiavelli claimed to present everything he knows only, but equally, in *The Prince* and the *Discourses* (*P* let ded; *D* let ded). Since they were written at about the same time and since the former seems favorable to princes and the latter to republics, one must conclude either that Machiavelli presented everything he knew in two ways or that he changed his thought entirely very rapidly. With this much scope for discovery, and with competition on a common problem, the scholars have exercised their faculties to the utmost.[4]

One scholar uses the techniques of textual criticism to suggest emendations of what he considers to be Machiavelli's loose insertions in favor of what he considers to be Machiavelli's settled intention.[5] Another uses Machiavelli's references to Livy to form a sequence that qualifies the stated plan of the *Discourses* and reveals two stages of composition, the first when Machiavelli had one conception and the second when he had another.[6] A third scholar finds by study of Machiavelli's sources that Machiavelli waited until 1515 to compose Book I of the *Discourses,* so that he could appropriate an important part of it from the translation of the sixth book of Polybius made by an obscure, itinerant Greek.[7] But no report can convey the subtlety of the arguments merely by giving their results. They must be seen to be believed, for they gain solidity by building on one another and against one another.[8]

One who decides not to join this controversy may think himself obliged to explain. It would be easy to say that some are interested in the dating of Machiavelli's works, and others in his meaning. This is insufficient because those interested in the dating are also interested in the meaning. Indeed, their inquiries begin by taking note of obscurity in Machiavelli's meaning, state as their purpose the clarification of his meaning, and then conclude with a statement of clarification. But to see the starting point of their inquiries is enough for our purpose. We must have, Felix Gilbert says, "otherwise inexplicable contradictions in our source material."[9] When contradictions appear in Machiavelli's text that cannot be explained in the text or on the basis of the text, then we must seek elucidation in what Machiavelli did not say. For example, Gilbert finds a contradiction between the "political realism" of *The Prince* and the "political idealism" of the *Discourses,* and by means of his researches on the dating of those works, concludes that it can be explained as "an intellectual development" not as "an expression of a tension in Machiavelli's mind"[10] (not to mention a consistent intention). Not only this conclusion but also the motive for the researches depend on the finding that Machiavelli's political realism contradicted his political idealism in the "source material." The motive depends on the finality of the contradiction in Machiavelli's text; that is, it depends on the failure of every attempt to resolve the contradiction in the text. After the failures it became necessary to resort to an "intellectual development" unavowed by Machiavelli for an explanation. Gilbert's starting point, then, was a certain understanding of Machiavelli's meaning that was definitive as regards the text, and his conclusion was a better understanding than the one available there.

What is omitted in the procedure is the attempt to clarify the obscurities and contradictions in Machiavelli's meaning—whose existence everyone admits—under the hypothesis that they were deliberately intended as rhetoric. This hypothesis, even if seemingly remote from the truth, takes precedence over an attempt to establish Machiavelli's meaning from the "otherwise inexplicable contradictions." It would forestall an appeal to sources outside Machiavelli for the purpose of understanding him, and it would eliminate the need to apologize for the unsystematic character of his thinking.

Obviously, Machiavelli was a penetrating and sagacious thinker, but obviously, too, his writings contain many inconsistencies and errors, not only in a comparison of *The Prince* and the *Discourses,* not only in widely separated parts of these works that might constitute different "stages of composition," but even on the same page of these and other works. Perhaps this makes him a poet rather than a philosopher—if a poet is a man whose thought is held in the grip of his imagination, instead of the reverse; and if a philosopher is defined, in contrast to Machiavelli's favorites, Lucretius and Xenophon, as a man who intends "to outline a philosophical system" or "to introduce new philosophical terms."[11] But what is it to be systematic?

A strictly systematic book would consider every subject once in one place, and to be sure of this result, it would deduce every proposition from distinct and irreducible propositions or axioms "in a geometrical manner." Spinoza's *Ethics* is almost such a book. An author can afford to be systematic in this way if his audience is open to every new opinion and not partial to the opinions it holds. In this case, strict system is the most economical way of presenting one's thoughts, for one could speak to others as to oneself. But if the audience is partial to its own opinions, and more resistant than receptive, then rhetoric is required for introducing new thoughts. Rhetoric is the deliberate distortion of system in deference to the opinions of the writer's audience. Nowadays "systematic" is often said loosely to describe an author who looks consistent. But looks consistent to whom? To the casual or to the careful reader? An author can be consistent without being systematic when his distortions, his apparent errors and inconsistencies, are made deliberately with an eye to his audience. This author has his own order; he treats each subject "in its place," as Machiavelli says. His order is part of his rhetoric; so he only hints at it, and sometimes does not seem to follow the plan that he does set for himself, as Machiavelli does not seem to follow the plan he gives at the end of the first chapter of the *Discourses*. This author is subtler and more difficult than the systematic author because his purpose must be discerned through his rhetoric.

It may seem arbitrary to attempt to distinguish an author's rhetorical statements from his true intention, but in truth it is difficult and uncertain. If the attempt is not made, one must assume that the author did not use rhetoric. This assumption—that every speaker is sincere and every statement literally intended—is truly arbitrary. Machiavelli tells us, indirectly of course, that it does not apply to himself. He says in the preface to Book I of the *Discourses* that he is bringing "new modes and orders," and in the dedicatory letter, that he deserves to be loaded with honors by men who deserve to be princes. In the twenty-sixth chapter we are told that he who becomes a new prince must make everything anew, so that "no rank, no order, no condition, no wealth is held by anyone that is not acknowledged as from you." Then how does Machiavelli make his way as a potential new prince or an adviser of potential new princes?

In a moment of doubt, Ernst Cassirer once said that Machiavelli was "perhaps one of the most sincere political writers,"[12] and in a moment of sincerity, Machiavelli said the following about rising from low to high fortune: "I do not believe that anyone can be found placed in low fortune who arrived at great power only by open force and ingenuously, but indeed it has been done by fraud alone" (D II 13). If Machiavelli is a new prince, or an inspirer of new princes, he must make his way by fraud at least in part, and since he himself is unarmed, wholly by fraud. Indeed, Machiavelli goes on to say that fraud "has always been necessary to use by those who wish to rise from small beginnings to sublime heights."

What then is rhetoric but written fraud, when the object of the writer is to rise in the world by the reputation or influence of his writings? In this chapter Machiavelli gives three examples of fraud in rising from small fortune to great as given by two writers, Xenophon and Livy, concerning two princes and the Roman republic. Then he exposes a technique of fraud in writing used by Livy to describe the Roman fraud, which is to put the writer's criticism of a powerful enemy in the mouth of an enemy of that enemy. Machiavelli seems not only to comprehend the writer's rhetoric under fraud, but to have it in mind more than any other kind of fraud.[13]

He also invites us to direct this reasoning to himself. At the end of the preface, he says that he undertakes to induce men away from the error of believing that the politics of the ancients cannot be imitated today: "And although this undertaking may be difficult, nonetheless, aided by those who have encouraged me to accept this burden, I believe I can carry it far enough so that a short road will remain for another to bring it to the destined place."[14] This is as plain a statement as one could have that Machiavelli has concealed his intention in the *Discourses,* leaving it to be discovered by "another" who can complete or execute it.

Machiavelli retains his distinction between the new prince and his adviser, between the man who has a short road to the destination and the man who first takes up the burden and carries it most of the way. But this difference is what makes his rhetoric necessary. If he could accomplish his undertaking "with one stroke," he would not need to advise others to adopt his new modes and orders. His undertaking consists precisely in overcoming the prejudice of his times that ancient politics cannot be imitated. Princes need advisers and advisers need princes for the same reason—because prejudices need to be overcome. They cannot be overcome except by fraud practiced upon both the prince and his people, for open and ingenuous force cannot succeed unless it is stronger than the existing order and all those whose rank, condition, and wealth are owed to the existing order. Open and ingenuous force is the weapon of the existing order; it keeps the existing order, rather than some other, in existence; it constitutes the existing order. Fraud creates and conceals a force against the existing order that does not seem to oppose it openly because the fraud does not seem to challenge the power of the ruling prince or government. Such fraud must be conceived and perpetrated by someone who does not seem to profit from it directly, or who is content to wait for that highest glory which comes only after one's lifetime, an adviser who is willing to remain an adviser and not become his own prince. Machiavelli, holding "the office of a good man" and in his "natural desire" to bring "common benefit to everyone," wishes to offer a teaching useful to humanity, not a mere fraud for the purpose of self-promotion. But his teaching includes a new praise of fraud and cannot succeed without the use of fraud and without bringing glory to himself (D I, pr; II pr; III 1, 8, 35, 37).

With the understanding that Machiavelli's rhetoric is the language of the weak to the strong, of the weak gaining in strength to the unwary strong, one might begin to see the difference between *The Prince* and the *Discourses* by considering the different rhetorical situations indicated in the dedicatory letters of those works, the former dedicated to an actual prince, and the latter to two men who deserve to be princes but are not. The reference to "reasoning about republics" in *The Prince* and the references to *The Prince* in the *Discourses* might then be understood as cross references by a writer who has put "everything he knows" into two books from the two essential points of view and who, knowing the malignity of his times and the strength of his enemies, and eager for the glory of fame after his lifetime, remains indifferent to the exact dating of those books.[15]

NATIVES AND FOREIGNERS

We can now consider the first chapter of the *Discourses* with the hypothesis that Machiavelli, in seeking to gain adherents to his new modes and orders, will not say everything about one topic in one place, but will develop his meaning through the whole work. Although he begins with the topic of the beginnings of cities, he will not give the final, unqualified truth about them in his first statement, especially in view of the connection between the topic of beginnings and writers who wish to propagate a new conception of politics. In fact, we find that Machiavelli returns to the topic of beginnings late in the *Discourses* to propound his celebrated thesis that states can survive only by periodic reversions to their beginnings (*D* III 1, 8, 22; cf. I 2, 17). Again Machiavelli's rhetoric duplicates his political teaching; he returns to the topic of beginnings to teach that states must return to their beginnings. After examining the text of the first chapter, we must see how it is provisional and why it is necessary to return to the topic later.

According to the chapter title, the first chapter is about the beginnings of any city and of Rome. It is not explicitly about the beginnings of man simply, like the Book of Genesis; but, as we shall see, Machiavelli seems to imply that man's political beginning, rather than his creation by God, is the beginning that rules his life. The first sentence of the chapter distinguishes between the beginning of the city of Rome, on the one hand, and its legislators and how it was ordered, on the other. The discussion in the first chapter moves from the kind of beginning Rome had to the virtue of legislators as shown, first, in the choice of site and, second, in the ordering of the laws. As a whole it justifies the suggested distinction between the beginnings and the regime, because it shows that at the beginning, the legislators of a city cannot determine its regime or how it will be ordered.

"Wishing first to discourse of the birth of Rome, I say," says Machiavelli, "that all cities are built either by men native to the place where they are built or by foreigners" (*D* I 1). What is the importance of the difference? Considering Machiavelli's examples, we see that Athens and Venice were begun by natives gathering together to resist attack, Athens under Theseus and Venice under no single legislator. A city may be built by natives whether they build either "by themselves or by someone among them of greater authority." When we come to cities built by foreigners, we find that some were built by free men and others by "those depending on others." Examples of the latter are colonies built by "the Roman people,"

Alexandria built by Alexander for the sake of his own glory, and Florence built "by soldiers of Sulla or perhaps by inhabitants of the mountains of Fiesole." By contrast, free men build cities when forced to abandon their native lands and find new seats, and either inhabit cities that they find in the lands they have acquired, like Moses, or build anew, like Aeneas. Free men may be either "under a prince" like Moses or Aeneas, or "by themselves"; here again Machiavelli expresses indifference to the regime. He then drops the discussion of native and foreign builders until the end of the chapter, when the difference reappears in order to be dismissed: "Whoever examining the building of Rome takes Aeneas for his first progenitor will consider it to be of those cities built by foreigners while whoever takes Romulus will think it to be of those built by men native to the place; and in whichever mode, he will see that it had a free beginning, without depending on anyone."

Men make a free beginning not by virtue of the regime or form of government but by not being dependent on others. Machiavelli uses the distinction between native and foreign builders or legislators to introduce a different distinction between peoples with a free beginning and those that begin dependent on others. Surprisingly, he at first identifies the free beginning of a city as a kind of foreign rather than native beginning. The foreign builder either conquers or builds anew, and thus his people do not depend on the prior or native inhabitants for their beginning. But the native inhabitants, he has said, build their own city in self-defense against foreign enemies, and therefore, it would seem, they build to avoid becoming dependent on others.

Moreover, natives as well as foreigners have to move in order to found a city, according to Machiavelli's own account. Athens was built "under the authority of Theseus" by a scattered population, and the Venetians had to move, as we learn in the *Florentine Histories,* from fertile lands around Padua and Aquileia to make their new home in a swamp. Leaving—if not the old site, at least the old modes and orders—seems to be characteristic of all beginnings. Machiavelli is reticent about the reasons that these men may have had for leaving their native lands, but we may supply the defect from his other writings and from other places in the *Discourses.* The Venetians are said there to have come together "because of the coming of new barbarians after the decline of the Roman empire." In the *Florentine Histories* we learn that the Venetians not only left their old homes; they were in fact the former inhabitants of Aquileia and Padua driven out by Attila, king of the Huns, who burned their cities and many others besides, and who refrained from destroying Rome only at the Pope's request.[16] In *The Prince* we are told not that Athens was built by its scattered inhabitants under the authority of Theseus, as here, but that Theseus had to find the Athenians dispersed in order to demonstrate his virtue in acquiring or founding a new kingdom (*P* 6, 26). In this chapter, again, Moses is said to have built a city by conquering one when the people under him were forced to abandon their native country; later it appears that Moses killed the former inhabitants of Syria (or "countless men"), seized their property, and set up a new kingdom with the new name of Judea (*D* II 8; III 30). Aeneas was of course forced to leave Troy, although Machiavelli does not mention it. Thus, leaving is the result of being forced out—and both "natives" and "foreigners" may be forced out—of their homes or their former names if not their land.

The distinction between native and foreign beginnings with regard to freedom does not survive an inspection of the examples that Machiavelli brings up to illustrate it. Rome, he concludes, had a free beginning regardless of the nativity of its "first progenitor," who was either the native Romulus or the foreigner Aeneas. Whether the first legislator was native or foreign does not matter, we can see, because he must be both. As a native who builds anew and reorders the city completely for the sake of self-defense, he makes himself a foreigner to the old ways of that city. As a foreigner he makes himself the first native of a new regime. Having been first in war and hence first in peace, such a founder easily makes himself first in the hearts of his new countrymen. Contrary to Machiavelli's first statement but consistent with his intention, native beginnings can be free beginnings. To see them as such, we must understand that natives build their city to become foreigners to their enemies, while foreigners become natives by leaving their former native land and starting again.

One may suspect that Machiavelli stresses the foreignness of free beginnings not to favor the pretensions of the adventurer or the conqueror (he does not deny them), but to make a deeper point. A beginning is a leaving, not an arriving; it is leaving blasted hopes, not arriving to a hope fulfilled. Although Machiavelli mentions Moses and the city he built, he does not mention the promised land toward which Moses led his people; he does not mention God or the gods in this chapter. Machiavelli does not give Moses a special status as founder here, but in *The Prince* he calls him "the mere executor of things that had been ordered for him by God" and the pupil of God in one chapter, so that we know he is aware of his claim to special status, and seems to forget that status in another chapter, so that we can guess that he rejects it (*P* 6, 26). Moses merely combines the religious aura of Aeneas (the son of a goddess) and perhaps the religious laws of Numa with the ruthlessness of Romulus, who killed his own brother in order to found a city by himself (*D* I 9, 18).

In this chapter the clearest allusion to Christianity is a remark about Florence, one of the two cities said to have begun depending on others, "because (whether built by the soldiers of Sulla or perhaps by the inhabitants of the mountains of Fiesole, who, trusting in the long peace that was born in the world under Octavian, came down to inhabit the plain by the Arno) it was built under the Roman empire. Nor, in its beginnings could it make any other gains than those conceded to it by courtesy of the prince."[17] The art of this sentence is to suggest an ambiguous source of protection and dependence, the prince who was son of Caesar or the one who was son of God.[18] Although silent about religion in this chapter, Machiavelli implies a conclusion about the promised land and the city of God, for the distinction between native and foreign beginnings leads to the question of the scope and use of human choice. Whether native or foreign, a true beginning is a free beginning; and a free beginning is an independent beginning—a human beginning. Men are forced to leave their old site or their old way of life to make a new life that is independent. Their old protection has failed them, as will every protection, including divine favor, and they must make themselves natives against the foreigners menacing their existence. This necessity sets men free, or rather forces them to free themselves, and it is to their own recognition of necessity that they are indebted, not to their creator.

FLORENCE'S BEGINNINGS

In the *Florentine Histories,* Machiavelli tells more about the dependent beginning of Florence than he does in the *Discourses,* and a brief excursion to that discussion will clarify the meaning of a free beginning. There he begins his account of the origin of Florence by praising the "great and marvelous orders of the ancient republics and principalities" for building at all times new lands and cities. These orders, which have disappeared "in our times," consisted in the practice of sending new inhabitants into conquered or empty countries "which they called colonies" (*FH* II 1). By this means conquered provinces were made more secure for the conqueror and the empty places within them filled with inhabitants. It is important to fill the places in a land that are not naturally healthful or productive because if this is not done, the fertile spots acquire an excess of inhabitants, who become poor. Machiavelli gives two examples of modern cities, Venice and Pisa, in which human "industry" made unhealthful places healthful. Then, he cites the city of Florence as the example of the ancient mode, now vanished, of building new cities by sending out colonies. Florence had an ancient beginning under the protection of Rome, and also a beginning in the ancient manner as a colony.

Thus the modern city, Machiavelli's own, which serves him as the exemplar of modern weakness in the *Florentine Histories,* is first presented as the example of the praiseworthy ancient method of building anew. Florence was built by merchants from the city of Fiesole under the Romans and further colonized by Romans, yet, we are told, it was built "anew." How can a colony be considered a new beginning? In this aspect, the means of a new beginning is to send colonies from an established state; it is an act of established power creating new power for itself. It would seem that every beginning of a city is both native, as an extension or a survival of some established power, and foreign, as a creation of power by intrusion into another land. Machiavelli says that colonies were sent into "conquered or vacant countries," but what is the difference? By sending out colonies, the ancients filled up their lands; so if they still had empty lands to colonize, and if no natural disaster had occurred, the lands must have been emptied by conquest. This is what happened at the founding of Venice; and Pisa, too, was filled only after Genoa and its shore were laid waste by the Saracens.

One could infer the necessity of conquest from the identification of new building as colonizing, for the colonists would force the old inhabitants into the barren and unhealthful sites. These old inhabit-

ants would in turn become new colonists of the sites they were
forced to occupy. The best sites are always occupied by the dominant
powers, and they must be ousted or obeyed. Every new beginning is
either the growth of an established power or an attack on an established power, in fact an attack either by or upon an established
power; it is not a voluntary, unhampered growth in empty places.
Some empty places must remain in the world for the health of mankind, since men must be able to move and change; and when the
world becomes filled, heaven or nature must empty it with floods,
plagues, and famines. But as the survivors of such a disaster descend
from their mountain refuges, "few and battered," they must occupy the best sites and make ready for contention with other men
(D II 5).

Yet Florence, it seems, had a protected beginning. It was begun
by ancients in the manner of the ancients, but with a difference. At
first it was a market on the plain for the merchants of Fiesole (situ-
ated on the summit of a mountain), which thrived after the Roman
conquest of the Carthaginians made Italy secure. Later, it was colonized as a result of the peace that "was born" after Rome's civil
wars. Florence was created not of necessity but "at the call of convenience" in an empty place that would have been exposed to attack
had it not been protected by the power of the Romans (FH II 2).
The beginning of Florence was not a true beginning because it was
derived from Rome. Florence was made for the convenience of local
merchants without any necessity of its own; it was made possible
by the necessity that pressed the Romans to defeat their enemies.
Machiavelli cites Florence as the example of one "among the great
and marvelous orders of ancient republics and principalities," but
in the first sentence of the first chapter of the *Discourses,* he says
that those who read of Rome's beginning, its legislators, and how it
was ordered, will not marvel that so much virtue was maintained
for so long. Florence's beginning is derived from a marvelous Roman
order, but Rome's ability to protect Florence is not marvelous. It is
a consequence of Roman virtue. Florence's beginning revealed as
little virtue as necessity of its own, so it points to Rome's beginning,
which was typical of beginnings as well as having been the ultimate
beginning of Florence. From the *Florentine Histories* we are led back
to the fundamental discussion in the *Discourses,* confirmed in the
understanding that every true beginning is free in the double sense

of independent and unprotected. Every true beginning is thus native and foreign.

In the first chapter of the *Discourses,* Machiavelli does not assert that the difference between native and foreign is conventional, and subject to swift and ruthless change; one must find that conclusion elsewhere in his writings. Here he wishes to show that men are forced to make this fundamental, political distinction when they build cities. If they could rely on the protection of nature or God, they would not have to separate themselves into natives and foreigners. If they could consider themselves natives of a mother earth or of an intended home, they could regard themselves as brothers. But necessity forbids it, and Machiavelli now brings up the topic of necessity in the legislator's choice of site.

## CHOOSE YOUR VICTIM

Machiavelli has said in the first sentence of the chapter that those who read of Rome's beginning, its legislators, and its ordering will not marvel at its virtue. Then, after discussing native and foreign beginnings, he speaks of free builders of cities, like Moses and Aeneas, who are forced to leave their native land to find a new seat; in their case "one can recognize the virtue of the builder and the fortune of what is built, which is more or less marvelous as the one who was the beginning of it was more or less virtuous. His virtue can be recognized in two modes: the first is in the choice of site, the other in the ordering of laws." We see that the legislators of Rome have become a single builder who is the cause of both the beginning of the city and the ordering of the laws. Virtue in a city seems to be caused by and visible in the builder; the fortune of Rome, which seems marvelous to the untutored, can be accounted for by the virtue of the builder. The builder chooses the site and orders the laws, whereas the legislators in one reading of Machiavelli's first expression (*latori di leggi*) might have been lawbearers, perhaps from above. What is notable is building, human building, in a site chosen by men.[19] Men do not receive a place or home from God. In the second chapter we are told immediately that Rome did not have one "orderer," and later we learn that this was very much to Rome's advantage. The first chapter exaggerates the scope of the single human builder in order to make human choice its theme.

What does the legislator choose? Machiavelli uses the answer to reduce the power of human building, just after he had seemed to raise human power by omitting all mention of divine power at the beginnings of cities. He says that the virtue of the legislator is made known first in the choice of site and second in the ordering of the laws—as if these were separate questions. As regards the site, Machiavelli asks whether the legislator should "choose" a barren or a fertile site (*D* I 20). This is a surprising question from him, for it was part of the utopianism of classical philosophers that they discussed this question under the very unrealistic assumption that the legislator would have the opportunity of choosing the site.[20] Machiavelli uses the assumption momentarily so as to make a turn in his argument.

A barren site has the advantage that men are "constrained to be industrious, less occupied with leisure, live more united, having less cause for discords because of the poverty of the site." This choice would be wiser and more useful if men were content to live on their own and did not wish to command others. But since men cannot secure themselves without power, it is *necessary* to avoid such sterility in a country and to live in very fertile places. What seemed to be a free choice is restricted as a choice between necessities and decided by the sovereign necessity, the desire of men to command others. Since the most fertile sites will already be occupied by men who have followed their own inclination or Machiavelli's advice, the factual truth of "choose your site" is "choose your victim." At the same time, after seeming to celebrate the marvelous virtue of the builder, Machiavelli remarks that virtue is seen more where choice has less authority.

In this chapter Machiavelli makes human freedom independent of divine power precisely at the time when most men (not to mention previous writers) have looked for a divine presence—at the beginning of cities; and he calls this freedom "building" and "choice." But out of the first choice he shows the power and virtue of necessity. Machiavelli substitutes necessity for divinity; he shows that since men are independent of divinity because of their necessities, they must decide independently according to those necessities. Men are independent of divinity but not free to build according to their own wishes, least of all in a state of hubristic rebellion against divinity. Men must measure their forces.

Having exposed the truth of "choosing," Machiavelli moves to the second way the legislator makes his virtue known, "building" or "ordering the laws." But the character of the laws is determined by the "choice" of a site; the laws must correct the leisure or laziness (*ozio*) of the people in the city that has been wise enough to choose a fertile site. The second concern of the legislator follows from the first; to avoid leisure, the laws of the wise city "should be ordered to constrain it by imposing such necessities as the site does not provide." The laws should reproduce the constraint of necessity or barrenness; they are a kind of artificial necessity contrived to replace natural necessity. They allow men to take advantage of natural fertility, which otherwise makes men lazy. Without laws, men are unsafe either because of their poverty or because of their laziness; with laws, men unlock the bounty of nature or of God. If the desire to command others is a sin, Machiavelli does not say here whether this sin is necessary (forced upon men from outside) or natural (prompted by their own nature); but this cannot be original sin in the Biblical sense of an unforced, voluntary act.[21] Machiavelli wants the government of laws in the Garden of Eden; he wants to combine the two states that the Bible had sundered and that Christianity had separated by the Fall. Such a combination is nothing mythical or imaginary, for two kingdoms, ancient Egypt by whose laws were produced very excellent men[22] and modern Egypt under the Mamelukes, are cited as examples of wisdom.

The first concern of the legislator is not the regime—the ordering of the laws by the men who rule—but the site. The site determines the choice of regime, not particularly by the climate but generally by the need to create artificial necessity. The laws are ordered so as to put pressure on men for the sake of their security. Their security is also the cause of the laws; so the end of the laws, once ordered, is the same as the need that prompts men to make laws. The laws answer the necessity imposed by the desire of men to command others, but they do not rise above that necessity.[23]

Aristotle explained that the reason for the coming-into-being of a polis is not the same as its reason for staying-in-being; men come together to protect life and stay together for the sake of the good life. According to Machiavelli, however, protection is the first and last goal of cities. He implies here what he argues amply elsewhere, that the danger of civilized enemies is as great and as fearful as the pressure of elementary necessities. Every state, however civilized or modern, is

liable to be destroyed by "the Grand Turk." How could it be otherwise? The solution for insecurity does not attempt more than security;
it accommodates—or rather feeds—the desire of men to command
others. The "city" of Rome, in which "so much virtue was maintained
for many centuries," grew to "the empire to which the republic attained."[24] The Roman republic virtuously attained an empire because
it obeyed the need to answer the danger from men who desire to command others. For Machiavelli, *Rome* means the Roman kingdom, republic and empire (not to mention modern Rome). So understood,
Rome detracts from the importance of the successive regimes, since all
fundamentally had the same end, security.

Machiavelli repeats a story about Alexander the Great and the
building of Alexandria to show what he understands by building a
city. Alexander, intending to build a city for his own glory, received
the proposal of a certain Deinocrates,[25] an architect, to build it on
Mount Athos in such a way as to give it a "human form." Their
city would be "marvelous and rare, and worthy of his [Alexander's?]
greatness." But, having asked the architect what the inhabitants
would live on and receiving the reply that the architect had not
thought of it, Alexander refused this marvelous project. He decided
to "set aside that mountain" and not to create a city in his own
image but to build Alexandria where the inhabitants "would have
to stay willingly because of the fatness of the country and the convenience of the sea and the Nile." The form of a city should not copy
the human form, as the city is modeled upon the soul in Plato's
*Republic.* The builder must be free to make his name by serving
human necessities instead of finding his glory in seeking the highest
human possibilities. If he does so, men will follow him willingly,
without imprudent trust in "the long peace that was born in the
world under Octavian."[26]

## NEW BEGINNINGS

When we look at this account of the beginnings of cities as a whole,
epitomized in the story about Alexander, it must appear fundamentally inadequate. It is also inconsistent with Machiavelli's further
thoughts on beginnings in the *Discourses,* and, as will be shown, for
a purpose. Machiavelli discusses here what the beginnings of any
city whatever *have been,* and what *was* that of Rome. He speaks of

beginnings in the past only and uses predominantly ancient examples, referring only to the Sultan and the Grand Turk of modern rulers, and not to them as "builders." He does not speak of beginnings that have been made recently or of the beginnings of modern times. Although he had announced his "new modes and orders" in the preface to Book I, he does not speak here in the first chapter of beginnings that might have to be made now. The new is underplayed in this treatment of beginnings. He mentions the new only three times in reference to or in association with lands newly acquired. The new is what has been acquired, but acquired from the old. The opposition between new and old is not set in view; as we noted, Machiavelli does not make manifest the conflict between natives and foreigners for the choice sites.

This reticence accords with the fact that Machiavelli chooses, in the preface to Book I, to present his new modes and orders as imitating the politics of the ancients. He therefore presents as the obstacle to his enterprise the opinion that the ancients cannot be imitated because the modern world has changed essentially: "as if heaven, the sun, the elements, men were changed in motion, order and power from what they were in ancient times." Machiavelli uses the sameness of moderns and ancients, of new and old, to introduce the possibility of changing the present. With this tactic he can deny that Christianity has made the modern world irrevocably different from the ancient. In silent contrast to Christian political science, he can deny an essential difference between the New Law and the Old Law and he can imply that the coming of Christ does not hinder, except through belief, the recourse of any prince or republic to ancient examples. Thus, he can begin his attack on what he calls here "the present religion" for the "weakness" and "evil" it brings,[27] without seeming to confront it with his own new modes and orders.

In this first chapter Machiavelli does not emphasize the new versus the old because he wants us to think of the old versus the divine. His account of old beginnings brings out the importance of necessity in beginnings, by which he means human as opposed to divine necessities. Alexander, though he built Alexandria for his own glory, built rightly because he built for human glory. His glory could not last if his city did not last, and his city would last, it seems, only if its inhabitants were willing to live there. His glory is in accord with human necessities, with what men choose in accordance with their necessities, as opposed to the glory that glorifies the human form and seeks the marvelous and the rare. Machiavelli desanctifies the old beginnings. They are not marvelous; they have lasted because of the virtue of the human builder choosing necessity, like Alexander. The old can be explained without reference to the divine.

The new, however, cannot be explained without reference to the divine, or in Machiavelli's term, to the extraordinary. He does not tell here of the beginnings of cities as they were to men living at the time, but as they seem to us living in the present. That is why his discussion of building and choosing a site seems so notably un-Machiavellian, with almost all of the nastiness, cruelty, and confusion suppressed. He makes the founding of a city seem like the choice of a site by a home buyer in a new suburban development. But having first taught the opposition between the old and the divine, he can proceed to oppose the new to the old. Having established the sovereignty of human necessity over the divine, he can interpret the divine in terms of human necessity. If Machiavelli had discussed religion in the first chapter he could not have demoted it so effectively, and thus could not have reconstructed it, when he does discuss it in the eleventh chapter and thereafter, so aptly to his own prescription. The opposition of the old versus the divine prepares that of the new versus the old.

One may oppose the new to the old by considering the old when it was new. When the old was new, it was humble and exposed. This much can be inferred from Machiavelli's description of the old beginnings of cities built to escape or anticipate necessity, but of course Machiavelli goes much further in later chapters. He shows that every man was once a man of "small fortune." Those who were born to rank or wealth have this same beginning if they look back far enough to the beginning of their rank or wealth. Every man either had a humble beginning in his own lifetime or inherited it from his ancestors who were not born to the purple. In any case, everyone inherits some important things from his city, and all cities had beginnings—that is to say, humble beginnings. All rank depends on rule, and all rule has beginnings of small fortune. Every man who reflects on his beginnings can see that his present place (if he has one) was not given to him without effort. Such reflection dispels the illusion of effortlessness that is the achievement of civilization. One cannot take for granted the place one has.

At the same time, reflection on one's beginnings reveals the assumption that he must make, which is that every place is occupied. If every reflective man can see that he and his city were once humble in fortune, he can also infer that other men and other cities were then in command. Every man was once a new man, and all who have made their way to power have done so by virtue of the displacement of other men who once held power. They may have made their way by pushing others aside, or their way may have been cleared by natural disaster or divine visitation. Every act of construction presupposes an act of destruction: to act anew is to renovate the old (*D* III 1, 22). The Good Book may say that men were originally placed where it was unnecessary to sin, and the good-hearted (who also enjoy *their* place) may accept the consequences of not pushing others aside. But this is merely a comfortable illusion, since the origin of present comforts is not comfortable to examine. Our friendly surroundings were once held by enemies who had to be displaced (*D* II, 5, 8; III 1).

Thus men must acquire their cities, their riches, and their security from others. Their necessity forces them to pursue the new. Machiavelli develops the necessity of security into the necessity of acquiring through Book I of the *Discourses,* so that in the preface to Book II, he is ready to condemn the usual praise of the ancients and to offer a new reason for imitating them. In II 5 he applies the necessity of the new to religion, showing how men who make new sects are driven to efface every sign of the old. This makes explicit that religion is included in the "everything" that the founder must make anew, according to I 26.

Making a new religion: this is the great omission of Machiavelli's first account of the beginnings of cities. He does not speak of religion and he speaks of "builder" instead of "founder." "Founder" first occurs in the ninth chapter, after a section of chapters, two to eight, on the regime. As we have noted, Machiavelli depreciates the importance of the regime in the first chapter. He does this because he suppresses the opposition between the old and the new, and therefore the difference between the two natural orders of men. When the necessity of acquiring new lands becomes evident, it also appears that some men are more apt and avid in acquiring than most other men. The necessity of acquiring reveals the two "humors" of "the people" and "the great" (*D* I 4). Whereas Machiavelli had said in the first chapter that "men" seek to command others, he now shows that men differ in this respect, some desiring to command and others not to be commanded. When acquisition becomes paramount, the regime becomes a problem; the two orders of men, naturally hostile to each other, must be "managed" by the ruling or princely order. In the first chapter he leaves the impression that laws can reduce discords in a people living at a fertile site by reproducing the necessity of a poor site, but in the following section on the regime he shows that the laws must tolerate discords so that the rulers can manage them. Such management is more difficult than "building" and must be continuous rather than once for all time. The easy harmony of glory for Alexander and security for Alexandria must be reconsidered when it becomes clear that Alexander and his people have opposed natures and hostile interests.[28]

Machiavelli considers the conventional division of men into natives and foreigners before he considers the natural division into princes and peoples. He conceals at first the difficulty of creating a regime of "natives" in order to show that men must divide themselves by their own effort. Before they can understand their own nature, they must distinguish themselves from the supernatural; and, in this distinction, the natural differences between men and the human creative power of overcoming them are lost to view. Machiavelli enlisted both the natural and the conventional against the supernatural, and confused them as "necessity." After the supernatural has been opposed, the necessity of dividing men into natives and foreigners can be analyzed as recognizing the division in human nature and managing it by human creation or convention.

In that management religion or its like is an indispensable instrument. Religion makes men faithful to the gods, and hence to the men the gods recommend. Founders creating a new regime must have recourse to religion as an indirect and apparently impartial recommendation of themselves, for they cannot offer themselves as rulers openly to the people. Their own nature urges them to arrogant mastery of the people, whose nature prompts them to fear and hatred of this mastery. Men cannot live unless they live together, and they cannot live together if the people see the rulers for what they are. The first necessity of ruling, then, is for the rulers to hide their own nature by means of religion, or in the Machiavellian equivalent, by fraud. Rulers would be as blind as the ruled and would never appreciate this first necessity if they did not see it as a human rather than a divine necessity. That men need religion should be a reproach to their creator, for if religion were gratitude, it would be offered willingly and could not be forced upon men. Man's need for religion is thus the cause of his independence, not of dependence. Only when rulers see or sense that men obey themselves in obeying necessity can human necessity appear as the foundation of human freedom.

So Machiavelli gave a first account of the beginnings of cities according to human necessities, which omits the first necessity in beginning a city. The first necessity of the beginning (*principio*) is a prince (*principe*) who makes everything anew.[29] As the *archē* is in the architect, Machiavelli finds the *principio* in a human *principe*. The human prince must "be alone" against God before he can be alone among other men, and he learns the necessity of acquiring from other men by "acquiring the world" from God. Man's necessity turns out to be this man's necessity, *your* necessity in Machiavelli's familiar address. One cannot speak of "one's own" always in the third person: your necessity is to be a new prince and make a new beginning.[30]

To indicate that religion made by a founder binds the regime, Machiavelli alternates sections of chapters on founders and religion through the fifty-two chapters remaining in Book I after the section on the regime.[31] For a time he separates the founding of the regime from the founding of religion by giving the fame of founding the Roman regime to Romulus and that of founding the Roman religion to Numa. But this separation proves to have been an accident of the opposite characters of Romulus and Numa, the first "very ferocious and warlike," the second "quiet and religious." Better than either is a king like Ancus, "gifted by nature in such a way that he could make use of peace and carry on war" (*D* I 9, 10, 11, 19). Founding a regime is founding "new orders," which are, with respect to the old orders, "extraordinary." "And truly there has been no orderer of extraordinary laws in a people who did not have recourse to God."[32] Such laws would also be "foreign" to the people receiving them. Religion communicates what is extraordinary and foreign to the laws, and revives the original fears as they were felt at the beginning.[33] The prince can therefore secure himself and his regime with both the recommendation and the fear of God.

It is the new, the humanly created, rather than the old as related in histories, that is connected to the divine. Wishing to teach princes how to make a new or reordered religion, Machiavelli had to begin by distinguishing his enterprise from "the present religion." To do this he made the histories of Titus Livy his Bible and offered his new modes and orders in the rhetorical guise of a commentary on a human book, "a fragment of an ancient statue" (D I pr).

# THREE

# BURKE AND MACHIAVELLI ON PRINCIPLES IN POLITICS

What is the place of principles in politics today? The first thing to notice is the plural: ordinary citizens in liberal democracies today are accustomed, as citizens, to a plurality of principles in politics. They do not have to stand above active political life, as philosophers, in order to observe the variety of regimes and the conflict of the principles of which one animates every regime. They find that conflict within their own regime.

## PRINCIPLES AND CONSCIENCE

The plurality of principles in liberal democracies is on view in the institution of party government. There liberal democracies seem to have accomplished in practice what had always before seemed marvelous even in theory, one society with many principles. The one society not only tolerates many principles, but through party government turns them to account; so pluralism seems not only harmless but healthy. Liberal democracies take pride in the toleration of exclusive principles and even in the encouragement of such principles as they contribute to the common good. Because in liberal democracies principles are plural, they are seen as essentially partisan. When a politician claims to be acting on principle, the obvious response is, which principle? On the other hand, although principles are seen as essentially partisan, partisanship is not seen as deep and divisive. Since each principle can make its contribution to the common good

This chapter was originally published as "Burke and Machiavelli on Principles in Politics," in *Edmund Burke: The Enlightenment and the Modern World*, ed. P. J. Stanlis (Detroit: University of Detroit Press, 1967), 49–79. Copyright © 1967 by Peter Stanlis.

in its party, or from its wing of the party, partisanship need not divide the country fundamentally.

In the Civil War the United States was divided fundamentally, but some revisionist historians, using this reasoning about the pluralistic party system, have argued that the Civil War was unnecessary.[1] In their opinion, the Civil War was the result of a misunderstanding of the pluralism of liberal democracy and mismanagement of its party system. Even differences as apparently deep as those between the North and the South are not too deep for party government to link and combine in a common or at least contiguous life. When those differences are combined as the revisionist historians argue, they will seem to be less noble principles than regional interests, less slavery and freedom than cotton and manufactures. It would be as silly to condemn the selfishness of the interests as to praise the nobility of the principles. Thus the reduction of principles to interests seems to be both a prerequisite and a consequence of the plurality of principles in one society. In this view, principles can be plural in one society only when they are moderate, that is, when they contribute to what might be overstated as the dialectic of freedom; but, in making this contribution, they are reduced to the modest function of interests. Principles in a liberal democracy do not stand for the whole; they merely claim for a part. Whatever the sincerity of men of principle—and no one should underestimate their faculty of self-deception—the actual function of principles is the promotion of selfishness which, incidentally, and with proper management, redounds to the general good.

Now it will seem that by beginning with the plurality of principles I have neglected the simple meaning of principle in politics, which still survives as conscience. In the strict sense, now rarely met, conscience is the receptivity of the human soul to a higher law, a divine law. Conscience has its source *above* politics, and for this reason it is taken to be authoritative *in* politics. A man who acts on conscience is guided by a principle higher than his interest, a principle above himself, above his own group or party or country. Such a person is raised by his transcendent principle above those who do not follow conscience, not for his own sake, not necessarily by his own choice, but for the sake of the principle and ultimately for the sake of the source of the principle, God. Conscience taken strictly restores the exclusiveness of a principle with a vengeance. It implies not the existence of a common good accommodating the interests of all but rather a communion of those who live according to conscience, which may be hostile to or forgiving of those who do not. But, whether hostile or forgiving, this communion does not accept a plurality of principles; it cannot agree that its principle is a part of the truth to be complemented by other parts, or an exaggeration of the truth to be offset by contrary exaggerations. It can be objected that there are many conceptions of conscience, of which this is the most extreme. But if this conception seems strange and obsolete today, then this is the very problem to which I call attention.

Liberal democracies pride themselves on the toleration of individual conscience, but they do so in the spirit of toleration, not of conscience. When conscience is received tolerantly, it is absorbed into the practices of liberal democracy. Conscientious objectors, for example, advertise not so much their pacifist principle as the plurality of principles in the society that allows them the privilege. They become "the conscience of society"; they serve the purpose of reminding us of the horrors of war. To serve this purpose, it matters little whether conscientious objectors are sincere in what they say or whether they really are guided by conscience. In liberal democracy there is a systematic preference for the tender conscience over the fierce conscience, for the social conscience over the antisocial conscience. But conscience in the strict sense thrives where the attractions and blandishments that appeal to one's interest are denied by stern intolerance, and every appeal to the higher law has to be paid for in the lower courts. At first it might seem that men of conscience would thrive where conscience is respected and even given a function in politics or society. But, after consideration, one may perhaps conclude that the embrace of liberal regimes is more dangerous to men of conscience than the hostility of illiberal regimes. Such men, who may be very successful in liberal regimes, are tempted to forget that conscience in the strict sense has its source above all politics, including the politics of liberal democracy.

The result of the argument hardly seems satisfactory. Is there no way to tolerate conscience without destroying it? Is it impossible to respect someone else's principle without debunking it?

To consider the problem I propose a comparison of Machiavelli and Burke. They are not commonly known as progenitors of liberal democracy, for they have many heirs and few disciples, especially

Machiavelli. Nor are they commonly compared with each other; for both in respectability and in devotion to principle Burke seems far removed from the sardonic, conscienceless Machiavelli. But they have three points of contact that also touch our concerns today. First, they both argued in support of party government. While Burke was the first respectable political philosopher to argue that parties can be respectable, Machiavelli was the first political philosopher to argue that they can be good. Second, they were both concerned with principles in politics, and agreed that politics is most healthy when there is a plurality of principles. Third, they both thought that conscience in the strict sense was, if not an intrusion of divine politics into human politics, a pretense of humans to cover their interests. This belief is notorious on the part of Machiavelli,[2] but Burke's partial agreement is less well-known. He criticized the public use of conscience by politicians, calling the conscience "that secret tribunal, where they are sure of being heard with favour, or where at worst the sentence will be only private whipping."[3]

## MACHIAVELLI ON MIXED GOVERNMENT

In considering Machiavelli it is useful to begin with his praise of party government and then to derive his argument against conscience. In this way we shall move from a familiar institution to Machiavelli's unfamiliar defense of it, and we shall be able to reproduce some of the reasoning of this most subtle and difficult writer. Machiavelli's praise of party government occurs near the beginning of the *Discourses on Livy,* the work in which he has put "everything he knows" and claims to present "new modes and orders," not in the *Florentine Histories,* where the sins of the Italian parties are put on view.[4] Machiavelli does not tell us directly what this first praise of party government in the history of political philosophy signifies.[5] Instead, with every appearance of impartiality, he allows his new conception of party government to emerge victorious from a competition with the classical doctrine of mixed government. Rather than proclaim the novelty of party government, Machiavelli seems to borrow extensively from the classical writer Polybius and to adopt his discussion of Sparta and Rome as examples of mixed government.

In the first chapter of the *Discourses,* as we have seen, Machiavelli takes up the beginnings of all cities and especially of Rome. It seems that Rome's beginning is responsible for Rome's virtue, but Machiavelli does not mean that Rome's first legislation was good because it was fashioned by Aeneas, the son of a goddess. Contrary to the myths to be found in Livy, Rome did not have a perfect, divine beginning. Nor was there a single legislator on the classical model of Plato and Aristotle whose human virtues infused the regime he formed. Machiavelli praises several Roman legislators for the proper use of necessity. Instead of choosing a poor, infertile site to keep men busy and content with each other, the Roman legislators chose a rich, fertile site so that Rome might be able to expand. Then they used laws, that is, an artificial necessity, to prevent men from becoming lazy and distracted by luxury.

The reason for preferring a rich site is that "men cannot make themselves safe without power"; so the seemingly innocuous topic of where to place a new city discloses the principle by which Machiavelli will reject the polis of the classical political philosophers. It was a vital provision of Plato's *Republic,* somewhat relaxed in the *Laws* and by Aristotle, that a city must live poor if it wishes to be self-contained or self-sufficient.[6] Machiavelli seems to exclude the possibility of self-sufficiency in denying that men are content to live on their own and do not seek to rule others. Machiavelli will show that party government and a self-sufficient regime are incompatible.

Chapters 2 to 8 of the *Discourses* are concerned with the regime, and Machiavelli gradually makes clear the issue between party government and the traditional mixed government. The second chapter is on the classification of regimes as it is complicated, or rather overthrown, by Machiavelli's understanding of Rome. Machiavelli presents the traditional classification of six types or reasons of government, consisting of principality, aristocracy, and popular government, and their perversions—the classification of those who are wiser "according to the opinion of many" than those who believe there are only three types of government. He proceeds, somewhat in the manner of Polybius,[7] to the traditional cycle of regimes by which each good regime degenerates into its corresponding perversion, and concludes rather strongly that all are "pestiferous," the three good ones being short-lived and the bad ones being malignant. Hence one should choose a mixed government containing all types—

that is, the three types named above.[8] The Spartan constitution of
Lycurgus was a government with a share for king, aristocrats, and
people, and it had a life of more than eight hundred years.

Rome, however, had no first, sovereign legislator like Lycurgus.
By "Rome" Machiavelli apparently means here the Roman kingdom, republic, and empire successively, with the consequence that
the many legislators of Rome were working on different, indeed
conflicting, regimes. Although they intended to form different
Romes, Machiavelli implies that their contradictory intentions had
a single result—for many centuries a free and powerful Rome. What
Sparta achieved by the intention of Lycurgus, Rome achieved contrary to the intentions of successive and competing legislators. Machiavelli says that Rome was achieved by chance, in the sense that it
was not planned all at once and from the beginning, which is to say,
by one legislator.[9] But the "many unexpected accidents" that defeated the separate intentions of Roman legislators had a constant
source in the disunion between the plebs and the Senate. Rome's
first laws were "defective," because they aimed to establish a kingdom, but "good" because they were adaptable to liberty. When the
kings were expelled, the kingly power was retained under the name
of consuls; and when the nobles became insolent and the people rose
up against them, the consuls and Senate retained their power after
the creation of the Tribunes of the plebs. Thus, despite an apparent
succession of "all three kinds of governing," Rome remained mixed
and made a perfect republic. Rome came to this perfection, Machiavelli says, through the very discord that prevented a stable, lasting
regime.

It is true that the Senate and the plebs were on good terms just
after the Tarquins were driven out, for the nobles had put away
their pride and adopted a popular spirit. But this seeming generosity
had a hidden cause in the pride of the nobles, since the nobles had
feared the Tarquins and had surmised that the people, if ill-treated,
would ally with them. When the Tarquins were gone, the pride of
the nobles was asserted against the people and their hidden enmity
came into the open. The willingness of the nobles to accept the
establishment of Tribunes of the plebs—indeed their general moderation—cannot be put down to their generosity: the hidden cause of
their moderation was their experience under the Tarquins.[10] The
enmity of the nobles and the people was as irrepressible as Rome

was durable and invincible. Machiavelli had said that Rome was a mixture of the three types of government, and that the consuls were the former kings without the name; but in the third chapter he shows how the Tribunes took over from the Tarquins the function of damping the insolence of the nobles and calls the Tribunes middle-men between the plebs and the Senate, thus disregarding the difference between the kingly and the aristocratic power. It seems, then, that the Roman mixed government is constituted by a fundamental tension of two elements with the third in the middle; it is neither a unity of three elements in which their hostility is resolved, nor a kind of equilibrium system of three independent elements. The understanding of Roman mixed government as a fundamental tension casts doubt on the traditional classification of regimes, whether threefold or sixfold. Contrary to Polybius, the traditional classification does not provide a proper preparation for mixed government; at least in Rome, mixed government is twofold rather than threefold.[11]

## PARTY GOVERNMENT AND IMPERIALISM

In Chapter 4 of the *Discourses* Machiavelli opposes the opinion of the many that the dissensions in Rome were injurious to the republic. He does not say so, but this was the opinion of Livy, based on classical political philosophy and also found in the medieval tradition. This chapter is the *locus classicus* of the argument for party government, the first argument that party government is good. "Party government" means the open and public practice of partisanship and the public praise of it as good or respectable; for Machiavelli shows us that, in this broad meaning, party government must be justified before any particular kind can be proposed. The dissensions in question were Roman, but Machiavelli's argument that they were not injurious constitutes the first modern argument for party government. When Machiavelli recommends imitating the ancients, he refers to the ancients as newly interpreted by himself.[12]

After saying in the second chapter that Rome came to perfection through discord, Machiavelli says in the heading of the fourth chapter that discord *made* the Roman republic free and powerful. In the chapter itself, Machiavelli retreats somewhat from the assertion of the chapter heading, saying that the dissensions were the first cause of *keeping* Rome free. He deplores those dissensions considered in themselves and excuses them by remarking how few were exiled or put to death as a result. Finally, he suggests sardonically that, as laws for liberty were the result of the dissensions, one ought to consider that "so many good effects as emerged from that republic were not caused if not by the best causes."

The suggestion is explained in Chapters 5 and 6, where an alternative of Rome or Sparta is developed. The premise of the alternative is that there is no unmixed good, or that no decision is without its inconveniences, and hence that good effects do not come from simply *good* causes, but, as Machiavelli so precisely said, only from the best causes—that is, the best existing causes. Machiavelli makes his decision for Rome for this very reason: the legislation of Sparta turns out to be an attempt to have an unmixed or self-sufficient political good, and that is impossible. We discover in Chapters 5 and 6 that the liberty of the Roman republic was an unintended consequence of its desire for power and its many conquests. Rome's domestic arrangement—its party government—was a by-product of its imperialistic foreign policy. Machiavelli presents his argument for party government by stages; and, just as his meaning seems to become settled, he brings up a new consideration to disturb it.

The alternative of Rome or Sparta arises from the problem of finding the most secure guardian of liberty; is it the nobles or the people? The Spartans and, among the moderns, the Venetians, made the nobles guardians of liberty; the Romans relied on the people. There are reasons on both sides, Machiavelli says, although the liberty of Sparta and Venice lasted longer than that of Rome. On the Roman side, it can be said that nobles clearly desire to dominate, whereas the ignobles (*ignobili*), or the people, desire not to be dominated;[13] and it is better that the guardians cannot seize the liberty they guard. On the Spartan and Venetian side, it is argued that guardianship in the hands of the powerful (*potenti*) keeps them better satisfied and removes from the people the restless spirits who usually rouse the people against the nobles. Machiavelli summarizes this argument with a question: which humor of men is more harmful to a republic, that which desires to keep acquired honor or that which desires to acquire what it does not have? Then he asserts that, after subtle examination of the whole, one can resolve this argument into another: is it better for a republic to wish to make an empire, like Rome, or to be satisfied with maintaining itself?

Venice maintained itself because it had relatively few inhabitants; and, although it was very cosmopolitan and its laws allowed foreigners to settle, the people were governable because they were not entrusted with arms. Machiavelli tacitly rejects this possibility in Chapter 6, since it requires reliance on mercenaries, on the arms of others.[14] The choice is between Sparta and Rome, two states that armed their peoples. Sparta did not admit foreigners, and so did not have occasion to become corrupted or to grow so much that it was unmanageable by the few who governed it. We note that Machiavelli here treats Sparta as an oligarchy made moderate by the presence of kings, not as a true mixed government with a share of power for prince, aristocracy, and people. The vital feature of Sparta was its prohibition against foreigners. Rome, however, did not "remain quiet." The Roman legislators (Machiavelli keeps the plural) welcomed foreigners and armed them, which gave the people force, increased their number, and afforded them infinite occasions for raising tumults. Thus the causes of tumult were the causes of growth.

> In all human things he who examines well sees this, that one inconvenience can never be cancelled without another's cropping up. Therefore if you want to make a people numerous and armed, so as to be able to make a great empire, you make it of such a quality that you cannot then manage in your mode; if you keep it either small or unarmed so as to be able to manage it, then if you acquire dominion, you cannot hold it or it becomes so vile that you are the prey of whoever attacks you.

The question now seems to be whether it is necessary to desire to have great empire, since Machiavelli seems to allow that a small armed state would be feasible if it did not seek empire. "If someone wanted therefore, to order a republic anew, he would have to examine whether he wanted it to expand like Rome in dominion and power or truly to remain within narrow limits."[15] Whether to seek empire seems to be a matter of choice. But, in the last part of Chapter 6, Machiavelli gradually withdraws the possibility of choosing to seek empire, and, with it, the alternative of Rome or Sparta.

First, it appears that Sparta had an empire after all and lost it, having revealed "its weak foundation in one slightest accident." Venice also had conquered much of Italy, and then lost it in one battle (or in one-half of a battle). But, if Sparta and Venice fail to certify the possibility they seemed to embody, perhaps a republic "like Sparta or Venice" can be placed where it could not easily be conquered and also kept small in order not to cause fear in her neighbors. If this could be done, Machiavelli believes,[16] "the true political way of life and the true quiet of a city" would prevail. It cannot be done, however: "But since all things of men are in motion, and cannot stay steady, they must either rise or fall; and to many things that reason does not bring you, necessity brings you." (D II pr, 19; FH III 5, V 1). The argument between Rome and Sparta is decided by necessity rather than reason; or, when we remember the effect of Machiavelli's reasoning, the argument is decided by reasoning about necessity.[17] A republic organized to maintain itself may have to grow, and will be unprepared to grow successfully; or, even if it is not forced to grow, the ease of quiet living will make it effeminate or divided. Machiavelli concludes with his characteristic blandness: "In ordering a republic there is need to think of the more honorable part, and to order it so that if indeed necessity brings it to expand, it can keep what it has seized."[18]

Human things are in motion, and human affairs must therefore rise or sink. The world is unfriendly, and the political skill of men must be devoted to the competition for the catch. Politics cannot bring respite from the primitive necessities in order to aim at the good life, Machiavelli thinks, because those necessities are too powerful to be suppressed by civilization. They are too powerful because they are in motion. A man or a country may be able to afford generosity today but what of tomorrow? Anxious foresight is the only unqualified rule of Machiavellian prudence;[19] and human progress toward the better things and the better life is indistinguishable from unending flight from the fears relentlessly pursuing men.

## THE ILLUSION OF SELF-SUFFICIENCY

We are accustomed today to distinguish between the "haves" and the "have-nots." In discussing Sparta and Rome in Chapter 5, Machiavelli asks whether those who desire to keep or those who desire to acquire are more harmful to a republic. In his answer he first indicates that those who desire to keep fear to lose, and then says that the fear of loss produces the same will as the desire to acquire; for the haves are not secure in what they have unless they get something new. The haves can indeed cause more tumults than the have-nots because they can use greater power and motion in making changes, and because they inspire ambition in the have-nots for revenge or for riches and honors. Machiavelli is not opposed to unrestrained ambition, unless the restraint is rival ambition; and his question is answered in such a way that ambition must be on the whole useful to a republic.[20] Since the haves must seek to acquire as avidly as the have-nots, acquisition must be the guiding necessity of any republic or any political order.

The desire to keep having thus the same effect as the desire to acquire, the legislation of Sparta is based on an illusion. Sparta was forced to expand abroad, yet its internal order presupposed that keeping can be accomplished without new acquisitions. Its internal order aimed at a just balance between the classes, a balance that resolves the private claims to justice advanced by each class in a public order. Lycurgus maintained unity, Machiavelli says, by keeping property nearly equal and the citizens equally poor, though not equal in rank; and he tried to secure the rigor of his laws by excluding foreigners (D I 6; II 3). Lycurgus, so to speak, admitted that his internal legislation depended on the exclusion of foreigners, or, more generally, that his domestic policy depended on the primacy of domestic policy over foreign policy. His domestic policy was the primacy of the public over private interests and private considerations; so one may say that the primacy of the public over the private depends on the primacy of domestic policy over foreign policy. If laws made for domestic unity require the exclusion of foreigners, Lycurgus should have known that, sooner or later, and sooner than eight hundred years,[21] Sparta would have to repel foreigners by conquering them—which is to say that it would have to include foreigners.

If foreigners are so powerful and hostile that they must be excluded from a republic, they are powerful and hostile enough to force themselves upon that republic eventually as conquerors or conquered. That is the self-contradiction of Spartan legislation: the need to *require* domestic self-sufficiency shows the impossibility of *attaining* it. The Spartan legislation arbitrarily divides men into those who can be integrated into the public order and those who cannot, but if foreigners cannot be integrated, how can citizens? Today we would say that those of a common culture can be integrated more easily than those of diverse cultures; but Machiavelli would ask:

where does the common culture come from? Culture comes from education, and, he reminds us, education comes from laws, that is, from a political order in the widest sense.[22] Since the difficulty of integration is universal, domestic and foreign policy must be made to correspond rather than kept separate with different rules for each. The virtue of the Roman legislation is that it treated the plebs as a large neighboring nation, actually or potentially hostile, somewhat as the Romans treated the Samnites.[23] The Roman nobles made the plebs their *ally*, according to Machiavelli's account; one could not say that the nobles and plebs were merged into the public order of a traditional mixed government.

In Rome, the primacy of foreign policy over domestic policy led to the primacy of private interests over the public good. The Roman regime shifted rapidly to reflect the current balance of power between nobles and plebs. As Rome acquired more and more territories, the plebs became less and less manageable, until the nobles were overthrown entirely by an alliance between Caesar and a corrupt plebs.[24] Until this time Rome had party government at home as a consequence of its imperialistic foreign policy; Rome was forced to tolerate the pursuit of private interests, whether those of individuals or of classes, because it was forced to expand. Faction comes with glory and both contributed to the advance of Rome; but the self-sacrifice of Spartans is suited only to the modesty of their original orders. If classical republican virtue is self-sacrifice, Machiavelli finds it inadequate to the acquisitive tasks of republics.

The traditional argument for mixed government, which Machiavelli almost reproduces in his second chapter, neglects foreign affairs, and proceeds as if the cycle of simple governments took place on an island where there were no neighbors or other enemies. Machiavelli had indicated as much in the second chapter when he said that a state that staggers through the cycle of governments will probably become subject to a neighboring state better ordered by laws. But it becomes clear in his discussion of Rome and Sparta that due attention to foreign policy casts a new light on domestic policy. Machiavelli overthrows the traditional distinction between friends and enemies, and holds that all men must be considered enemies. Not only must the legislator presuppose that all men are evil or criminally inclined, for all agree that this presupposition is necessary (*D* I 3). The legislator must presuppose in addition that all men are enemies of one another, and therefore not try to make some of them friends. Machiavelli does not deny that men can be trusted, but he asserts that the basis of trust is the confidence of the prudent and the strong in their own forces.[25]

When the connection between party government and imperialism is properly weighed, one can see that it amounts to a profound rejection of the self-sufficient polis of classical political philosophy. The Spartan illusion that domestic policy can be planned and carried on in a world apart is the very theme of Plato and Aristotle. Sparta is not a solution to the traditional problem of the decay of regimes because that problem is misstated. In the traditional view it is assumed that self-sufficiency is possible at least in some circumstances and hence it is supposed that the greatest difficulties are internal. Machiavelli finds that the greatest difficulties are both internal and external, but of the kind that had traditionally been considered chiefly external—those arising from the hostility of enemies or the conflict of hostile interests. His discovery of the primacy of foreign affairs had the effect of dissolving the traditional mixed government; for imperialism, by allowing the people to become large, well-armed, and diverse, makes them unmanageable. Those who do not attempt an imperialistic policy must nonetheless face the necessities to which that policy is the only prudent response. In the event, their states must rise or fall.

But even before necessity becomes so clear that it cannot be mistaken, the "hidden cause" is effective. In Rome, the nobles kept up a false democratic spirit to hide their true malignity to the people before the Tarquins were expelled. In Sparta, the unity and quiet of the state were similarly false, hiding the oppression not merely of the helots but also of the common people. In Chapter 6, Machiavelli debunks the threefold harmony of Sparta on which Lycurgus's reputation (not to mention the authority of Polybius) rests (Cf. D I 1, 9, 35 and I 2, 6). There Machiavelli says that Sparta was governed by a king and a limited Senate,[26] and that the nobles did not treat the people so badly that the people wished to hold offices. But the moderation of the nobles was enforced by the Spartan kings, just as in Rome under the Tarquins; moreover, Machiavelli later refers to the Ephors in a way that intimates that the Spartan people were not so quiet after all. Rome and Sparta differed not so much in structure as in the policy of imperialism; and, even here, the Spartans were not guiltless but ineffectual.[27] The manageable plebs of Sparta, so far as it was manageable, seems to have been merely oppressed.

There is one aid for the Spartan way, however. Machiavelli seems to allow that, when Sparta has been debunked, it need no longer be rejected. The alternative of Rome or Sparta can be restored if it is understood as a choice not between imperialism and self-sufficiency but between oppression of foreigners and domestic oppression. The necessity to expand can be answered by means of a confederation of republics, each of which remains small and hence oppressive to its own people. From the connection between party government and imperialism we can see why another possibility remains. Since party government is a substitute for domestic oppression and must be combined with oppression of foreigners, it is not simply a substitute for oppression; and therefore it is not absolutely required. Machiavelli's rule that every good has its inconvenience means that in some *foreseeable* circumstances any good can reasonably be rejected. If a "free republic" like Rome is a republic that oppresses its neighbors instead of its own people, Spartan oppression could become choice-worthy.[28]

I conclude that, for Machiavelli, mixed government in the traditional sense is undesirable because it is impossible. Machiavelli divides all states into republics and principalities in defiance of the cyclical analysis that requires six types, including the perverted types. His usage deserves a more detailed treatment, but clearly he prefers a twofold classification of regimes that roughly corresponds to the two classes within regimes. In comparison with the traditional classification, he drops the perverted forms of government; and he amalgamates aristocracy and democracy under "republic," which is to say that he drops democracy as a form of government (*D* I 16, 37, 44; III 29).

CLASS ANALYSIS OF POLITICS

The reason for Machiavelli's new classification of regimes is to be found in his new analysis of classes within a regime. In Chapters 4 and 5 of the *Discourses,* Machiavelli makes two statements about the classes in a republic that must be quoted for careful inspection.

> In every republic are two diverse humors, that of the people (*popolo*) and that of the great (*grandi*). (I 4)

In every republic there are great men (*uomini grandi*) and popular
men (*popolari*). (I 5)

These statements seem to be the same and are not. Popular men are
not the people; they have the favor of the people but they have the
humor of the great, which is ambition. "The great" can be understood to include the popular men because popular men are ambitious, or to exclude them because they have no power and hence no
titles and honors;[29] likewise "the people" can be understood to include or exclude popular men.[30]

The discord between the nobles and the people has two aspects,
the difference in humor between the people and the great, and the
ambitious rivalry of the nobles and the popular men. The people by
themselves are not ambitious, as they wish merely not to be oppressed; but the popular men are ambitious and not content to be
left alone. Thus "managing the people" is a complex task. The Roman nobles showed their moderation (that is to say, their enlight-
ened selfishness) in yielding some honors to "the restless spirits of
the plebs" as well as maintaining the religion of the people.[31] The
people can of course become excited; so Machiavelli says that "every
city ought to have its modes with which the people can vent their
ambition, and especially those cities that wish to make use of the
people in important things" (D I 4). But the ambition of the people
is the ambition of the popular men, for the people quickly become
weak and inert without a head or a leader (D I 7, 44, 50, 57, 58). The
people are fearful and religious, or perhaps simply fearful, without a
leader; and their desire to avoid oppression is more a consequence
of their weakness than of their virtue (D I 13, 39, 58; II 16; III 12,
32). By themselves the people are inactive. Their virtue is constancy,
Machiavelli says, opposing the view of Livy and "all the other historians." Whereas the princes or nobles are superior to the people in
establishing laws and new orders, the people are superior in keeping
things already organized. To be constant, the people need the good
laws and orders that superior princes give them, but once given such
laws, the people hold them tenaciously, as for example the Roman
people were for four hundred years an enemy to the name of king.[32]

Machiavelli announces the novelty of his argument that the multitude is constant, while he somewhat conceals the novelty of his
argument for party government; but the two arguments are necessar-

ily connected. If without a leader but under good laws and orders
the multitude is constant, party conflict is in fact confined to the
"princes," actual and potential—to those who hold versus those
who wish to hold power. The dispute between the nobles and the
people is in fact between the nobles and the popular men who look
to the people for support, that is, between legitimate and illegitimate
nobles. The people are constant, contrary to the view of Livy; hence
the people do not attempt to rule, contrary to the view of Aristotle.
The "popular men" of Machiavelli are essentially different from
demagogues according to Aristotle, since Aristotle supposed that
demagogues are indeed democratic, merely giving effect to the popular will.[33] To ascribe constancy to the people, however, is to absolve
them of responsibility for their moods and deeds when excited; these
are the work of their heads (*capi*), not of themselves. The multitude
is mere body or mere material without a head or form of its own,
and therefore democracy in the strict sense of the rule of the people
is impossible. The people do not wish to rule and cannot rule; they
are superior to princes in goodness, but the goodness of the people
does not make democracy possible. On the contrary, goodness seems
to make men less fit to rule.[34] The prosy assertion of "elite" theory
today that every popular movement is the work of a disguised elite
was anticipated, if not forestalled, by Machiavelli.

The constancy of the people means that they are nonpartisan
when they are not led into partisanship; and such partisanship is the
work of their leaders. The constancy of the people supplies the context of partisanship so that the prizes of party conflict are to some
extent held clear from the conflict and partisans have something
constant to fight for. It makes party government possible by maintaining the necessary nonpartisan context, the established laws and
orders. Thus party government is made possible by the very fact,
the constancy of the people, that makes democracy impossible. Today we have almost lost sight of the importance of this fact, since
we use the term *democracy* not in its strict sense but loosely to mean
representative government or representative democracy.

Yet, although the conservative function of the people is vital,
we should not suppose that the nonpartisan context of party government is permanent, according to Machiavelli. In general, no mixed
body is permanent, and the constancy of the people often, perhaps
usually, pertains to the name rather than the thing, as in the hatred

of the Roman people for the name of king (*D* I 25). Moreover, the laws and orders that the people maintain were once founded for them by a prince or princes, perhaps in the course of party conflict, as when the Tribunes were instituted. And third, party government is dynamic because it requires and produces expansion. The new prince in a republic who makes new institutions is likely to be a "popular man" since, being new, he *must* be illegitimate. The need for new institutions is a consequence of the motion of human things, and so illegitimate nobles or new princes are favored by the nature of human things. A venerable oligarchy like the Roman Senate survives because it makes room for new men and finds new sources of energy within its ranks. The Roman consuls had such short terms that many of them could show their energy; and they had to show it so quickly that the glory of a new conquest rather than leisurely superintendence was the way to fame.

The diverse humors of the great and the people are thus kept apart by the turbulence within the class of the great. Some of the great may wish to keep the established laws and orders—those who profit from them; but even they are forced to innovate as the means of anticipating the innovations of those who would replace them. The only way to maintain any regime for a long time (never permanently) is to put an innovating tendency into the works of the regime. But this tendency runs contrary to the natural inclination of the people to conserve: the context of party government, being nonpartisan, is essentially hostile to party government. The republican regime is an arena of action and reaction by conflicting impulses. The two classes cannot be put together to live for the sake of a common good that all citizens more or less consciously make their own. The regime does not aim at the common good; it has two classes that contribute diversely to the common good. Insofar as the people are religious, they are dedicated to the common good; but the people do not rule. The religious and patriotic class is not the ruling class.

The ruling class must manage the people so that their conservatism helps the enterprises of the state, and, to manage conservatism, the rulers cannot *be* conservative. On the contrary, they must be prudent and bold. To be prudent, one must anticipate misfortune and the hostility of one's neighbors; that is, one must grasp in the manner of the avaricious. To be bold, the innovating rulers also require an incentive, the love of glory. Great deeds are born in great natures and need great motives. The prudence and the greatness of the man who restrains his ambition in order to help his country are merely imaginary, Machiavelli believes. A great man helps his country only by liberating and exercising his ambition. Thus the class that is dedicated to the common good—the people—will never be adequate to the common good. That is why Machiavelli does not include the perverted regimes in his classification of regimes into republics and principalities, for, according to Aristotle, the perverted regimes are those that do not *aim* at the common good except accidentally, when the common good coincides with the private good of the rulers. According to Machiavelli, it is impossible for a regime to *aim* at the common good; it can reach the common good, or majority good, only by not aiming at it. All regimes are perversions by the Aristotelian standard.[35]

Machiavelli replaces Aristotle's analysis of politics by regimes with a class analysis. For Aristotle, classes are understood as elements in a regime that is not merely a reflection of the classes within. The regime embodies a common conception of the good life that justifies the rule of one man, a few, or the many.[36] For Machiavelli, the ruling class is always a prince or princes; the people are not a self-subsisting class apart from the ruling class. They passively receive the imprint of the ruling class, and their function is to hold what they receive. The classification of principalities and republics is much less important than the understanding of the nature of princes and peoples, since the name of the whole does not identify the part that rules. The ruling part is always the same, and only the relation of princes to each other and of princes to the people discloses the nature of the regime. For Machiavelli, the fundamental question is not the Aristotelian question, *who* rules? It is, rather, *how* is this country ruled?

Machiavelli's class analysis has this grave implication: in politics, one cannot *be* good in order to arrive at a good *end*. The people, who are good, must be led by the princes, who are eager for glory, quick to find it, and utterly unwilling to share it, whose prudence is not moderation but the ability to "measure their forces well" (*D* II 23; III 2, 6), and whose thoughts reach far into the past and the future to seek comparison with other great men, but never turn to the things above men. Such men are "virtuous" in the Machiavellian sense. Their virtue does not aim at a good end, just as the people's goodness can never attain a good end. In politics, end in the sense of outcome is disjoined from end in the sense of purpose. Final cause is not a factor in politics. The beginning is everything, because the necessities of the beginning must be faced and conquered without cease. Politics affords no leisure for the good life, neither to those who rule nor to those who conspire to rule. Before final cause was removed from nature by modern science, it was expelled from politics by Machiavelli.[37]

## THE LIMITS OF PLURALISM

Although no common good exists at which all citizens *aim,* there remains a common good in which all citizens may *share.* Political philosophy stands or falls with the existence of a common good that in some way unites all citizens, including philosophers. As a political philosopher, Machiavelli could not argue that party government is a remedy for social conflict unless he believed that it was conducive to the common good. But he supported only that party government which is conducive to the common good. Like every other reasonable man who has thought on the subject, Machiavelli did not believe that all parties can be made to work in party government. Party government needs the nonpartisan context of the people, we have seen; yet the people can be misled into partisanship. The people must be properly managed to ensure that they provide a safe context for partisanship, and the wrong parties will disturb or destroy that context. For more than three hundred years, the tumults in Rome rarely caused exile and very rarely caused bloodshed. But in Florence the tumults were disastrous, as the people were insolent and unjust to the nobles, killing many and exiling many more (*FH* pr; III 1; VII 1). This contrast brings up the topic of the last two chapters in the section on the regime at the beginning of the *Discourses* (I 2–8), the distinction between accusation and calumny.

Machiavelli says that accusation is essential to keeping a republic free, whereas calumny is as pernicious to a republic as accusation is useful. Accusation is the power of the guardians of liberty in a city to bring charges before the people[38] against citizens who "sin" against free government. Calumny is private slander that produces the parties that ruin states. Now Machiavelli brings up not the alternative of Rome or Sparta, but the difference between Rome and Florence.

Rome managed partisan humors successfully with the institution of lawful accusation, whereas Florence lacked such a law and suffered repeated disasters. Why did Florence lack such a law? Why did Florence fail to provide for the proper context of party government?

Machiavelli does not answer directly. He remarks that one can believe that the appeal to "outside forces" arises from the lack of such a law, since a party seeking revenge and having no lawful outlet may vent its malignant humor in this way. But, in Chapter 8, Machiavelli shows that the Roman law on accusation was not self-executing; it had to be enforced prudently by a patrician dictator (D I 8; cf. I 24; III 8). Later, in Chapter 45, Machiavelli says that Florence did after all have a law permitting appeal to the people, proposed by Savonarola in 1494; but Savonarola himself allowed the law to be disregarded when it was to be applied in favor of his opponents. In Chapter 11 we are told that Savonarola persuaded the people of Florence that he spoke with God even though this people supposed itself neither ignorant nor rude. In Chapters 7 and 8, Machiavelli for the first time uses "sect" (*setta*) to refer to parties, and both uses refer to parties in Florence;[39] "sect" has religious connotations for him, though it often does not mean a "religious sect" strictly.[40]

I suggest that the difference between parties in Rome and parties in Florence is caused by Christianity. Christianity is an "outside force" for Machiavelli not merely because, like any religion, it claims a divine source. Christianity also teaches hostility to war and to politics, and is transpolitical in its intention. It supports a pope and a priesthood who are independent of political authority: when Savonarola claimed to speak with God, no political authority could gainsay him and the people were drawn into partisanship with his "sect."[41] Christianity destroys the nonpartisanship of the people by making it difficult or impossible for the political princes to appeal to them. The people, being naturally inclined to religion, are natural partisans of the side that can claim to "speak with God"; their "fear" of being oppressed turns into "hatred" of those pointed out as their oppressors. The people become cruel and commit the bloodthirsty partisan outrages detailed in Machiavelli's *Florentine Histories*. They are no longer conservative in function because their patriotism has been made to serve their transpolitical religion. Such is the "effectual truth," the practical effect, of the Christian conscience that claims to stand above politics. But if, on the other hand, the people are to serve as the judge to whom partisans may appeal, their nonpartisanship must be protected and their judgment must be guided by the political authorities. One "can believe" that the appeal to outside forces in Florence arose from the lack of a law on accusation, but in fact the outside forces already present in Florence prevented a workable law on accusation.

Christianity is of course not the only source of corruption that keeps party government from functioning in a free republic. Christianity came to Rome because Rome was already corrupt, and Rome's corruption had foreclosed party competition long before. Such corruption is the effect of prolonged intercourse with foreigners, which gives the people new tastes in earthly goods and in religion, and of obvious and long-continued inequality in wealth. By such causes also, the people are seduced from their nonpartisanship and led to take the part of a Caesar against the nobility. Their corruption is inevitable because it follows from success in acquiring empire, and the policy of acquiring empire is necessary to a free republic. The non-Christian causes of corruption, therefore, destroy a free republic at the same time that they make party government unworkable; and they may be allayed indefinitely (though not forever) by prudent policy aroused, perhaps, by the shock of a timely defeat (*D* I 17, 18; III 1).

The question of the limits to party government opens up the evils of Christianity, as Machiavelli saw them, and one understands why the *Discourses* seems so much more favorable to parties than the *Florentine Histories*. Machiavelli's argument for party government is directed against both the Aristotelian regime that implies a conception of the good life, and the Christian teaching on conscience. The virtue of the princes, which is vigorous and glorious selfishness, must oppose the goodness of the people, which is constancy, honesty, and piety. Machiavelli allows the competition of several "principles" in politics—virtue against goodness and the rival achievements of glory, old and new, which result from the struggle of legitimate and illegitimate princes. But, by allowing such competition, he seems to have blasted all principles from politics. We cannot help being sympathetic to Burke's view that it is possible to practice several principles without abandoning all principle. But we must be impressed by the difficulty of maintaining that position without the support of either the classical good life or the Christian conscience.

It is Machiavelli's argument that civilization emerges from savagery by primitive acts of savagery occasionally repeated. Fine things have a nasty beginning and, by the motion of human things, a repeated necessity to return to their nasty beginning. The pluralism on which we pride ourselves seems to illustrate this argument, for it had a very disreputable beginning in the political philosophy of Machiavelli.

But, given this beginning, do we have to return to it? Perhaps it is possible to admit that civilization has a nasty beginning and that human things are in motion, but then to deny that this motion forces us to return to the beginning. That is the possibility explored by Burke. He agreed with Machiavelli and Aristotle that civilization had a nasty beginning, and he agreed with Machiavelli against Aristotle that pluralism was the correct response to the motion of human affairs. But he tried to show against Machiavelli that the motion of human affairs can and must be managed without reenacting the oppression of every human founding. If Burke sustained this point, he would be entitled to "forget" his indebtedness to Machiavelli;[42] and so would we, with a sigh of relief. Pluralism would have become respectable in the way that every human institution becomes respectable, by making its beneficiaries—all of us—oblivious of its origin.

One can see Burke's agreement and his disagreement with Machiavelli in a famous passage on the great law of change:

> We must all obey the great law of change. It is the most powerful law of nature, and the means perhaps of its conservation. All we can do, and that human wisdom can do, is to provide that the change shall proceed by insensible degrees. . . . This mode will, on the one hand, prevent the *unfixing old interests at once:* a thing which is apt to breed a black and sullen discontent in those who are at once dispossessed of all their influence and consideration. This gradual course, on the other side, will prevent men long under depression, from being intoxicated with a large draught of new power.[43]

Change cannot be avoided, but the true method of change is "by insensible degrees." Change by insensible degrees is legal change, since it does not call the established laws into question. On the contrary, insensible change protects the established laws against the natural law of change by keeping change from being felt, if not from becoming visible. Legality is so much the true method of change for Burke that it is the most important part of natural law; for the most important part of natural law must be that which answers to "the most powerful law of nature."

Legality does not mean mere resistance to change; it is justified because it permits a prudent reform of the former system of interests. Legality prevents sullen discontent in the haves, as they lose power, and intoxication in the have-nots, as they gain power. How reasonable it seems to take a little and give a little! We begin to wonder at Machiavelli's shocking extremism. But when Burke's words are examined more closely, one may suspect that, according to him, the haves and the have-nots are not a necessary feature of politics, and that there is no ultimate conflict of interests. The haves can be confident that a small concession will not hurt only if the have-nots can be satisfied that a small gain will help. Then haves and have-nots do not really exist: all have an interest in the laws as they are or will be and all can be convinced of this interest. If the constitution, gradually developed, does not have to contain an ultimate conflict of interests, Burke's definition of party as a body of men united upon a particular principle is no longer unrealistic. Men can afford principles when their interests are well satisfied.

Contrary to Machiavelli, Burke believed in the possibility of a balanced constitution, in which all interests would receive due recognition, though not equal power. He therefore profoundly distrusted new men, although he was himself a new man and the England of his century offered great opportunities to new men. New men were so dangerous to the balanced constitution that Burke was unwilling to let them suffer the natural penalty of intoxication; he would not let them learn, like Machiavelli's new princes, to "measure their forces."[44] Burke's hostility to new men and his consequent indulgence for his Whig patrons have earned him both contempt for his self-neglect and reproach for his subservience from some commentators.[45] Why did he prefer his dull employers, at least in politics, to the brighter lights of his age? The reason is not merely that the ruling Whig families were safer than new men or that comfortable men can afford to live and rule by principles because their interests are satisfied. Burke believed the comfortable Whig families to be more prudent than Machiavelli's virtuous new princes.

Comfortable men of inherited wealth are less likely to be constantly occupied with their wealth; since they did not acquire it, they are freer to spend it and less eager to acquire more. Having received what they hold, such men do not live in an atmosphere of acquisition, even when they engage in commerce. Such "princes" have some of the conservative mood of Machiavelli's people. Machiavelli knew this, and, believing in the necessity of acquisition, he rejected the rule of comfortable men, of those he defined as "gentlemen" (D I 55). But Burke saw that, by tempering the glory of rule with the feeling of inheritance, the comfortable Whig princes can aim at the common good, instead of obliquely helping to effect it. Because they are "bred in a place of estimation" and "see nothing low and sordid from . . . infancy," they "stand upon such elevated ground as to be enabled to take a large view of the widespread and infinitely diversified combinations of men and affairs in a large society."[46] Because they are elevated above the necessities of acquisition, they may be presumed capable of seeing the whole and hence capable of seeing what they are doing. Their dedication to the common good is secured by the interest they hold in it, but it is informed by their elevation above acquisitive interests.

It is not that Lord Rockingham, Burke's Whig patron, was more sharp-eyed than Pope Alexander; according to Burke, Lord Rockingham could see farther because of his very innocence. Innocence implies both presumption and modesty: the presumption to take one's place by right, as if no taking were involved; and the modesty to be satisfied with the place that one is not forced to take and defend. Burke's innocent gentlemen, not blinded by glory and connected to the people by their property and by their honesty, see the common good of their society tolerably well. Parties formed of these gentlemen restrain themselves from the fierce action and reaction of Machiavelli's party government.[47] They uphold principles not as a foolish luxury that innocent gentlemen do not know they cannot afford, but by virtue of what they see because they are free from the need to acquire. A stern moralist might despise this difference, but Burke was a more exact, and more politic, moralist.

One may call the large view of elevated gentlemen "prudent" because of Burke's notion of the general bank of reason. Burke would not allow "men to live and trade each on his own private stock of reason" but would require individuals "to avail themselves of the general bank and capital of nations and ages." There is a general bank of reason greater than any individual man's reason; it is the "collected wisdom of mankind," and goes proudly under the name of prejudice.[48] By drawing on the bank of reason, gentlemen who act in association may control the motion of human things. Burke's gentlemen may act together because they do not seek glory, and must act together if they are to act for the common good. Nothing is more suspect to Burke than the individual prudence of Machiavelli's founder-prince. The general bank of reason enforces change by insensible degrees in the cautious adjustment of interests, so that reasonable men can be modest for themselves and optimistic for the whole. The paradoxical result is that insensible change is rational change; in politics, what is least felt is best thought.

Change is "the most powerful law of nature" but blind in itself, like the law of gravity in physics. The proper response of human wisdom to the law of change, Burke says, is change by insensible degrees. Insensible change means legal change or legality, implying a balanced constitution in which all interests may be satisfied. The balanced constitution requires a common good that is the aim of the leaders; otherwise it will be out of balance, like Machiavelli's regime of princes allied to peoples, and must resort to internal or external oppression. A common good that the rulers aim at reopens the possibility of natural law or natural right that Machiavelli had foreclosed; for the disjunction between the common good and the virtue of rulers is overcome. Change by insensible degrees is the rational part of natural law in response to the blind part of natural law, which is mere change. Rational, insensible change is explained in Burke's theory of prescription.

IMPARTIAL NATURAL LAW

Prescription is a "great fundamental part of natural law," according to Burke.[49] He borrowed prescription from the Roman private law, where it describes how title to property may be gained without a deed by long-continued use or lost with a deed after long-continued disuse. Burke made this principle of private law a fundamental part of public law and hence of natural law. In private law, prescription

gives title without a deed, and, in public law, it gives authority without a return to the beginning, as opposed to Machiavelli. Prescription describes a manner of growth by insensible degrees without
acquisition in the Machiavellian sense. By means of prescription,
Burke was able to convert acquisition and inheritance, which seem
to be opposites, into equivalents; for insensible increments to authority and refinements of its exercise come to the citizen as interest on
his public inheritance. Burke said that "the desire of acquisition is
always a passion of long views"[50]—with which Machiavelli would
have agreed in regard to the motive of glorious deeds. But for Machiavelli, the most glorious deeds change all the orders of a state in a
stroke, making everything anew. Burke was able to avoid the turmoil
of glory and to oppose the harsh splendor of Machiavellian virtue
with his theory of prescription. At the same time, he did not have
to deny that all human things are in motion; he did not attempt to
sustain the Spartan illusion of self-sufficiency.

Burke's political philosophy depends on the establishment, after
Machiavelli, of a form of natural law that opposes yet yields a fundamental point to Machiavelli. The liberal natural law of Hobbes and
Locke rescued the idea of the common good from Machiavelli's
destructive class analysis by showing that all men are equal in a
prepolitical state of nature. According to their natural law, all men,
being naturally equal, can aim at a good common to them, security;
and the common good is not the result of different and complementary motives, as for Machiavelli. But this common good is not the
highest good, as either philosophers or political men see the highest
good. Natural law in this form contains no *summum bonum* and
recommends no particular end or way of life. On the contrary, being
concerned only with the necessary condition of civilization, which
is security, it keeps politics impartial among the ends men pursue.
An impartial natural law yields the fundamental point to Machiavelli
that politics must not be concerned with the highest good. Liberal
natural law must be seen as an improvement upon Machiavelli's
new way, not as totally different.

An impartial natural law does not favor one regime over another; it favors a regime of liberty in which men live securely, actively, and as virtuously as they will. In Burke's version, impartial
natural law decides among regimes according to their policy of prescription. It leaves the state free as to its end because the state can

be self-restrained in the manner of reaching its ends. The state, according to Burke, is "a partnership in every virtue, and in all perfection," but, unlike Aristotle's regime, it does not aim at a certain partisan version of the good life. It facilitates every virtue, but does not choose among them. It is not a jointstock company "in things subservient only to the gross animal existence of a temporary and perishable nature,"[51] but it is also not a *polis* with a directed end. By respecting inheritance in all its forms, by polishing the manners and securing the establishments of society, the state achieves a noble and liberal liberty. Burke's state is limited, because natural law is impartial, and yet comprehensive, because natural law is prescriptive. The turn from the origins to the manner of growth of society directed Burke to a comprehensive view of the subpolitical aspects of society and makes him look "sociological."

Impartial natural law in Burke's version is also pluralistic. Without abandoning the absolute sovereignty required by Hobbes's natural law, he defended the balanced constitution and party government. For the first time, he argued the view now taken for granted, that reasonable men can and should openly express different political opinions regarding the common good and form public organizations reflecting those differences. The theory of prescription is again responsible: when the beginning of society is not thought to determine its working, the original institution of sovereignty is less vital than the developing patterns of its exercise. These patterns will reflect the circumstances of different parts of society more than the original need for unity.

## PRINCIPLES AND PROVIDENCE

We may now set forth Burke's solution to the problem of principles in politics posed at the beginning of the chapter. For Hobbes and Locke, the purpose of the state was to serve society by securing the condition of the ends men pursue in society. But curiously the result is the opposite: principles become subordinate to the need for security. The interest of the sovereign (or society) in security is so overwhelming that society must suit its principles to this need. Perhaps the best example is Hobbes's refutation of the fool who "hath said in his heart, there is no such thing as justice." The argument is simply that, without justice, prudent men cannot "reasonably reckon upon" the misplaced trust of the foolish.[52] Thus, to make justice secure as a principle, Hobbes reduced it to an interest or to self-interest. Burke avoids this result because the institutions or "establishments" of society do not have to be referred back to the original need for sovereignty. Government for him is a partner in every virtue, not the indispensable agent who becomes the master of every virtue;[53] and in this way liberal principles are lifted above the interests of liberal society. Burke's pluralism is rich and comprehensive in order to promote the cultural diversity on which liberal society prides itself today. He was one of the select spokesmen for the spirit of liberty—a group that includes also Montesquieu and Tocqueville—whose purview was neither formal nor narrow.

The sanction for impartial natural law, according to Burke, is providence, and a brief survey of Burke's thoughts on providence can secure the difference between Burke and Machiavelli on the principles that can be reflected in party government. For Burke, providence is not simply inscrutable: "the rules of prudence . . . are formed upon the known march of the ordinary providence of God."[54] "The known march" of "ordinary providence" must be distinguished from "the hand of God in those immense revolutions by which at certain periods He so signally asserts his supreme dominion and brings about that great system of change, which is, perhaps, as necessary to the moral as it is found to be in the natural world."[55] The supreme dominion of God allows the lesser dominion of rules of human prudence to take effect in the ordinary course of events and reserves only "those immense revolutions" in human affairs to demonstrate its supremacy. Ordinary providence is accessible to man as man, it seems, without divine revelation; for Burke does not say that the rules of prudence must be learned from or even be congruent with the truths of biblical revelation.[56] Burke's understanding of providence does not seem to be specifically Christian. He does not indicate that God has chosen a church, or a people for special favor. God is impartial among the religions of the world, or among most of them, and perhaps also among the great moral systems whose immense revolutions He uses to assert His supreme dominion.[57]

Is God then impartial among the just and the unjust, among those who stand on principle and those who are led by interest? Such is the Machiavellian view. Machiavelli believed that it was necessary to sin and hence that God was the origin of evil; God is then impartial or neutral among the just and the unjust and fortune favors those who do not rely on providence—the armed, the prudent, and the fortunate.[58] Burke escapes this conclusion through the working of prescription. The known march of providence, he thought, shows how worldly benefits in the high sense are returned for obedience to the rules of prudence understood in the wide sense: how civilization requires and repays the efforts of duty and the subjection to manners. Civilization accrues to its beneficiaries by prescription, by small reforms done gradually and legally. The necessary condition for such reform is neither Christian revelation nor Machiavellian virtue; it is an ordinary providence that teaches the true manner of reforming. Burke's natural law directly requires certain means rather than certain ends. It is not enforced by conscience, in which God is the witness of sin and His providence is the test and reward of virtue. Burke agreed with Machiavelli that a godly conscience can give principles a despotic rule over worldly interests. But he conceived a religion of providence to sanction and sanctify a natural law of prescription in the middle between the cruelty of divine conscience strictly considered and the brutality of principles reduced to low interests.

In consequence but not directly, providence favors the just over the unjust, while permitting the growth of pluralism. That is why the parties of Burke's party government are respectable, whereas Machiavelli's are merely good. Burke's partisans combine some of the prudence of Machiavelli's princes with all of the honesty of his people. They are incapable of the best in order to be prevented from the worst, whereas Machiavelli's princes are capable of the worst in order to make possible a common security and individual glory. Burke's pluralism is rich and comprehensive so as to dull the brilliance of glorified interests in the shock of rivalry; to avoid a vicious conflict of interests, he proposed an honest competition of principles.

Yet it remains doubtful whether the principles of Burke's free society are far enough above its interests. Burke seems to have supposed that the principles available to gentlemen must occasionally yield to the higher principles of men of higher prudence like himself. And, for him, these occasions were decisive: the first argument for the respectability of party government, the "Bristol Speech" against compulsive instructions to representatives, the attack on the French Revolution, the impeachment of Warren Hastings.[59] In each case

Burke did not wait for action by the leisurely gentlemen whom he served, and he took no more guidance from them than the encouragement he sometimes received. The principles of gentlemen are honorable but not perspicuous, consistent but not discriminating; although distinct from the interests of Machiavellian new men, they are insufficient protection against such men.

Burke's prescriptive, impartial natural law does not include the highest good of man, and hence it does not permit an appeal to principles above politics. Having found that respectable gentlemen and their principles were insufficient, Burke had to seek principles above the idea of providential inheritance to justify and enlighten his own interventions and innovations. These principles are above politics for two reasons: because they point to a life above the political life and even above the motion of human things, and because they are not guaranteed to emerge from the political process of prescriptive inheritance and from the known march of ordinary providence that sustains prescription.

From Machiavelli we can learn to doubt the value of respectability, but from Burke we can learn how to transcend respectability without despising it.

# FOUR

# MACHIAVELLI AND THE
# IDEA OF PROGRESS

$M$achiavelli is not often given credit for the revolutionary change
he initiated and in time accomplished. He began a project, later
picked up and developed by other modern philosophers, for a permanent, irreversible improvement in human affairs establishing a
new political regime. The project is often called "modernity,"
though modernity is understood no longer as a project but rather as
a historical force—one that may now have come to an end. To
Machiavelli's new political science was added a new natural science,
together with a protective blanket known as "epistemology," which
science still cannot quite do without. How Machiavelli was responsible for modernity I shall outline as I have been able to perceive it.

Perhaps one reason that Machiavelli is not often given credit as
founder of modernity is that he does not claim it. He does not put
himself at the head of a party of progress claiming to speak for all
mankind. So far as there exist Machiavellians, they have always been
known as enemies of mankind. And if one wishes to take a more
generous view of Old Nick, one still finds his humanity to be
bounded, envenomed, and contradictory. In the last chapter of *The
Prince,* he surely calls for progress in Italy, but by an exhortation to
seize Italy and free her from the "barbarians"—who must be the
civilized monarchies of France and Spain. And even Machiavelli's
patriotism is divided between Italy and Florence, whose interests he
well knew were not identical. He says that "by experience one sees
that only princes and armed republics make very great progress"

This chapter was originally published as "Machiavelli and the Idea of Progress," in
*Democracy, Progress, and Universal History,* ed. Arthur M. Melzer, Jerry Wein-
berger, and M. Richard Zinman (Ithaca: Cornell University Press, 1995). Copyright
© 1995 by Cornell University. Used by permission of the publisher.

(*grandissimi progressi*, P 12), but the statement is made in the context of rejecting the use of mercenary arms and does not seem to promise more freedom for everybody. How can one promote the happiness of all unless mankind is at peace?

Yet at the beginning of the *Discourses on Livy* Machiavelli states that he is driven by a "natural desire," as if it were not merely his choice, to "work, without any respect, for those things I believe will bring common benefit to everyone." Those things are "new modes and orders," political arrangements in the widest sense of everything pertaining to rule. Here Machiavelli claims to work (*operare*), if not speak, on behalf of humanity, and humanity is described as what is common to everyone individualized (*ciascuno*). The promised benefit does not appear to be a collective project, such as modern science, to which all might variously contribute. Such a project might actualize humanity as a progressive force regardless of its political divisions. But Machiavelli works through those divisions, the princes and armed republics. Each individual, it is true, has a common interest with all other individuals in being well governed, but it is obviously not an interest held in common because governments oppose one another. How will Machiavelli make each one the beneficiary of political innovation—innovation that not only maintains political divisions but also enlivens them with new modes and orders of war?

## THE CYCLE OF SECTS

Another, insufficiently noticed, subdivision of humanity besides the strictly political ones can be found in Machiavelli: the sect. The sect, sometimes identified with religion, is a more comprehensive phenomenon than the government. It includes language, customs, and morality; it is the whole climate of opinion surrounding and inspiring government. It can be understood as government in a wide sense, as Machiavelli shows by speaking of the "Christian republic" that comprises Christian states (*D* I 12). But of course the Christian republic is divided, and Machiavelli does not hesitate in his exhortatory mood to call some of its states barbarians, as we have seen. Nonetheless, it is by attending to the phenomenon of sect that we may approach Machiavelli's thought on progress.

Machiavelli faced two main obstacles to the idea of progress, and both are involved with sect. They are the notion of the cycle, arising from classical political philosophy, and Christianity. The notion of the cycle says that all human things change by turning in a circle, of which progress is merely one phase, to be followed by decay. Christianity says that human events began from a perfect beginning, followed by the Fall and the Redemption, and look forward to the Second Coming. Here too progress is only part of the story, and it is not achieved by man unaided. The modern idea of progress had to overcome the classical cycle and Christian redemption in order to establish itself. A careful study of Machiavelli on the two points would help us understand progress better than we can through our contemporary perspective, for it would make us aware of possible alternatives. Then we could see how the idea of progress looks as a choice, before the alternatives have receded from view. Our perspective is posthistorical; it is disillusionment with the idea of progress that takes for granted the establishment of that idea against its rivals. Our objection is to the situation in which history has left (or thrown) us, not to history itself. But Machiavelli had to defeat his two main rivals, and he did not yet speak of "history" in any but the classical sense of "inquiry."

The cycle and Christianity come together in Machiavelli's discussion of the cycle of sects (D II 5; cf. FH V I). There Machiavelli considers the causes of the oblivion of sects. Sects change; they even have life-spans limited to between 1,666 and 3,000 years. So the world is older than any sect, including the "Christian sect." Those who survey the changes of sects, the philosophers, have a longer and broader view than those founders who are concerned merely with "the ordering of a new sect." Although the causes of change are three—men, heaven, and nature—Machiavelli suggests the possibility that a single man surviving a near-universal natural or heaven-sent disaster might be able to control the "human generation" that remains. Such a man, blessed as it were with the opportunity Noah had, could remake the past *a suo modo* and so project his new enterprise (*impresa*) into the future. He could actualize the power (*potenza*) of humanity, not merely its possible intellect in the Averroistic sense. The Christian sect, unlike other less universal and less competent religions, has shown men how to unify mankind and capture the world for their own benefit.

That partial and compressed interpretation of a single Machiavellian discourse hurries his argument, but since there is no room for patient interpretation, let it suffice to note the strategy.[1] Machiavelli brings together his two enemies and uses the one against the other. On the one hand, the Christian sect is treated like any other as within a natural cycle according to the classical conception. On the other, the superiority of the Christian sect, which lies not in its truth or divinity but in its political acumen, is used to suggest how men might escape from the cycle and create a universal sect that would lead mankind to progress. To explain Machiavelli's strategy, I discuss the cycle and Christianity in turn.

Machiavelli's consideration of the cycle depends on Polybius (*D* I 2), but it is easier and still faithful to his intent to look to Aristotle for the classical notion of the cycle. Aristotle understands the cycle as one of three kinds of revolution, all of which are endemic to the human situation. Machiavelli means to replace them with one revolution, the modern revolution, a revolution that puts an end to revolution, at least in the grandest sense.

### ARISTOTLE ON REVOLUTION[2]

For Aristotle, the first meaning of revolution is *stasis,* or uprising, a public disturbance visible to all. The second meaning is a change of regime, a new beginning or a new principle of rule. *Archē* means both rule and beginning. It is simultaneously a beginning in accordance with a principle and ruling in accordance with a beginning. Such a beginning is never *de novo,* as from a state of nature in which there was no previous regime. For Aristotle, man is a political animal by nature. So every new regime consists in the change of an old regime. Every regime moves in a certain direction in accordance with its principle, the principle that is reflected in its form, or structure, of government. For example, democracy moves toward the end reflected in its democratic form; that end is to live democratically. The rulers of the regime have a certain awareness of their direction toward an end, which they declare or claim to be just. Being partisan creatures, they do not have a full awareness of the end, but they have a certain awareness; and with it they take responsibility for the character of the regime. They blame others, their enemies foreign and domestic, and they praise themselves, always insisting on a contrast between the two. Every regime, therefore, has a self-definition that is partisan.

A stasis can occur, however, without a change of regime. A coup d'état in an unstable republic would be an example: a public change that does not alter the nature of the regime. Or, one could have a change of regime over decades or centuries without a stasis—a gradual change that steals over a government without its consent or even recognition, as from new ideas or new technology not initiated by the government, or initiated without comprehending the consequences. But the most dramatic event is an uprising together with a change of regime, as in the French Revolution.

A third meaning of revolution is revolution in the literal sense of cycle (*kuklos*). In that meaning we see that regimes have an end that they do not foresee or desire: their death. They may degenerate from internal causes, or they may be destroyed by a natural catastrophe external to them, a flood or an earthquake. The third meaning is connected to the partial or partisan nature of the regime. Since every regime is partisan, no regime does full justice to the facts. But the facts, because they are facts, will eventually catch up with the regime. Since every regime is partial, no regime is permanent. No regime can last in perpetuity because none rules in accordance with truth and nature. So the likely course of such revolutions is a cycle—a return to the beginning so that we can make the same mistakes all over again.

What is the role of the philosopher, that is, the political philosopher, in the context of imperfect regimes fated in the long run to die? It is to improve his own regime and others if he can. Such a task could possibly lead to revolution or urging a revolution if the philosopher lives in a bad regime or sees bad regimes around him. But he would also point out the limits of action. Good regimes tend to be followed by less good or even bad regimes, bad or less good regimes by good ones. Aristotle says that the most virtuous are least likely to rebel (*Politics* 1301a38–40). The most virtuous for him would be philosophers. Philosophers are few. Those who are very few will always need allies to make a revolution, and those allies being less virtuous, they will always be dubious and untrustworthy (*Politics* 1304b3–5). If philosophers make a revolution in their company, the result may be no better than the regime they rebelled against.

With modern revolutionaries, however, we find on the contrary that the most virtuous are thought most likely to revolt. The culmi-

nation of the most dramatic modern revolution was called the reign
of virtue by Robespierre (not a philosopher but the disciple of Rousseau). From his new modes and orders, Machiavelli expected a revival of "ancient virtue." Modern revolutions are not shunned but
led by philosophers. A modern revolution in thought precedes the
great modern revolutions in deed. So said Tocqueville in his book
on the *ancien régime,* the prerevolutionary regime in France. The
French Revolution was prepared by the destructive work of philosophers throughout the eighteenth century under the protection and
sometimes the encouragement of the *ancien régime.*[3] Edmund Burke
declared that the French Revolution was "the first, complete revolution." It was a revolution in sentiments, manners, and moral opinions that reached "even to the constitution of the human mind."[4]
In speaking of a revolution in the constitution of the human mind
Burke probably was referring to the unprecedented atheism of the
French Revolution. This was the first revolution to be founded on
the idea that there is no power in the human mind superior to human
reason or human will. But that principle one can find already in the
philosophy of Descartes as the principle of doubt, and in Locke as
the denial of innate ideas. Machiavelli's slogan "one's own arms"
has the same meaning.

Thus the French Revolution brings the modern philosophical
revolution into view. It tears away the veil covering the cowardly
hesitations of philosophers who did not openly proclaim their atheism. Modern revolutions were inspired by political philosophers
seeking a permanent improvement in human affairs. They envisaged
a permanent regime that would be the best regime actualized by *The*
Revolution, which would be a combination of stasis and change of
regime. The change of regime might begin before the stasis, as with
the intellectual changes in eighteenth century France. Intellectual
change produced social and cultural changes by which, for example,
the Church became a less reactionary force. And then the stasis
brought the latent principle into broad daylight by a change of
regime.

But even The Revolution, begun by modern philosophers and
actualized in modern governments, is not accomplished all at once.
Rather than being unchanging like the regime of ancient Egypt, the
new regime has a principle of change, a direction that cannot change.
Its permanency is not in being changeless but in being irreversible.

One cannot go backward: That is what is meant by progress. In the notion of progress, the cycle or circle that Aristotle spoke of is flattened out to a linear motion that has one direction and does not return to the beginning. The linear progress may indeed proceed by dialectical stages, as with Hegel and Marx, rather than by simple accumulation of improvements. But that complication does not affect the single essential direction of human history.

### THE IMPARTIAL REGIME

The consequence of replacing Aristotle's revolutionary cycle with the modern revolution of progress is to overcome the limits to the possible achievements of human politics. First, those limits arising from the supposed fixity of human nature can be surpassed. Men are much more malleable than Aristotle and his friends believed. And second, one can institute an impartial regime not essentially subject to revolution, as was Aristotle's regime. The problem in Aristotle's regime arose from the fact that he accepted the inevitability of human partiality in politics. His remedy for partiality was the mixed regime. But the remedy was not a cure, and the mixed regime was, for the most part, an aspiration based on arguments requiring an ability to persuade, along with people who were persuadable. It was, therefore, very unlikely, if not utopian.

What is the general character of the modern impartial regime? For Aristotle, the typical partisan conflict is between the many and the few, the people and the nobles. To replace that conflict, the general formula for the modern impartial regime is to remove one of the two parties, the people, as a political actor. Then let the elite compete before the people for its favor. The idea begins with Machiavelli, who makes a distinction between peoples and princes, a distinction of human natures (or humors, *umori*) that can be found in all regimes, whether popular or oligarchical. Today we say that the people elect the government. The people thereby become the judge of all government. They do not form a government themselves; the people do not rule. Today's liberal democracy is, of course, very different from Machiavelli's harsh preferences for martial republics and Borgia-like principalities. But there is a certain generic resemblance in the impartiality of outlook and new attitude toward the people. Both we and Machiavelli are more favorable to popular judgment than were the ancients, and less favorable to popular rule. The impartial regime is actualized by lowering the moral standard: if the people are not competent to rule, at least they can judge the competence of those who are. Virtue comes to mean something closer to stability, or survival, because that is what the people can understand. Indeed, outstanding virtue is dangerous. Virtue can lead to revolution because it turns people against consensus and compromise. But a certain minimum or mediocre virtue is guaranteed by the impartial regime—or is required by it. Such, especially, is the virtue of respecting others' rights.

The revolution establishing the new regime is, to repeat, The Revolution, because it is irreversible. Machiavelli's role in it is commonly underestimated, not to say overlooked, not only because he does not head a party of humanity but also because he admires the ancients and appeals, as I said, to "ancient virtue." His treatment of the cycle in *Discourses* I 2 is often misinterpreted as favorable, hence hostile to the idea of progress; and his proposal in *Discourses* III 1 for reviving republics, kingdoms, and sects by returning them back "toward the beginnings" (*verso i principii*) is also thought to be reactionary rather than progressive. A quick look at these two chapters will help to overcome such misunderstandings.

Machiavelli begins *Discourses* I 2 by distinguishing two kinds of republics according to their beginnings. One kind receives its laws from "one alone" and "at a stroke," for example Sparta from Lycurgus; the other gets its laws by chance, at many times, and through accidents, as did Rome. At first it seems that the first kind is better, but Machiavelli gradually makes us see that the second kind can become perfect, even if it does not begin so, by the occurrence of accidents. These two kinds of republic suggest the difficulty Machiavelli himself faces in legislating his new modes and orders; he casually mentions here the "accident" in 1512 that displaced him from office as secretary to the Florentine republic. Machiavelli must legislate with his books alone and at a stroke, yet he must do so with a view to the accidents that will displace him and his influence. He who begins the progressive revolution must take thought for the followers who will both succeed and supersede him.

Machiavelli then confronts Rome's accidental perfection with the classical cycle. He follows the argument in Polybius's text so closely that the differences become obvious to anyone making the comparison (though some commentators, content to find a "source," note only the similarities). He seems to have chosen Polybius to represent classical political science since Livy does not discuss the cycle, and Plato and Aristotle do not discuss Rome, Machiavelli's exemplar of accidental perfection. Machiavelli begins by saying "in the beginning of the world," a Christian notion of unique creation obviously contradictory to the notion of a cycle in human affairs, yet un-Christian in denying a perfect beginning. Again we see Machiavelli using the ancients and Christianity against each other. Among many revealing differences of detail between his account and that of Polybius, the main one is that what Polybius attributes to nature Machiavelli attributes to chance.[5] Not being political animals by nature, men are free both to behave like beasts in accordance with their origins and to advance toward a perfect republic not subject to the vicissitudes of a natural cycle.

At the end of the chapter, Machiavelli denies the endogenous premise of the cycle of regimes that regimes fail because of their own faults; he simply remarks that any republic revolving in the cycle would fall subject to a better-ordered neighbor. Contrary to the assumption of the ancients, foreign policy is more vital than domestic policy. Rome was the regime whose domestic order—or disorder between the Senate and the people—was determined by its readiness to seek empire through conquest. Like Polybius, Machiavelli mixes together two distinct cycles, the cycle of regimes and the cycle of civilizations. The former presumes, as I said, that regimes fail because of their own faults; the latter, that they are destroyed from without by natural catastrophes. But while Polybius mixes them to show that nature is a force greater than Rome, and human partisanship generally, Machiavelli does so to suggest an expansion of human power. A cure for human partisanship can be found, not the classical palliative that mixes virtues in a mixed regime and holds nature in reserve so that men can start again after they fail, but a new mix of partisan humors loosed from restraint. Machiavelli's new regime, not subject to the "pestiferous" faults of the six classical governments, can save civilization without the necessity for outside intervention. He does not refer again in the *Discourses* to the cycle (he does in *FH* V 1, also leaving a way out); it has been replaced by his "perfect republic." Instead of using the cycle to signify the circular inevitability of good and bad in politics and the ultimate weakness of human will, Machiavelli appropriates the classical cycle to introduce the very contraries of those limitations.

Nor is his call, in *Discourses* III 1, to return toward the beginning, if one means a sect or republic to live a long time, a move against progress. In his statement, returning toward (not to) the beginning is neither conservative nor cyclical. Human institutions must have had some goodness in them, he says, to gain their first reputation; but the goodness becomes corrupt in time. Returning toward the beginning, then, means returning to the condition of being new and exciting, and it is done not by resuming the original constitution but by curing the corruptions that come with growth. The aim is not to curb growth, but to further growth. As compared to *Discourses* II 5, where Machiavelli speaks of "purges" and thus implied that early men were healthy, he now offers as a cure changes (*alterazioni*) for the better that both return toward the beginning and maintain one's acquisitions. "Mixed bodies," he says, do not last if they are not renewed. Perhaps the mixture in mixed bodies is of natural limitation and human improvement. Then Machiavelli's idea of progress is toward the overcoming of natural limitation, but in such a way as never to leave necessity behind. A state must return toward the beginning that nature provides while making that beginning its own, but without conquering the necessity that makes men operate well.

The Roman republic had "orders" that returned it toward the beginning, such as tribunes and censors and other institutions to oppose ambition, but they had to be "brought to life" by the virtue of "one citizen" who "spiritedly" seeks to execute them against the ambitious. Not a renewal of piety but sensational executions are the device of recall. Such executions revive in men the fear of punishment, the original fear from which government, whether human or divine, protects them. To protect men from fear, governments must periodically (Machiavelli proposes every ten years) remind them of fear, lest they become complacent, corrupt, and lawless. Progress cannot take itself for granted; it cannot continue without a vivid reminder of the contrast with the beginning. Returning toward the beginning applies the spur necessary to progress. Machiavelli even promises that had Rome followed his recipe of sensational executions and virtuous examples, "it follows of necessity" that it would never have become corrupt. This amazing possibility, the first statement of the modern impartial republic, shows how far Machiavelli has departed from the classical cycle.

Sensational executions are not, I said, a renewal of piety—or are they? Machiavelli continues in this same chapter to consider the renewal of the Christian sect, when it had fallen into corruption, by Saint Francis and Saint Dominic. The renovation, he says with superb impudence, succeeded by reinspiring Christian priests to do the worst they can "because they do not fear that punishment they do not see and do not believe in." In plain words, the renovation merely confirmed Christianity in its corruption. But of course it cannot be an accident that the chosen instrument of republican reform, the sensational execution, is also the central mystery of the Christian religion. Nor can we fail to note Machiavelli's particular interest in the executions by Junius Brutus, in which a father kills his sons (D I 16; III 3). It is time to turn to the other obstacle to progress, Christianity.

## MACHIAVELLI'S PERPETUAL REPUBLIC

In *The Prince* 12 Machiavelli speaks of Savonarola's prophetic denunciation of Italy and Florence at the time of the French invasion of 1494: "And he who said that our sins were the cause of it spoke the truth. But the sins were surely not those he believed, but the ones I have told of." This may be taken as representative of Machiavelli's appropriation, for his own project, of Christianity, the sect that conquered much of the world through unarmed prophets. Machiavelli's view of his situation was the following. He saw, first, that the ancients were strong and the moderns are weak. This was nothing but the common perception of the Renaissance applied to politics as well as the arts (and that application was not new). Moreover, he believed that the cause of modern weakness was Christianity: still nothing new. But he went on to ask himself why the strong ancients of pagan Rome were defeated by the weak moderns of Christian Rome. The very cause of weakness appeared in a new light as the cause of strength.

Machiavelli, himself not fearing the punishment he did not see, dismissed divine providence as the cause of the Christian triumph. So he looked for a thisworldly explanation of that success, found it, and took it up for himself to make Christianity serve his end, the liberation of mankind through the use of "one's own arms." For Christianity is strong enough to defeat the strong, but not strong enough, because of its dependence on arms in an otherworldy sense, to be strong on its own. Machiavelli noticed that the unarmed prophets are armed in that sense, that they even speak of a holy war; perhaps they are possessed of the art of war (*P* 14) by which a prince can gain converts. They know how to make a virtue out of weakness—the virtue of humility (*D* II 14). Their militant orders can be described as military orders, which Machiavelli proceeds to do in the second book of the *Discourses*. There Machiavelli describes the three orders of an army—infantry, artillery, and cavalry—with a view to the contrast between the strong ancients and weak moderns who somehow seem superior to the ancients in artillery and cavalry! Manfully Machiavelli struggles to argue that the ancients are nonetheless superior. But only when one applies the analogy between ordinary and spiritual warfare does his argument reveal itself. One sees that the modern superiority in artillery and cavalry and inferiority in infantry (in stubbornness, *ostinazione*, the quality of infantry) refers especially (though not only, of course) to Christianity, and one sees further how Machiavelli's army, the army of the Romans as he reinterprets it, will be better in all three orders. To state these conclusions, to hand them over on a silver platter, is a far less valuable gift than to prove any one of them in the text. Indeed, it is better to let the reader share the excitement of discovery by finding them himself. The highest reaches of Machiavelli's ambition are to be found in the details, the *cose piccole* (*D* III 33) of his writings.

Machiavelli believes he can carry his enterprise to the point that "another" will have but a brief walk to take it to its destined place (*D* I pr). He founds the modern impartial republic but leaves something—not so much!—for others to do, according to their competence in perceiving the magnitude of his intention. But he who adds the last bit always seems to have brought the whole thing (*D* III 17); so by leaving a little at the end, Machiavelli leaves most of the glory to his followers, especially to those who do not understand him well and believe that in reading his books *they* are patronizing *him*. Machiavelli's princes belong to his principality, but since they get most of the glory, his principality can also be understood as a republic in the larger sense, the sense in which he speaks of the "Christian

republic" (*D* I 12). The difference is that Machiavelli's sect appeals
to all mankind. Princes and republics in the usual sense will continue
to rise and fall in accordance with their virtue and fortune. The
impartiality is in Machiavelli himself and in the indifference he
teaches to the partisan principles of Aristotelian regimes.

Thus the "perpetual republic" is both impossible, as Machiavelli
says in *Discourses* III 17, and possible, as he says five chapters later.
No single state within Machiavelli's system can last forever, but the
whole can be perpetual because the various fortunes, or the fates,
of its members have been anticipated by Machiavelli. His books will
neither be lost nor superseded, though they may be covered over by
later books written by princes of similar quality but not of the same
priority as Machiavelli, to whom he leaves most of the glory. These
authors fill out and develop Machiavelli's enterprise—for example,
Bacon and Descartes—so that they can be understood as his captains. Book 3 of the *Discourses* is about the relationship between
"one" who commands an army and his captains. (The Roman army
in the *Discourses* corresponds to the ecclesiastical principality in *The
Prince*.) Machiavelli is in no position to be severe with his captains;
he cannot keep his republic uncorrupt with sensational executions.
When he says in *Discourses* III 17 that to order a perpetual republic
is impossible, it is because of the possible vengeance of an offended
captain. But to deal with the difficulty Machiavelli follows the path
of Valerius's kindness rather than Manlius's harshness (*D* III 22).
By allowing princes to be harsh and cruel, he himself can be kind
to them and to mankind; for by allowing them worldly vengeance
he prevents the build-up and release of far worse vengeance from
an otherworldly captain. So, with the problem solved, his republic
will be perpetual.

What distinguishes Machiavelli's idea of progress from following ideas, the ideas of his followers, is the point mentioned at the
beginning: he does not appear at the head of a party on behalf of
humanity. "Machiavellian" does not refer to a progressive. But for
the same reason, a Machiavellian is not a totalitarian claiming to
represent all humanity in the name of the universal class or race.
Machiavelli's revolution is intended to be irreversible only in regard
to the cyclical change of sects or civilizations; revolutions in Aristotle's first two senses of uprising and change of regime will continue. Like any other multitude, humanity needs a head (*capo, D*

I 44), but Machiavelli's Valerian kindness requires him to remain concealed. His revolution is partly open because it gives politics a new freedom in new modes and orders, but it is also partly concealed because it appears to continue politics as usual.

Machiavelli accepts the political division of mankind because he wants to retain politics, which is the realm of virtue. Any supposed betterment of mankind at the cost of virtue is no bargain. It is a new virtue to be sure, the virtue of overcoming fortune. But to overcome fortune, virtue is in need of fortune to provide risk and challenge. Machiavelli, the true and only prince, has overcome fortune, but he allows it to his captains and unwitting subordinates. Whether modernity has taken its intended course is doubtful, however. In attempting other, more regular and scientific modes of overcoming fortune, Machiavelli's successors formalized and emasculated his notion of virtue. They created pitiful creatures seeking security instead of risk who are oblivious to virtue. Despite Machiavelli's best efforts the weakness of the moderns continues.

THREE

# MACHIAVELLI'S
# BOOKS

Machiavelli made himself a prince by writing books. His readers are his army, the subjects of his principality, or the citizens of his republic: he uses all three images. The images come out of his analysis of politics. But since his analysis is directed toward a great reform of which he is in charge, the army, subjects, and citizens are more essentially true in their metaphorical sense than as description. Metaphor is necessary because Machiavelli is not *the* prince out in broad daylight, where everyone can see him. As a prince he addresses his readers for the most part obliquely, using the terms by which he describes directly as an author.

Each of Machiavelli's books must be treated as a whole by itself and as a part of his enterprise. Why did he write it? one must ask. In accordance with custom, each of his main works is introduced by a dedicatory letter or preface which seeks the protection of a patron: Lorenzo de' Medici (*The Prince*), Lorenzo Strozzi (*Art of War*), Pope Clement VII (*Florentine Histories*). The *Discourses on Livy* is dedicated to his friends Zanobi Buondelmonti and Cosimo Rucellai, on whom he places the responsibility of having required this book from him. The *Discourses,* in which Machiavelli announces that he is bringing "new modes and orders," is his boldest work; *The Prince,* in which he complains at the beginning of a "great and continuous malignity of fortune," and in the middle announces that he "departs from the orders of others," is his most dramatic. Both these books stand out from the others because they contain, he says, everything he knows. With this special status, and with cross references to each other, they constitute a pair. *The Prince* is for the busy executive; the *Discourses* is for the potential prince with time on his hands. This does not mean, obviously, that *The Prince* is a mere summary of the *Discourses*. Machiavelli can explain certain matters more easily to a prince with experience of politics, who takes for granted the identity of kingship and tyranny, and other matters to those with opportunity for reflection, to whom that identity needs to be shown.

The *Discourses* is not written within an established literary genre, as are the other three works. *The Prince* is in the tradition of Mirror of Prince tracts that began with Xenophon's *Cyropaideia*. But in so clearly rejecting any reliance on imaginary goodness, Machiavelli obviously separates himself from that genre. In both *The Prince* and the *Discourses* he goes beyond imitating the ancients to improving on them. The *Florentine Histories* and the *Art of War*, however, remain within the humanist outlook. The superiority of the ancients to the moderns is never challenged, and the humanist compromise with Christianity is not put in doubt. The two works do not raise fundamental questions; they are more "contextual" than *The Prince* and the *Discourses*. They show us what Machiavelli wanted to do in his own time—to mount a short-term project for the reform of humanism—as opposed to his long-term design for entirely new modes and orders. What he wanted immediately was a less rhetorical humanism that would tell Italian republics how to live with party conflict (*Florentine Histories*) and how to improve their military by learning from a humanist condottiere (*Art of War*). These contextual works have their place in Machiavelli's grand scheme, but they do not reveal that scheme. From them alone we get little that is distinctively Machiavellian, except for the self-caricature of Machiavelli in the guise of a plebeian leader in the *Florentine Histories* (*FH* III 13).

One cannot see how each work fits in the whole unless one is mindful of each work as a whole in itself. Each work has a plan with a rhetorical movement reflecting the interaction between author and reader as the reader begins to catch on or drop out, as the case may be. Leo Strauss was the first scholar to expose the character of Machiavelli's books, and my defense of his scholarship belongs with my studies of the books. If someone wants to know why the *Discourses* is missing, the answer is that I have had my say on that at length in another place.

# FIVE

# AN INTRODUCTION TO MACHIAVELLI'S *FLORENTINE HISTORIES*

Machiavelli's title for the *Florentine Histories* is usually less accurately translated as the *History of Florence*. The latter title makes it seem that Machiavelli is writing history as we know it today. In using the more literal one, I mean to indicate a specific doubt as to whether Machiavelli has written "history" in the *Florentine Histories*.

Machiavelli's work does resemble a present-day history book in certain respects. It selects an object of narration, Florence; it describes a particular period, from the origins of the city to the death of Lorenzo de' Medici in 1492; and it presents a problem or theme, the causes of the remarkable hatreds and divisions within Florence. But it is not a history of Florence in the sense we are accustomed to, which requires that Florence have or have had a history. Machiavelli does not use the word *istoria* to refer to an object of study; he uses it to mean only the study itself. Whereas for us history is both the object of study and the study itself, for Machiavelli history is a study, apparently, of something other than history. Thus, when he speaks of "our history" or "my history," he refers to a study or an inquiry that he also calls "my narrations" or "my description" or "my undertaking" (see the letter dedicatory). And since he does not have in mind history as an object, he can say "Florentine histories" in the plural if he wishes, contrary to usage today, which admits that many histories of Florence have been written but denies that Florence could have had more than one history. Further contrary to

This chapter was originally published as "An Introduction to the *Florentine Histories*," in *Machiavelli's "Florentine Histories,"* trans. Harvey C. Mansfield and Laura Banfield (Princeton: Princeton University Press, 1988).

current practice, Machiavelli does not speak of "historiography": for him, history *is* historiography.

Machiavelli's usage of the word "history," therefore, is enough to make us doubt that the *Florentine Histories* is history as we know it. But perhaps history as we know it would never have allowed us to suppose otherwise. History as we know it, in the sense of an object as well as a study, embraces Machiavelli in a context that could not fail to differ profoundly from our context, from our history. His historical context includes both the facts of his time, which would have influenced his writing of history, and the historiography characteristic of his time, together with the conception of history underlying those historiographic methods.

To begin with the latter, we find preceding Machiavelli humanist historians (as well as chroniclers) who titled their works *histories* in the plural, above all, Leonardo Bruni's *Historiae florentini populi.* More important, their histories incorporate certain features that do not appear in today's history books: the division of the history into books with general, nonhistorical introductions; invented speeches presented as if they were actual speeches taken down verbatim or paraphrased; and the presentation of a political history so much to the neglect of economic, cultural, social, and intellectual history as to imply that political history is the chief or even the only history. Machiavelli's adoption of these conventions of humanist historiography suggests that his conception of history and even historical context differs from ours.

In the preface, Machiavelli says that his purpose in this work is "to write down the things done at home and abroad [or, inside and outside] by the Florentine people." In the first book, as he says in the preface, he narrates "all the unforeseen events [*accidenti*] in Italy following upon the decline of the Roman Empire up to 1434." He shows how Italy from the time of the barbarian invasions "came to be under those powers that governed it" in 1434. Florence had its origin earlier than the barbarian invasions, we learn in II 2, at the time when the Roman Republic was dissolving; but we would say, and Machiavelli seems to mean, that his first book sets Florence "in context." The difficulty is that he calls this context "our universal treatise" (II 2). Although the first book appears to be merely a narration of events in Italy, Machiavelli invests it with a significance more than historical. Also, each of the following seven books begins with a chapter that discusses some general topic nonhistorically: colonies, natural enmities between men of the people and the nobles, liberty and license, the natural cycle of order and disorder, the advantage of victory in war, the difference between divisions with "sects" and those without them, and conspiracies. To be sure, Machiavelli typically contrasts the ancients and the moderns in each regard in a way that might seem historical, but he does so to explain the superior virtue of the ancients, not merely to adduce a difference in historical context.

In the broad sweep of his outlook, and in his attention both to the rise and fall of states and to their internal divisions, Machiavelli is alive to the fact of "historical change," as we would say. But he interprets it differently. For him, historical change is either the motion of nature—not perhaps random but not intended by men—or the order and ordering ("orders and modes" in the preface and VIII 29) that men intend. Since nature's motions do not make men feel safe or grateful, they appear to men as "fortune," sometimes good and sometimes bad but never reliable. Because nature looks to us like fortune, it is in effect reducible to fortune. Instead of the classical opposition, first discerned by philosophers, between nature as unchanging and fortune as fickle, Machiavelli adopts the popular attitude, as he sees it, that neither nature nor fortune can be trusted. And since human order made by human virtue is designed to overcome this sense of lack of support, and to create reliable principles and states, the context of history must be understood as a contest between virtue and fortune. Possibly this contest may be won definitively by virtue, that is, at some historical time. But the contest itself, because it explains history, is not historical and will not be decided by history. If the contest between virtue and fortune is the context of history, then the context of history is not history. That is why the word "history" for Machiavelli means a study or an inquiry and does not refer to history as an object.

To vaunt the worth of his history, Machiavelli makes a statement in the preface that we would regard today as unhistorical, but one that fits the practices of humanist historiography. "And if every example of a republic is moving," he says, "those which one reads concerning one's own are much more so and much more useful; and if in any other republic were there ever notable divisions, those of Florence are most notable." He offers a practical and a theoretical inducement to his readers, neither of which resembles a question of historical interest in our regard. A historian, for us, is supposed to be above concern for "one's own" and would not admit to choosing a topic for its utility to his own country. Yet he is not so abstracted from historical fact as to believe that his topic is a mere "example" out of some general category, whose selection must be justified by a theoretical interest, say, in republics. If Florence is merely an example of a republic, then it is hard to find a boundary between the *Florentine Histories* and Machiavelli's apparently more theoretical works, *The Prince* and the *Discourses on Livy*—that is, between history and political science. True, the *Florentine Histories* is devoted mainly to a republic, not to both republics and principalities as a work of political science might require. But the *Discourses on Livy* is also devoted mainly to a republic (the Roman), and *The Prince* is mainly about principalities. More important, the reader soon discovers that the Florentine republic, whose leaders are frequently called "princes" by Machiavelli and which is once referred to as a principality (I 26), shares many of the institutions and much of the behavior of principalities. It is no wonder that many scholars have sought to find Machiavelli's political science in his *Florentine Histories:* it is left quite visible in the beginning chapters of its books and in many pungent judgments throughout. In VIII 1 Machiavelli refers his readers to the *Discourses on Livy* for a longer discussion of conspiracies, not for a more abstract or scientific one.

Thus Machiavelli, as author of the *Florentine Histories* and in common with humanist historians, has two different but not exclusive motives—practical and theoretical—the first of which seems to us beneath history and the second above it. From this double motive for history, Machiavelli's concentration on the political can be derived. Historians today, rightly doubting that politics can explain all human activities, are drawn beyond political history to establish and investigate social, economic, cultural, and intellectual history. Confident that history exists as an object, they look for another kind of history if the dominant one seems unsatisfactory. But for Machiavelli, as we have seen, history is not an object; rather, the object of history is the contest between virtue and nature or fortune. To go beyond or beneath political history is to leave the realm of what we can do with "our own arms" and to enter that of nature or fortune, where we seem powerless. Machiavelli would want to know from the modern historian whether social, economic, cultural, and intellectual history could come under human control, that is, under politics. He would want to know whether the other kinds of history could become political history by being raised to our awareness or lowered to our reach. What is unconscious can be made conscious through politics, and what is above common consciousness can be simplified through politics.

In the *Florentine Histories* Machiavelli does not disregard the other kinds so much as he politicizes them. In what might be social history, he considers divisions among various classes of the "people" and dwells on the rise of the guilds (Book II) and the revolt of the plebs (Book III), but always for their political consequences. For economic history, he discusses the opening of an alum mine in Volterra (VII 29) as the cause of war and the operations of the bank of San Giorgio in Genoa (VIII 29) as an instance of free government amidst corruption. To keep up with culture, he mentions the "most excellent" architect Brunelleschi (IV 23), but then relates how an experiment of his at a siege of Lucca backfired (or backwatered) against the Florentine army (see also his political comment on the architecture of the Pitti Palace in VII 4). Marsilio Ficino, Pico della Mirandola, and some others are mentioned as recipients of Medici patronage and thus as occasions of praise for the Medici (VII 6, VIII 36). Dante appears in the role of historian of Florence's origins and of the cause of its parties (II 2), as the man who had the prudence to call the people to arms (II 18), and as one of those expelled from Florence (II 24)—whether justly or not, Machiavelli does not say. Donato Acciaiuoli, "a man very learned in Greek and Latin," is mentioned as spokesman for the Florentines on one occasion (VIII 14).

Besides the uncertainty as to whether his work is history or political science, and in addition to the concentration on politics, Machiavelli shares with humanist historians the device of inventing speeches. Even though he was not present and could not have been present, he puts appropriate speeches into the mouths of actual historical figures as if they were characters in a play of his. In "my history," as he calls it, he even provides "private reasonings" that no one could have overheard (letter dedicatory). Sometimes he introduces the speeches with the formula "in this sense"; often there is no such announcement. Sometimes the speeches are given indirectly, sometimes directly, as if these were the exact words. Such license on Machiavelli's part seems to defy the obligation binding historians to respect historical fact and to leave his history to wander in the neighborhood of poetry and rhetoric. But Machiavelli is so far from casual or forgetful in his use of invented speeches that this technique appears to be one of his themes or preoccupations. The phrase "in the mouth of" someone, though not occurring in the *Florentine Histories,* is one of his favorites elsewhere. In the *Discourses on Livy* he refers nearly a dozen times to instances in which Livy makes someone say or do something. The practice he discovers in the historian Livy seems difficult to distinguish from that of the poet Virgil, who, according to Machiavelli in *The Prince* (P 17), says something interesting "in the mouth of Dido."

And yet Machiavelli prides himself on "the dignity and truthfulness of the history" (letter dedicatory), as did the humanist historians, who expressly claimed to be speaking truth. It might be better to infer, then, that Machiavelli and the humanists have a notion of the truth of history that does not concede the sovereignty of historical fact. Fact, in their view, needs to be filled out with opinion, and it is the duty of the historian, in the absence of scribes and witnesses, to infer human intention and to make it explicit in speeches, adding sense to actions in order to arrive at truth. And if the speeches had been recorded, he might even have been compelled to change them for their own good. Thus, in the humanist (as well as the classical) conception, historical truth is not only compatible with patriotism and rhetoric but in need of them. Historical truth is not simply opposed to what historians today call "myth"; somehow it must be reconciled with myth because everyone, even the historian, has a fatherland (*patria*) and because all facts need to be interpreted with speech to gain significance. On behalf of truth, the historian may— or must—criticize the actions he relates. But if his criticism is to serve a practical end and is to be accepted by the citizens to whom it is directed, it must appear to be patriotic. Judged by the sovereignty of historical fact, this conception does not allow, much less encourage, historical research as practiced today. But before dismissing this conception of historical truth as odd and primitive, we should be sure that our historians can meet, or successfully evade, the requirements that history be patriotic and interpretive.

The facts of Machiavelli's time—the pressures and influences of power bearing on his writing—are the other element of his historical context, in addition to the dominant forms of discourse. These facts come to a focus in Machiavelli's relationship with the Medici, the ruling family in Florence when he wrote the *Florentine Histories.* Machiavelli was commissioned to write this work on November 8, 1520, at the instance of Cardinal Giulio de' Medici, who had become Pope Clement VII by the time Machiavelli finished. When Machiavelli presented eight books of the *Florentine Histories* to the pope in May 1525 (from the second sentence of the letter dedicatory it seems he may have intended to write more), he was paying homage to the ruling power in both his city and the Church. In his letter dedicatory, introducing himself as a humble servant, Machiavelli acknowledges the problem of flattery when one writes by commission. He nonetheless proudly proclaims "the dignity and the truthfulness of the history." He begins the letter by saying that he was commissioned for the work; at the end he calls it "my undertaking," and next he begins the preface very firmly in his own name: "My purpose, when I first decided to write . . ." Then, grasping his commission as if it were his idea, he proceeds to reveal in the outline of his history that it centers on "the year of the Christian religion 1434," the year when the Medici family gained the greatest authority in Florence. Machiavelli is so far from unaware of his historical context that he makes it the crux of his work, and we learn of his context from the text. Indeed, a survey of all his works might lead one to say that the *Florentine Histories* is his most contextual work, the one where he makes the powers impinging on him, which he is neither free of nor subservient to, the subject of his reflection. That is perhaps why the *Florentine Histories,* as opposed to *The Prince* and the *Discourses on Livy,* makes so little of innovation and founding in politics and does not dwell on the "new prince" or "new modes and orders." These are the themes, respectively, of the two works into which he said he put everything he knows. In the *Florentine Histories,* by contrast, he says he has striven to satisfy everyone "while not staining the truth."

Two of Machiavelli's surviving letters contain remarks about the *Florentine Histories,* and another comment was reported after his death by his young friend Donato Giannotti. All three tell of his concern with his context and suggest how he may have dealt with it. In his letter to Guicciardini of May 19, 1521, he says:

> Concerning the *Histories* and the republic of wooden sandals [the monastery where he was staying], I do not believe I have lost anything by coming here because I have learned of many of their institutions and orders that have good in them; so I believe I can make use of them for some purposes, especially in comparisons. For where I have to reason about silence, I will be able to say: "They stay more quiet than the brothers when they eat." And so one will be able to adduce many other things through me by the means that this bit of experience has taught me.

In a fragment of another letter to Guicciardini of August 30, 1524, Machiavelli says:

> I have been staying and stay now at the villa to write the history, and I would pay ten *soldi*, I will not say more, to have you at my side so that I could show you where I am; for, having to come to certain particulars, I would need to learn from you whether I offend too much either by exalting or by abasing things. Yet I shall keep on considering by myself and shall strive to act so that, while I am speaking the truth, no one will be able to complain.

Giannotti reports that Machiavelli said to him:

> I cannot write this History from when Cosimo took the state until Lorenzo's death as I would write it if I were free from all hesitations [*respetti*]. The actions will be true, and I shall not leave anything undone; only I shall not tell in what mode or by what means and tricks one arrives at so great a height. And whoever wants to learn this also may note very well what I will make his adversaries say, because that which I will not want to say myself, as from me, I will make his adversaries say.[1]

Thus by the first remark it would seem that Machiavelli lets actions speak louder than words; by the second, that he exaggerates and understates so as to forestall complaints; and by the third, that he criticizes indirectly by speaking through adversaries.

We cannot say, however, that Machiavelli was unwilling to flatter the Medici because he put virtue above power and success. For him truth was not so distant from flattery as to leave him serenely unconcerned with the causes of greatness. Nor can we say that Machiavelli's attention to his own city comes from a desire, both responsible and patriotic, to improve its virtue, as virtue is ordinarily understood. It is time to take notice of Machiavelli's rebellious criticism of his two humanist predecessors as historians of the Florentine people, Leonardo Bruni and Poggio Bracciolini. They were, he says in the preface, "two very excellent historians" and "very diligent" in describing the wars of the Florentine people. But they went wrong in regard to "civil discords and internal enmities, and the effects arising from them." Believing that these divisions were unimportant and that to describe them might offend the living, they failed to see that discord revealed the greatness of Florence, and they failed to understand that greatness. For they did not consider that "actions that have greatness in themselves, as do those of governments and states, however they are treated, or whatever end they may have, always appear to bring men more honor than blame" (pr). In cruder words, Bruni and Poggio overestimated the power of morality in determining reputation, and the particular inadequacy of their histories in regard to civil discords is the result of a deep and general mistake that infected their work as a whole and rendered them incapable of understanding human ambition and the desire men have to perpetuate their names.

However much Machiavelli's methods resemble those of the humanist historians, he separates himself deliberately and decisively from them, basing his advice on what is done rather than what should be done. (He took the same departure in Chapter 15 of *The Prince*.) When reading the humanist historians, one breathes the spirit of Cicero, and one is particularly reminded of the second book of *De Republica* (a part of the work they did not know), where Cicero, with fine irony and careful responsibility, blends an account of the origin of his own republic with the development of the features of the best regime. This kind of history is both theoretical and practical because it supposes that nature and virtue are not so much in contest as in cooperation. Machiavelli, on the other hand, who did not think highly of Cicero (see especially D I 52), was no mere observer of the contest between nature or fortune and virtue; he was no Stoic nobly but passively resigned to the limits of politics. For him the end and consequence of theory are to expand the possibilities of practice. To attempt this "undertaking," he opposed himself to the

entire tradition preceding him—classical, medieval, and humanist—as too dependent on the force of morality. Whatever he borrowed from that tradition was used against it.

To conclude, I may briefly suggest what follows upon Machiavelli. If Machiavelli does not accept the sovereignty of historical fact,
he does appear to set forth the sovereignty of historical *effects*. When
virtue is understood not as acting in accordance with moral precepts
but as producing impressive effects, we are, perhaps, on the way
toward the sovereignty of fact and the study of history as an object.
As long as Machiavelli's effects are products of human virtue and
his "actions that have greatness in themselves" are human actions,
then what men do matters more than what happens to them. And
Machiavelli's peculiar humanism, however morally dubious, survives. But as soon as the effects are thought to come from forces
larger than human, though less than divine, then human fortune
subsumes human virtue and acquires patterns of its own. In these
patterns the historian's facts come to life and quickly learn to speak
for themselves. History is no longer an opposition between virtue
and fortune; it has become a mixture of the two, in which virtue is
diminished by its historical conditions and fortune is enhanced by a
new predictability, even rationality, when seen in the guise of those
same conditions. With a view to Machiavelli, one might be induced
to doubt that our notion of history was made for us by history.

It is enough for an introduction to introduce; in chapter 6 I
begin an interpretation of this marvelously intricate work. Having
seen that the *Florentine Histories* is not the sort of history we today might expect, we are left in pleasurable bewilderment as to
what sort of history it may be. To echo the recent question of one
scholar: What, then, did Machiavelli want to teach with his *Florentine Histories?*[2]

# SIX

# PARTY AND SECT
# IN MACHIAVELLI'S
# *FLORENTINE HISTORIES*

M achiavelli's *Florentine Histories* resembles a history book of our day in having a period of narration and in presenting a problem. After the dedicatory letter to Pope Clement VII, who commissioned the work, Machiavelli states the problem in the proemium. Despite his commission, he calls the *Florentine Histories* "my undertaking"; and "my intent," he says, is to write on "the things done inside and outside by the Florentine people," especially on the former, "the causes of the hatreds and divisions in the city." If any republic has notable divisions, he adds, those of Florence are "very notable." Most republics have had one division between the nobles and the plebs, as Rome or Athens, but Florence has suffered from many divisions in the winning party, which have produced "as many deaths, as many exiles, as many ruined families as ever appeared in any city of which we have record."

Machiavelli's undertaking, then, is to seek the causes of the divisions in Florence as contrasted to those in Rome or Athens. Yet in the rest of the work we are given only two explicit statements on the causes. In the first chapter of the third book, Machiavelli says that whereas the Roman people desired to share supreme honors together with the nobles, the Florentine people fought to govern themselves without participation by the nobles. The refusal of the Florentine people to share supreme honors with the nobles is puzzling, however, because Machiavelli began the chapter with the remark that popular men do not wish to obey and the implication

This chapter was originally published as "Party and Sect in Machiavelli's *Florentine Histories*," in *Machiavelli and the Nature of Political Thought*, ed. Martin Fleischer (New York: Scribner, 1972), 209–66. Copyright © 1972 by Martin Fleischer. Reprinted by permission of Scribner, an imprint of Simon and Schuster, Inc.

that they do not wish to rule. What makes the Florentine people thirst for partisan victory?

In the first chapter of the seventh book, Machiavelli gives his only explicit characterization of the Florentine parties. Some divisions, he says, are harmful to republics; others are beneficial. Harmful ones are "accompanied by sects and partisans," while beneficial ones are not. The founder of a republic cannot prevent enmities, but he can provide against sects. The enmities of Florence were always sects or "mixed with sects." But what are sects? Nowhere in the *Florentine Histories* does Machiavelli define "sect." He uses the word in several meanings, but always in connection with religion; and the religion of Florence was Christianity.[1] We are led to the suggestion, which I shall develop, that Christianity is responsible for the special character of the parties in Florence.

Christianity, with its otherworldly understanding of "supreme honors" and its consequent superpolitical claims and transpolitical organization, is a sect essentially different from the ancient sects. It could not be managed or controlled by the Florentine princes in the way that the Roman Senate was able to manage the more political sects of pagan priests. The Christian sect (in the sense of "religion") became the context of the modern sects (in the sense of "parties"), and determined the play of modern politics by deprecating its prizes in favor of rewards in the other world. In a work commissioned by and dedicated to a Florentine Pope, Machiavelli does not make the point directly. Since the publication of that fundamental work of Machiavelli scholarship, Leo Strauss's *Thoughts on Machiavelli,* scholars have begun to explore Machiavelli's methods of indirect statement. In the *Florentine Histories* he makes his point indirectly both in the form of the work and in the content of his narrations. To begin with the form of the book, one must consider its period of narration.

THE MEANING OF 1434

In the dedicatory letter Machiavelli excuses himself for the things he will say against the Medici by pretending that, contrary to the instructions of the pope (formerly Giulio de' Medici), he may have seemed to flatter them. Thus he forestalls the charge of hostility by denying the charge of flattery. In the proemium he says that it was "my intent" to begin "my narrative" at 1434, when the Medici had become the most powerful family in Florence, because "two most excellent historians" had told of the things that happened before that time. But on examination, their works proved inadequate on "the civil discords and internal enmities" and indeed, because of the importance of these matters, altogether defective.[2] This is the kind of examination that ambitious young princes of scholarship apply to the established authorities, and it might seem that Machiavelli was merely enlarging a gap in the scholarly literature to make a place for himself as a narrative historian. The *Florentine Histories* is often translated *The History of Florence*, as if this were his intention, whatever his success in it.

The *Florentine Histories* is the only work of narration that Machiavelli wrote, but, as we have seen in chapter 5, its resemblance to a modern history book is merely superficial. He speaks of "my narrative," "my narratives," and "our narrative"; once when he interrupts the narrative briefly he speaks of returning to "our order." But he also speaks of "our history" (*la istoria nostra*), of "my history," which he determined to begin at the beginning of "our city" and of "all parts of my history," which include "speeches and private reasonings, direct as well as oblique."[3] The "history" is not identical with the "narrative"; it determines where the narrative begins and contains invented speeches and reasonings that mere narrative would not include.

Moreover, the "history" has parts; as we know from the title of the work, it is divided into "histories." The obvious divisions are the eight books, of which seven begin with a discussion of some general political topic in the first chapter, in five cases an explicit comparison of ancient and modern practice. Perhaps it would be better to understand these "histories" as in the classical sense "inquiries."[4] The master inquiry, stated in the proemium, would be "to show the causes of the hatreds and divisions" in Florence as opposed to Rome or Athens, and the seven following inquiries would serve this end. The master inquiry is not a historical problem in the current meaning, since its end is not to characterize the "history" of Florence but to use narratives of events in Florence to characterize certain parties and sects. It does not assume, as historians do today, that "history" is a thing to be studied or an aspect of reality as well as a certain kind of study. Correspondingly, the seven inquiries do not each introduce a historical period whose course of events illustrates some general human propensity in favor at that time, like the periods that make chapters in our history books. Machiavelli's inquiries overlap and do not seem to begin or end a course of events.

Most important, the narrative does not proceed without interruption or complication. It is constructed to and from 1434, the date of Cosimo de' Medici's return to Florence from exile, which was the coming to power of the Medici in Florence; and it is divided in four parts according to a distinction between things inside and things outside Florence. In giving the plan of the work in the proemium, Machiavelli divides his task at 1434, before which he will, in view of the scholarly literature, discuss "particularly" things that happened inside the city and those outside things necessary to know the inside things. After this date, he will describe both the one and the other. Then he says that before dealing with Florence, he will show how Italy "came to be under those powers that governed it in that time"—a guarded expression suggesting the wide scope of things outside Florence. Machiavelli then gives an outline of the first four books; the first book describes "briefly" events in Italy to 1434 and the second to fourth books on Florence also close at 1434. From that time, he will present things happening inside and outside Florence "up to our present times." In fact, he tells first of things outside Florence to 1463 in Books V and VI, and then returns to 1434 at the beginning of Book VII to catch up on things within Florence. From the seventh chapter of the seventh book, that is, from the death of Cosimo de' Medici, Machiavelli relates events inside and outside Florence together.

The reader thus expects 1434 to be a crucial year.[5] It seems to be connected to the distinction between things inside and things outside Florence, for the narrative is told in such a way that the things outside Florence are brought ever closer to the things inside. In the first book, only events outside Florence to 1434 are narrated; in Books II to IV (before 1434) only those outside events relevant to events inside Florence are narrated; from the beginning of Book V to Book VII 6 (after 1434), outside events are assumed to be relevant to inside events but are narrated separately; and from VII 7 (1464) they are narrated together. The year 1434 divides exactly in half not only the eight books but the 286 chapters of the *Florentine Histories*.[6] The precise difference, as given, is this: before the coming to power of the Medici, it is necessary to distinguish between things outside Florence necessary to know the inside things and things outside unnecessary to know for that purpose; and afterward it is no longer necessary to make this distinction. With the return of Cosimo, things outside Florence are automatically relevant to things inside, and this result is given emphasis by the change in narrative method used after the death of Cosimo.

The meaning of 1434, though not obvious, seems surely grand. But when we turn to Machiavelli's description of this event in the last chapter of the fourth book and the first chapter of the fifth, we find no discourse on "the meaning of 1434." Instead we find a trifling turn of fortune caused by impotence and foolish confidence. It appears at the end of Book IV that the Medici did not first become prominent in 1434. In that year Cosimo de' Medici was restored from exile to Florence in triumph over the chief of the opposing party, Rinaldo degli Albizzi, himself now sent into exile. "Rarely does it happen that a citizen, returning triumphant from a victory, has been received by his fatherland by such a crowd of people and such a demonstration of good will as he received when he returned from exile." But how did he get the victory and what was the nature of the triumph?

Cosimo had been sent into exile by a party of "nobles" whose divided counsel had allowed him to bribe his way to this easy fate, leaving his own party strong in Florence.[7] When Cosimo's partisans captured the Signoria by the usual method of lot from elected or prearranged eligibles, Messer Rinaldo and his party were again divided and irresolute. Though aware of the danger, they could not decide to prevent the new Signoria from taking office. As soon as it showed its intention of restoring Cosimo, Messer Rinaldo took arms, but those of his party who had argued against precipitate action, as they called it, had no stomach for fighting an opponent who by their inactivity had won public authority. Messer Rinaldo upbraided them for their sluggishness, receiving a feeble excuse from one and muttered incoherence from another. He took the time to declare to them that if disaster followed he would have the satisfaction of having given advice of the danger and of having been present at it with force. But in fact, Machiavelli says, Messer Rinaldo had sufficient force to capture the *signori*, and lost his opportunity by waiting for more. In the time he spent in upbraiding his friends, the *signori* recovered their spirit, made preparations for their defense, and sent some citizens to Rinaldo to exhort him to lay down his arms, assuring him the *signori* had no intention of restoring Cosimo. One of Rinaldo's lieutenants accepted this assurance, and went with his followers into the palace of the Signoria to signify his acceptance. Rinaldo saw his own followers begin to lose their warmth of spirit.

At this point the pope intervened. He was staying in Florence because he had been chased from Rome by the Roman people. "Hearing of these tumults and feeling it his duty to quiet them," he sent for Rinaldo and persuaded him, with a guarantee of the good intentions of the Signoria to disarm himself. Whereupon the *signori* secretly arranged to seize the city's fortresses, and having done so, brought back Cosimo and exiled Rinaldo. Pope Eugene, seeing the ruin of those who "at his prayer" had laid down their arms, was "very ill content." He lamented the injury "done under his faith" and asked Rinaldo to have patience and to hope much "from a change of fortune." Rinaldo accepted these priestly condolences in the spirit with which they were offered: he blamed himself more than anyone else, he said, for putting too much faith in the Pope and for believing that "you who had been driven from your own fatherland would be able to keep me in mine."[8] He said that he had had much experience of the senselessness of fortune, and that if fortune did not show itself favorable to him, he did not desire anyhow to live in a city where the laws were less powerful than men. Rinaldo stalked out of Florence in high dudgeon, and Cosimo returned "triumphant."[9]

Machiavelli's *Florentine Histories* thus turns on what may be called the comedy of 1434. The contrast of Cosimo's triumph with a Roman triumph is humiliating for Italy, Florence, and Cosimo himself. Cosimo's triumph established the hegemony of the Medici family, but a Roman triumph brought glory to the individual and acquisitions to the republic. A Roman triumph could not occur in Florence because the Florentine nobility, disunited and weak, was unable to manage Cosimo; it thought only of exile or death for him and could not find a task that would attach his interest and glory to the common good.[10] In the end Cosimo was permitted to back his way into power in a kind of "restoration."[11] He did not have to gain power with his own arms.

Cosimo's triumph, therefore, was "Roman" in the modern rather than the ancient sense. It was accomplished partly by "the authority of the Pope" (*FH* IV 31), who at the time was staying in Florence and who thereafter was united with Florence as members of the Medici family became popes. In submitting the *Florentine Histories* to a Medici pope, Machiavelli asserted that Florence remained divided "until it began to be governed under the protection of Your House (*Casa Sua*)." "Your House" contains the ambiguous reference to both the Medici and the papacy that is needed to confirm the "Roman" triumph of Cosimo.[12] We may wonder what made that triumph possible. What cause but the character of the Christian sect makes possible the authority of the pope and establishes his "office" as a regent above human polities and as intermediary and peacemaker between human parties? We shall find a similar explanation for the obvious fact that the Medici house was made more prominent by its ecclesiastical attainments. A private house like the Medici was enabled to rise above public control because Christianity had weakened or destroyed the basis of public control.

## THE EXTRAORDINARY FORCE

The account of Cosimo's triumph is immediately followed, at the beginning of Book V, by a discussion of "nature" and man's place in nature. Machiavelli says that "nature does not allow worldly things [*mondane cose*] to remain fixed"; hence order is followed by disorder, and disorder by order, unless men are stifled by "an extraordinary force." This "extraordinary force" outside the working of "nature" and superior to the "worldly things" that move makes one think of the supernatural. Elsewhere in this work Machiavelli describes a whirlwind as driven by "superior forces, whether natural or supernatural"; thus an extraordinary force outside the natural would seem to be the supernatural. One recalls a statement in the eleventh chapter of the *Discourses* (ambiguously titled "Of the Religion of the Romans"): "And truly there has been no orderer of extraordinary laws in a people who did not have recourse to God, for otherwise they would not be accepted."[13] Perhaps the "extraordinary force" that keeps modern men in disorder results from having recourse to the Christian God.

This chapter (V 1) is also the only one in which the Tuscans, as distinguished from the inhabitants of the region of Tuscany, are mentioned.[14] The Tuscany of the Tuscans (or, as we would call them, the Etruscans) is pre-Roman Italy, hence not only pre-Christian Italy, but considering that ancient Rome is partly continuous with modern Rome, pre-pre-Christian Italy. It recalls the context of "nature" in which the Christian sect is only one among many sects. Machiavelli does not say what the "extraordinary force" could be that has prevented the return of virtue and order out of the ruins of the Roman empire. He merely wonders at the ease with which "weak and poorly administered armies" have held in check "so many very noble peoples." He remarks that since philosophers corrupt "the strength of armed spirits" with honorable leisure (or laziness), Cato introduced a law that "no philosopher be received at Rome."[15] What is the leisure, honorable or pious, that prevails in modern Rome? If it arises from an "extraordinary force," can it be controlled by political authority? These high thoughts on order and disorder in nature follow a domestic comedy in Florence and introduce a criticism of the conduct of modern "princes, soldiers, and chiefs of republics" in warfare.

We have, then, a transition from domestic to foreign affairs at the beginning of Book V, as accords with Machiavelli's plan. The foreign policy of Florence becomes necessarily relevant to its domestic policy after the Medici achieve power in Florence through the unwitting agency of the pope, who could not manage his own domestic troubles and yet thought himself qualified to pacify Florence. Because he does not recognize the distinction between domestic and foreign, he meddles where he can in the domestic affairs of princes and republics.

Thus the meaning of "foreign" is also ambiguous. It refers to the external relations of men with men and of men with God. The ambiguity is implied in Christian doctrine, which says that men live as friends with one another in peace, as they live at peace with God: the brotherhood of man under the fatherhood of God. Machiavelli might have supposed from this doctrine that man's distance from God, which he thought too great for gratitude or filial piety on the part of man to God, makes God a foreigner to man.[16] Ultimately, he might infer, the remoteness of God the Father is also responsible for the unfraternal distances between human societies and hence for the distinction men make, in "ordinary" usage, between domestic and foreign affairs.

Christianity is the context of the *Florentine Histories*, since Florence, as Machiavelli shows in Book I, was from its beginnings a Christian state. Christianity is not the open theme of the work, however. As compared to the *Discourses* (*D* I pr, 12; II 2, 5; III 1), Machiavelli says little in the *Florentine Histories* about Christianity. Although he states the problem of the work in a comparison of ancient and modern politics, he never describes Christianity, as he did in the *Discourses,* as the decisive difference between ancient and modern politics. The only book without an inquiry, the first, is the book that discusses Christianity by describing the activities of Christians and popes. Machiavelli remarks here that men are now Pieros, Giovannis, and Matteos instead of Caesars and Pompeys, and he gives some idea of the effect of "the Christian religion" by discussing the effects of its heretical (as opposed to its catholic) sects.[17] The reader is left to surmise the meaning of "catholic sects" just as he was forced to discover the meaning of 1434.

In a book on his own city, commissioned by a Florentine pope, Machiavelli could not speak as boldly about Christianity as he did in *The Prince* and the *Discourses;* and he does not claim for this work, as he did for those, that it contains everything he knows. But he constructed it with a division in the middle suggesting a thought that points directly at the pope in Florence and indirectly at a Medici, that is, Florentine pope. Machiavelli's rhetoric more than his historical accuracy is at issue here. But which is his historical argument? Did Cosimo capture Florence and then did the Medici capture the papacy for Florence, or by capturing Florence did he and Florence become unconscious tools of the pope, or was neither of these the case?

Cosimo was a "disarmed man" (*FH* I 23), and he proved unable to expand "Florentine power with an honorable conquest" (*FH* VII 5). To capture Lucca, he had put his faith in the "mercenary and faithless arms" of Francesco Sforza (*FH* VII 6). He had great authority in Florence, but it was left to his "descendants" to acquire authority in all Christendom (*FH* VI 20). Yet if his "descendants" include the Medici popes, they too were forced to depend on faithless mercenaries. It seems that under Christianity it is difficult for a prince to acquire anything, whether he is a "secular prince" or a pope (*FH* VII 11, 17). Because Christianity is above politics, the prince must be disarmed either of this world's weapons, like a pope, or of the other world's weapons, like a mercenary captain. Cosimo seems to

represent the modern prince whose "greatness of spirit" is reduced
to private "magnificence," whose ambition is restricted to peacemaking in his own city, and whose authority is dissipated in the ecclesiastical attainments of his "descendants." At Cosimo's triumph in 1434
and again at his death, Machiavelli quotes the epitaph on his tomb-
stone, *padre della patria,* ambiguous as to the sacred or the secular
hierarchy.[18]

## THE ABSENCE OF SAVONAROLA

The importance of Christianity is openly slighted and covertly emphasized. In view of this rhetorical tactic, it is significant that Machiavelli fails even to mention Savonarola in the *Florentine Histories.*
He says in the proemium that he will describe things inside and
outside Florence "up to our present times," but he ends Book VIII
at the death of Lorenzo in 1492. Lorenzo, he says ominously, was
mourned with just cause, for after his death those who were left
found no way to satisfy or check the ambition of Lodovico Sforza,
a situation "which began the growth of those evil seeds that, in a
short time, since no living man knew how to destroy them, have
ruined and still ruin Italy" (*FH* VIII 36). Thus Machiavelli quickly
shifts his gaze from Florence to Italy, overlooking the then-imminent
rule of Savonarola, whom Lorenzo had already invited to Florence.
Since he apparently does not keep his promise to carry the narrative
"up to our present times," it is easy to conclude that the *Florentine
Histories* is unfinished. Yet the arrangement of chapters indicates
that it is not simply unfinished.[19] Machiavelli submitted it as finished
and surely polished his first draft.

In the dedicatory letter he offers an apology for not writing up
to the present: "And since I have come now, in my writing, to those
times which, through the death of the Magnificent Lorenzo de' Medici, brought a change to the form of Italy, and because the things
that followed afterward were higher and greater, and are to be described with a higher and greater spirit [*spirito*], I judged it would
be well to reduce to one volume all that I had described up to those
times and to present it to Your Most Holy Blessedness, so that you
may begin to taste in some part the fruits of your seeds and of my
labors."[20] It is as if a second volume were promised that would
contain a full description of everything "higher and greater" than

the contents of the first volume. Yet the first volume is a fruit that may have a taste of the second volume, and it seems to end in a way that suggests the higher and greater things of which Machiavelli could not speak explicitly.

Machiavelli had said in the *Discourses* (in the eleventh chapter, discussed above) that one must speak of "so great a man" as Savonarola "with reverence," but he did not hesitate to display "his life, doctrine and the plan he undertook" as an example to confirm the feasibility of bringing new orders even to civilized men, such as the people of Florence supposed themselves to be (*D* I 11). Surely a *Florentine Histories* completed "up to our present times" would describe the new order of Savonarola, unless we are to impute reverence to Savonarola in Machiavelli's mention of the "higher and greater" things to come after Lorenzo. At the end of Book VIII, he speaks only of the calamities to come after Lorenzo, the evil seeds whose growth would begin, in the absence of Lorenzo, through the ambition of Lodovico Sforza (*D* II 15; III 11; *P* 3). The passage must refer to the invasion of Italy by Charles VIII, king of France, in 1494. These calamities were signified, Machiavelli says in the same place, by a bolt of lightning that struck the cathedral of Santa Reparata.[21] In the *Discourses,* however, in the chapter devoted to signs (I 56), he mentions this event as occurring before the death of Lorenzo (1492) but without saying what it signified and with the prosaic remark that it caused "very great damage to that building." He must have known Savonarola's interpretation of the event, also as a sign of calamities, but of domestic calamities in Florence. They were the scourge of God—*Ecce gladius Domini*—to punish the Florentines for their sins.[22] Just before he mentions this event without its interpretation, he tells "how much was predicted by Brother Girolamo Savonarola before the coming of King Charles VIII of France into Italy." So in the *Florentine Histories* he uses the wrong sign of the two available, the one referring to domestic calamities rather than foreign invasion; and he omits any connection with Savonarola by failing to mention either his name or the domestic changes in Florence that would put him in mind immediately.[23] Machiavelli leaves a false trail that points away from Savonarola and therefore, after the proper "inquiries," leads back to him.

We are at first confused by the fact that the *Florentine Histories* ends with the foreboding of a foreign invasion, when we expect, in a work whose theme is internal divisions, to hear of a striking change of government to come in Florence. But in the refined meaning of "foreign," the coming of Savonarola rather than the king of France constituted a foreign invasion. In V 1, Machiavelli says that by the cowardly wars in Italy, "as will be made clearly known by what we shall describe from 1434 to 1494," a new road was opened to the barbarians and Italy put herself back into slavery under them. But Savonarola, in 1494, hailed the coming of the French king as the purgation of Florence and the Church. In consequence of the invasion, the Medici were expelled from Florence and Savonarola seized the opportunity of bringing new orders to men who thought they were civilized. Truth is stranger than fiction, and Machiavelli did not have to make the metaphor of "foreign" that he could find in events.

### THE INQUIRIES

To understand the *Florentine Histories,* one must make the importance of Christianity explicit. To do this for 1434, the crucial event of the work, it was necessary to consider the inquiry on order and disorder at the beginning of Book V as a transition rather than an introduction. At the beginning of Book VIII, Machiavelli says that it would seem proper, "wishing to follow our custom," to speak of "the quality of conspiracies and their importance" between the narrations of two actual conspiracies. This he would do, he says, if he had not done so in another place or if he could do so with brevity.[24] So these things will be put aside, and he will turn to "another matter"; the seventh inquiry, it seems, will be omitted. But in fact it is not omitted. Machiavelli does speak of "the quality of conspiracies and their importance," and in such manner as to suggest the quality and importance of his "inquiries."

Passing to the other matter, he says that after "the state of the Medici" had overcome all the hostilities of those who opposed it openly, it had to overcome those who schemed against it secretly.[25] Such conspiracies succeed with difficulty, for they usually bring ruin to "those who move them" and greatness to the man conspired against. Unless the latter is killed, which rarely happens, he rises to greater power. Then he often becomes wicked, as these conspiracies by their example give him cause to fear; fear causes him to secure himself; securing himself causes him to injure; injuring gives birth to hatreds "and many times his own ruin." Thus, Machiavelli concludes, such conspiracies quickly crush "those who move them" and with time, harm "those against whom they are moved."

These remarks serve as a prelude to a fascinating narration of the Pazzi conspiracy against the Medici brothers Giuliano and Lorenzo. The conspiracy was executed inside Florence and by a last-minute change of plan inside a church, and it failed because the executioners, lacking "a great and firm spirit [*animo*]," killed only Giuliano and not Lorenzo.[26] Lorenzo, rid of a brother who was bound to cause him trouble, did indeed rise to greater power in a city "that judges things by success and not by counsel" (*FH* VIII 2, 22). Why, then, did Machiavelli make so much of the indirect consequences of conspiracy, since apparently they did not follow from the Pazzi conspiracy? His discussion hints that not every conspirator need "move" his conspiracy. It suggests the possibility of an indirect conspiracy that uses other conspirators to "move" the conspiracy and make the first—ordinarily unsuccessful—attempt. Then the patient master conspirator can watch the indirect consequences develop. In fact, there was a master conspirator behind the Pazzi conspiracy, the pope—and he was foiled by the refusal of one executioner "to accompany treason with sacrilege."[27]

It would be prudent to suppose that Machiavelli considered himself a master conspirator who intended, however, not to be hoist on his own petard. He remarks mildly that this pope was "the first who began to show how much a pope could do." The first words of the *Florentine Histories* are *lo animo mio* ("my intent") and the last words are *la Italia*. The chapter on the "extraordinary force" that stifles a return to order ends with a recommendation to study modern things as well as ancient, for while "free spirits" (*liberali animi*) can imitate the latter, they can avoid and abolish the former (*FH* V 1; VII 22). Having an aim at least partly practical and reforming, the *Florentine Histories* must have been written not with the methods of scientific history but with the devices of reformers or "new princes." Like any new prince, Machiavelli began by being weaker than the existing princes, and he must have been forced to express himself disingenuously, or as he says, with fraud.[28] If he could have said openly all he intended against "this corrupt world," he would not have had to say it. In the *Florentine Histories,* his method of fraud

is to conduct the reader by stages in histories or inquiries that bring
him to understand what is wrong with the modern world and offers
an opinion that points beyond itself to a better understanding; the
inquiries overlap each other because each is provisional and hence
transitional. Machiavelli makes his hostility to the modern world
plain and clear so that everyone, at whatever level of understanding,
can find a reason for changing it, but only at the last stage of the
conspiracy does one learn of the extent of the conspiracy or even
that one has joined a conspiracy. Thus the inquiries of the *Florentine
Histories,* being transitional from and to the matter surrounding
them, are transitional to each other; and they culminate in an inquiry
on conspiracy that impudently claims to be omitted.

The first inquiry (II 1) compares ancient and modern policy on
colonies: "Among the other great and marvelous orders of the ancient republics and principalities that in our times have been eliminated was that by which they used to build many towns anew and
at all times." This statement equates colonizing with new building
and implies that political vitality demands growth. Yet Machiavelli
conceals the harshness of imperialism by attributing it solely to a
defect of "nature." Nature, not "history" as we know it, is the
problem of Machiavelli's "histories." Nature does not provide an
even fertility of land, and in the absence of human "industry" or
"culture," fertile lands become crowded and poor, while unfertile
lands remain desert. That explanation does not account for the phenomenon of conquest, although Machiavelli refers to the policy of
colonizing in lands "either conquered or empty." And why do the
moderns not send colonies? "Because princes have no desire for true
glory and republics no order that deserves to be praised." The defect
of the moderns is political, for Machiavelli condemns modern
princes and republics impartially and separately. We note that the
moderns are not lacking in industry or in the pacific art of farming
but it may be that they somehow place too much confidence in
nature, as though forgetting its failure to provide the most elementary necessities and the consequent need for human "culture" or
cultivation.[29]

The second inquiry (III 1) discusses "the grave and natural enmities . . . between the men of the people and the nobles" in Rome
and Florence. In the description of *natural* enmities we have an inti-
mation that nature is not to be understood simply as distinct from

human culture nor human culture simply as supplying the defects of nature. Within human culture, among "human things," these natural enmities are "the cause of all evils that arise in cities." Yet "diverse effects" can be observed in Rome and in Florence; in Rome, the enmities were brought to an end by disputes, in Florence, by fighting; in Rome, they ended with a law, in Florence, with the exile and death of many citizens; in Rome, they always increased military virtue, in Florence, they destroyed it entirely; in Rome, they brought very great inequality out of equality, and in Florence, they reduced inequality to a "wonderful [*mirabile*] equality" (*FH* III 1). For the cause of this difference, Machiavelli blames the Florentine people. Unlike the Roman people, who wished to enjoy supreme honors with the nobles, the Florentine people fought to govern by themselves without the participation of the nobles. Their desire was "harmful and unjust" but it is not fully explained. Why did the Florentine people wish to govern by themselves, despite the fact that peoples do not naturally desire to command? The consequence of their rule has been to destroy in Florence "that virtue in arms and generosity of spirit [*animo*]" possessed by the nobility, with no stated advantage to themselves.

Machiavelli shows in the next inquiry (*FH* IV 1) that he does not accept the partisan view of either the people or the nobles. "Cities, and especially those not well ordered that are administered under the name of republic, frequently change their governments and their states not between liberty and servitude, as many believe, but between servitude and license." The ministers of license, he says, are the people, and the ministers of servitude are the nobles; both claim the name of liberty. Thus the alternative of liberty and slavery would be the popular view that "many believe" and that Machiavelli chooses to expose as partisan. Then how can a city be free? A city "can be called free" when by good fortune a good, wise, and powerful citizen orders the laws so as to quiet the humors of the nobles and people or to restrain them so that they cannot work for evil. Founded on good laws and orders, such a city would not need to be maintained, as other cities are, by the virtue of one man. "Many ancient republics," Machiavelli says, had this good fortune, but cities where such laws and orders are lacking vary between a "tyrannical and a licentious state." Now, since the tyrannical state does not please the good and the licentious does not please the wise, these cities have to be maintained by "the virtue and fortune of a single man."

Natural enmities, it seems, can be repressed with impartial laws and orders established by a "good, wise and powerful man" who makes the "virtue of a single man" unnecessary thereafter. Such a man is "the good fortune of the city": good fortune would then seem to be the solution for natural divisions. How likely is good fortune? By moving from the division between nobles and people regarding liberty to the distinction between a tyrannical state that does not please the good and a licentious state that does not please the wise, Machiavelli indicates the existence of a natural division between the good and the wise regarding good laws and orders. If a powerful citizen appears who is both good and wise, he must have coincidentally two qualities not only different but contrary.[30]

Thus the problem of natural divisions between the nobles and the people continues among those who might be thought above the quarrel; it cannot be solved by the legislation of an impartial man. Yet "many ancient republics" were gifted with good laws and orders and long lives. Perhaps they used "the virtue of a single man," as opposed to goodness, and with good laws and orders managed not to depend on "the virtue and good fortune of one man," like the modern states. Machiavelli's regime is impartial, while his conception of virtue emphatically is not. The regime achieves impartiality by using the virtue of many men, each of whom is partial to himself, for virtue is always "the virtue of a single man." Since Florence failed to restrain the conflict between nobles and people with the proper mixture of rewards and punishments, the city could not make use of its supply of virtuous men, as each was dangerous to every other.[31] It became dependent on the good fortune, as well as the virtue, of one man. The reason for this failure is not explained, but a lack of tolerance for the partiality of virtue, for the desire of princes for true glory, is suggested.[32] Machiavelli does not mention the possibility, dear to Aristotelian political science, of a mixed regime sustained by an impartial middle class, but the reasoning that separates the good from the wise would bear against this possibility.[33]

The central inquiry has been considered. It seemed to show the contrast between the natural order of "worldly things" in movement, within which men contrive their own order and suffer through its decay, and the supernatural, which can stifle at least the return to good order with an "extraordinary force." This contrast modifies the farmer's view of nature given in the first inquiry, that nature and culture are distinct, in the direction suggested by the second inquiry, that natural order applies to human things, especially the divisions in human societies. But now we have a reason why "natural divisions" can have "diverse effects" in Rome and in Florence: not the chance of a good and wise lawgiver, but a supernatural force or the belief in a supernatural force. Virtue needs arms to bring forth "quiet," a kind of disorder to create order. Since order does not create itself, men can be held in disorder by an opinion, a belief in the extraordinary force of the Christian God, which keeps virtue disarmed.

In accordance with his introduction of the supernatural in contrast with the natural, Machiavelli now blames princes rather than peoples; for it is princes who introduce new orders and new ways of life.[34] He wonders "how so many very noble peoples were held in check by such weak and badly directed armies." "Princes, soldiers, and heads of republics" were able to maintain their reputations only by the use of frauds, tricks, and arts (*FH* V 1). This criticism is continued in the next inquiry (VI 1) on the costly indecisiveness of modern wars. Modern wars are as expensive for the victors as for the vanquished because they are fought by mercenaries who take the spoils if they win and wait to be reequipped if they lose. In either case, the prince must take money from his subjects. Victory brought nothing to the benefit of the people and only made the prince more pressing and less respectful. "Ancient and well-ordered republics were accustomed to fill their treasuries with gold and silver from their victories, to distribute gifts to the people, to forgive payment of tribute by their subjects, and to entertain them with games and solemn festivals. But victories in the times we are describing first emptied the treasury, then impoverished the people, and still did not protect you from your enemies" (*FH* VI 1; cf. I 39).

It is no wonder, then, that the Florentine people did not wish to share "supreme honors" with the nobles; there were few of the worldly kind to be shared. Why were there few such? Why were mercenaries, "the two sects of armies" that Machiavelli describes in Books V and VI, allowed to engross the profits of victory and live comfortably in defeat? One cannot help but recall Machiavelli's remark in the *Discourses* about "our religion . . . which makes us esteem less the honor of the world."[35] For a Christian people, the "supreme honor" is salvation in the afterlife, in which all men may share a "wonderful equality"; but the desire for this honor is consistent only with the nature of a people, since it does not desire to rule. Mercenaries, who play their own game while holding the fate because they hold the arms of the prince, remind one of other intermediaries who set themselves up as necessary to salvation and who thrive in good times and bad.

The sixth inquiry returns to domestic matters after 1434, although the narrative on the "two sects of armies" (Sforza's and Piccinino's) in the two preceding books had touched on Florentine internal divisions when necessary (FH V 4, 15, 27; VI 6, 7, 23). Machiavelli begins his inquiry by stating that he wishes to explain "why those who hope that a republic can be united are very much deceived in this hope." This is surprising, because he himself had seemed to plant and nourish this hope in his readers. In the proemium he promised to show the causes of the hatreds and divisions in Florence, so that "citizens who govern republics" can keep themselves united; and he had said that if Florence had had a form of government that would keep it united, it would have been the equal of any republic, ancient or modern. Now we are told that unity is impossible, and we are given an explanation for the diverse effects of the natural enmities in Rome and in Florence. Florence suffered under harmful divisions, those accompanied by "sects and partisans," as opposed to the beneficial divisions "that are maintained without sects and partisans." Until this point in the Florentine Histories, Machiavelli, while admitting that divisions are natural, has treated kindly the opinion hostile to parties that he dismisses at the beginning of the Discourses.[36] He needed the protection of this opinion in teaching the causes of weakness in his own city in his own times, and he did not reveal its inadequacy before he was ready to say that some divisions are beneficial. Even so, he soothes the shock of discovering that republics can never be united with a continued hostility to partisans, if not to all parties.

Bearing in mind that he cannot prevent enmities, then, the founder of a republic must seek to prevent sects. "Therefore," Machiavelli says to introduce a well-concealed consequence, he must know "that citizens in cities acquire reputation in two modes: either by public ways or by private modes." The public ways are "winning a battle, acquiring a town, carrying out a mission with care and prudence, advising the republic wisely and happily." Private modes are "benefiting this or that citizen, defending him from magistrates, helping him with money, getting him unmerited honors, and ingratiating oneself with the plebs with games and public gifts." From the latter way of proceeding come sects and partisans, but the former way is "not mixed with sects, because that reputation is founded on a common good, not on a private good." This distinction, we note, is between private and public ways of gaining reputation, that is, of gaining a private end; that is why the public ways are said to be "founded on a common good" instead of "aiming at the common good."

Machiavelli makes this implication explicit by almost abandoning the distinction in the next sentence: citizens who use private modes will not harm the republic if they do not have "partisans who follow them for their own profit." On the contrary, they will be useful because to succeed, they must try to effect "the exaltation" of the republic, and "watch one another particularly so that civil bounds [*i termini civili*] are not transgressed."[37] The founder of a republic must admit the need for honors and use them to unite private advantage with the public good. Machiavelli said in the first inquiry that modern states do not send colonies "because princes have no desire for true glory and republics no order that deserves to be praised." Now he combines the two reasons. Praiseworthy order in a republic would encourage the desire for true glory or reputation in its princes, offer prizes to them, and manage the competition.

When the reader understands the need for worldly honor in politics, he will join Machiavelli's conspiracy against Christianity; for Christianity clearly denies the desire for worldly honor. But the precise effects of this denial are unclear, since Christianity despite its intention cannot dispense with worldly honor. Florentine parties may have been "mixed with sects," but the Guelfs and the Ghibellines were not doctrinal parties of priests, and few Florentine politicians were notably pious or easily obedient to sacerdotal authority. In politics, Christianity does not necessarily make men into zealots for otherworldly honor, especially not in its time of corruption. Rather, it prevents the princes who desire worldly honors from pursuing them wholeheartedly, attaining them completely, and enjoying

them without a bad conscience. At the same time it offers an illusory
protection for the weak that keeps them weak—an excuse for defeat,
a consolation in failure, and an avoidance of the natural punishments for imprudence. Christianity keeps men in dependence to God
or to themselves, a condition that Machiavelli represents as that of
a colony. Florence began as a colony of ancient Rome and now
continues as a colony of modern Rome.

### THE COLONY OF FLORENCE

Since the Florentine parties took their special character from their
origin, it is necessary to attend particularly to the first two books of
the *Florentine Histories*. Machiavelli shows that parties arose from
the dispute between the emperor and the pope, between the heir to
the vestiges of the Roman empire and the representative of its sancti-
fied spirit. The first book, he says dryly, "tells briefly all the unforeseen events in Italy following upon the decline of the Roman empire
up to 1434" (*FH* pr). Its theme is Rome, not Florence, not even the
origins of Florence, as we would expect from Machiavelli's decision
"to begin my history with the beginning of our city"; Florence is
mentioned only three times and carefully not discussed.[38] Its theme
is Rome because Florence had its origin in Rome, a protected beginning as a colony of Rome. Thus the first book does not have as its
theme "beginnings," for Florence did not have a true, unprotected
beginning, as did Rome. Accordingly, the first inquiry does not occur
at the beginning of the first book, and when it occurs, it discusses
colonies rather than beginnings. The beginnings of Rome suggest
the beginnings of any city, as we know from the first chapter of the
*Discourses*.[39] But the origins of Florence must be seen in the decaying
empire and growing Church that gave it protection. Florence is kept
out of the first book of the *Florentine Histories* so that its protector,
Rome, can be examined for the cause and manner of its protection.

In the first chapter we are told that the Roman empire was
destroyed by barbarians who followed a policy of colonizing their
excess inhabitants. They lived up north in a prolific and healthful
region where population often increased to such a multitude that a
province would "divide itself in three parts" and send the lucky third
south "to seek its fortune." It was fitting that to overthrow so great
an empire, founded on the blood of so many virtuous men, the

Italian princes not be less sluggish than they were, the ministers less faithless, nor their attacks less forceful and persistent than they were. Then in the first inquiry (II 1), we are informed of the "great and wonderful order" of ancient republics for colonizing in the same way, except that Machiavelli here stresses the filling of empty lands rather than the emptying of full lands. Florence, it seems, was a product of this very praiseworthy order, having "its beginning from Fiesole and its growth from colonies."[40] In keeping with his avoidance of beginnings, Machiavelli discusses only its growth as a market town under the protection of the reputation of the Roman republic, that is, the Roman empire; he says nothing here of Fiesole or of the "ancient Tuscans." This protection weakened as Rome lost its power and its opportunity to colonize, and Rome was destroyed by barbarians with the vigor to imitate its "great and wonderful order." To protect is to colonize; to be protected is to be a colony; to be a colony is to be conqueror or conquered.

The Roman empire was destroyed by barbarians, but they were given the opportunity to destroy by the emperors who abandoned Rome for Constantinople and left the western part of the empire weak. Later we learn that "the emperor became a Christian, left Rome, and went off to Constantinople."[41] The disorder that followed was terrifying because not merely princes or governments were changed, but laws, ways of living, and especially religion. The new religion with its miracles fought the customs of the ancient religion, and men died wretchedly, uncertain to which god they should turn, even to which sect of the Christian God, for the disunity of Christianity caused as much affliction as the cruelty of the barbarians. During this disorder the popes gained authority. The first popes after Saint Peter, because of their holy lives and their miracles, became respected by the people; Christianity was from the first a religion of the people. Then princes found it necessary to adopt the Christian religion "so as to dispel the great confusion abroad in the world" (*FH* I 9; cf. I 25; II 6). Still, before the coming of the Longobards, the popes had no other power than the respect they earned for their habits and their teaching; in secular matters they obeyed the kings and emperors and were sometimes killed by them or used as ministers. The pope acquired some power in Rome by default when Theodoric made himself king of Italy in Ravenna, and when the Longobards came, they allowed the pope to become almost the

chief of Rome. But as the eastern empire declined and the Longobards grew stronger, the popes began to seek help in France. The
many wars of the barbarians in Italy from those times to the present
were largely caused by the popes' summoning help, Machiavelli concludes.[42] The greatest instance was the pope's summons for Charle-
magne, who crossed the Alps and visited Rome, where he "judged
that the pope as vicar of God could not be judged by men" and was
proclaimed emperor by the pope and the Roman people (*FH* I 11).

The popes used the opportunity of barbarian invasions, which
Machiavelli fails to call heaven-sent, to create the power that could
only be maintained by further barbarian invasions. These two powers depended on each other, the popes on the barbarian kings for
that "kingly power" that true princes supply (*D* I 34), and the kings
on the pope to rectify the great disorder and introduce quiet and
obedience to their kingdoms. Together, they corresponded to the
two elements of ancient Rome or any regime: people and princes.
But in decadent Rome, the two elements worked badly and could
not act and react against each other in a manner conducive to the
common good.

Why the ancient Roman system failed in modern Italy could be
seen in the actions of the crucial factor in the system, the pope. The
pope was head of a religion that, scorning worldly honor and political glory, appealed to the people rather than princes; according to
the ancient Roman system, he was therefore in the equivocal position
of the plebeian prince, ambitious above his rank yet hostile to all of
noble rank. Such a man could be "managed" in the Machiavellian-
Roman sense by a policy of co-optation into the nobility, in which
the plebeian princes were first made rivals to each other for military
prizes and afterward the best or the luckiest selected for noble rank.
The "policy" did not require that the nobles in power stay in power,
since no harm was done if the plebeian prince defeated his managers
and vaulted into the office where he would have to manage others
like his former self. All the system seemed to need was the avarice
all nobles hold from nature and the prudence some of them display
in rising to the highest offices. But to form the combination of prudent avarice, prudence must be free of hostility to avarice and eager
to cooperate with it. This was the difficulty in managing the pope.

The pope was a prince of the people, who because of the character of the "sect" that gave him office, could not be bribed or re-

warded in the usual way with honors. He and the Church he heads have renounced both the use of arms and self-advancement, and so he can neither be offered nor can he accept worldly honors that require the use of arms in one's own advancement. To accept worldly honors in the spirit with which they are offered would reduce him to the level of the other worldly princes in this world and would require him to renounce his claim to superiority over them, yet his office is constituted by that claim alone. As pope, he cannot be a prince of any kind unless he is superior to the worldly, or the natural, princes. It is his very "spiritual power" that makes him faithless in his worldly engagements (*FH* VIII 17).

The pope exercised his authority "first with censure, then with censure and arms," as in time he acquired the inferior status of a worldly prince in addition to his superior status, but he acquired worldly status because he had a superior status. His "censures" could inflict "spiritual wounds," whose importance the Emperor Henry IV was the first prince to learn. It was through the power of censures, however, not through fair or equal competition with worldly princes on their level, that the pope acquired "arms." Henry IV, suffering the spiritual wound of excommunication, came to Canossa to ask pardon of the pope because he was "obliged by his peoples."[43]

Spiritual wounds do not hurt the spirit merely, but they also undermine the worldly rule of princes through the belief of their peoples in the supremacy of otherworldly salvation. The pope, therefore, wields arms as a consequence of his censures, but he does not hold his own arms. Granted the superiority of the divine, he is only the vicar of God, and God does not choose to make himself the agent of the pope's worldly designs as if they were directed by a worldly purpose. Machiavelli gives a thisworldly explanation that accounts for both the pope's existence as a worldly prince and his failure to prosper in that office: "So much are the things that appear feared more at a distance than nearby."[44]

Not wielding his own arms, the pope must exercise his authority "at a distance." He must work on princes through their peoples; he does not confront them as the prince of his own people. As vicar, he cannot govern directly. In the matter of Thomas à Becket, he imposed a judgment on King Henry II "that a private man would be ashamed to submit to,"[45] but he could not make himself obeyed at home in Rome and often had to live elsewhere. As he himself was unmanageable, so for the same reason, lacking his own arms, he could not manage his own people.[46] Therefore his arms had to be foreign.[47] Urban II, hated by his own people and doubting his security amid the divisions of Italy, "turned to a generous enterprise" against the Saracens, "with all other similar enterprises later called the Crusades" (FH I 17; cf. VI 33; VII 9).

These were the reason (to distract popular discontent) and the occasion (a foreign expedition) that together built the Roman empire; but they did not build a modern Roman empire. By the virtue of Saladin and the discords of the Christians, all the early gains were lost. Moreover, the Crusades were only one episode in the use of foreign arms by the popes. From the beginning it was their policy to summon foreign arms, the descendants of barbarians, into Italy (FH I 13). They governed or managed Italy so weakly, and yet persisted despite their weakness so obstinately, because they had inducements or sanctions sufficient to command foreign arms. Thus their power was based on foreign arms in both Machiavellian senses of "foreign," foreign to one's own country and foreign to this world. Their power could not operate for the common good of Italy or any city of Italy or any city.

The foundation of the common good, according to Machiavelli, is the preference for one's own, as this preference makes it possible for orders naturally disparate to coexist if not to live in union. Nobles and people will coexist when the city can expand to serve their needs and provide both glory and security. The common good, to speak plainly, is a good taken from foreigners that is common to one people and its princes;[48] it can subsist only so long as human beings are divided in political allegiance, and understood to be divided by their sects, into natives and foreigners.[49] The Christian Church does not observe this distinction, but the effectual truth of its internationalism is subservience to foreigners. If the common good is at the expense of foreigners in booty and glory, princes cannot operate for the common good with foreign arms; the foreigners, that is, the mercenaries, will keep the spoils intended for their employers.[50] At the same time, every Christian prince knows that the people of his land are not his own, but in some part at some times are the pope's. The pope has no home and many colonies, especially the colony of Florence.[51] The disaffection of his own people is compensated by the allegiance of other peoples, and his incompetence as a worldly prince does not receive its natural punishment.

## PARTIES IN ITALY

Machiavelli does not believe that the papacy has become corrupt through its temporal possessions. He objects to its *not* being corruptible in the worldly way. His objection, therefore, goes to the otherworldly essence of Christianity, and could not be satisfied by a Protestant or even a Puritan rearrangement of the sacerdotal hierarchy. The pope acquired his temporal possessions out of the necessities of ruling, which are the same for all princes in this world, including the princes of a church. In the absence of a direct providence of God, ruling men in this world is necessarily worldly. That is why the popes stirred up new dissensions in Italy "now through the charity of religion, now through their own ambition."

It is true that Pope Celestine, "being a hermit and full of holiness," renounced the papacy after six months, and on the other hand that popes have increasingly promoted their relatives to the extent that in the future one may expect the popes to try to make the papacy hereditary.[52] The ratio of piety to ambition has diminished through the history of the papacy, and the Church could now be considered corrupt in the Christian sense. In this condition the Church is now also perhaps open to attack as never before. But whatever the current mixture of motives, piety and ambition in the popes tended to the same result of disunion and enfeeblement. Pope Nicholas III was the first to promote his relatives; yet Machiavelli says only that "he was the first of popes who openly revealed his own ambition" (*FH* I 23). Boniface VIII seems to be criticized for "desiring too much to satisfy his appetite" in using the "weapons" of excommunication and of crusade against the Colonna family in Rome; they might have been used "virtuously through the charity of faith" but instead were turned against Christians "for his own ambition" (*FH* I 25). But what other use could he make of his arms? Excommunication is a weapon that cuts Christians only; crusades are directed against foreigners. By confusing the two, Machiavelli seems to indicate that the pope is compelled to treat all men, including the people of Rome, now as brothers, now as enemies. If pious, the popes could not ignore the necessities of ruling in this world; if ambitious, they could not obey them. They have "used badly" both censures and arms because they must (*FH* I 9; cf. I 21, 22).

In the thirty-ninth chapter of the first book of the *Histories,* Machiavelli lists the five principal powers of Italy, all of them "disarmed of their own arms." The pope is in the center of the list, disarmed "because arms are not suitable for him as an ecclesiastic." The other four powers are disarmed for reasons that describe, in Machiavelli's characteristic translation of divine politics into human terms, various features of papal rule. Duke Filippo Visconti of Milan is disarmed; "shut up in his rooms and not letting himself be seen, he directed his wars through commissioners." The Venetians were disarmed because "as they turned to land, they threw aside the arms that had made them glorious on the seas" and like the other Italians managed their armies under someone else's rule. Queen Joanna of Naples and the Florentines were disarmed of necessity, the former because she was a woman, the latter because frequent divisions had destroyed the nobility and left the republic in the hands of "men nurtured in trade." Florence continued in "the orders and fortune of the others" at this time, in 1434.[53]

The system of modern parties is disposed by the influence of the disarmed prince of Christianity and his commissioners. Since modern princes and peoples cannot operate with and against each other for the common good, their parties seek foreign alliances. Whereas the party system of Rome was domestic, based on the common good acquired by common hostility to foreigners, the modern party system is between states or international. It consists essentially of leagues between peoples who favor the pope as opposed to princes who favor the emperor, aided by exiles expelled by their people. Modern states, incapable of allying their own princes and peoples, are captured by one party or the other in league with its counterpart in a foreign state (*FH* V 6). The modern parties seek help from those who are like-minded elsewhere, since they cannot operate successfully with their complements at home.

We might say today that the basis of parties had become ideological rather than territorial, but Machiavelli would say "foreign" rather than "domestic," divine rather than worldly. This world, he thought, is divided into lands by differences so exclusive that they can be overcome only by neglecting the interests of this world.[54] But the interests of this world are split, for men are divided by nature into princes and peoples. Thus if a common good in this world is possible only in a territory, it must consider the interests of both the local princes and the local people. Leagues of the like-minded, ignoring the difference between natives and foreigners, produce partisan victories and never achieve a common good (*FH* VII 21). Such victories often wear the appearance of justice because they right a preceding wrong, but, because they also create a new wrong, they must be repeated in series or else in alternation, to the result of misery in the people and death and exile for the princes. The dead are gone and the miserable are not obvious; so the surest sign of corruption in party politics is the crowd of exiles who have suffered partisan defeat. They find themselves in the hard position of being impotent except to hurt the country they love, for the exile without a fatherland can at best attain the reputation of a mercenary.[55]

The pope, we have seen, needed the kingly power of the emperor to sustain the power of the Church in Italy. He also had to fight the emperor, who could not be expected to serve as a mere subordinate in this design. The dispute between Pope Alexander II and Henry IV, in which the latter suffered "spiritual wounds," was, Machiavelli says, "the seed of the Guelf and Ghibelline humors," the parties of the pope and the emperor. This single dispute is made responsible, like a seed, for continuing domestic party conflict: Why? The mutual hostility of the pope and the emperor was sustained and rendered permanent in the modern party system by the mutual dependence that has been explained. Since each power was, as it were, a factor in the regime of the other, neither could destroy or ignore the other as a foreigner; and yet they could not combine in one regime to support a common good.

As a result of the "Guelf and Ghibelline humors, Italy, when without barbarian invasions, was torn apart by internal wars."[56] Internal wars were the disease left by the barbarian cure, for with its Christian constitution, Italy could never unite against a foreigner. In every Italian city the people had a common otherworldly, that is, ecclesiastical allegiance; and in consequence their opponents had a common need to league with each other and with the emperor or some other counterweight to the pope (*FH* I 21, 22, 26, 27, 28). If a single prince had succeeded in uniting Italy in one kingdom, he would still have encountered the power of the Church in the extraterritorial allegiance of the people to the ecclesiastical hierarchy within his territory; he would have substituted for Guelf and Ghibelline party conflict the episcopal disputes of the Christian kings outside Italy. But a single prince could not succeed in uniting Italy because of the temporal possessions of the pope; in Italy, the pope had a territory, not merely an office, to defend. He therefore brought in foreigners to Italy more readily than he could send one Christian king to enforce his will against another. It was easier to pay the doctors' fees by allowing them to feed on the patient than to get them to collect from each other.

Affairs in Italy were complicated by the number of participants, for there were many powers and both princes and popes had short lives (*FH* I 23). The alignment of Guelf and Ghibelline powers was surely not perfect, unaffected by circumstances. At one point the pope, to keep the emperor out of Italy, deserted the Guelfs and welcomed the entry of John, king of Bohemia, who had been summoned by the Ghibellines. This overturn of established allegiances did not change the system, however; the pope gained nothing from his faithlessness and the king of Bohemia nothing from his faith (*FH* I 28).

Thus the dispute between pope and emperor was the prototype, as well as the origin, of the modern parties. In all the events, what remains constant as the essence of the system is the inability to achieve a domestic regime. Foreigners were not merely the material of the regime, the booty and the victims of a domestic alliance between princes and people of a common land; they were a factor in the regime itself. Modern government is confused between "things outside" and "things inside," [57] and the cause is a deeper confusion of allegiance between the other world and this. "Barbarian invasion" and "intestinal wars" were fundamentally identical; so it was no wonder that they were politically connected. This bad system was against nature, by which Machiavelli means this world. It denies the claims of this world, in particular the claims that princes make because of their ambitious natures. Yet, though unnatural, it continues; the system, as we say today, was in equilibrium, and by the operation of an "extraordinary force."

THE FIRST DIVISION IN FLORENCE

The Florentine parties were modern parties of this description. Machiavelli shows this by separating his account of the origin of the modern parties in Italy, given in Book I, and his account of the origin of the Florentine parties in Book II. By this rather artificial procedure he gives the Florentine parties a chance to begin, as it were, on their own, in conformity to the natural partisanship of men. When the characteristic modern corruption appears, as it does very soon, we know it must be attributed to a general context of corruption rather than to a bad beginning peculiar to Florence. "The later Florence was in joining the sects of Italy, by so much more was it afflicted by them" (*FH* II 2; cf. VI 9).

Machiavelli relates "the cause of the first division" in Florence, even though it is "very well known" from being celebrated by Dante and many other writers. The cause turns out to have been "the chance" that a young knight could be tempted to break his pledge of marriage to one rich and well-born girl for another, equally rich and well-born but more beautiful.[58] This act of infidelity brought revenge from the family of the slighted girl, who killed the knight and with "this homicide" divided the city between partisans of the Buondelmonti, the knight's family, and partisans of the Uberti, relatives of the girl. After relating this incident, Machiavelli in the next chapter begins to speak of the Guelfs and Ghibellines in Florence: "Thus was our city divided, just as Italy had been for a long time, into the Guelfs and the Ghibellines." He does not say how the small incident of imprudence and private revenge was absorbed into the grand dispute between the pope and the emperor. Though he lists the Buondelmonti in the group of families belonging to the Guelf party and the Uberti among the Ghibellines, he does not say why the chance division into partisans of the Buondelmonti and the Uberti became the all-Italian division into Guelfs and Ghibellines, which had its seed in a great confrontation between the pope and the emperor and its necessity in their mutual hostility and dependence. The sequence of chance incident and great division recalls Aristotle's remark that "factions arise not over small things but out of small things, and they are carried on over great things."[59] But what is the precise connection between the small matter and the great?

When the Uberti party was meditating revenge, some of its members feared the evils that might result from their retaliation; but one man, Mosca Lamberti, stilled these doubts, saying that those who think of many things never finish them, and he concluded with the adage: "A thing done is ended" (*Cosa fatta capo ha*). He could not have been more wrong—but why? Why did the sense of injury linger in the form of party rivalries? In Dante's version of the story, this incident is called "the seed of ruin and misery" for Italy, while for Machiavelli, Canossa was the seed of the Italian parties and this incident merely the cause of the first division in Florence. Dante quotes the adage in the mouth of Mosca, who now knows he forgot about divine retribution.[60] Machiavelli carefully says nothing of divine retribution, and we note only that Florence had no institution for public retribution to replace private revenge. As in the case of accusation and calumny,[61] it lacks the practice of management, which could focus punishment on the faithless young knight, his bride's mother, who tempted him, or Mosca Lamberti, who loosed the revenge. Christianity is responsible for this lack both because it weakens public authority and because it excites and sustains private revenge. The sin for which Mosca suffers in Dante's *Inferno* is not injustice but too much justice and not enough prudence. Machiavelli seems to agree, and in regard to a later division of parties he implies that the blame for this sin is on Christianity itself.

The Albizzi and the Ricci families had long hated each other when in 1353 they nearly clashed as the result of a false rumor to each that one was using the opportunity of a general call to arms to attack the other. Uguccione de' Ricci, head of his family, then decided to gain superiority "through the ordinary way" by the renewal of an old law. Established after the victory of the Emperor Charles I in 1267, the law reserved authority to the Guelfs over the Ghibellines (*FH* II 10). In time, Machiavelli says, through various accidents and new divisions, this authority has so nearly fallen into oblivion that many descendants of the old Ghilbellines held the chief magistracies.[62] Uguccione proposed to renew this law against the Ghilbellines, since it would exclude the Albizzi, who "many thought" were descended from Ghibellines. Piero degli Albizzi discovered this intention and decided to favor it, thinking that if he opposed it, he might be declared a Ghibelline. Those who were declared Ghibelline and excluded from office were called "the admonished." "Admonishing" then became a regular institution in Florence of purging through calumny; so the renewal of this law was "the beginning of many evils."

"Nor can a law be made more damaging to a republic than one

that looks back a long time," Machiavelli says without elaboration.[63] Since he rarely commits himself without possibility of escape,
it will be worthwhile to see what he is saying; and to do this, it is
necessary to translate in the usual way from human politics to divine
or divine-human politics. The most damaging law might be the one
that looks back the longest time; and that would be the law of
obedience to God, by which all men are sinners because they are
involved in the original sin.

Original sin is *the* cause of divine retribution; it is *the* reason
why, in the Christian doctrine, what is done by men is not ended
for God, and consequently not for men. Since original sin makes all
men sinners, it justifies an absolute revenge or retribution appearing
in the minds of the godly or of those who have persuaded themselves
they have been forgiven their sins. Belief in divine retribution, since
it confers grace on the godly, gives a sterner cogency to human
retribution, instead of the patience with human weakness one might
otherwise expect.[64] If every injury must be paid for, men are more
rather than less eager to exact the payment.

When this belief in divine retribution reaches back to the sin of
the first men, and so includes the present rulers no less than the
meanest subject or strangest foreigner, it becomes politically unmanageable.[65] Only the transpolitical priests who bear no arms can absolve, and their interest is not that of the princes nor of the republic.
Indeed, they can defend their worldly status only by dividing their
enemies, and for this purpose they can never allow old wrongs to
lose their stink. The freedom of priests and the fervor of the godly
set the ends and means of politics among politicians who were in
neither category but had to accept the condition of unmanageable
partisanship. As these were the great majority of rulers, and as they
were condemned and opposed not only by Machiavelli but also by
reforming priests like Savonarola, it took a sharp eye to discern
overmuch religion as the cause of the many evils of Italian politics.
Machiavelli had a sharp eye.

Florentine partisanship feeds on the Christian spirit, as Machiavelli sees it, of absolute revenge. This revenge may not have been
intended by the religion that endorses the statement "judge not that
ye be not judged," but the natural desire for revenge in men is too
powerful. If that desire is condemned and denied, it will expand and
find expression in the belief that God has judged in favor of oneself

or one's party.[66] It is much safer and more humane to control the
desire than to deny it, for men will feel it themselves and must incur
it in others. Human necessity operates through the movement of
human things as new dangers and new attractions come to view.
When men see these things, for instance a more beautiful girl, men
separate themselves from their old loves and hates; they are faithless.[67] They incur the revenge of their old loves or of their fathers.
Since one's faith is to one's own as formerly understood, or to one's
*old* own, the fundamental distinction in Machiavelli's thought is not
between one's own as the customary and the good (as for the classical political philosophers) but between one's own as the customary
and one's own simply.[68] "One's own simply" is expressed in Machiavelli's phrase "one's own arms." Necessity rightly understood and
properly accepted forces men to place faith in their own arms rather
than "with mercenary and faithless arms" (*FH* VI 20). This principle
limits the desire for revenge because it teaches men to avoid the
revenge that promises the consequence of "many evils." Indeed, it
could be stated in the adage "a thing done is ended," because properly applied by Mosca Lamberti that adage would have precluded
revenge against a youth who broke his faith by falling in love with
a more beautiful girl. But the principle also justifies revenge to the
limit of prudence, for men cannot afford the humility of placing
their lives in the hands of foreigners (*FH* VI 12).

Parties in Florence had evil effects because they were used, under
the influence of the Christian religion, as instruments of private revenge. This transpolitical religion does not distinguish between domestic and foreign affairs; it keeps modern princes from seeing the
distinction clearly, and its priests, so far as they can, prevent princes
from acting on the basis of the distinction. But the distinction between domestic and foreign affairs, as we have seen, is necessary to
the distinction between public and private affairs, for the public is
based on the common good of two disparate orders of men who
happen to inhabit a locality together. They will ally if they have
enemies to oppose; and if they ally, they will sustain the public good
against private interests within. There will be no natives if there are
no foreigners, and no public good if there are no natives. The very
universality of Christianity causes it to support private attachment
to one's own against public control. When that universality is ap-

plied to the belief in absolute revenge, the result is violent excitement of a private passion.

Machiavelli shows the necessary condition for the primacy of the public good in his discussion of the two conspiracies in Books VII and VIII. Both took place in churches, and with encouragement from Christian offices that Machiavelli relates in detail; and both were directed for private revenge against allies of the moment and enemies of the Pope, Duke Galeazzo Sforza and the Medici brothers. Both were moved by men of frustrated ambition, the first by ardent youths and the second by a family of high position that could not bear continued injuries from the Medici. Christianity, Machiavelli seems to say, lets revenge loose but holds down ambition. It imposes on the human spirit (*animo*), and especially on the princes whose character is spiritedness, a goal of vengeance that can be traced ultimately to divine vengeance for the original sin; at the same time it denies the value of the worldly honors and rewards by whose attraction human spiritedness can be made to serve the needs of mankind. "So much did our Italian princes fear in others the virtue that was not in themselves, and they eliminated it" (*FH* VII 8; cf. VI 4, 7, 21). Machiavelli does not take a high view of the public good; he does not suppose it to be nobler than private goods. He frowns on revenge, but not on ambition; and in this, as in many other ways, he argues the reverse of Christianity.

## FLORENTINE AND ITALIAN PARTIES

Machiavelli mentions three separate divisions that produced parties in Florence. The first was the dispute between the Buondelmonti and the Uberti, which began with a broken pledge of marriage and became accidentally involved with the Guelfs and Ghibellines when Emperor Frederick II used the Uberti to strengthen his power in Tuscany against the Church. In time the Uberti were defeated, and by 1298, though some anger and suspicion remained between the nobles and the people, "everyone lived united and in peace" (*FH* II 15). Then arose the division between the Cerchi and the Donati families, or the Whites and the Blacks, as they called themselves. This division was imported from Pistoia where a card game between members of two families had led to quarrel, injury, and harsh revenge. One of these families was related to the Donati in Florence, whose head was Messer Corso Donati, at that time one of the chief men in the city; and in exhaustion and despair, this family came to Messer Corso for support, while the other came to Messer Corso's rival in Florence, Messer Veri de' Cerchi. By these interventions the ancient hatred between the Cerchi and the Donati was so aroused that the pope sent for Messer Veri and ordered him to make peace.

The result of the pope's interference was, as always in Machiavelli's account, unfortunate. Messer Veri pretended not to be at war, so that he did not need to make peace, and when he returned from Rome without any settlement, "humors" grew so hot that "every little accident could make them spill over, as indeed did happen" (*FH* II 17). It came at a funeral, when both parties came to blows; after this the *signori,* acting with "the advice and prudence" of Dante, called the people to arms and expelled many of the Blacks and some of the Whites. Messer Corso went to the pope, and the pope sent Charles of Valois, brother of the king of France, to Florence to secure the return of Messer Corso and the triumph of the Blacks.

In the first division the connection between the sects of Italy and the Florentine parties was accidental; indeed, we had to search for a connection in the influence of Christianity between the unmanaged revenge of the incident in Florence and the dispute between the pope and the emperor. Then in the second division, the domestic incident led to the politics of the Italian sects through the pope's partisan peacemaking. The third division, between the Albizzi and the Ricci, was simply imposed on Florence through the dispute between the pope and the emperor. Those families had taken arms and through a false rumor had nearly used them against each other, because they were defending Florence against the menace of a band of mercenary adventurers left unpaid after a war between the pope and the emperor. Though the old division between Guelfs and Ghibellines had nearly fallen into oblivion, Uguccione de' Ricci revived it with his proposal to "admonish" the Ghibellines.

Machiavelli thus presents three possibilities: generation of parties from within through uncontrollable revenge; imposition from without of the parties of the Christian system; or the central case of both generation and imposition. From within or without, the Florentine parties received their special character from Christianity. Moreover, Machiavelli moves his explanation from parties generated from within, accidentally (it seems) related to the "sects" of Italy, to parties imposed from without by those sects. As the *Florentine Histories* progress, Florence becomes more and more "foreign," barbarian, Roman. The early separation of Rome and Florence in Books I and II prepares and displays the gradual overcoming of that separation in a work dedicated to a Florentine Pope.

### THE DIVISIONS OF MODERN PRINCES

What distinguishes ancient from modern party conflict, in Machiavelli's first statement, is the number of divisions in modern party conflict. He says the Florentine divisions are "very notable" because they were many; Florence was "not content with one." Of these many he specifies three: among the nobles, between the nobles and the people, and "lastly" (*in ultimo*) between the people and the plebs. "It happened many times that the winning party was divided in two" (*FH* pr; cf. II 21). We are left uncertain about the number of kinds of divisions and the number of divisions, as Machiavelli does not make the distinction. Only the third division is of a new kind, and it apparently exhausts the three kinds, which are not "many." The new division presupposes that the people have won over the nobles; and they have won, we have seen, because the nobles were divided into armed and disarmed princes. The difference between ancient and modern party politics is that in modern party politics the people have won.

Accordingly, Machiavelli says that by repeated divisions the Florentines had destroyed the nobility and the republic put in the hands of "men nurtured in trade" (*FH* I 39); and as he describes toward the end of Book II events in the rule of the duke of Athens, in which the nobility of Florence was finally destroyed, he refers to the "middle citizens" (*i mediocri cittadini*). He also lists three kinds of citizens, the great, the people, and the artisans (*grandi, popolani, e artefici*), and in another place speaks of the great, the lesser people (*il popolo minuto* or *la plebe minuta*), and the people (*il popolo*), a middle class of men.[69] In Books II and III, Machiavelli considers the possibility that modern politics is characterized by a party of the middle, but then afterward for some reason he resumes his view of the division of all men in politics into nobles and peoples. He seems to discover a new party division in modern politics arising from the victory of the people and then to lose interest in it. In the very inquiry that divides the material on the middle party (*FH* III 1), Machiavelli speaks merely of "the grave and natural enmities . . . between the men of the people and the nobles," or "between the people and the nobles."

The ambiguity between "men of the people" (*popolari*) and "the people" (*popolo*) can be found in Machiavelli's discussion of Roman parties in the *Discourses on Livy* (*D* I 4-6). "Men of the people" come from the people but are not of the people; they share the natures but not the honors and titles of the nobility. Machiavelli uses this ambiguity in the *Florentine Histories* to show how "the grave and natural enmities" operate unmanageably in the modern setting. He has a leader of the plebs, "one of the most daring and more experienced," speak to the other "men of the plebs," urging them to continue their crimes until they are completed, until "either we shall be left princes of all the city or we shall have so large a part of it that not only will our past errors be pardoned but we shall even have authority enabling us to threaten them with new injuries." Take no account of shame, conscience, or reputation, the speaker advises, for those who conquer are never disgraced because of the way they conquer; and all who conquer do so either by fraud or force. Then he urges further force against the wealthy and the heads of the guilds. "I confess," he says, "that this course is bold and dangerous; but when necessity presses, boldness is judged prudence, and spirited men never take account of the danger in great things, for those enterprises that are begun with danger always finish with reward" (*FH* III 13). But whose reward? The frank immoralism of this unnamed speaker, whom Machiavelli chose to speak in his account of the year 1378, conceals the purpose of the speaker. We see that he asserts all conquest is by force or fraud and does not mention any fraud in his own plan. The fraud is in the difference between his bold nature and the nature of his audience; as he says, the reward comes to the "spirited men" (*uomini animosi*), not to the plebs. When the people conquer, the popular men become nobles.

This speech occurs in Book III, after the people have won their victory over the nobles and then have divided themselves. Indeed, this division took place immediately. The duke of Athens had been brought to Florence by the nobles to frighten and awe the people, much like a Roman dictator. But the Florentine nobles were incapable of managing him to their end. On the contrary, they were exposed and punished as the promoters of his odious tyranny;[70] so they went down after him. Yet after "the great" were conquered, Machiavelli notes that three kinds of people, "powerful, middle, and low" (*potente, mediocre, e basso*), remained to share the government (*FH* II 42). Included among the powerful of the people were the Medici and the Rondinegli, and Machiavelli says of the later division begun by the Ricci and the Albizzi that the Albizzi party, the revived Guelf sect, contained *all* the ancient nobles with the greater part of the most powerful men of the people" (*FH* III 8, 21; cf. II 11).

Thus the new division of modern party politics into people and plebs, which might seem to create a new middle class between the nobles and the plebs of ancient party politics, results merely from the natural differences between princes and people as they appear in the modern setting. The people as opposed to the plebs, or the powerful people as opposed to the low, are merely plebeian princes generated from below, the Tribunes of modern politics, but with the difference that they have defeated the ruling princes, the "ancient nobles." When the "men of the people" win, they displace the "nobles," killing many and exiling more, but under the conditions of modern politics, they can manage new plebeian princes or absorb the ancient nobles who may remain, no better than their predecessors. After 1378, they were divided into princes of the people and of the plebs, and the middle had disappeared (*FH* III 18; IV 2, 27; V 4). This new division is a consequence of the division within the nobility, which permitted "the people" to conquer, and the nobility was divided by the interference of Christianity.

The middle class between nobles and people was really a half-armed or disarmed nobility ignorant of the practices of mastery yet by nature incapable of tolerating subjugation.[71] Their guilds had been endowed with a kind of political power by the Ghibellines, acting in fear of the Guelfs and their champion, Charles of Anjou. When the Ghibellines tried to take back this gift and were defeated and expelled, the guilds thereafter supported the Guelfs. From this time (1266), each guild received a magistrate to administer justice to all under its jurisdiction, and it enjoyed the power of presenting armed men under its banner when called upon (cf. *FH* II 5, 8, 11, 22). In a few years, according to Machiavelli, the guilds took over all government in the city. Indeed, it was they who established the magistracy of the *signori* from which nobles were excluded. They were themselves divided into more and less honored guilds, called "greater" and "lesser," which sustained the difference between the people and the plebs. The greater guilds were favored by the captains of the Guelf party, who had acquired rights to certain magistracies at the time of the expulsion of the Ghibellines and constituted a separate power within the city, somewhat like the Church itself, with a palace of their own (*FH* II 11, 12, 13; III 10 12).

Thus the guilds did not head a middle class by whose commercial vigor and skill the ancient nobility was displaced and debased; they were, rather the undeserving beneficiaries of ecclesiastical interference in politics. They replaced the nobility because the nobility had been sapped by the Christian disdain for honors of this world and then had been directly attacked by the pope, the Church, the Guelfs, and their foreign allies. In replacing the nobility they complicated the nomenclature of Florentine party politics to the point that it became necessary for Machiavelli to refer to "a very noble popular family,"[72] yet it was not they fundamentally, but the Church, that ruled the city. When politics is divided into sacred and secular as defined by the sacred, secular politics can fall into the hands of merchants, "men nurtured in trade." Such men are the remnant of a spirited nobility, not the leaders of a rising class.

In ancient party politics, the plebeian princes, intermediaries between the two natural parties of men, are managed and absorbed by the princely party. But in the modern system, leagues of partisans are managed by the intermediaries, both sacred and secular, who scurry through many complexities and confusions to the business of cunning and bungle. The difficulty is that the modern system puts too great a burden on the princes: they have not only to seek the honors of this world against other princes, but also to maintain the interest of the world itself against those who place the supreme honors in the afterlife. Under Christian politics, one of the two natural parties, the popular as embodied in the Church, advances the argument for the supernatural; the other natural party is left to defend the notion of natural partisanship, which is to say the desirability of this world's honors.[73] No man can reach for honors while he is considering or defending the very status of honor; nor can he defend honor in general while his own honor is at stake.[74]

The princely party is in the position of a party having to defend partisanship and the party system, for in modern politics the status of honor cannot be taken for granted. Lacking ambition, the people never understand it or appreciate the necessity for it; and when they are fortified in the fortresses of Christianity, they can succeed in defeating the natural party of the ambitious. This party, because of the nature of ambition, is always potentially at odds with itself; it can achieve unity by extending the ambitions of individuals to the highest political glory that exacts attention to the common good, the glory of founding new orders. In the widest sense, these new orders must be understood as "sects," for politics, culture, and religion are connected, and the glorious prince makes everything anew. The "new orders" of *The Prince* and the *Discourses* appear in the *Florentine Histories* as "sects." The disease of modern politics, then, can be summarized as the inability of the princely party to control the making of sects. Sects cannot be made or maintained by being remade because the Christian sect controls the popular party. The remaining natural party, since it cannot make the conventional, must confront the supernatural. In this conspiratorial work Machiavelli tries to show Italian princes how to regain control of the supernatural.

# AN INTRODUCTION
# TO *THE PRINCE*

Anyone who picks up Machiavelli's *The Prince* holds in his hands the most famous book on politics ever written. Its closest rival might be Plato's *Republic,* but that book discusses politics in the context of things above politics, and politics turns out to have a limited and subordinate place. In *The Prince* Machiavelli also discusses politics in relation to things outside politics, as we shall see, but his conclusion is very different. Politics according to him is not limited by things above it, and things normally taken to be outside politics—the "givens" in any political situation—turn out to be much more under the control of politics than politicians, peoples, and philosophers have hitherto assumed. Machiavelli's *The Prince* then, is the most famous book on politics when politics is thought to be carried on for its own sake, unlimited by anything above it. The renown of *The Prince* is precisely to have been the first and the best book to argue that politics has and should have its own rules and should not accept rules of any kind or from any source where the object is not to win or prevail over others. *The Prince* is briefer and pithier than Machiavelli's other major work, *Discourses on Livy,* for *The Prince* is addressed to Lorenzo de' Medici, a prince like the busy executive of our day who has little time for reading. So *The Prince,* with its political advice to an active politician that politics should not be limited by anything not political, is by far more famous than the *Discourses on Livy.*

We cannot, however, agree that *The Prince* is the most famous book on politics without immediately correcting this to say that it

This chapter was originally published as "An Introduction to *The Prince*," in *The Prince,* trans. Harvey C. Mansfield (Chicago: University of Chicago Press, 1985). Copyright © 1985 by the University of Chicago. All rights reserved.

is the most infamous. It is famous for its infamy, for recommending the kind of politics that ever since has been called Machiavellian. The essence of this politics is that "you can get away with murder": that no divine sanction or degradation of soul or twinge of conscience will come to punish you. If you succeed, you will not even have to face the infamy of murder, because when "men acquire who can acquire, they will be praised or not blamed" (*P* 3). Those criminals who are infamous have merely been on the losing side. Machiavelli and Machiavellian politics are famous or infamous for their willingness to brave infamy.

Yet it must be reported that the prevailing view among scholars of Machiavelli is that he was not an evil man who taught evil doctrines, and that he does not deserve his infamy. With a view to his preference for republics over principalities (more evident in the *Discourses on Livy* than in *The Prince,* but not absent from the latter), they cannot believe he was an apologist for tyranny; or, impressed by the sudden burst of Italian patriotism in the last chapter of *The Prince,* they forgive him for the sardonic observations that are not fully consistent with this generous feeling but are thought to give it a certain piquancy (this is the opinion an earlier generation of scholars); or, on the basis of Machiavelli's saying in Chapter 15 that we should take our bearings from "what is done" rather than from "what should be done," they conclude that he was a forerunner of modern political science, which is not an evil thing because it merely tells us what happens without passing judgment. In sum, the prevailing view of the scholars offers excuses for Machiavelli: he was a republican, a patriot, or a scientist, and therefore, in explicit contradiction to the reaction of most people to Machiavelli as soon as they hear of his doctrines, Machiavelli was not "Machiavellian."

The reader can form his own judgment of these excuses for Machiavelli. I do not recommend them, chiefly because they make Machiavelli less interesting. They transform him into a herald of the future who had the luck to sound the tunes we hear so often today—democracy, nationalism or self-determination, and science. Instead of challenging our favorite beliefs and forcing us to think, Machiavelli is enlisted into a chorus of self-congratulation. There is, of course, evidence for the excuses supplied on behalf of Machiavelli, and that evidence consists of the excuses offered by Machiavelli himself. If someone were to accuse him of being an apologist for tyranny, he can indeed point to a passage in the *Discourses on Livy* (II 2) where he says (rather carefully) that the common good is not observed unless in republics; but if someone else were to accuse him of supporting republicanism, he could point to the same chapter, where he says that the hardest slavery of all is to be conquered by a republic. And, while he shows his Italian patriotism in Chapter 26 of *The Prince* by exhorting someone to seize Italy in order to free it from the barbarians, he also shows his fair-mindedness by advising a French king in Chapter 3 how he might better invade Italy the next time. Lastly, it is true that he sometimes merely reports the evil that he sees, while (unnecessarily) deploring it; but at other times he urges us to share in that evil and he virtuously condemns half-hearted immoralists. Although he was an exceedingly bold writer who seems to have deliberately courted an evil reputation, he was nonetheless not so bold as to fail to provide excuses, or prudent reservations, for his boldest statements. Since I have spoken at length on this point in another place, and will not hesitate to mention the work of Leo Strauss, who first made the point, it is not necessary to explain it further here.[1]

What is at issue in the question of whether Machiavelli was "Machiavellian"? To see that a matter of the highest importance is involved, we must not rest satisfied with either scholarly excuses or moral frowns. For the matter at issue is the character of the rules by which we reward human beings with fame or condemn them with infamy, the very status of morality. Machiavelli does not make it clear at first that this grave question is his subject. In the dedicatory letter he approaches Lorenzo de' Medici with hat in one hand and *The Prince* in the other. Since, he says, one must be a prince to know the nature of peoples and a man of the people to know the nature of princes, he seems to offer Lorenzo the knowledge of princes he does not have but needs. In accordance with this half-serious promise, Machiavelli speaks about the kinds of principalities in the first part of *The Prince* (P 1–11) and, as we learn of the necessity of conquest, about the kinds of armies in the second part (P 12–14). But at the same time (to make a long story short), we learn that the prince must or may lay his foundations on the people (P 9) and that while his only object should be the art of war, he must in time of peace pay attention to moral qualities in such manner as to be able to use them in time of war (P 14, end).

Thus are we prepared for Machiavelli's clarion call in Chapter
15, where he proclaims that he "departs from the orders of others"
and says why. For moral qualities are qualities "held good" by the
people; so, if the prince must conquer, and wants, like the Medici,
to lay his foundation on the people, who are the keepers of morality,
then a new morality consistent with the necessity of conquest must
be found, and the prince has to be taught anew about the nature of
peoples by Machiavelli. In departing from the orders of others, it
appears more fitting to Machiavelli "to go directly to the effectual
truth of the thing than to the imagination of it." Many have imagined republics and principalities, but one cannot "let go of what is
done for what should be done," because a man who "makes a profession of good in all regards" comes to ruin among so many who
are not good. The prince must learn to be able not to be good, and
use this ability or not according to necessity.

This concise statement is most efficacious. It contains a fundamental assault on all morality and political science, both Christian
and classical, as understood in Machiavelli's time. Morality had
meant not only doing the right action, but also doing it for the right
reason or for the love of God. Thus, to be good was thought to
require "a profession of good" in which the motive for doing good
was explained; otherwise, morality would go no deeper than outward conformity to law, or even to superior force, and could not be
distinguished from it. But professions of good could not accompany
moral actions in isolation from each other; they would have to be
elaborated so that moral actions would be consistent with each other
and the life of a moral person would form a whole. Such elaboration
requires an effort of imagination, since the consistency we see tells
us only of the presence of outward conformity, and the elaboration
extends over a society, because it is difficult to live a moral life by
oneself; hence morality requires the construction of an imagined
republic or principality, such as Plato's *Republic* or Saint Augustine's
*City of God.*

When Machiavelli denies that imagined republics and principalities "exist in truth" and declares that the truth in these or all matters
is the effectual truth, he says that no moral rules exist, not made by
men, which men must abide by. The rules or laws that exist are
those made by governments or other powers acting under necessity,
and they must be obeyed out of the same necessity. Whatever is

necessary may be called just and reasonable, but justice is no more reasonable than what a person's prudence tells him he must acquire for himself, or must submit to, because men cannot afford justice in any sense that transcends their own preservation. Machiavelli did not attempt (as did Hobbes) to formulate a new definition of justice based on self-preservation. Instead, he showed what he meant by not including justice among the eleven pairs of moral qualities that he lists in Chapter 15. He does mention justice in Chapter 21 as a calculation of what a weaker party might expect from a prince whom it has supported in war, but even this little is contradicted by what Machiavelli says about keeping faith in Chapter 18 and about betraying one's old supporters in Chapter 20. He also brings up justice as something identical with necessity in Chapter 26. But, what is most striking, he never mentions—not in *The Prince* or in any of his works—natural justice or natural law, the two conceptions of justice in the classical and medieval tradition that had been handed down to his time and that could be found in the writings on this subject of all his contemporaries. The grave issue raised by the dispute as to whether Machiavelli was truly "Machiavellian" is this: does justice exist by nature or by God, or is it the convenience of the prince (government)? "So let a prince win and maintain a state: the means will always be judged honorable, and will be praised by everyone" (*P* 18). Reputation, then, is outward conformity to successful human force and has no reference to moral rules that the government might find inconvenient.

If there is no natural justice, perhaps Machiavelli can teach the prince how to rule in its absence—but with a view to the fact that men "profess" it. It does not follow of necessity that because no natural justice exists, princes can rule successfully without it. Governments might be as unsuccessful in making and keeping conquests as in living up to natural justice; indeed, the traditional proponents of natural justice, when less confident of their own cause, had pointed to the uncertainty of gain, to the happy inconstancy of fortune, as an argument against determined wickedness. But Machiavelli thinks it possible to "learn" to be able not to be good. For each of the difficulties of gaining and keeping, even and especially for the fickleness of fortune, he has a "remedy," to use his frequent expression. Since nature or God does not support human justice, men are in need of a remedy; and the remedy is the prince, especially the new prince. Why must the new prince be preferred?

In the heading to the first chapter of *The Prince,* we see that the kinds of principalities are to be discussed together with the ways in which they are acquired, and then in the chapter itself we find more than this, that principalities are classified into kinds by the ways in which they are acquired. *Acquisition,* an economic term, is Machiavelli's word for *conquest;* and acquisition determines the classifications of governments, not their ends or structures, as Plato and Aristotle had thought. How is acquisition related to the problem of justice?

Justice requires a modest complement of external goods, the equipment of virtue in Aristotle's phrase, to keep the wolf from the door and to provide for moral persons a certain decent distance from necessities in the face of which morality might falter or even fail. For how can one distribute justly without something to distribute? But, then, where is one to get this modest complement? The easy way is by inheritance. In Chapter 2, Machiavelli considers hereditary principalities, in which a person falls heir to everything he needs, especially the political power to protect what he has. The hereditary prince, the man who has everything, is called the "natural prince," as if to suggest that our grandest and most comprehensive inheritance is what we get from nature. But when the hereditary prince looks upon his inheritance—and when we, generalizing from his case, add up everything we inherit—is it adequate?

The difficulty with hereditary principalities is indicated at the end of Chapter 2, where Machiavelli admits that hereditary princes will have to change but claims that change will not be disruptive because it can be gradual and continuous. He compares each prince's own construction to building a house that is added on to a row of houses: you may not inherit all you need, but you inherit a firm support and an easy start in what you must acquire. But clearly a row of houses so built over generations presupposes that the first house was built without existing support and without an easy start. Inheritance presupposes an original acquisition made without a previous inheritance. And in the original acquisition, full attention to the niceties of justice may unfortunately not be possible. One may congratulate an American citizen for all the advantages to which he is born; but what of the nasty necessities that prepared this inheritance—the British expelled, Indians defrauded, blacks enslaved?

Machiavelli informs us in the third chapter, accordingly, that "truly it is a very natural and ordinary thing to desire to acquire." In the space of a few pages, "natural" has shifted in meaning from hereditary to acquisitive. Or can we be consoled by reference to Machiavelli's republicanism, not so prominent in *The Prince*, with the thought that acquisitiveness may be natural to princes but is not natural to republics? But in Chapter 3 Machiavelli praises the successful acquisitiveness of the "Romans," that is, the Roman republic, by comparison to the imprudence of the king of France. At the time to which Machiavelli is referring, the Romans were not weak and vulnerable as they were at their inception; they had grown powerful and were still expanding. Even when they had enough empire to provide an inheritance for their citizens, they went on acquiring. Was this reasonable? It was, because the haves of this world cannot quietly inherit what is coming to them; lest they be treated now as they once treated others, they must keep an eye on the have-nots. To keep a step ahead of the have-nots, the haves must think and behave like have-nots. They certainly cannot afford justice to the have-nots, nor can they waste time or money on sympathy.

In the dedicatory letter Machiavelli presents himself to Lorenzo as a have-not, "from a low and mean state"; and one thing he lacks besides honorable employment, we learn, is a unified fatherland. Italy is weak and divided. Then should we say that acquisitiveness is justified for Italians of Machiavelli's time, including him? As we have noted, Machiavelli does not seem to accept this justification because, still in Chapter 3, he advises a French king how to correct the errors he had made in his invasion of Italy. Besides, was Machiavelli's fatherland Italy or was it Florence? In Chapter 15 he refers to "our language," meaning Tuscan, and in Chapter 20 to "our ancients," meaning Florentines. But does it matter whether Machiavelli was essentially an Italian or a Florentine patriot? Anyone's fatherland is defined by an original acquisition, a conquest, and hence is always subject to redefinition of the same kind. To be devoted to one's native country at the expense of foreigners is no more justified than to be devoted to one's city at the expense of fellow countrymen, or to one's family at the expense of fellow city-dwellers, or, to adapt a Machiavellian remark in Chapter 17, to one's patrimony at the expense of one's father. So to "unify" one's fatherland means to treat it as a conquered territory—conquered by a king or republic from within; and Machiavelli's advice to the French king on how to hold his conquests in Italy was also advice to Lorenzo on how to unify Italy. It appears that, in acquiring, the new prince acquires for himself.

What are the qualities of the new prince? What must he do? First, as we have seen, he should rise from private or unprivileged status; he should not have an inheritance, or if he has, he should not rely on it. He should owe nothing to anyone or anything, for having debts of gratitude would make him dependent on others, in the widest sense dependent on fortune. It might seem that the new prince depends at least on the character of the country he conquers, and Machiavelli says at the end of Chapter 4 that Alexander had no trouble in holding Asia because it had been accustomed to the government of one lord. But then in Chapter 5 he shows how this limitation can be overcome. A prince who conquers a city used to living in freedom need not respect its inherited liberties; he can and should destroy such cities or else rule them personally. Fortune supplies the prince with nothing more than opportunity, as when Moses found the people of Israel enslaved by the Egyptians, Romulus found himself exposed at birth, Cyrus found the Persians discontented with the empire of the Medes, and Theseus found the Athenians dispersed (*P* 6). These famous founders had the virtue to recognize the opportunity that fortune offered to them—opportunity for them, harsh necessity to their peoples. Instead of dispersing the inhabitants of a free city (*P* 5), the prince is lucky enough to find them dispersed (*P* 6). This suggests that the prince could go so far as to make his own opportunity by creating a situation of necessity in which no one's inherited goods remain to him and everything is owed to you, the new prince. When a new prince comes to power, should he be grateful to those who helped him get power and rely on them? Indeed not. A new prince has "lukewarm defenders" in his friends and allies, because they expect benefits from him; as we have seen, it is much better to conciliate his former enemies who feared losing everything (compare Chapters 6 and 20).

Thus, the new prince has virtue that enables him to overcome his dependence on inheritance in the widest sense, including custom, nature, and fortune, and that shows him how to arrange it that others depend on him and his virtue (Chapters 9, 24). But if virtue is to do all this, it must have a new meaning. Instead of cooperating with nature or God, as in the various classical and Christian conceptions, virtue must be taught to be acquisitive on its own. Machiavelli teaches the new meaning of virtue by showing us both the new and the old meanings. In a famous passage on the successful criminal Agathocles in Chapter 8, he says "one cannot call it virtue to kill one's fellow citizens, betray one's friends, to be without faith, without mercy, without religion." Yet in the very next sentence Machiavelli proceeds to speak of "the virtue of Agathocles."

The prince, we have seen in Chapter 15, must "learn to be able not to be good, and to use this and not use it according to necessity." Machiavelli supplies this knowledge in Chapters 16 to 18. First, with superb calm, he delivers home-truths concerning the moral virtue of liberality. It is no use being liberal (or generous) unless it is noticed, so that you are "held liberal" or get a name for liberality. But a prince cannot be held liberal by being liberal, because he would have to be liberal to a few by burdening the many with taxes; the many would be offended, the prince would have to retrench, and he would soon get a name for stinginess. The right way to get a reputation for liberality is to begin by not caring about having a reputation for stinginess. When the people see that the prince gets the job done without burdening them, they will in time consider him liberal to them and stingy only to the few to whom he gives nothing. In the event, "liberality" comes to mean taking little rather than giving much.

As regards cruelty and mercy, in Chapter 8 Machiavelli made a distinction between cruelties well used and badly used; well-used cruelties are done once, for self-defense, and not continued but turned to the benefit of one's subjects, and badly used ones continue and increase. In Chapter 17, however, he does not mention this distinction but rather speaks only of using mercy badly. Mercy is badly used when, like the Florentine people in a certain instance, one seeks to avoid a reputation for cruelty and thus allows disorders to continue that might be stopped with a very few examples of cruelty. Disorders harm everybody; executions harm only the few or the one who is executed. As the prince may gain a name for liberality by taking little, so he may be held merciful by not being cruel too often.

Machiavelli's new prince arranges the obligation of his subjects to himself in a manner rather like that of the Christian God, in the eye of whom all are guilty by original sin; hence God's mercy appears less as the granting of benefits than as the remission of punishment. With this thought in mind, the reader will not be surprised that Machiavelli goes on to discuss whether it is better for the prince to be loved or feared. It would be best to be both loved and feared, but, when necessity forces a choice, it is better to be feared, because men love at their convenience but they fear at the convenience of the prince. Friends may fail you, but the dread of punishment will never forsake you. If the prince avoids making himself hated, which he can do by abstaining from the property of others, "because men forget the death of a father more quickly than the loss of a patrimony," he will again have subjects obligated to him for what he does not do to them rather than for benefits he provides.

It is laudable for a prince to keep faith, Machiavelli says in Chapter 18, but princes who have done great things have done them by deceit and betrayal. The prince must learn how to use the beast in man, or rather the beasts; for man is an animal who can be many animals, and he must know how to be a fox as well as a lion. Men will not keep faith with you; how can you keep it with them? Politics, Machiavelli seems to say, as much as consists in breaking promises, for circumstances change and new necessities arise that make it impossible to hold to one's word. The only question is, can one get away with breaking one's promises? Machiavelli's answer is a confident yes. He broadens the discussion, speaking of five moral qualities, especially religion; he says that men judge by appearances and that when one judges by appearances, "one looks to the end." The end is the outcome or the effect, and if a prince wins and maintains a state, the means will always be judged honorable. Since Machiavelli has just emphasized the prince's need to appear religious, we may compare the people's attitude toward a successful prince with their belief in divine providence. As people assume that the outcome of events in the world is determined by God's providence, so they conclude that the means chosen by God cannot have been unworthy. Machiavelli's thought here is both a subtle attack on the notion of divine providence and a subtle appreciation of it, insofar as the prince can appropriate it to his own use.

It is not easy to state exactly what virtue is, according to Machiavelli. Clearly he does not leave virtue as it was in the classical or Christian tradition, nor does he imitate any other writer of his time. Virtue in his new meaning seems to be a prudent or well-taught combination of vice and virtue in the old meaning. Virtue for him is not a mean between two extremes of vice, as is moral virtue for Aristotle. As we have seen, in Chapter 15 eleven virtues (the same number as Aristotle's, though not all of them the same virtues) are paired with eleven vices. From this we might conclude that virtue does not shine of itself, as when it is done for its own sake. Rather, virtue is as it takes effect, its truth is its effectual truth; and it is effectual only when it is seen in contrast to its opposite. Liberality, mercy, and love are impressive only when one expects stinginess (or rapacity), cruelty, and fear. This contrast makes virtue apparent and enables the prince to gain a reputation for virtue. If this is so, then the new meaning Machiavelli gives to virtue, a meaning that makes use of vice, must not entirely replace but somehow continue to co-exist with the old meaning, according to which virtue is shocked by vice.

A third quality of the new prince is that he must make his own foundations. Although to be acquisitive means to be acquisitive for oneself, the prince cannot do everything with his own hands: he needs help from others. But in seeking help he must take account of the "two diverse humors" to be found in every city—the people, who desire not to be commanded or oppressed by the great, and the great, who desire to command and oppress the people (*P* 9). Of these two humors, the prince should choose the people. The people are easier to satisfy, too inert to move against him, and too numerous to kill, whereas the great regard themselves as his equals, are ready and able to conspire against him, and are replaceable.

The prince, then, should ally with the people against the aristocracy; but how should he get their support? Machiavelli gives an example in the conduct of Cesare Borgia, whom he praises for the foundations he laid (*P* 7). When Cesare had conquered the province of Romagna, he installed "Remirro de Orco" (actually a Spaniard, Don Remiro de Lorqua) to carry out a purge of the unruly lords there. Then, because Cesare thought Remirro's authority might be excessive, and his exercise of it might become hateful—in short, because Remirro had served his purpose—he purged the purger and one day had Remirro displayed in the piazza at Cesena in two pieces.

This spectacle left the people "at the same time satisfied and stupefied"; and Cesare set up a more constitutional government in Romagna. The lesson: constitutional government is possible but only
after an unconstitutional beginning.

In Chapter 9 Machiavelli discusses the "civil principality,"
which is gained through the favor of the people, and gives as example Nabis, "prince" of the Spartans, whom he calls a tyrant in the
*Discourses on Livy* because of the crimes Nabis committed against
his rivals. In Chapter 8 Machiavelli considers the principality that
is attained through crimes, and cites Agathocles and Oliverotto, both
of whom were very popular despite their crimes. As one ponders
these two chapters, it becomes more and more difficult to find a
difference between gaining a principality through crimes and
through the favor of the people. Surely Cesare Borgia, Agathocles,
and Nabis seemed to have followed the same policy of pleasing the
people by cutting up the great. Finally, in Chapter 19, Machiavelli
reveals that the prince need not have the support of the people after
all. Even if he is hated by the people (since in fact he cannot fail to
be hated by someone), he can, like the Roman emperor Severus,
make his foundation with his soldiers (see also *P* 20). Severus had
such virtue, Machiavelli says, with an unobtrusive comparison to
Cesare Borgia in Chapter 7, that he "stupefied" the people and "satisfied" the soldiers.

Fourth, the new prince has his own arms, and does not rely on
mercenary or auxiliary armies. Machiavelli omits a discussion of the
laws a prince should establish, in contrast to the tradition of political
science, because, he says, "there cannot be good laws where there
are not good arms, and where there are good arms there must be
good laws" (*P* 12). He speaks of the prince's arms in Chapters 12
to 14, and in Chapter 14 he proclaims that the prince should have
no other object or thought but the art of war. He must be armed,
since it is quite unreasonable for one who is armed to obey one who
is disarmed. With this short remark Machiavelli seems to dismiss
the fundamental principle of classical political science, the rule of
the wise, not to mention the Christian promise that the meek shall
inherit the earth.

Machiavelli does not mean that those with the most bodily force
always win, for he broadens the art of war to include the acquisition
as well as the use of arms. A prince who has no army but has the

art of war will prevail over one with an army but without the art. Thus, to be armed means to know the art of war, to exercise it in time of peace, and to have read histories about great captains of the past. In this regard Machiavelli mentions Xenophon's "Life of Cyrus," as he calls it (actually "The Education of Cyrus"), the first and best work in the literature of "mirrors of princes" to which *The Prince* belongs. But he calls it a history, not a mirror of princes, and says that it inspired the Roman general Scipio, whom he criticizes in Chapter 17 for excessive mercy. Not books of imaginary republics and principalities, or treatises on law, but histories of war, are recommended reading for the prince. Last, the new prince with his own arms is his own master. The deeper meaning of Machiavelli's slogan, "one's own arms," is religious, or rather, antireligious. If man is obligated to God as his creature, then man's own necessities are subordinate or even irrelevant to his most pressing duties. It would not matter if he could not afford justice: God commands it! Thus Machiavelli must look at the new prince who is also a prophet, above all at Moses. Moses was a "mere executor of things that had been ordered by God" (*P* 6); hence he should be admired for the grace that made him worthy of speaking with God. Or should it be said, as Machiavelli says in Chapter 26, that Moses had "virtue," the virtue that makes a prince dependent on no one but himself? In Chapter 13 Machiavelli retells the biblical story of David and Goliath to illustrate the necessity of one's own arms. When Saul offered his arms to David, David refused them, saying, according to Machiavelli, that with them he could not give a good account of himself, and according to the Bible, that the Lord "will deliver me out of the hand of this Philistine." Machiavelli also gives David a knife to go with his sling, the knife which according to the Bible he took from the fallen Goliath and used to cut off his head.

Must the new prince—the truly new prince—then be his own prophet and make a new religion so as to be his own master? The great power of religion can be seen in what Moses and David founded, and in what Savonarola nearly accomplished in Machiavelli's own time and city. The unarmed prince whom he disparages in Chapter 6 actually disposes of formidable weapons necessary to the art of war. The unarmed prophet becomes armed if he uses religion for his own purposes rather than God's; and because the prince cannot acquire glory for himself without bringing order to his principality, using religion for himself is using it to answer human necessities generally.

The last three chapters of *The Prince* take up the question of how far man can make his own world. What are the limits set on Machiavelli's political science (or the "art of war") by fortune? At the end of Chapter 24 he blames "these princes of ours" who accuse fortune for their troubles and not their own indolence. In quiet times they do not take account of the storm to come, but they should— they can. They believe that the people will be disgusted by the arrogance of the foreign conquerors and will call them back. But "one should never fall in the belief you can find someone to pick you up." Whether successful or not, such a defense is base, because it does not depend on you and your virtue.

With this high promise of human capability, Machiavelli introduces his famous Chapter 25 on fortune. He begins it by asking how much of the world is governed by fortune and God, and how much by man. He then supposes that half is governed by fortune (forgetting God) and half by man, and he compares fortune to a violent river that can be contained with dikes and dams. Turning to particular men, he shows that the difficulty in containing fortune lies in the inability of one who is impetuous to succeed in quiet times or of one who is cautious to succeed in stormy times. Men, with their fixed natures and habits, do not vary as the times vary, and so they fall under the control of the times, of fortune. Men's fixed natures are the special problem, Machiavelli indicates; so the problem of overcoming the influence of fortune reduces to the problem of overcoming the fixity of different human natures. Having a fixed nature is what makes one liable to changes of fortune. Pope Julius II succeeded because the times were in accord with his impetuous nature; if he had lived longer, he would have come to grief. Machiavelli blames him for his inflexibility, and so implies that neither he nor the rest of us need respect the natures or natural inclinations we have been given.

What is the new meaning of virtue that Machiavelli has developed if not flexibility according to the times or situation? Yet, though one should learn to be both impetuous and cautious (these stand for all the other contrary qualities), on the whole one should be impetuous. Fortune is a woman who "lets herself be won more by the impetuous than by those who proceed coldly"; hence she is a friend of the young. He makes the politics of the new prince appear in the image of rape; impetuous himself, Machiavelli forces us to see the question he has raised about the status of morality. Whether he says what he appears to say about the status of women may be doubted, however. The young men who master Lady Fortune come with audacity and leave exhausted, but she remains ageless, waiting for the next ones. One might go so far as to wonder who is raping whom, cautiously as it were, and whether Machiavelli, who has personified fortune, can impersonate her in the world of modern politics he attempted to create.

# EIGHT

# AN INTRODUCTION
# TO MACHIAVELLI'S
# *ART OF WAR*

M achiavelli's *Art of War* does not appear to be as Machiavellian as his other major prose works. *The Prince*, the *Discourses on Livy*, and the *Florentine Histories*, all first published in 1531 and 1532, after Machiavelli's death in 1527, are studded with wicked sayings—some of them pungent, some bland, all of them memorable. For examples: "Men forget the death of a father more quickly than the loss of a patrimony" (*P* 17); "When the act accuses, the result excuses" (*D* I 9); "Faithful servants are always servants and good men are always poor" (*FH* III 13). But beauties such as these do not occur in the *Art of War*, published in 1521.

There is, to be sure, a list in Book VI of thirty-three deceits that a captain might find necessary (*AW* VI 482–90), supplemented by a list in Book VII of tricks that those besieged in a town might have to expect from their besiegers (*AW* VII 505–11). But these "Machiavellian" sections of the *Art of War* are relatively mild, exuding none of the venom that Machiavelli can produce when he wants to. Moreover, their wickedness is excused by the context of war, and thus limited. In the circumstances of war good men are of course compelled to commit wrongs they would not conceive of doing when at peace. Machiavelli does not attempt to extend the utility of evil practices from the battlefield into peacetime politics, as he does in his other works. Rather than being proposed as weapons for all those on the make, they seem to remain deplorable necessities for those who must fight.

Most striking, however, is the modest view taken of the art of war in Machiavelli's *Art of War*. In *The Prince* Machiavelli pro-

This chapter was originally published in French in *L'art de la guerre* (Paris: Editions Flammarion, 1991). Page number references are to NM's *Arte della guerra*, ed. S. Bertelli (Milan: Feltrinelli, 1961).

nounces that the art of war is the "only art which is of concern to one who commands":

> A prince should have no other object, nor any other thought, nor take anything else as his art but the art of war and its discipline, for that is the only art which is of concern to one who commands. (*P* 14)

And, he goes on to say, a prince who has the art but no state will often gain a state, while a prince who has a state but not the art will lose his state. Indeed, for a prince to be "armed" means not that he holds a weapon or has an army but that he knows the art of war. Machiavelli cites the case of Francesco Sforza, who, because he was "armed," became duke of Milan from a "private individual." All he needed was to learn to be a military professional, it seems; the knowledge he had of war enabled him to succeed in politics. That knowledge is not only the sovereign but also the comprehensive art; no other knowledge is required, perhaps only good fortune. From this it would seem that war and politics are identical.

Yet if we turn to the *Art of War* for an explanation of this startling remark in *The Prince*, we are disappointed. No definition of the art of war is supplied, and the interlocutors seem to remain comfortably within the conventional distinction between wartime and peacetime, which would deny the imperialist claim for the art of war made in *The Prince*. Only occasionally, as we shall see, does the conversation carry the logic of war far enough to press against the boundary that keeps the art of war within its usual confines.

In the preface to the *Art of War*, Machiavelli announces that he is writing against the opinion powerful in modern times that civil life is dissimilar from military life. But this proves to mean that military life should be brought closer to civil life, that professional mercenaries should be replaced by citizen armies—not that civil life should be brought closer to military life and politicians encouraged to think of their competence as the art of war.[1] Although one interlocutor, Cosimo Rucellai, is praised by Machiavelli for teaching "many useful things" for civil life as well as military (*AW* I 329), the main impression of the work on most readers is that the military should be subordinated to civilian authority. After implying in the preface that military and civilian life are not so dissimilar, Machiavelli likens the military to the roof of a sumptuous palace and assigns it the function of defense. In this picturing of protection, the possibility—rather, the *necessity*—of acquisition, so prominent in *The Prince* and the *Discourses on Livy*, is passed over in silence here and hardly appears elsewhere in the *Art of War*.[2]

Nor does Machiavelli regale us with a lively account of the career of Francisco Sforza, his model of professional success in the art of war in *The Prince*.[3] That account is given in Book V of the *Florentine Histories*. Instead, in the *Art of War* we receive the wisdom of Fabrizio Colonna, the principal interlocutor, a condottiere who has just completed an assignment for Ferdinand of Aragon ("the Catholic King," *AW* I 329). Fabrizio does not appear to share the thought Francisco Sforza must have been entertaining when he was considering how to deceive the Milanese citizens who had hired him and become prince over them (*AW* I 335).

Fabrizio seems to blame that deed; he himself has moral qualms about following the art of war as a profession. Despite that profession, he strongly opposes the use of mercenaries and he constantly recommends the military methods of "my Romans," the Romans of the republic. His name reminds us of Fabricius, a republican Roman general who was noted for his moral uprightness and whose example is cited at the beginning of the *Art of War* (*AW* I 332). Machiavelli also cites that "Fabrizio" in two places in the *Discourses on Livy* for having given a "rare and virtuous example" of himself (*D* II l) when he revealed a threat of poisoning to an enemy general from a familiar of his (*D* III 20). Machiavelli remarks that with this act of "liberality" Fabricius was able to expel Pyrrhus from Italy when Roman arms had proved incapable. But in the *Art of War* a similar incident appears inconspicuously as the thirty-third in the list of deceits mentioned above (*AW* VII 490); Machiavelli does not seize upon it to teach us a lesson about the nature and uses of moral virtue, as he does in the *Discourses on Livy*. There he indicates that moral virtue must be judged for what it can do, from outside itself, not in its own terms as good in itself.[4] No such Machiavellian lesson appears here. In sum, I think it is safe to say that Machiavelli would not have his reputation as the inventor of Machiavellism if all we had to judge were the *Art of War*.

Why the discrepancy between the modesty of this work and the scheming evil set forth in the other works? We do not know exactly when Machiavelli wrote his books, but it appears that in the time from 1513 to 1525 he produced *The Prince* and the *Discourses on*

*Livy* before the *Art of War,* and the *Florentine Histories* afterward. This is not a schedule that would permit us to infer a change of mind, for which there is, in any case, no evidence external to the text. As I said above, the *Art of War* is the only major prose work that Machiavelli published in his lifetime. Obviously, one could assume that Machiavelli had to be more careful about challenging the morals and religion of his native country when he was alive to suffer the consequences of doing so. But he had found a way around that difficulty simply by publishing the other three works after his death. Why did he write the *Art of War* in such a way as to make it publishable in his lifetime? To ask the same question more broadly, how does this apparently limited work share in Machiavelli's ambitious enterprise (*impresa*), proclaimed in *The Prince* and the *Discourses on Livy,* of introducing a new political, moral, and religious order for the benefit of mankind? That is the guiding question to be addressed in studying the *Art of War.*

### THE CRITIQUE OF HUMANISM

Machiavelli's *Art of War* is a dialogue that takes place in the garden, known as the Orti Oricellari, of his friend Cosimo Rucellai.[5] Cosimo and his friends Zanobi Buondelmonti, Battista della Palla, and Luigi Alamanni appear as interlocutors in the dialogue, respectfully questioning the visitor Fabrizio Colonna, who is their authority in the art of war. Although the group of friends also included Machiavelli (who dedicated the *Discourses on Livy* to Zanobi Buondelmonti and Cosimo), Machiavelli does not take part in the dialogue; he remains silent and merely narrates it. He is prominently identified as the author of the preface, "Niccolo Machiavelli, Florentine citizen and secretary"; and he introduces the first book with repeated use of "I believe," "I know," "I confess." But then, having stated his purpose in the preface to Lorenzo Strozzi, and having set the stage at the beginning of Book I, he withdraws and neither continues as narrator nor appears in the conversation himself. The narrated dialogue becomes a performed one, with the excuse that it is burdensome to repeat "he said" and the like; and the characters give their own speeches as in a play.

Thus Machiavelli carefully introduces himself and removes himself. He must, therefore, be identified with the whole of the dialogue but not with any particular character—especially not with Fabrizio, the military authority who is usually assumed to be his spokesman.[6] Machiavelli apologizes in the preface by saying that the errors in his writing can be corrected without harm to anyone, whereas those of doers cannot be found out without bringing ruin to empires. But of course Machiavelli, instead of giving his views directly, puts them in the mouth of a doer, a military professional. The result is to give his opinions more authority and himself less responsibility for the errors he warns of. In his own name Machiavelli speaks of "sinister opinions" that cause the military to be hated and their company to be avoided. But in the dialogue, Fabrizio does not identify the opinions or seek to oppose and replace them. He himself is an ambiguous figure. Perhaps he is intended to represent the humanists and their Renaissance of ancient thought that does not reach to deeds, their praise of republicanism that compromises with the power of princes and of the Church, and their reluctance to admit that a return to the ancients would require a revolutionary new order for moderns. Fabrizio is not Machiavelli but rather Machiavelli's half-hearted ally.

In the introduction to Book I, Machiavelli describes but does not name the garden of the Rucellai family; nor does he remark that conversations such as the one he begins to narrate were frequent there. According to contemporary accounts, the Orti Oricellari were a center of both philosophical and political discussion not only in the 1520s, when the *Art of War* was written, but from the beginning of the century at least.[7] Thus the setting signifies humanist reflection, but the topic is war and Fabrizio is a man of war. The characters are said to have just finished a sumptuous meal; the day is hot, and they head for the "most secret and shady part" of Cosimo's garden. Satiated as they are, they are in a mood to listen to the expert Fabrizio. The questioners are acute and often show skepticism concerning Fabrizio's expansive regard for the methods of the Romans, but they do not challenge him or attempt to set forth alternative opinions.[8] The discussion takes place in the shade of ancient trees, Cosimo says, that his grandfather had cultivated. But Fabrizio replies that it is better to seek to imitate the ancients in "strong and harsh things, not in delicate and soft, in things that are done under the sun, not under the shade" (*AW* I 331). "My Romans," he reminds them, became corrupt from studies in delicate and soft things.

Thus Fabrizio aims a Catonic reproof at humanist garden salons, which reminds us of Machiavelli's complaint at the beginning of the *Discourses on Livy* that the ancients are imitated in all but politics. Yet Machiavelli's opinion here seems to differ somewhat from Fabrizio's. Machiavelli does not entirely despise the shade. He uses the leisure of self-satisfied, cultivated gentlemen to argue on behalf of the unleisured, indelicate profession of war. He claims the protection of "ancient" trees—the ancients—for a harsh politics that the ancient philosophers would have wanted to condemn, and where necessary to accept, would have concealed.

By contrast to Plato's *Republic,* in which the sun represents what is intelligible, Machiavelli allows Fabrizio to identify being in the sun not with the philosopher's yearning but with a soldier's life in the field. This is "hard" humanism as opposed to the soft neo-Platonist humanism of rhetoric and philosophy brought to Florence by Machiavelli's immediate predecessors, Marsilio Ficino and Pico della Mirandola, and practiced by many lesser figures, including Cosimo's uncle Bernardo in the Orti Oricellari, as Fabrizio points out. Machiavelli's appeal to the prevailing esteem for the ancients seems designed to transform the object of that appreciation from Greek literature into Roman deeds. Such a change may be accompanied by sincere admiration for the ancients, but it is an undertaking for the purpose of meeting contemporary necessities in a way that the ancients would not have approved. The trees in the Orti Oricellari stand for the ancients who create shade for the moderns (I 330).[9] The shade is both a help and a hindrance: a help because it offers an authority alternative to modern belief; a hindrance because it softens the moderns. The setting of Machiavelli's dialogue thus serves as counterpoint to its theme. The dialogue is an argument in the shade to encourage marching and fighting under the sun.[10]

Yet, in response to Cosimo, who excuses the talks in the shady garden of his uncle, Fabrizio says that the ways he recommends are not hard living in the Spartan manner; they are "more humane" (*piu umani*). And what are the ancient ways Fabrizio would like to introduce? "Honoring and prizing the virtues; not despising poverty; esteeming the modes and orders of military discipline; constraining citizens to love one another; living without sects; esteeming the private less than the public; and other similar things that can easily accompany these times" (*AW* I 332).

Fabrizio's answer sounds like a program for what recent historians have called "civic humanism" in contrast to literary humanism. In their description, never too exact, civic humanism blends moral virtue with patriotism so that neither element makes uncompromising demands on the other.[11] Moral virtue regarded civically signifies self-sacrifice, as what one would give up for the republic or for the common good. This is opposed to Aristotle's emphasis on the pleasure of being virtuous and on justified pride in moral self-perfection.[12] Nor, in civic humanism as presented, does patriotism require injustice or any other vice. Patriotism in this optimistic view would never be narrow, cruel or fanatical. Such a mixture of civic advantage and virtue is too nice to be true in any well-considered view, not to mention Aristotle's or Machiavelli's.

In the pioneer version of Hans Baron, civic humanism is said to have its source in the work of Leonardo Bruni (1374–1444), the Florentine secretary who wrote a history of Florence and made translations of Aristotle's works.[13] Exactly a century before Machiavelli's *Art of War*, Bruni also produced a treatise on the military, called *De militia*.[14] But that work, in marked contrast to Machiavelli's, has a strong flavor of aristocracy in its republicanism.[15] Citing the Roman example, it praises and justifies the preeminence of the equestrian order in the army—just the contrary of the extreme denigration of cavalry and elevation of infantry by Machiavelli. Bruni does not confine himself to actual regimes in Rome and Florence. In his preoccupation with the honor of the military, he considers their status in the best regime as conceived by Plato and Hippodamos (according to Aristotle, the first political scientist[16]). That regime is the same imaginary republic rejected as a model for politics by Machiavelli in the famous fifteenth chapter of *The Prince*. Bruni's concern for the nobles and for the best regime accords with the rhetorical form and exhortative tone of his text that has been noted by its recent editor, C. C. Bayley.[17] The work is devoted to a harsh subject, the necessity of war, but treats it as an opportunity for honor rather than acquisition. Instead of treating virtue as an instrument of war, Bruni looks to war as an arena of virtue. In spirit he is as far removed from Machiavelli as are Plato, Aristotle, and Cicero,[18] and although it is firmly civic, it is as surely moral, literary, and rhetorical as is the nonpolitical tradition of humanism. One could say that it is above all concerned for the dignity and elevation of man. Machiavelli's topic, as we learn in the preface to the *Art of War,* is the defense of man and of men's cities. For him, the question becomes whether the defense of man does not require the subordination, or the abandonment, of human dignity.

In Bruni's *De militia* there is no mention of the art of war; the only mentions of "art" distinguish it from the virtues and strength of a soldier.[19] But Machiavelli writes on the *art* of war as distinct from the military in general. Considered as an art, war need not necessarily be either civic or moral. The military professional who possesses that art does not as such have the civic motive of the citizen, and he is skilled in defeating others by immoral means. The art of war seems difficult to reconcile with civic or any other humanism.

### CLAUSEWITZ AND SOCRATES ON THE ART OF WAR

Machiavelli's *Art of War* has attracted a number of military commentators who treat it with a seriousness unfortunately not achieved, or even attempted, by commentators on his other works.[20] The military scholars may think well or ill of Machiavelli's insight, but they judge it as an essay on the art and nature of war, as war was practiced then or is always practiced. Even if these commentators ignore the dialogic presentation of Machiavelli's work and its deeper resonances, as they uniformly do, their directness is refreshing. It bears witness to the integrity of the art of war, where argument is conclusive because victory is clear, as compared to the contestable superiority of one political regime over another. But the very idea of an *art* of war deserves more consideration than the military commentators give it.

In an early work Clausewitz praises Machiavelli's "very sound judgment in military matters."[21] He likes Machiavelli for his appreciation of the psychology of warlike spirit. Then in *On War,* Clausewitz expresses his distrust of any art or science of war to the extent that it treats the human subjects of war as mechanical objects.[22] Clausewitz seems unsure whether a true art of war can be adjusted to this difficulty, of which Machiavelli too was aware. Clausewitz remarks perceptively in a letter that Machiavelli's *Art of*

*War* lacks the "free, independent judgment of his other works."[23]
But the reason is perhaps that Machiavelli, as we have noted, does
not give the "art of war" the same expansive meaning in the dialogue
of that name as in *The Prince* or the *Discourses*.[24] For the expansion
of the art of war to include all politics gives Machiavelli's doctrine
a new psychology that frees it from tradition and morality. Before
we see how the issue arises in Book I of the dialogue, we need to
look at its origin in the Socratic tradition for a fuller explanation.

Machiavelli's principal sources for the *Art of War* are, following
Burd,[25] commonly taken to be Frontinus, Vegetius, and Polybius.
They supply him with necessary information on the order of battle
of the Roman legion and the Macedonian phalanx, on the recruit-
ment of soldiers, on the march and the encampment of armies, on
discipline and on weapons. All these are ancient "orders," as Machiavelli calls them, which he wishes to recommend for imitation. But
prior to the ancient orders is the very notion of the art of war; and
indeed he takes that for his first topic in the dialogue. The "art of
war" is Greek in origin, more precisely Socratic. The very Socrates
who made so much of virtue, and especially justice, is the one responsible for supposing that war can be an art. But Socrates did not
make that supposition as a matter of course.

The advantage and the difficulty of that hypothesis can be illustrated in two passages out of the twenty-odd references on the art
or science of war to be found in Plato and Xenophon. In Plato's
*Republic* we learn that the art of war should be exercised by skilled
practitioners who devote themselves to that single activity. Like the
other arts, this one has a limited field of competence that can be
articulated and taught, in which excellence can be discerned. Nothing in the art prevents a woman from acquiring it. The art of war
sustains its rationality by refusing to entertain extraneous questions
about who exercises it and for what end.[26] But in contrast to the
picture of an articulated art, Xenophon tells a story that expands
the art of war past all recognition as a purely military competence.
Socrates urged a young companion of his to learn the art of war if
he wished to become a general. But on returning from his lessons,
the pupil confessed that tactics was all he had learned. Socrates
reminded him that good tactics requires careful disposition of men,
thus knowledge of their characters—indeed all knowledge necessary

to distinguishing good men from bad.[27] Under his seemingly innocent questioning, Socrates transforms the art of war into knowledge
of the good life, the object of philosophy. The artisan's concern with
the boundaries of his art suddenly becomes the philosopher's love
of knowledge as a whole. After discussing the nature of the art of
war, Machiavelli's Fabrizio proceeds to the choosing of an army and
thereby confronts the same difficulty. Is the man who is good at war
the same as the good man? If not, how can we guarantee that the
art of war will be used for a good end? Is a victory that brings
corruption to the victor so clear a victory? The purely military view
dissolves in the doubt and uncertainty that inspire philosophy.

Xenophon suggests an answer to the question in a comic episode
from the *Cyropaedia*—a work recommended by Machiavelli in the
same chapter of *The Prince* (14) where he says that the art of war
is all a prince needs to know. After the conquest of Babylon, his
last, Cyrus addressed the leaders of the elite guard of Persians who
were to hold their empire, and insisted that they retain for themselves, and not share with the conquered, "the science and care of
war" that would sustain their superiority.[28] The Socratic version of
Cyrus's warning asserts that men willingly obey their superiors,
those whom they believe to be best because they have knowledge.[29]
Thus the natural right of the best will, or should, prevent the art of
war from being abused. By validating the art of war, natural right
confines it within its bounds, and reconciles the articulation of the
art with its thrust toward wholeness. Whether such natural right
exists is of course open to question. Fabrizio, whose name reminds
us of the high-minded Fabricius, in effect presumes upon some such
natural right. He quotes a proverb that reflects his overconfidence:
"War makes thieves, peace hangs them" (*AW* I 336).

Machiavelli never attacks the notion of natural right expressly.
He says as much as he can or wishes to say by never mentioning
"natural right" or "natural law" in any of his works or correspon-
dence. Such resounding silence cannot mean that Machiavelli was
unaware of the foundation of morals and politics according to the
Socratic tradition. He left many signs of his deliberate rejection in
his ferocious Machiavellisms (of which I have given samples), not
to mention in his less conspicuous departures from the meaning of
the ancient writers he so frequently cites or refers to.[30] Those who

regard Machiavelli as a civic humanist should be gravely concerned at this absence of natural right in his thought. They seem not to have considered what might keep the civic spirit humane if there is no justice in nature.

After Machiavelli, natural right reappeared in a new form as a right of equality rather than of the best. The new doctrine was applied to war and international relations by the seventeenth century jurists Hugo Grotius and Samuel Pufendorf, who conceived an international law based on the equality of nations that still today defines legitimacy in international behavior. The legal equality of nations derives from a doctrine of sovereignty in which a determinate test of who is sovereign replaces a contestable judgment of who is the best ruler. Thus the art of war, when used in defense of sovereignty, is both justified and limited—an important advance, one could suppose, over the ancient conception that fails to set determinate limits on the exercise of that art. But the cost of the modern doctrine of natural right is a certain loss of understanding. That doctrine creates a legalistic separation of the military from the political that does not acknowledge the unity so well recognized by Socrates and Machiavelli. The result is to underestimate the moral problem of war rather than to solve it because the doctrine denies any justifiable motive for aggression. Nations that do not know that they themselves can be tempted by aggression will always be surprised by the aggression of others and will have difficulty in identifying and resisting it. Moreover, the notion of the military professional subordinate to political authority exaggerates the controllability of war. Machiavelli is criticized, with some reason, for being a military reactionary who not only denied the value of artillery, cavalry and fortresses, but also failed to notice the beginnings of modern military professionalism in his time. What he did see, however, as Piero Pieri has noted, was the possibility of total war.[31]

Machiavelli prepares the development of modern natural right, apparently so contrary to his own intention, by undermining and refuting classical natural right. For him the natural superiority of the best has no standing, at least in all those political situations where "best" would be understood as the rule of the morally best or gentlemen he so despises.[32] But of course, in contrast to the equality of modern international law, Machiavelli maintains the natural superiority of the best prince or captain, that is, of the most capable aggressor. In his other writings he is therefore hostile to the professional soldiers who do not fight on their own account; they are mercenaries. His hostility turns to warm approval if the mercenary captain undertakes to become a prince and uses the art of war to promote himself like Francesco Sforza. With this act mercenary arms, which Machiavelli scorns, are transformed into "one's own arms," his very motto. Later, by the genius of Thomas Hobbes above all others, "one's own arms" became equalized in the principle of self-preservation; the Machiavellian conquering prince was made into government by consent, and his incitement to conquer the world (D I 20) was limited by the creation of international law discussed above. Thus the Machiavellian spirit of selfishness was redirected to a non-Machiavellian conclusion setting moral limitations on the art of war.

In the *Art of War,* however, Machiavelli's gentleman mercenary Fabrizio represents the innocence of classical natural right as it reflects the obtuseness of moral persons. Fabrizio praises the Romans for using their own arms (*AW* I 348–49) but never thinks of doing the same for himself; instead, he soldiers for the "Catholic King." The effectual truth of the gentleman professional—or of classical natural right in general—is fighting for the Catholic King. Filled with moral disgust for his own aggression, he dutifully aids in the aggression of others. Machiavelli wants to make him consistent in his indulgence, not in his disapproval, of aggression. To see his adverse judgment on Fabrizio one must appreciate his need to use Fabrizio's authority; one must understand that he intends to use the Renaissance of classicism in his time against the tradition of classical natural right. Writing a dialogue permits both aims to be achieved, first the installation of Fabrizio as the authority, then the gradual sapping of his authority by questioning from Machiavelli's characters, for whom Machiavelli does not take responsibility. The movement of Machiavelli's dialogue undermines Fabrizio's presumption of natural right as Fabrizio is, by implications that he never fully appreciates, compelled to abandon the moral restrictions on the art of war that he himself lays down. To see Machiavelli at work, we must follow that movement closely and respectfully. To understand the *Art of War,* it is not enough to quote isolated statements of Fabrizio's as if they were Machiavelli's opinions.

COSIMO'S ACCUSATION

Critics of the *Art of War* have noted disapprovingly that Fabrizio, the principal interlocutor, makes his way through the dialogue without facing any open challenge from the other participants. Since the critics understand dialogue democratically as equal exchange, this seems to them unfair. But Fabrizio is an accomplished expert in the art of war to whom it is reasonable for young men to listen. As noted, he has been fed a sumptuous dinner, after which it would be rude to question his assumptions and spoil his digestion. But this does not mean that an alert reader must accept the assumptions. Machiavelli does not offer an equal combat of opinions, leaving the reader to choose. Instead, he has a dominant thesis, imitate the ancients in the art of war—and a quieter counterpoint, improve on them.

Nonetheless Cosimo Rucellai, who speaks with Fabrizio in the first two books, promises to question him "without respect" (*sanza rispetto, AW* I 331). Cosimo had died by the time of Machiavelli's narration of the dialogue; so the dramatic date of the *Art of War*, taken to be September 1516 by Sergio Bertelli (*AW* I 310) because Fabrizio was then at leisure after the treaty of Noyon, differs from the date of narration, which is soon after Cosimo's death in 1519. Machiavelli begins Book I with a tearful tribute to Cosimo, believing such praise could never be suspected of "adulation": as if no one had ever adulated a dead young man.[33] As the conversation begins, Cosimo enters an apologetic defense of his grandfather in response to Fabrizio's reproof of him for having imitated the ancients in delicate things. He asks Fabrizio what things similar to the ancient he would introduce, producing in reply the items of civic humanism that we have discussed. Then Cosimo questions Fabrizio about his art.

How is it, asks Cosimo, that although you condemn others who do not imitate the ancients in their actions, in war, which is your art, you yourself do not appear to use any ancient provision (*termine*)?[34] Cosimo apparently means that Fabrizio is a mercenary captain contrary to the practice of the ancients (but not of the Carthaginians, whom Fabrizio will mention presently). "Your art" is a skill to the practice of which Fabrizio is supposedly devoted, an art in the Socratic sense, which we would call a profession.[35] Fabrizio answers to Cosimo's "accusation" that he has not yet found an occasion on which to demonstrate the "preparations" he has made toward returning the military to its ancient orders. Perhaps this dialogue is that occasion, but the dialogue was initiated by Cosimo and recorded by Machiavelli. Fabrizio adds, weakly, that youthful listeners are more likely to believe him than are graybeards who are normally enemies of war and do not see that "wicked ways" are the cause of modern neglect of it. He says nothing of the "sinister opinions" mentioned by Machiavelli in the preface as standing in the way of military reform. The art of war, we see, is bounded by the necessities of awaiting opportunity to use it and of respecting human nature. It cannot by means within its own competence achieve its own adoption and use.

Then Cosimo's accusation suddenly becomes Fabrizio's self-accusation, as he attempts a further excuse. "My art," he says, is not one by which one can live honestly at any time—ancient or modern—unless it is used by a republic or kingdom (*AW* I 334). A good man (*uomo buono*) would never practice it as his particular art (*per sua particulare arte*) because it requires him to be rapacious, fraudulent, violent—qualities that necessarily make him not good. And he cannot do otherwise because the art of war does not support its practitioner in time of peace; so he has to make great profit during war or contrive to turn peace into war. Thus the art of war is really the art of being hired, of "soldiering" (*arte del soldo*). Professional dedication is not possible in war because it transforms the professional into a wicked man devoted no longer to his client but only to his own support and aggrandizement. If he uses the art in the service of a "well-ordered republic or kingdom" (*AW* I 337; cf. I 334), the art is washed clean of its moral taint. But a well-ordered state is precisely one that does not permit the professional to follow the art of war to its end; it requires him to return to "his [peaceful] art" to support himself. One must distinguish Pompey and Caesar, who were able (*valenti*) in the art of war, from the captains of the early Roman republic, such as Scipio and Marcellus, who were both able and good.

So much for Fabrizio's admired ancients! They prove to be divided into those who should and those who should not be imitated. Fabrizio has a dim awareness of the expansive potential of the Socratic art of war, but he has no remedy for it. A moral man himself, he wants the art of war to be moral; and he seems to think that his desire alone will make it so. His personal apology to Cosimo for not imitating the ancients himself turns into an accusation against all who are dedicated to the art of war, including himself; the professional is understood as a mercenary. But then the licentious behavior of modern mercenaries is excused as something they are compelled to do in the absence of well-ordered states. Fabrizio ends up contradicting himself. Having begun by saying that the art of war is "my art," he denies it (*AW* I 334, 342) and claims that "my art" is to govern and defend my subjects. The art of war appears to be bounded and governed by the art of politics. The civic humanism that Fabrizio wanted to introduce by "due degrees" (*debiti mezzi*, *AW* I 332) now seems to be a necessary condition for adopting the art of war. What is the sense, then, in giving a discourse on the art of war as if it were separate from politics? In trying to make the art of war compatible with honesty, Fabrizio seems again to represent the half-hearted humanism of his day and, more deeply, to reflect the problems and paradoxes of ancient virtue. We must not suppose that Machiavelli shares Fabrizio's confusion, but we do need to consider what might have been his way out of the difficulty.

### FABRIZIO'S PRESUMPTION

Fabrizio in his embarrassment now takes refuge in promoting the value of infantry, which he says are the nerve of armies (*AW* I 339). The infantry have the merit of returning to their homes in time of peace to practice their arts without tyrannizing over other citizens. Their merit is *not* to be professional military. But will a nonprofessional army of infantry win battles?[36] In the remainder of the dialogue, Fabrizio tries manfully to argue, while dodging many objections, that the infantry are militarily as well as morally superior to an army of mounted professionals, and that the ancients so believed. Thus his problem is neatly solved: by imitating the ancients one can win battles and not risk trouble afterward from those persons necessary to the winning. Infantry is the answer. By using infantry, the art of war will generate both victory and the moral goodness needed for its own restraint.

That is Fabrizio's presumption, coming to light from Cosimo's question about the art of war at the beginning of Book I. On that basis he makes a new beginning (*AW* I 343) and continues through the dialogue to discourse on more strictly military matters. But the moral and political difficulties in the presumption keep cropping up, though often in the form of military problems. I have given the reader a taste of the close interpretation that would be necessary to follow Machiavelli's presentation diligently. The literary form he has adopted is far from a mere formality, and the interlocutors (particularly Cosimo) are hardly harmless listeners to Fabrizio's discourse. Without challenging him, indeed while agreeing with his arguments, they bring out the weaknesses in them.

With his new beginning Fabrizio turns to the choosing (*deletto*) of soldiers. Using diligence (*industria*), he says, one can make good soldiers anywhere; he does not say this is a matter of art, or part of the art of war. But to choose his soldiers, the captain must have the authority of a prince; soldiers come to him on a middle way (*via di mezzo, AW* I 347) between voluntary will and force.[37] But suppose the captain does not have a state and so is not in a position to select his army? Cosimo's questioning brings to light Fabrizio's presumption that the captain is in a position to choose whom he pleases; or more generally, Cosimo shows that the art of war depends on political authority. Machiavelli's solution in *The Prince,* that the captain must become a new prince, is only hinted at.[38] For Fabrizio is not the man to appreciate the moral liberties that a new prince must take in order to succeed. When speaking of his soldier's qualities, he casually equates moral goodness (*bontà*) with virtue (*virtù, AW* I 350). But he is led by Cosimo (*AW* I 353-56) to admit the necessity of a large army with heads loyal to the prince, or at least harmless to him, through rotation—a democratic rather than an aristocratic ordering. Fabrizio's choice is guided by necessity, but he does not seem to recognize the fact. He has too much confidence in the power of law to keep a people unified (*AW* I 356).

It is Cosimo, not Fabrizio, who brings up the necessity for relying on one's own arms, a great theme of *The Prince* and the *Discourses on Livy* that receives only a narrow, strictly military interpretation here. Cosimo asks Fabrizio whether he would have an ordinance similar to that "in our countries," apparently a reference to the 1506 proposal for a military ordinance in Florence, authored by Machiavelli himself.[39] Fabrizio approves of it, and then, again prompted by Cosimo, moves to a defense of "one's own arms," which, as we have seen, he does not understand in a selfish sense.

There is an advantage in the fighting spirit of one's own arms over expert, professional arms, which is represented in the superiority of infantry over cavalry. But can that spirit be aroused and managed by the art of war, or is it a passion independent of the art, on which in fact the art is dependent? Fabrizio wavers between claiming that such spirit (*animo, AW* I 347) can be brought to life with good orders, and allowing that it (*spirito, AW* I 354) must be sought out in those chosen for the infantry. The question is still about the sovereignty and comprehensiveness of the art of war: does the art depend on the availability of a certain human material (men of fighting spirit), or can it create that material?

This question leads back to the moral dubiousness of the art of war. Fabrizio has said that the moderns, despite their military weakness, paradoxically practice the art of war with full devotion. Thus making war in time of peace, and against friends as well as enemies, they are required to transform the art of war into the art of getting hired—of remaining soldiers in the literal sense. Their art compels them not to serve their clients, like Socratic artisans, but rather to be loyal only to themselves: hence the necessary immorality of the art. On the contrary, the ancients in Fabrizio's account were half-hearted military professionals who returned home to peacetime arts after the war was over. They did this because they were good, it seems, though Fabrizio does not say why their goodness could be depended on. Perhaps it could be because it was supported by fighting spirit in the common defense, a loyalty to others that makes use of the art of war but also restrains it.

If this were true, the art of war would remain within moral bounds, not subject to the excesses of mercenaries. But the art would also be powerless to create the generous fighting spirit that seems to be independent of it, and the weakness of the military in modern times would continue or would need some other remedy than the art of war. In the *Discourses* Machiavelli says that "those who fight for their own glory are good and faithful soldiers" (*D* I 43). Here is a denial that fighting spirit is really so generous and a suggestion that it might be generated through sound policy. Machiavelli has said in the preface of this work that he is writing on the art of war to show that some form of past virtue is not impossible in his time. Remarkably, he uses the word *arte* very densely in Book I (forty-four times),[40] and then not at all in Books II and III.

In the first book Machiavelli holds out the promise of an over-arching art that would combine professional dedication, and its at-tendant self-aggrandizement, with the amateur spirit of infantry and its accompanying goodness. Such an art, for example, would not merely wait for the appearance of a supply of spirited volunteers for the army but would actively seek to recruit them by finding a motive for their conversion to the military. In this way the art of war would overcome the difficulties that made Clausewitz hesitate to use the term. Those difficulties are raised in Books II–VII in the *Art of War,* as can be seen in the summary interpretations that follow.

## ORDER AND VIRTUE

Once the troops are chosen according to the method in Book I, they must be armed. Fabrizio immediately recommends the arms of the Romans, with which "they seized the whole world" (*AW* II 361). But, under prodding from Cosimo, Fabrizio is forced to retreat from his insistence on the superiority of the ancients. Modern infantry have pikes to defend against cavalry, and after boasting that the Romans were better nonetheless, Fabrizio accepts a compromise of half-Roman, half-German arms. He has to admit that modern cav-alry, with stirrups and improved saddles, is superior to the ancient. Even in ancient times Parthian cavalry defeated the Romans, Fa-brizio concedes; but then he adds petulantly that he is speaking of warfare only in Europe, not Asia (a resolution he soon abandons). The "natural virtue" of infantry works only where the battlefield is cramped so as not to permit the maneuver of cavalry. Thus Roman success depended on finding a narrow site to fight on; it was limited to particular circumstances. If modern arms are in fact superior to those of the ancients, what accounts for the weakness of modern armies?

Fabrizio turns with evident relief to the second topic of Book II, the need for military exercises. Here we are reminded that the art of war is not like other arts that are complete when they are acquired as knowledge. War requires exercise and habit as well as rational calculation; so exercises lead one to the need for order in the mili-tary. "Order chases fear from men; disorder lessens ferocity" (*AW* II 375). So a spirited army is a well-ordered army, not one composed merely of spirited men, Fabrizio asserts as he composes the battalions of his army. When Cosimo asks him why there is such cowardice, disorder, and negligence in the exercise of armies today, he answers with the confidence of a general "willingly" delivering his thoughts on politics (*AW* II 392–95). The problem does not seem to be in misunderstanding the art of war.

Europe, Fabrizio says, has many well-known military names, Africa a few, and Asia the least. (In naming some of them, Fabrizio with his pro-Roman bias forgets to mention Hannibal from Africa.) The reason is that Europe has republics rather than kingdoms, and whereas republics most often honor virtue, kingdoms fear it. Fabrizio, like Machiavelli elsewhere, speaks not of "republican virtue" but of republics honoring the virtue of their leaders or princes. He surely abandons the praise of both republics and kingdoms earlier (*AW* I 334), when he said that either form, when well-ordered, could keep military professionals under control. But, he continues, the virtue in many ancient republics and princes was destroyed by the Roman empire, which thereafter became corrupt so that virtue was stifled everywhere. Nor has virtue been reborn there, because it takes time to revive "orders" once they are spoiled and also because of the Christian religion. That religion, Fabrizio says, does not impose the necessity to defend oneself that formerly existed when men conquered in war suffered "every last misery" (*AW* II 395). Now losers in war have little loss to fear and so men do not fight.

Fabrizio's speech mentions virtue fourteen times and art not at all. The art of war seems here to yield its efficacy to virtue and fear. They are in a relationship Fabrizio does not explain and are in turn controlled by an opinion in the Christian religion that prevents men from fighting to the death. Christianity in Fabrizio's view is hostile to republics, which are arenas of virtue; the monarchies he sees growing in France and Spain are signs of modern weakness, not beginnings of the powerful modern state. The "ultimate ruin" facing the defeated in ancient times was not loss of the republican form of government but of one's home and property in this world. A belief that these things ultimately do not matter could be among the "sinister opinions" mentioned in Machiavelli's preface as causing the military to be hated. But Fabrizio does not say what should be done to combat an opinion that surely stands as an obstacle to imitating the

ancients in the art of war. He considers Christianity in a narrow
military view that gives only a hint of Machiavelli's broader criticisms elsewhere.

## CHANCE

In Book III Fabrizio's new questioner, Luigi Alamanni, the youngest
in the company, is treated to a stirring imaginary battle. "Our
army"—Fabrizio's and Luigi's—wins an easy victory in a battle on
paper, resembling a planned triumph by Socrates in one of Plato's
dialogues. In such a battle the enemy has no chance; and in fact, the
theme of Book III appears to be chance.[41] Fabrizio begins by asserting that the greatest disorder in modern armies is their use of a
single front. The Roman armies, by contrast, kept three ranks in
battle (known as *astati, principi,* and *triari*) so that the first, when
hard pressed, could retreat into the second, and if necessary, the first
and second into the third.[42] Fabrizio remarks that the formation was
Roman; the Greek phalanx did not allow one rank to retire into
another. Imitating the warfare of the "ancients" again faces the difficulty of deciding which ancients to imitate.

After listening to Fabrizio's enthusiastic account of the paper
victory, Luigi screws up his courage to ask why Fabrizio had made
so little use of his artillery, shooting just once, and indeed whether
it is not madness to retain the massed formations of the ancients in
face of the fury of modern artillery (*AW* III 411). Fabrizio admits
that the question requires a long response, and he provides a long,
unconvincing one, full of obvious shifts and damaging concessions.
In fact his imaginary battle had been lacking in any plan of attack,
its tactics being determined by the necessity of charging the enemy
before it could fire its artillery a second time (the first salvo had gone
over their heads!). With Fabrizio's forced conclusion that modern
artillery does not impede the use of ancient modes Luigi is silenced
but clearly not impressed that Fabrizio has made his case. He asks
whether Fabrizio would always use the Roman formation and is
told no, but that knowing this one permits the use of other formations; "for every science has its generalities" (*AW* III 418). Fabrizio's
imaginary battle in his science of war is the analogue of the best
regime in classical political science. Behind the art of war, for Fabrizio, lies a science that essentially consists in wishful thinking, and

that is unprepared to meet the chance of a technological innovation such as artillery. Instead of an imaginary science behind the art, perhaps Fabrizio should be looking for a way to make the art of war operative. An art in the classical sense is indifferent to whether it is applied, as for example the art of the shoemaker is not affected by whether the customer can afford to buy. Can an art of war be conceived that would contrive to propagate itself and to create its own fortune by awakening potential clients to its necessity? Such an art would no longer be dependent on chance, on the chance of its being exercised.

AUTHORITY

The new questioner in Book IV, Zanobi Buondelmonti, would prefer to continue listening to Fabrizio's discourse, but Fabrizio asks him whether he has anything to add to the material discussed. The addition that gradually emerges is the authority of a captain, which, it appears, is not guaranteed by his knowledge as with other arts than the art of war. A competent artisan does not have to establish his authority; a captain does. Zanobi desires to be informed on two things: whether there is any other form than the Roman in which to order an army (he is apparently dissatisfied with Fabrizio's answer to Luigi in Book III); and what cautions (*rispetti*) a captain should have before engaging in battle. Fabrizio replies to the two points together because the "other form" he has in mind turns out to be simply the captain's authority.

On the first point Fabrizio gives more importance to the site of a battle as compared to the order of an army than he had been willing to say before (*AW* IV 426; cf. II 371); the site can sometimes determine the proper ordering. He lists a number of accidents that can occur during battle and tells how to deal with them. We learn, for example, that the Romans did not always use their formation of three lines; once, when Scipio had to oppose Hannibal's elephants, he had his first line withdraw to the wings, not into the second line.[43] In response to such accidents requiring ingenuity in a captain, *arte* reappears in the sense of trickery; a captain, Fabrizio says, should do by art what Fabius did in one instance by chance (*AW* IV 430, 433, 439). The consideration of chance in applying an art (from Book III) suggests an additional, morally dubious, meaning of art and requires a renewed emphasis on the virtue of a captain. For Machiavelli, a chief task of virtue is to surmount the inhibitions of morality.

Fabrizio then turns to cautions after and before battles, and among the latter mentions the need for prudence and counsel to a captain. For example, which does he trust more, his infantry or his cavalry—that is, the spirit of his troops or his own authority? (*AW* IV 437). It is easy to persuade a few men with whom you can use authority and force, but the difficulty is in removing a "sinister opinion" from a multitude (*AW* IV 440). So, excellent captains such as Alexander the Great were compelled to be orators, and Fabrizio lists thirteen functions of those speeches. In Book IV more than elsewhere Machiavelli seems to put himself in Fabrizio or to make Fabrizio his authority. To apply his doctrine, his art of war, Machiavelli must address a multitude as well as persuade a few; for the former he needs the authority of spokesmen like Fabrizio, and for the latter his own authority will do.

What constitutes the authority of a captain? Returning to his point in Book II, Fabrizio mentions the religion and the oaths of ancient soldiers that disposed them to war. But this time he omits the contrast between paganism and Christianity, and to our surprise, he includes the use of Joan of Arc by Charles VII among instances of successful manipulation of religion, as if forgetting his contention that Christianity detracts from the desire to win. Perhaps he wants to suggest that even Christianity, when properly interpreted—better to say manhandled—is no obstacle to the imitation of the ancients. Yet he repeats his insistence on the good effect of necessity in removing the soldiers' every hope of salvation save in victory. Their obstinacy is increased by love of the fatherland—caused by nature—and by love of the captain—which comes from his virtue more than any other benefit. It seems that the captain's virtue is above military order and is perhaps responsible for his authority, and that virtue and nature added to necessity are more powerful than religion. Machiavelli does not speak of "republican virtue," but again reduces republican loyalty or republicanism to patriotism and confines virtue to a few.

The need to establish authority shows that competence in the art of war has to be supplemented by the virtue of captains. Machiavelli himself does not have this virtue; his art works through the virtue of those whom he unofficially commissions. Fabrizio is an example, created by Machiavelli. In the dialogue, Fabrizio, no longer working for the Catholic King, becomes Machiavelli's captain, illustrating what such a captain might say to move educated opinion toward a healthier, more worldly spirit. But, to repeat, Fabrizio and Machiavelli are not identical. Fabrizio would not be Machiavelli's captain if he had Machiavelli's opinions. As we have seen, the interlocutors who subtly question Fabrizio's confidence give better clues to Machiavelli's understanding than do Fabrizio's long, somewhat boastful, somewhat inconsistent, speeches.

## THE CAPTAIN'S SOLDIERS

In Book V Fabrizio takes his army on the march against a mysterious enemy it does not see but from whom it fears attack. As with the order of battle, Fabrizio's disposition is defensive; he does not share the intent on acquisition so prominent in Machiavelli's other works. To combat fear the army must be disciplined and must keep to its order; such an army in these times would never be defeated, Fabrizio asserts (*AW* V 452). In an earlier discussion of the exercises of his army, Fabrizio had said that a captain would be honored for an army well turned out even if he lost the battle (*AW* II 371), but by now the necessity of overcoming accidents has come to the fore. The captain can hardly deal with the fear of soldiers by pointing to the beautiful formation in which they are drawn up and offering this as compensation for defeat.

In the matter of fear and authority, Fabrizio, or through him, Machiavelli, makes us aware of the context in which a modern army lives. Fabrizio criticizes the modern army as opposed to the ancient for carrying bread and wine in its provisions. This obtrusive allusion to Christianity invites us to consider the spiritual armies of the Church as an analogue to temporal ones and enables us to interpret Fabrizio's next criticism of modern armies, where the allusion is less obvious. He says that in modern armies booty is left to the discretion of the soldiers, while the ancients reserved all booty to the public. By the same analogy between temporal and spiritual armies, we have a reference to individual salvation under Christianity. What Fabrizio says about booty can be considered as an elaboration of his earlier remark that Christianity imposes no necessity to win or die. A Christian can die and still win in the next world.

The topic in Book V is the captain and his soldiers, "my own soldiers," Fabrizio calls them (*AW* V 453). They are his because he has trained them in a discipline under his authority; they are not mere instruments of his art. Zanobi remarks that an army on the move can hardly avoid dangerous accidents where it needs the "diligence [*industria*] of the captain and virtue of the soldiers" (*AW* V 456). Through the captain's authority his virtue has become theirs. Fabrizio readily agrees and adds that he wants to give "perfect knowledge" (*perfetta scienza*) of this exercise, which is thwarting ambushes (note: not setting them). When he had mentioned science before, he had spoken of its generalities (*AW* III 418); now he says he has a perfect science that includes the particulars of warfare. He is moving, or being pushed, toward a master art of war of the kind adumbrated in *The Prince,* but he has not yet arrived at it.

## THE CAPTAIN'S POLITICS

The last two books deal with politics, but only indirectly and grudgingly: encampment in Book VI and the besieging of towns in Book VII. A military camp reminds us that an army is not always fighting or on the march; it also desires "repose" (*AW* VI 462). With the change of subject (*ragionamento*) Battista della Palla takes the place of Zanobi as Fabrizio's interlocutor. In a speech resounding with high philosophical terms, Fabrizio says that necessity has compelled us in discussion to reverse the order of action from camping to marching to fighting. He could have included the political decision to send out an army if he had wanted to expand the art of war, but he hesitates to carry his argument back to that first cause until he is compelled to do so by military necessity.[44] Following Polybius in his comparison,[45] he prefers the orderly Roman form of camp to the haphazard adaptation to the natural shelter of the site that the Greeks practiced. Where the Greeks sought for the advantage of nature, the Romans relied on art.

It soon becomes clear, however, in response to a question by Battista, that art does not suffice. Guards are required to watch even an orderly camp, and severe punishments are needed to enforce discipline there.[46] The ancients added the fear of God to enforce such punishments, Fabrizio says approvingly. Soon he volunteers that the nature of the site matters after all (*AW* VI 479). And then he offers a summary that raises a new point unprompted by his questioner: the army at camp not only needs rest but also needs to think how to finish the war, since the enemy remains.

The battle, therefore, is not the end, as Fabrizio had insisted in Book I (*AW* I 334; cf. VI 463, 481). A decision to go to war precedes it, and win or lose, enemies remain afterward. Fabrizio proceeds to give the list mentioned earlier of thirty-three deceits in dealing with enemies, a list that amounts to a recognition from a military point of view that winning the battle is not the only goal. In two of them (nos. 13 and 17) he mentions art in the sense of trickery—the arts of dividing enemies and eliminating seditions. He says (no. 19) that what keeps an army united is the reputation of its captain, which comes from his virtue, not his birth or authority. And as the last advice he urges that a captain gain a people to his side with examples of chastity and justice—an overtly political message.

Fabrizio almost makes his captain into a Machiavellian prince, but not quite. At the end of the book he shows the contradiction that prevents him from going the way of *The Prince*. The Romans, he says, realizing that harsh sites and bad weather were inimical to order and discipline in an army, always avoided fighting in winter or on mountains or in any situation that would prevent them from showing their art and their virtue (*AW* VI 493). Thus in order to be independent of nature's harshness, the Romans, whose example Fabrizio recommends, were dependent on nature's bounty. In his other books Machiavelli develops a conception of necessity, merely alluded to here, as a remedy for this difficulty. By anticipating necessity, one can choose in advance on better terms what one would later be compelled to do at a disadvantage.

Book VII begins with the subject of defending and attacking towns and ends with an exhortation to new political orders. Fabrizio acknowledges the political obstacles in the way of reviving the ancient art of war, but in his very resignation one can see the gleam of Machiavelli's hope. As to defending fortified towns, Fabrizio is compelled to allow that the "fury of artillery" (*AW* VII 496, 498) has become the dominant consideration. He does not admit but cannot deny the superiority of the moderns in gaining and losing whole cities. One should not construct bastions far from the walls, Fabrizio explains, because artillery will always destroy the bastions and the defenders will seek safety within the walls. If defense is to succeed, defenders must never believe they may retreat. Fabrizio gives a "fresh instance" of this in which he describes the "virtue" and "magnanimous enterprise" of Caterina Sforza while defending her fortress unsuccessfully against Cesare Borgia (AW VII 497). No one receives higher praise than she in the Art of War.

Nothing encourages an enemy more than to know that the city it attacks is not used to seeing the enemy; and conversely, to defend a city one must place strong men where the enemy attacks those who are frightened not by opinion but by arms. Does this mean that pious men are not strong defenders? In this work as elsewhere, Machiavelli's defense of religion when it serves political goals implies the possibility of a more vigorous politics that has no need of religion. At this point Fabrizio inserts twenty-two tricks of besiegers of cities, useful both for them and for the besieged (AW II 505-10), followed by twenty-seven "very familiar" general rules on war (AW II 511-13). The rules are familiar to Fabrizio's literary companions because they come mostly from Vegetius, with minor changes useful to Machiavelli.[47]

That is the end of "my discussion" (mio ragionamento), Fabrizio says with insufficient regard to the quietly skeptical contribution of his interlocutors. "My intention," he claims, has been not to show exactly how the ancient military was composed (a remark unnoticed by literal-minded source-seekers in the scholarship on the Art of War), but how to order the military today with more virtue (AW VII 513). He does not mention the art of war. He soon refers to a captain's profession as his mestiere, not his arte (AW VII 514). And he returns to Cosimo's question about his own imitation of the ancients (AW I 333) but this time omits mention of the art of war. His desire to carry ancient modes into effect has been frustrated; a revival of those modes in the military would be easier than any other for a prince with a sufficiently large state. Thus the application of Fabrizio's art is defined by politics, and politics is out of its control. That is his apology.

Or is it possible, though very difficult, for a captain to form and order his own army? Fabrizio names a small number of ancient captains who succeeded in making their own armies before fighting, and singles out "Philip of Macedonia, father of Alexander" as his exemplar for both princes and republics. This is as close as he comes to Machiavelli's description elsewhere of Philip as a new prince.[48]

He laments that nature should either have not made him recognize the possibility of another Philip today, or should have allowed him to carry it out. But he also blames his bad fortune in not being granted enough of a state to succeed in such an enterprise. To show why he cannot attain the "perfection of the ancients," he asks thirteen rhetorical questions denouncing the corruption of the moderns in the military. Thirteen is Machiavelli's number; the seventh question is: why should soldiers who do not recognize me have to obey me? So we ask, how can we recognize Machiavelli in Fabrizio?

Fabrizio says that Caesar and Alexander fought at the head of their troops; if they lost their states, they wanted to lose their lives. Machiavelli is, and is not, at the head of his troops. He has the intrepidity to raise new questions and propose new remedies, but he also has the caution to appoint captains to do his "fighting" for him. Such captains must win or lose on their own; so they will not be mere duplicates of Machiavelli. Many of them will suffer from the moral fastidiousness of Fabrizio, who is brought to a certain self-awareness by the dialogue he believes he controls. But at the end he shows still that he thinks goodness and virtue are the same thing, that Caesar's and Alexander's ambition is to be condemned, and that he does not know how to overcome fortune. Fabrizio can overcome the chance of military success or failure by becoming a teacher—by transforming the accident of this meeting into a dialogue that conveys a complex teaching.

On one level—Fabrizio's—the *Art of War* is a document of the Renaissance; on another, it penetrates to the contradictions of the Renaissance and suggests the new remedy that Machiavelli makes more explicit elsewhere. Machiavelli's situation can be compared to the collapsible formation of the Roman legion that he so insistently praises. He himself is out in front in the first line of *astati,* making contact with the enemy. But when the enemy attacks, he withdraws to the *principi,* more or less friendly political authorities who fight for him while fighting for themselves. And when they get into difficulties, suffer from inhibitions, and fall prey to contradictions, he is there among the *triari,* ready to help.

The *Art of War* is singular among Machiavelli's works because he does not display his boldness in it. His enemy is the same as in his bolder writings: classical political and moral philosophy and its popular derivative, Christianity (for Nietzsche was not the first to think that Christianity is Platonism for the people). But in the *Art of War* Machiavelli does not fight in the front line, drawing attention to himself with sardonic wit and sensational maxims. Instead, he allows a prince to campaign on his behalf, a Renaissance captain, but not the Cesare Borgia who teaches cruel lessons in *The Prince*— rather, a gentleman condottiere designed to appeal to, and to correct, the literary and the moral. This work is too ironic to be a serious study in the usual sense; but it establishes and promotes the serious study of war in modern times.

# NINE

# STRAUSS'S MACHIAVELLI

Leo Strauss once was heard to say that he had written *Thoughts on Machiavelli*[1] in order to be surpassed. Something of incompletion might also be inferred from the title of the book, which promises neither an order nor a whole. But for the reader—for us ordinary readers always and perhaps even for an extraordinary reader the first time—it is a book to be achieved. This again might be inferred from the foregoing, since Strauss in his humanity would surely have given an aid to surpassing by forcing an effort to achieve. My own experience is all on the side of achieving, for when studying Machiavelli, every time that I have been thrown upon an uninhabited island I thought might be unexplored, I have come across a small sign saying, "please deposit coin." After I comply, a large sign flashes in neon lights that would have been visible from afar, with this message: Leo Strauss was here.

*Thoughts on Machiavelli* is an esoteric book, that is, a book containing much that is appreciably esoteric to any ordinary reader stated in a manner either so elusive or so challenging as to cause him to give up trying to understand it. In this it is to be distinguished from the books with which it is concerned, Machiavelli's *The Prince* and the *Discourses on Livy,* which, though shocking, do not appear to be so difficult. Almost all readers, and especially scholarly readers, believe they understand Machiavelli's books, and only Strauss has shown they do not. Croce's complaint that the question of Machiavelli will perhaps never be solved,[2] though frequently quoted, does not refer to the difficulty of understanding Machiavelli's books, and

This chapter was originally published as "Strauss's Machiavelli," *Political Theory,* November 1975, 372–84. Copyright © 1975 by Sage Publications, Inc. Reprinted by permission of Sage Publications, Inc.

it is quoted as often to close off an inquiry as to begin one. Strauss seems determined to disturb the overconfident reader.

The first sentence announces an appeal to "the old-fashioned and simple opinion according to which Machiavelli was a teacher of evil." It is an appeal to the people as repository of good and evil, holding both moral opinions and the beliefs in causes that constitute the basis of such opinions, that is, maintaining both morality and religion. Like Machiavelli, Strauss appeals to the people, but he does so with a different intent: to ascend from them to a better understanding, not to ascend by their means while fooling them, as Machiavelli recommends. Strauss appeals to the people against scholars whom he accuses of being infected by Machiavelli, and he claims that Machiavelli's evil reputation in "Machiavellism" is the proper beginning of inquiry.

Present-day scholars assume to the contrary that Machiavellism will never lead them to Machiavelli. In dismissing his reputation as false, they depreciate his influence to the role of being widely misunderstood. They deny his power to introduce "new modes and orders" so that the question of his responsibility for modernity is not raised or not raised in sufficiently broad and uncompromising terms. For them, he is only a harbinger of later developments of nationalism, of science, and in Isaiah Berlin's interpretation, even of liberalism.[3] He is seen as a man of the Renaissance, hence encumbered by the past and distracted by a futile dream of reviving it. Strauss himself held a version of this opinion when he wrote the book on Hobbes, published in 1936, in which he claims that Hobbes is the originator of modern political philosophy. He confesses his mistake in the second preface to that book, written in 1951, and there asserts on Machiavelli's behalf that the difference between Machiavelli's claim to originality and Hobbes's is in the degree of outspokenness, not of clarity of thought.[4] Since I believe that Strauss's relationship to present-day Machiavelli scholarship was far from being a matter of unconcern to him, I suppose that I will be faithful to his intent, if not obedient to his example, in devoting this chapter to it. I will discuss his reception in that scholarship and his treatment of it in *Thoughts on Machiavelli*, as preparation for the question of Machiavelli's responsibility for modernity.

Strauss's first sentence, again, is this: "We shall not shock anyone, we shall merely expose ourselves to good-natured or at any rate harmless ridicule, if we profess ourselves inclined to the old-fashioned and simple opinion according to which Machiavelli was a teacher of evil." The result was as predicted. None of the first reviewers was shocked, either because they were all somehow aware of this old-fashioned opinion or because it is no longer considered shocking to be a teacher of evil, or both. Good-natured ridicule could be found in the expansive and relaxed praise of Herbert Butterfield, who, while indulging Strauss's conceit that a Livy reference in the *Discourses on Livy* is "quite a separate thing" from a Livy quotation, describes him (or is it Machiavelli?) as "a man who attaches special meaning to numbers"[5] and gives several absurd examples of this attachment.

The other kind of ridicule was visible in a review by another historian or (in Butterfield's phrase) "a student of the historical process in general," Felix Gilbert.[6] Gilbert made two points concerning the beginning of the *Discourses on Livy* which were intended to be devastating to Strauss's book. In the dedicatory letter Machiavelli says he has told as much as he knows and has learned in a long practice and continual reading of "things of the world." And in the proemium to Book 1, he compares himself to Columbus and announces that he is bringing "new modes and orders" of common benefit to everyone. Without any prompting from Strauss, Gilbert decided that Strauss's reading "between the lines" of the latter "key passage" was crucial to his enterprise of proving Machiavelli to be a "superdevil." Then he solemnly informed readers of the *Yale Review* of something "we know": "We know the passage from handwritten notes by Machiavelli, but it was not printed in the first edition, because Machiavelli cut it out when he had the manuscript recopied for presentation." Second, Gilbert asserted that the *cose del mondo* about which Machiavelli had been continually reading were "political affairs" in the narrow sense and not "things of the world," as the Italian would seem to imply. In translating *cose del mondo* as "worldly things" Strauss had overlooked a "traditional view" (or meaning?) that Gilbert certified as correct.

On the first point, Gilbert misrepresents a disputed hypothesis as established fact. The passage in question does not appear in the first two editions of the *Discourses on Livy,* which were published posthumously, nor in a later manuscript regarded as sounder, but it does appear in what Gilbert incorrectly calls "handwritten notes," in fact the only fragment of the *Discourses* in Machiavelli's hand known to exist. Though handwritten, the whole of the fragment, including the undisputed portion, is in polished prose, not in notes. Although it is true that the only major textual question in the *Discourses* concerns the excision of a portion of the only fragment of that work now existing in Machiavelli's handwriting, it is not true that all scholars believe it should be excised. Still less do they "know" that Machiavelli cut it out and on what occasion. As for *cose del mondo,* it is enough to say that in Gilbert's book, published in 1965, he translates or paraphrases *tutte le cose del mondo* from *Discourses* III 1, as "everything on earth." In this book he also quotes from the very passage that he had condemned Strauss for relying on, without mention of the established certainty that it deserves to be excised, and without referring to Strauss.[7] Both of Gilbert's points, then, are retracted in his own book, though silently and between the lines. I have dwelt on this example of harmless ridicule because it has been cited as damaging, but also to give myself practice with the bayonet. Strauss says that many of Machiavelli's outrageously ruthless sayings are not meant seriously, but designed to force his pupils through a process of brutalization in order to free them from effeminacy, "just as one learns bayoneting by using weapons which are much heavier than those used in actual combat."[8]

There was indeed praise for Strauss from students of political theory, John Hallowell and later Willmoore Kendall in a longer review of enthusiastic reappraisal.[9] In 1967 Arnaldo Momigliano introduced Leo Strauss to Italian scholars as "the author of one of the most elaborate and minute condemnations of the immoralism and atheism of Machiavelli."[10] Momigliano's acquaintance with both men and books was of such vast extent that he may have seemed to leave only the position of Machiavelli the teacher of piety as safe to occupy. That position had been suggested if not taken up by Dante Germino in his "Second Thoughts on Leo Strauss's Machiavelli."[11] There, with many respectful expressions to both Strauss and Machiavelli, he took issue with the opinion that Machiavelli was an atheist on the basis of a certain "Exhortation to Penitence" composed by Machiavelli, where he too professes to encourage second thoughts. For if God forgave David and Saint Peter, what sins will He not forgive? It was Croce, not Strauss, who naughtily described this exhortation as a "frivolous joke"; but it might be taken more seriously for an early attempt at interpreting Christianity "according to virtue" (*D* II 2), Machiavellian virtue, that is. It is not quite an exhortation, but it is an invitation, to do the things for the doing of which one must be exhorted to penitence.

Robert McShea, in his long but short-winded review,[12] contends that the distinction between exoteric and esoteric doctrine that Strauss claims to discern in Machiavelli applies rather to Strauss's book itself. Strauss's secret teaching is classical natural right, but he chose to ally this with, or express it in, the tradition of religious belief. It is as if one professor of political philosophy might anticipate that another would go to scientists or historians for alliance and support, and decide to secure himself with the aid of the pope's numberless divisions. To adopt that policy one would have to give the pope's army at least a glance of assessment, and apart from this, it may fairly be observed that Strauss's book is salted with remarks against modern religiosity that are hardly compatible with detente, much less alliance. His esotericism, or reserve, is designed to force his readers through a process of learning in which the most meticulous attention to detail is required for the highest flights of speculation, and almost nothing is made available without effort on their part.

McShea's attempt to turn Strauss against himself has been repeated and developed in a serious appraisal by Claude Lefort.[13] While praising Strauss for his attention to the problem of reading Machiavelli, Lefort claims to have found a contradiction between Strauss's high esteem for Machiavelli as a philosopher and his assumption that everything in Machiavelli's works is planned. The assumption implies that philosophy is a teaching and the philosopher a master, but precisely according to the classical tradition, philosophy cannot be understood as an artificial product of the philosopher. It is necessary to suppose, in accordance with Strauss's own exposition of Machiavelli's own exposition of his methods, that the contradiction is deliberate and that Strauss has put a teaching in Machiavelli's mouth in order to prepare a return to his own classical teaching. But Lefort overlooks Strauss's emphasis on the necessity of an ascent, and he confuses what a philosopher arranges for his readers, which is his artifice, with what he recognizes for himself and asks his readers to recognize, which is not. Strauss speaks of the "charm of competence" that Machiavelli imparts,[14] the charm one sees dimly reflected in what certain scholars say "we know." The art of *Thoughts on Machiavelli* is designed to combat this charm by showing that after "human craft and malignity have attained what they can attain" (*D* II 5), the questions of the classical political philosophers remain. This "teaching" is the consequence of subjecting Machiavelli's every word to the assumption that he means it.

Yet when these criticisms have been recounted and others noted, it remains a fact that Strauss has for the most part received the silent treatment from the scholarly community. Strauss recommends silence as the most effective way for a wise man to show his disapproval of the common opinion,[15] but the talkative common opinion falls silent only when it is at a loss. Even the Italians have been silent; or especially they, for they are anxious possessors of the historians' historical Machiavelli. When Gennaro Sasso edited *The Prince* in 1963, he noted Machiavelli's use of the story of David and Goliath to illustrate the need for making war with one's own arms, and remarked that it was "surely singular" for Machiavelli in his version to have provided David with a knife to go with his sling, when the lesson is the value of one's own arms (not to mention what the Bible says), but Strauss in his interpretation of the example had produced results that were "absolutely unacceptable" (*assolutamente inaccettabili*).[16] In 1972, however, Sasso relented so far as to say that the complicated exegesis of this interpreter, intelligent but controversial (*discutabile*) deserved at least to be refuted.[17] But if Machiavelli scholars had read Kendall's enthusiastic review, they would have been chilled by his insouciant remark that in order to come to terms with this book, it was necessary to kiss goodbye to six month's of one's life.[18] That is too long for a digestion or for a vacation or even for a conversion.

It might be urged that the silent treatment for Strauss is just revenge for his silence on present-day scholarship. For Strauss mentions only three scholars by name: Jacob Burckhardt of the nineteenth century, who will now be forever famous less for his interpretation of the Renaissance than for his remark that philology used to like to embarrass theology with the distinction between *animo* and *anima*; William H. Prescott, also of the nineteenth century, to which far-off time Strauss went in search of "a historian who is well-known for his strict adherence to moral principle," who could then be quoted in a statement destructive of moral principle; and Mr. A. H. McDonald of Clare College, Cambridge, who helpfully, perhaps incautiously, vouches for the fact that it was once common knowledge that Livy's *History* consisted of 142 books.[19]

Yet as I have implied, Strauss is far from silent on Machiavelli scholarship. When all the various allusions have been collected to "the observations of a modern critic," to "the many writers" who have called Machiavelli a pagan, to "certain scholars" who believe that every difficulty vanishes once one assumed that Machiavelli is copying Polybius, to the "more sophisticated views which are set forth by the learned of our age," to "the modern historian" who disposes of an immense apparatus supplying him with information that can be easily appropriated because it is superficial, and so on,[20] it may well appear that Strauss's only fault in scholarly courtesy was an inability to remember names. In *Thoughts on Machiavelli* he treats the following issues in the scholarly literature directly and at some length: whether Machiavelli was a philosopher, the relation between *The Prince* and the *Discourses on Livy*, the meaning of *virtù*, the problem of Chapter 26 of *The Prince*, Machiavelli's relationship with Lorenzo de' Medici, the question of Machiavelli's own desire for office, and the places of Tacitus and of Polybius in Machiavelli's thought. Of course, he also raises issues of his own, but in raising his own issues, he does not ignore those raised by others. On the contrary, he relates them to his own understanding and answers them when he can.

Strauss, then, accepts the distinction between Machiavellism and Machiavelli, but believes it necessary to begin with Machiavellism in order to ascend from it. But how should one ascend? If one suspects that Machiavellism has distorted Machiavelli, one must test the suspicion by attempting to take an undistorted view of Machiavelli. Since Machiavelli is most helpful when he is making his own choices and developing his own designs, one must look for his intention. His intention is most visible not in his actions or writings as Florentine secretary, where he is subject to others, but in his books, especially, or rather only, in the two books in which he claims to have presented everything he knows, *The Prince* and the *Discourses on Livy*. These books have a special status and are to be read each by itself without any reference whatever to anything outside them, except in pursuit of Machiavelli's intended meaning and under his direction. Any reference to what Machiavelli must have meant because of some external circumstance unrecognized by him will prevent an undistorted view of Machiavelli's meaning and will impose the interpreter's view instead, so that the whole inquiry results merely in another Machiavellism. It would be foolish to deny oneself the aid of historical knowledge in understanding Machiavelli's allusions and stories, and to overlook other writings of his that might confirm one's interpretation; but it is futile to make one's understanding of Machiavelli's intention depend on them.

In examining these two books, one sees immediately that they are, and are said to be, written on sensitive topics, introducing "new modes and orders" in face of the "envious nature of men" and advising suspicious princes who are rightly suspicious of ambitious advisers. One must then infer that even where Machiavelli is most himself, he is subject to others or subject to the necessity of using others to further his design. He will have to be careful in communicating that design to say neither too much nor too little. But one can legitimately ask: does he have a design or an intention? He surely says that he has a design in the dedications to both *The Prince* and the *Discourses,* more openly in the latter. Whether he has a design, whether it extends as far as Strauss believes, and whether any human being can have intended so much are matters to be resolved as we look for evidence of his intention, and must not be foreclosed prior to inquiry. One cannot prove that Machiavelli has an intention until one has discovered what it is, nor can one deny that he has a consistent intention until one has surely failed to find it. Therefore Strauss's refutation is an urgent necessity, which must not be postponed for one minute, even if it threatens to take six months to accomplish. One cannot say that the refutation has even begun, because as far as I know, among hundreds of statements in *Thoughts on Machiavelli* susceptible to mistake, not one single mistake has yet been exposed.

Following these necessities, Strauss made a careful inspection of *The Prince* and the *Discourses,* looking for an intention that one would expect to be only partly visible in broad daylight. The phrase "in broad daylight" occurs four times in *Thoughts on Machiavelli,* if I am not mistaken. Since Strauss always claimed to be an empirical social scientist, he did not overlook the "little things" that might seem to be mindless accidents, though he stressed that they became meaningful only in relation to large things. In attending to "little things" he was taking a hint from Machiavelli. For in *Discourses* III

33, Machiavelli praises a Roman consul for not despising the *cose piccole* by which the intentions of the gods are discerned, or should we say interpreted and bent to suit human, political designs; but he also praises Livy for putting these words in the mouth of the consul, and thus suggests that authors too can leave auspices of their meaning. Strauss took his cue also from Machiavelli's remark that Livy indicates his opinion by failing to mention something when one would expect him to mention that thing;[21] it is possible, then, for an author to contrive a pregnant silence, and make it distinguishable from doltish silence. Strauss says and shows that Machiavelli's use of Livy is the key to his plan in the *Discourses,* which is a longer and more leisurely work than *The Prince.* The plan of *The Prince* is made more obvious by its subject-matter to suit the requirements of the busy executive.

Strauss also takes note of a chapter in the *Discourses* on manifest blunders (III 48). Machiavelli says there that when an enemy makes a great error, one should believe that some deceit lies hidden underneath; then in illustrating this maxim, Machiavelli makes a manifest blunder by giving an example in which an enemy did not make a manifest blunder. It is, I believe, a fact that no scholar before Strauss has ever recorded his suspicion that a deceit of Machiavelli's might lie underneath this manifest blunder. One scholar, Father L. J. Walker, S.J., a pre-Straussian commentator of some considerable innocence whose invaluable edition of the *Discourses* shows how far innocence can go, has compiled a list of Machiavelli's mistakes, totaling twenty-three.[22] The list is much too long because every one of them can be explained as a manifest blunder deliberately contrived by a deceitful enemy (or does your friend sometimes deceive you?), and it is also much too short because it fails to count the hundreds of manifest blunders in *The Prince* and the *Discourses,* including the one just alluded to.

Although Strauss cannot fully prove that Machiavelli has an intention until he can prove what it is, he can at least offer incontrovertible evidence, with each item of regularity where one does not expect to see signs of human intent, that something mysterious exists to be explained. One reviewer had the courage to dismiss the fact that Machiavelli's *Discourses* has the same number of chapters as Livy's *History* (142) as a "curious coincidence."[23] But he had to admit it was a *curious* coincidence, and he did not test his courage on the many, or so to speak infinite, other coincidences that Strauss found and left to be found. Indeed, it is more prudent not to admit any curiosities, as most scholars have prudently or instinctively recognized, because just one instance of hidden intention, no matter what the hidden intention is supposed to be, is enough to show that Strauss was on the right track as he read Machiavelli, whatever his mistakes, and all other scholars wandering at a loss, whatever their insights or discoveries.

Consider this example of scholarly prudence. In *Discourses* I 13, Machiavelli discourses on how the Romans used religion to stop tumults, among other things. In example, he cites the tumults over the Terentillian law, proposed to limit the power of the consuls, and remarks that on one occasion they were stopped when "one Publius Ruberius, a grave citizen of authority, came out of the Senate and with words partly loving, partly menacing, pointed out to them the dangers to the city," and got the plebs to swear not to depart from the wish of the consul. Now the trouble is that the grave citizen's name according to Livy was Publius Valerius, not Publius Ruberius, and Machiavelli in fact names him correctly in the next sentence. Walker, the pre-Straussian commentator, looked high and low in the annals of the Roman republic to find "Publius Ruberius," and reports his failure. Strauss offhandedly suggested translating "Publius Ruberius" into Italian, by which it becomes "public robber." Two post-Straussian commentators, Sergio Bertelli and Mario Puppo, who are well acquainted with Walker's commentary and not afraid to borrow from it, pass over this difficulty in silence.[24]

Although Machiavelli scholars permit themselves most of the human indulgences, there is one rule of sobriety they observe with monastic strictness: never laugh! If they laugh just once, it may be because the preacher told a joke, and if he told a joke, how can he be a preacher? The obverse of the rule, never look for serious intent in Machiavelli's comedies, is not so well observed, possibly because of the difficulty of retelling jokes. It may be suggested, however, that no paragraph in *The Prince* and the *Discourses* has been understood until you have found something funny in it. If you are not in more or less constant amusement when reading Machiavelli's books, you should consider yourself bewildered. This is not to say that Machiavelli's true meaning is a joke; it is rather that Machiavelli sees grave things as ridiculous because they are manipulable by men, and yet grave because they answer human necessities. In one of his objections to the modern reliance on cavalry, he compares this situation to a spirited horse ridden by a cowardly man, or a cowardly horse by a spirited man (*D* II 18). This remark becomes more and more funny the longer one thinks about it.

Two objections to Strauss's way of discovering Machiavelli's intention were made by most of the reviewers. First, they said it was ingenious, but the ingenuity was Strauss's, not Machiavelli's. And second, they said that Machiavelli was admittedly and obviously a bold writer who was placed on the Index and persecuted with the evil reputation of Machiavellism for his boldness; so it would have been superfluous for him to conceal what he did not scruple to say aloud.[25]

If Strauss's ingenuity is merely his own, it ought to be possible to uncover it in the same way that he claims to have uncovered Machiavelli's. Discrepancies like those between Machiavelli's text and the original in Livy should be detectable between Strauss's text and the Machiavellian original. Such discrepancies are easy to find once one begins to look for them, and correspondingly difficult to conceal if one wished to do so. Anyone who thinks it possible to exercise his ingenuity with a consistent interpretation of an inconsistent text, and not be caught, should demonstrate that he can do it. The posture of dull honesty recoiling in shock and bewilderment before Strauss's diabolical cleverness is not sufficient to convince. Nonetheless, I will content myself with one example of a Straussian ingenuity. At one point Strauss says that Machiavelli imitates Brutus, "who, in order to liberate his fatherland, played the fool by speaking, seeing and doing things against his opinion, and thus pleased the prince." In Machiavelli's text (*D* III 2), Brutus is said to play the fool by praising, speaking, seeing, and doing things against his opinion. Strauss omitted "praising," I suppose, in order to bring "seeing" to our attention as of central importance[26] and perhaps to suggest that Machiavelli saw things against his opinion to please the prince.

Machiavelli is bold, but as Strauss says, his boldness is always muted.[27] His boldness consists in seeking new modes and orders, but that is a dangerous enterprise requiring caution. When he finds new modes and orders, or rather when he communicates them, he encounters the envy of those who begrudge him the glory of a founder, of a new prince. That is the reason for caution that Machiavelli gives at the beginning of the *Discourses on Livy*, where he speaks of the envious nature of men (*D* I pr). But in *The Prince* he says that the introducer of new orders faces the partisan zeal of those who defend the laws because they believe they benefit from them (*P* 6). The envy of rival princes and the indignation of frightened peoples are the obstacles in Machiavelli's way. But where is he going and how far? Is he one who scoffs at the moral and the pious, an anticleric critical of the Church and the pope and of the credulous who support them? Or do *new modes and orders* imply a much more fundamental intention, an *appropriation* and not merely a criticism of Christianity?

Just how far his boldness extends is the question that *Thoughts on Machiavelli* chiefly considers. The Machiavelli scholars have made Machiavelli a harbinger of modernity by presenting him either as scientist or as patriot, Strauss says.[28] As scientist, he did not develop a methodology that would enable him to be ranked among the founders of modern science; and as patriot, his loyalty was divided between Florence and Italy, not to mention wider multitudes, so that his intention is reduced to his influence, thus dissipated, in Italian history. On both counts he is summed up as the man who said that he loved his fatherland more than his own soul. Strauss has shown, however, how unwise it is to assume that Machiavelli's fatherland was anything less than the world which human beings acquire for themselves and that Machiavelli had not reflected on what made his soul less dear to him than his fatherland.

At the end of *Thoughts on Machiavelli* Strauss asks what essential defect in classical political philosophy could have made Machiavelli's enterprise seem reasonable, and he answers on a seemingly narrow ground. Even the ancients had to admit, he says, that the good city could not remain indifferent to the state of military technology and might have to subordinate its goodness and its concern for the soul to the requirements of self-defense. One of Strauss's friendly reviewers, Carl J. Friedrich, objected: "But is this merely a question of weapons? What about propaganda, for example, or subversive activities?"[29] Yet Strauss had developed the analogy between weapons of ordinary warfare and weapons of spiritual warfare of which Machiavelli made such elaborate use. In stating the ground of difference between ancients and moderns so narrowly, Strauss was indicating how the ascent from Machiavellism to Machiavelli must continue as an ascent from Machiavelli.

FOUR

# MACHIAVELLI'S
# POLITICS

$M$achiavelli's political science has not received the attention it deserves. All commentators are attracted, with a force they often seem not to understand, by the question of his notion of virtue: is it a compromise with evil or is it innocent? So stark a formulation is not usual, but the sophisticated attempts to evade that question end up by coming back to it or by assuming some answer to it. I too began with Machiavelli's virtue. But after concluding that it does indeed compromise with evil for the sake of political success, one needs to know how the compromise is fashioned and how success is to be achieved. What is the political science of Machiavelli's politicized virtue?

Unfortunately the *classical republican* interpretation of Machiavelli offers little help. Despite the name, it is preoccupied with Machiavelli's morality and almost unconcerned with his politics. The classical republican view does not offer a sophisticated excuse for Machiavelli's little divergences from the straight and narrow path of strict virtue. It supposes, in its supersophistication, that Machiavelli's republican virtue amounts to unsophisticated self-sacrifice to the common good. How Machiavelli's republic actually *works*—which is not so different from the working of his principality—is, in this view, of little interest.

Yet Machiavelli's wonderful innovations—his new modes and orders—are in his political science. One of them is indeed the sacrifice of a self, but it is an involuntary sacrifice of a scapegoat whose sensational execution makes everyone except him feel virtuous. Accusations precede executions, and elections are a kind of accusation by which the candidate is first humiliated, then released for public service. Republics thrive on emergencies and should avoid too much respectable stability. To deal with emergencies they need dictators, and to deal with dictators, they need counterdictators. Their "orders" are distinct from illegal or extraordinary modes and yet originate in the resort to such modes. The only way they know how to live is dangerously.

The animating principle of Machiavelli's political science is to get people to impose harsh necessities on themselves, so that the government can escape responsibility. A self-inflicted wound hurts less than one done to you by someone else, he remarks. When one thinks about this principle, is it not the basis of modern, democratic, representative government? Our government gets the people to tax and punish itself. Does one have to be a cynic to see that an elected government is a kind of self-inflicted wound? Machiavelli was not a cynic; he expected great progress from his innovations. Nonetheless, his specialty was uncomfortable truth, his own effectual truth. From his political science we can learn the effectual truth not so much of the politics of his time as of ours. He was hostile to his time but a founder of ours. The modern impersonal state, seemingly so different from Machiavelli's personal *stato,* works on his principle and uses his manipulative devices. Machiavelli is no longer a discernible influence on us under his own name; books on how to succeed in business that mention him use his name, not his wisdom, but his wisdom is all around us.

Machiavelli's political science leaves room for, and gives evidence of, his own politics. It describes his own principality and the republic to which he is devoted. Like the argument of design proving the existence of God, only more seductively, the indirect government described by Machiavelli's political science suggests the presence of a master manipulator behind the scene that is revealed behind the scenes. Our brave liberalism assures us that we are in charge of our self-government. But just to be sure we are not deluded, here is another conspiracy theory to check out.

# TEN

# MACHIAVELLI'S
# NEW REGIME

In the preface to the first book of the *Discourses on Livy,* Machiavelli says that he is bringing "new modes and orders," a new regime, to men. That regime is far more than a collection of the pungent Machiavellisms that frighten and delight Machiavelli's readers. Although not presented systematically, it is in fact a system of a new type that I shall call indirect government, which was intended to oppose the classical understanding of the regime that prevailed in his day. Although Machiavelli had his eye on the troubles of Italy and Florence, he was prompted, he said, by a "natural desire" to bring "common benefit to each" in his new regime. It is based on a new view of the natural classes or "orders" of men that underlie all regimes and on a borrowed insight into the importance of punishment in government. As preparation for the main point, therefore, I shall briefly consider the classical understanding of the regime and the two preliminary stages of Machiavelli's attack on it. Machiavelli begins to present his new regime in the *Discourses* when he discusses the Roman institution of accusation, an institution not important in itself but characteristic, as one learns, of Roman government as a whole. My method will be to follow Machiavelli's method and to show how the orders of the new regime emerge from a careful examination of accusation.

## THE CLASSICAL REGIME

Machiavelli opposed his idea of indirect government to the direct government of the regime (*politeia*) as presented in the political sci-

This chapter was originally published as "Machiavelli's New Regime," *Italian Quarterly* 13 (1970): 63–95.

ence of Plato and Aristotle and their tradition. The classical notion
of the regime is most easily available in the third book of Aristotle's
*Politics* and was known to Machiavelli from Livy and Polybius as
well.[1] According to this notion, the regime is the rule of the whole
of any society by a part of that society, which by its rule, gives
that society its particular character. Men can live together in many
different ways, but *these* men live in *this* way because, by choice or
accident, they are kept to this way by the more powerful among
them. Since men are variable and no one regime is dictated unambig-
uously by nature, societies must be made to cohere by legislation.
The group—whether one, few, or many—that has made and can
remake the laws, customs, and beliefs of a society, is responsible
for the particular way in which this society coheres. Thus the most
important question to ask about any society is: who rules? When
that question is answered, one has learned the ordering principle of
the society, for rulers make laws that conform to their rule. Some
rule is indispensable to human society, and rulers try to make *their*
rule indispensable to this society by forming the society so that it
respects and needs them.

Ruling shows itself, therefore, in the most open and public ways.
Since the ruling part of every society is the most powerful part of
the society, it is the most *visible* part. It *is* the public, for the public
is what shows, and what shows is the power that does not need to
hide. Of course, in every society hidden powers exist that may affect
or even for a time determine the rule of the society, but the reason
these powers remain hidden is that they are weaker than the power
that does not have to hide. The "grey eminence" is weaker than the
king whose open majesty he uses and needs, and assuming that he
wished to improve his power, he would make himself king if he
could. In every established society, according to the classical notion
of the regime, the most respected power is the most powerful and
vice versa; and in a revolutionary situation, groups are fighting to
become the public power. Classical political science takes the fact
about any society that is most obvious to any member or observer
of the society, who rules, and designates it the most important fact.
It considers most important what seems most important to the citizen or statesman.

Machiavelli proposed to replace this notion of direct government with indirect government carried on by a hidden power. In-

stead of ruling in open light, government would be "management." Machiavelli speaks frequently of "managing" (*maneggiare*) men in the up-to-date, business-school sense of the term: ruling without seeming to. Management is not merely a clever improvement on direct government; it is made necessary by the division of men into two different natural orders. Some men, Machiavelli says, love to master other men; others only want not to be dominated and to live in security with wife and property (*D* I 4, 5; *P* 9, 19; *FH* III 1). He agrees with Aristotle that the regime, the ruling part, forms society, and does not accept the present-day opinion first advanced by the theorists of representative government that politics takes the shape of the society.

Machiavelli was too sensitive to the virtue of political men to use the passive verb of sociology. Yet he believed that the division of human beings into political and nonpolitical men, princes, and peoples precedes every political opportunity or decision. The regime forms society, but every regime is constituted by the natural political order, the princes. All politics is traceable directly to the nature of some men, not to an act of legislation by the regime, as for Aristotle. One cannot characterize a society by seeking to identify its legislators, because the legislators have the same nature in every society. Aristotle said that man is by nature a political animal, from which it follows that one cannot explain from human nature the presence, in a certain time and place, of a certain kind of politics.[2] But for Machiavelli, only some few men are political, and they rule in every regime, whatever it is called. The people do not wish to rule, and when they seem to rule, they are being managed by their leaders. They are matter without form, body without head. Since they cannot rule, the regime is always the rule of a prince or princes; it is not the settled primacy of one of the three formal groups in society (one, few, or the many) by a political act.

In the second chapter of the *Discourses,* as we have seen in chapter 3, Machiavelli shows the inadequacy of the traditional three-fold (or sixfold) classification of regimes. The regime is indeed constituted by a political act, the founding, but always by the same natural group or party, the princes, the few, each of whom tries "to be alone" (*D* I 9, 18). Hence the founding merely expresses the nature of founders, and not the particular character of those who happened to be founders of a particular regime. The fundamental fact for Aristotle, who rules, is political; for Machiavelli, that same fact is merely natural. But since Machiavelli agrees that politics is too varied to be determined by human nature, the fundamental fact for him cannot be *who* rules. Instead, it is *how* the princes rule. When nature determines the character of political men, and hence the end of politics, the varieties of politics must arise from differences in technique. Yet there is only one technique, corresponding to the one natural political order, the technique of management. The differences must then be accounted to the "times" or "the degree of corruption" in this particular society (*D* III 8, 9). With all his appreciation for quick, ruthless action in politics, Machiavelli is forced to anticipate the passive, gradual, and constricted politics of present-day social science because he saw the political end as the fulfillment of a political nature in some men, not in man as such.

The people do not wish to be ruled, but for their own good they need to be ruled. The end they desire, security, cannot be achieved by the passivity with which they enjoy that end. Security comes only with acquisition, not in enjoyment after acquisition but in the continuous acquisition of this world's goods before one's brother or neighbor can take them first or take them from you. Restless "virtue" in Machiavelli's sense, repulsive to the people and unappreciated by them, is the condition of their desire to be left to live as they please. The necessity of acquisition makes possible a common good between the two naturally disparate orders of men. When a founder makes a regime entirely anew so as to acquire the highest glory for himself, he incidentally gives the people their heart's desire, so far as it is attainable. Although he cannot bring them peace, he can establish relative security and overshadow their fear of natural evils with artificial fear of the laws and the gods. Security is achieved for those who want it by those who scorn it.

As "human things are in motion," (*D* I 6) a political founding is never permanent and security is never assured. One founder must be succeeded by another, and in the economy of human goods it is fortunate that the acquisitive nature of the princes matches the need of men to acquire continuously. But since "acquisitive" means "acquisitive for oneself," the problem of rewarding the acquisitive class arises: How can one satisfy the desire for glory that moves princes to be acquisitive, and thus makes peoples secure, without endangering that security? The princes serve the foremost human need, but they serve it for themselves, neither for the people nor for humanity at large. They must be rewarded and they must also be controlled.

## REWARDING PRINCES

The method of rewarding princes cannot be simply according to their deserts, or with justice. A state that adheres to a policy of justice makes few friends and many enemies. It makes enemies of all who might benefit from injustice. At the same time, it does not make friends of those whom it rewards, for no one admits that he is obliged to anyone for honors and benefits that he deserves. Just as a student who writes an excellent paper is not grateful for receiving an excellent grade, a prince collects his rewards with complacency rather than humility because he thinks he has earned them. Moreover, no man is so modest about his own merits as to think he is not entitled to security for himself, his property and his wife and children. Since no one is thankful for receiving his due, justice cannot be the source of trust or obligation. The just state might not need the gratitude of its friends if it did not, by its very justice, create so many enemies and if it were not liable, whatever its justice, to attack from enemies it has not created. But, given the fateful disproportion between the friends that justice attracts and the enemies it makes or fails to win over, the just state cannot afford to be satisfied with the cool acknowledgment of the man who has been justly treated (*D* I 16, 18).

In rewarding princes, then, something must be added to simple justice—which means in effect that something must be subtracted from simple justice. This could be either favor or severity, and Machiavelli chooses the latter. The state that rewards by a system of favoritism discourages meritorious princes and loses the acquisitions they bring. Those who are not favored become enemies to the regime, and those who are favored come to expect their favor as a matter of right. They grow arrogant and ungrateful to the dispenser of rewards. These favorites behave in the way that just men duly rewarded come to behave; for Machiavelli, having shown that justice must be supplemented either by favor or by severity, takes this opportunity to suggest that the cool acknowledgment of the man who has been justly rewarded is soon replaced by an arrogant presumption of reward and by heated resentment when it is denied. No state

240 MACHIAVELLI'S POLITICS

can be perfect in its justice, but the man who is used to receiving justice will not only expect it but will also be impatient with any lapse from perfection in the system of delivery, at least in his own case. Favoritism is the "effectual truth" of justice, because too much merit has the same effect as too much presumption. Thus Machiavelli praises the example of Junius Brutus, the founder of the Roman republic, who in an access of statesmanship killed his own sons to prove that the new regime would not allow favoritism (D I 18; III 1, 3, 5, 6). Since it is unwise to fall short of justice by favoritism, it is necessary to exceed it by severity.

Severity in the rewarding of princes requires the use of punishment. Machiavelli says that no well-ordered republic cancels the demerits with the merits of its citizens. For example, the Romans deserve blame for having acquitted Horatius of the murder of his sister because of his service to Rome in overcoming the champions of the Albans. Moreover, if one considers that the meritorious man will or may become arrogant, it is necessary to anticipate possible demerits in the future when rewarding men for past services. Therefore, while it is useful to reward merit when that merit helps you, it is necessary not to reward it fully and to keep everyone, not only the unjust but also those whom you anticipate may become unjust, under the fear of punishment. Fear of punishment will produce gratitude, for when a man believes that he may suffer punishment, despite his merits or services, then he will be grateful if he does not suffer it. A justly rewarded man is not grateful, but a citizen who fears punishment, even *unjust* punishment, is grateful for justice when he gets it. His fear makes him value his rewards and obliges him to the giver of rewards (D I 24, 28–32; II 23).

In terms of the professor grading students' papers, the prince or republic makes no friends by grading an A paper with an A. He could make friends by giving a B paper an A, but this is expensive and arouses envy. It is much better to give an A paper a B—not usually, but occasionally. Then the A student will be grateful for his A when he gets it. In the full knowledge that perfection is impossible—for even the best hero may murder his sister—the state must punish every lapse from perfection regardless of previous services. "What have you done lately?" is the demand of Machiavelli's policy; and the meaning is, "What can you do now?" To repeat: the state must reward according to merit as a rule; but it must also learn to depart from merit on occasion, for gratitude draws its power from fear. Prudence consists in knowing when and how to depart from justice in the management of rewards and punishments. One may surmise that Machiavelli found this idea in "the present religion," as he once referred to Christianity, where men are held to a standard of perfection so that remission for their sins replaces rewards for their good deeds.

## PUNISHING PRINCES

In the *Discourses* Machiavelli first discusses punishment in regard to accusation and calumny, at the end of the section of chapters on parties and the regime (I 2–8). The seventh and eighth chapters on accusation and calumny are explicitly connected with each other and with the sixth chapter, to show that they belong to this section. In the titles, Machiavelli says that accusation is necessary to keeping a republic free, while calumny is as pernicious to a republic as accusation is useful. Accusation is the power of the guardians of liberty in a city to bring charges before the people or some magistrate or council against citizens who "sin" against free government, and calumny is private slander. It is not at first clear whether a calumny is also a lie or a false charge, for the emphasis is on its delivery in private rather than to "authority" (*D* I 7, 8).

To us, it is surprising that political parties should be discussed with accusation and calumnies, or with the more familiar and somewhat narrower institution of impeachment. While parties today are considered essential to the practice and honored in the theory of modern government, impeachment is thought to be a relic from the history of free government at its fighting origin, an early, clumsy, and obsolete weapon against malefactors in office. In a political science textbook today, one would expect to find "parties and elections" discussed together, not parties and accusation or impeachment. Machiavelli does not discuss elections as such, but he does discuss ways of gaining the favor of the people. The people grant their favor as a reward for merit or good birth, actual or presumed in both regards (*D* I 18). Election is a kind of reward, whereas accusation is a kind of punishment. But since Machiavelli believes that punishment is more fundamental than reward, it seems reasonable for him, when treating political parties, to discuss accusation rather than elections.

Accusation is a kind of legal punishment, as opposed to calumny. Machiavelli says that a law providing for accusation, by forcing calumniators to make their charges in public, will prevent them and their victims from pursuing private revenge and from making a consequent appeal to the "outside forces" of foreigners. But in developing his argument, he shifts attention from the good effects of legality in itself to the way in which the legal punishment is enforced. He says that this law has two very useful effects for a republic: first, by fear of being accused, men do not attempt anything against the state, or if they do, they are put down instantly and without respect; second, it is a way of purging humors that arise in cities against a certain citizen. Then he gives two Roman examples to show the success of this law, the trial of Coriolanus and the imprisonment of Manlius. Neither Coriolanus nor Manlius was affected in the least by fear of accusation; neither was put down instantly; and both were treated with the respect of their noble rank. If they had been put down instantly or treated like ordinary criminals, their punishment would not have served to purge the humors of the people against a particular citizen. In the case of Coriolanus, we can reflect (for Machiavelli does not say) that the law failed completely, because after he was exiled to the Volsci, he led them against Rome in a marvelous invasion that nearly succeeded (D I 7, 29; III 13). Machiavelli tells of this event much later in the *Discourses* without reference to the law on accusation. It was the Tribunes, who had been created by the Senate and whose authority Coriolanus opposed, that saved him from the mob. Not only did the law of accusation prove dangerously lenient, but it also had to be invoked by the very Tribunes who would have profited in this case from its absence.

In the example of Manlius, the law was not used at all. Manlius was envious of the honor and glory awarded to Camillus, whose services to Rome (he believed) were no greater than his, but more recent. Unable to remain quiet or to show discord in the Senate, he spread word among the people that a certain treasure gathered from the people had been taken by private citizens for their own use. To check this calumny, the Senate appointed a dictator to conduct a public investigation. The dictator appeared with the nobles to confront Manlius, appearing with the plebs; and he asked Manlius which private citizen held the public treasure Manlius had said was hidden. Failing to name a specific culprit, Manlius was put in prison, Machiavelli says.

This praiseworthy result was effected by an arrangement similar to accusation; so accusation proper does not seem to be necessary. Machiavelli also shows this by varying his estimation of accusation. In the heading of Chapter 7, he promises to inquire "how much accusation in a republic is necessary to maintain liberty." He immediately pronounces that it has "most useful" effects, then warily asserts he has shown "how much it is useful and necessary" and blames the "bad orders" of a city, not merely the lack of accusation, for an appeal to outside forces. He says that Florence lacked "such methods" as accusation. At the end of Chapter 7 and in the heading of Chapter 8, he allows merely that accusation is "useful." Then he says that this matter was well ordered in Rome and badly ordered in Florence; if Florence had had an arrangement (*ordine*) for accusing citizens and punishing calumniators, "countless troubles would not have followed that did follow" (D I 8).

Accusation, then, is more an order or arrangement than a precise law. It depends on enforcement by prudent princes whose prudence seems very unobtrusive. It was invoked against Coriolanus by the Tribunes, who had been created by the Senate; and it was used against Manlius by a dictator, also appointed by the Senate. It is not incidental to note that in both cases, the Senate had something to gain or nothing to lose from either the actual or the alternative result. If Coriolanus had won his campaign against the Tribunes, the Senate would have profited from their defeat, just as it actually profited from the removal of a troublesome man of ambition. If Manlius had pointed out a private citizen who appropriated public treasure, this citizen and perhaps the dictator would have suffered punishment, but not the Senate. As it was, the Senate was again rid of a trouble-maker and excused from a more searching investigation of his "calumnies" against "private citizens," who in fact were Senators.[3] By varying his judgment on the specific necessity of accusation, and by dwelling on the prudent management of accusation, Machiavelli suggests how important is the enforcement of accusation and also reflects, in his own rhetoric, the unobtrusiveness of that enforcement.

In the case of Manlius, Machiavelli, as it were, leaves the enforcement incomplete. He says that "the Dictator had put him in prison" and at the end of the chapter he says blandly that when charges turn out untrue, calumniators "should be punished as Manlius was punished."[4] Only later (I 24) are we reminded how Manlius was finally punished: "he was without any respect for his meritorious actions thrown from that Capitol which before, with so much glory to himself, he had saved."[5] We see first that the power of accusation "without respect" (mentioned in I 7) refers not merely to respect for noble rank but more generally to respect for debts of gratitude (D I pr, 8, 52; III 35). Since the Romans properly punished misdeeds without respect for previous good deeds, their punitive justice contained a proper dose of ingratitude.

### EXTRAORDINARY MEANS

It is more surprising that the dramatic and definitive nature of Manlius's punishment was withheld, for Machiavelli is not always reserved about the use of "extraordinary means."[6] The reason for his reticence in I 7–8, however, can be seen in the understanding of punishment he wishes to develop. At first, accusation seems to have the advantages of deterring attempts against the state and of allowing the purging of humors against a single citizen by legal means. Legal means proceed "ordinarily" as opposed to "extraordinary means." "Oppression" of such a citizen by ordinary means causes little or no disorder because "the execution is done without private forces and without foreign forces." This remark pays no attention to the justice of any particular "oppression," but still it only hints at the turn to come. Machiavelli says that much "novelty" would have been avoided in Florence if such a man as Francesco Valori could have been stopped by ordinary means, for the extraordinary means used against him killed him and many other noble citizens besides. Ordinary means would have killed him alone, like Manlius, and perhaps in an extraordinary way too. Accusation is an ordinary means of keeping order in a republic, but it issues in extraordinary punishments.

Machiavelli's strange use of the distinction between ordinary and extraordinary means in Chapter 7 is explained by his pregnant reserve regarding Manlius's punishment in Chapter 8. Ordinary means include occasionally extraordinary demonstrations; indeed, they seem to conclude in such demonstrations. Machiavelli uses the connection between "order" (*ordine*) and "ordinary" (*ordinario*) to suggest that order is not the rule of the lawful over the unlawful but the result of calculated violence prudently managed (*D* I 7, 8). In a formula, he replaces the distinction between lawful and unlawful with the continuum between ordinary and extraordinary means.[7] This is to bring the perspective of the founder into ordinary political life, for the founder recognizes that he who establishes order is outside or beyond order, in that sense "extraordinary." The ordinary, law-abiding citizen, on the other hand, merely lives with the difference between lawful and unlawful, and does not reflect on the dubious means by which the lawful was created. For a citizen, the lawful determines what is unlawful, but for a prudent prince, extraordinary means make possible ordinary means. "Manlian severity" in the sense of severity to Manlius should set the tone of punishment by accusation, for in the other ancient example, the law on accusation did not prevent the return of Coriolanus, and Rome barely survived.

Florence had no ordinary way of allowing humors against a single citizen to be purged, and so its purging involved partisanship. In the example of Coriolanus in *D* I 7, Machiavelli refers to "purging of the anger [*ira*] that the generality [*universalità*] conceives against one citizen." When he comes to the case of Florence, he says that "the multitude [*moltitudine*] was not able to purge its anger [*animo*] ordinarily against a single citizen." Since purging was impossible in an ordinary way, "many other noble citizens" besides Valori were killed. If Rome had not had ordinary means of purging, and had suppressed Coriolanus "in a tumult," each one may judge how much evil would have resulted to the republic: "for from that arises offense by private individuals to private individuals, which offense generates fear; fear seeks for defense; for defense they procure partisans; from partisans arise the parties in cities; from parties their ruin" (*D* I 7). So soon after the praise of partisanship in *D* I 4–6 does Machiavelli admit the dangers traditionally ascribed to it. How may they be avoided?

In the trial of Coriolanus, the "universality" purged its anger. Machiavelli had said that accusation provides a way of purging the humors that arise in cities against a single citizen. These humors, as regards Rome, are not the diverse partisan humors of the nobles and the people that he spoke of before (*D* I 4–5). Although Coriolanus was "an enemy to the popular faction" and wished "to punish" (*gastigare*) the plebs, the issue did not become (according to Machiavelli) a partisan conflict involving the desire of the great to dominate and the desire of the people not to be dominated. Instead, the result was apparently a universal purging in which both parties, mixing or forgetting their diverse humors, turned their anger on Coriolanus. Livy reports the episode as more of a partisan conflict, the Senate proceeding to Coriolanus's trial in a united body and the Tribunes perhaps guilty of having excited the popular exasperation that they then directed to legal punishment of Coriolanus. But Livy remarks that the anger of the plebs was such "that the senators were obliged to extricate themselves from the danger by the punishment of one."[8] This seems to be Machiavelli's recommendation as well: replace the anger of the many against the few with the anger of all against one alone. Popular anger, which is normally directed against those who wish to dominate the people, can be managed when it is adopted by the nobles and focused against one individual. Such management is included among the "ordinary means" of prudent princes in a republic.

Ordinary means yield to extraordinary remedies, we learn, when calumniators are not required to make public accusations (*D* I 8). Popular anger cannot be focused on an individual unless those who make charges are forced to put up or shut up. When they have been forced to do one or the other, the Senate—that is, the ruling princes—can step quietly to the rear and allow the people to make its choice between accuser and accused. Accusation is a two-edged sword: It may cut accuser or accused, but neither edge cuts the Senate. It becomes clear that accusation is essentially the recourse of a plebeian prince, which is to say a prince out of favor with the rulers.[9] Manlius, despite his noble birth, was driven by envy of Camillus to seek favor among the plebs by spreading calumnies against the Senate. He could not "sow discord among the Fathers" because they were determined to honor Camillus for his more recent benefit to Rome. When a prince is out of favor, he must go to the people like Manlius or else flee the city like Coriolanus. Since Coriolanus had to flee to another city, where he found favor, the only recourse for a prince out of favor is the people. Whether fallen from above or risen from below, the plebeian prince has the nature but not the office of a prince. He can therefore be managed by the ruling princes because, having the same nature and belonging to the same natural order, they know what he wants. He may be adopted into the ruling order, as the Senate adopted plebeian princes to be Tribunes and used them against Coriolanus; or, like Manlius, he may be exposed as a mere rival of the ruling princes rather than a friend of the people.

## INDIRECT GOVERNMENT

Since extraordinary means make possible ordinary means in a republic, they must be legalized. If they are not, good and necessary deeds that are unlawful will become examples to be followed for bad purposes by ambitious men (D I 34, 46). Since it would have been necessary to break the laws for good purposes, it would become excusable to break them for bad purposes. Machiavelli's solution is simply to provide in the laws for extraordinary means that "ordinarily" would be unlawful. Such was his defense of the Roman institution of the dictator, who had power, for a limited term, to find his own remedies and to punish without appeal, but not to take authority from the Senate or people or to make new institutions in the city (D I 34, 35, 40; cf. I 60). Note that the dictator could punish without appeal, that is, without reference to the laws on accusation. From the standpoint of the Senate, he was an accuser who had to make his accusations stand.

In the two Roman examples of accusation (D I 7–8), the accusers were not the Senate but the Tribunes and the dictator. Machiavelli's Roman republic was not ruled by the Senate; it was managed by the Senate. Instead of holding all power directly, the Senate allowed institutions to exist permanently or temporarily that apparently derogated from its authority, like the Tribunes, the Dictator, the Censors, and even the Decemvirs. In fact, these institutions made the position of the Senate more secure by handling emergencies for it. No emergency, Machiavelli well knew, can be resolved merely by referring it to an institution whose name is the Department of Emergencies, for men of routine, wherever placed, produce routine solutions only.[10] A most virtuous prince is required. But given this prince, a republic finds itself in a dilemma between the cure and the disease. Its emergency typically includes the dangerous ambition of the only man who can save it (D I 18, 33, 34; III 3). In this emergency once removed from the first danger, indirect institutions can permit the Senate to use the virtue of an outstanding prince without succumbing to his ambition. His extraordinary intervention does not undermine the laws, and hence the ordinary authority of the Senate, because the laws have been stretched to include him and to limit him. Ordinary authority must bow to extraordinary means in an emergency, and it is better, Machiavelli argues, that this be done legally. He praises the Senate for its willingness to yield to necessity and for its noble condescension in the business of management (D I 37, 38, 51).

We may take as an example the interlude of government by the Decemvirs, presented by Livy and usually accepted by others as a revolution in regime that overturned the government of the Senate.[11] Machiavelli says more mildly in a chapter heading that the creation of the Decemvirate was "harmful to the liberty of the Roman republic," as if the Decemvirate were merely a departure from the ordinary within the system of that republic. Then he contrasts the limited power of the dictator, who could not take power from the Tribunes, Consuls, and Senate, to the greater power of the Decemvirate, "thus finding itself alone, without consuls, without tribunes, without appeal to the people and therefore not having anybody to watch them" (D I 35). So in describing the power of the Decemvirate, he omits the Senate, an unseen watcher. Five chapters later, he again takes up the Decemvirate. In the interval he had described and praised the prudence of the Roman nobility, which was chiefly shown in willingness to put its property above its honor. The Senate habitually yielded names and honors when it had to and tried to keep its property inviolate against plebeian disorders and also against individual nobles who valued glory above all else.

Now he says one will see "many errors made by the Senate and by the plebs not in favor of liberty, and many errors made by Appius, head [capo] of the Decemvirate, not in favor of the tyranny that he had supposed he would establish in Rome" (D I 40). The error of the plebeians, arising from too great a desire to be free, was to suppose that Appius had become one of the popular party while he was attacking the nobles. To attack the nobles with the aid of the people and then to oppress the people is the method of "all those who have founded tyrannies in republics." But Appius did not use this method. He made the "most evident error" of abandoning the people before he had secured himself against the people. His error saved the Roman people from their error, in Machiavelli's neat analysis, which equates the error of inviting tyranny with the error of failing to seize it (Cf. *D* I 52). How had Appius made his error? He betrayed himself by "showing his inborn pride" to the people while he still had need of their friendship. When it came time to reelect the Decemvirs for another year, the nobles, "hesitating to oppose him openly, decided to do it artfully" and gave him authority to propose himself, "a thing not done and disgraceful in Rome." But he named himself among the first, and soon "showed the people and the nobles their error" by reverting to his arrogant nature.[12]

The people's error is clear, but where is the nobles' error? It seems that they, knowing their man, artfully caused Appius to expose himself and to alienate his popular support. At the end of the chapter, Machiavelli says that the people's error was to take away their guard over the magistrates, which was effected partly through the excessive desire of the Senate to be rid of the Tribunes. But in the place where he explains this excessive desire, he shows that the Senate allowed the Decemvirate to stay in power to meet the emergency of war, in which it failed (*D* I 40, 43). The Senate thought, Machiavelli says, that if the Decemvirs resigned voluntarily, the Tribunes might not be restored. Instead, they were expelled and the Tribunes were restored. This "error" is like the previous "error"; it consisted in forcing Appius to make one of two bad choices and wrongly supposing which of the two he would choose. If he proposed himself for reelection, he exposed his design; if he did not, he was out. Similarly, if he remained in power to meet the threat of war, he was responsible for securing a victory while hard pressed at home; if he resigned, he was out and the Senate, having saved Roman liberty, might not have to restore the Tribunes. In the event, the people got the Tribunes back, but they were also glad to have Consuls again. As a whole, the episode of the Decemvirate confirmed the Senate's authority.[13]

The Senate, however, "did not wish to show its authority" (*D* I 40). This was the guiding principle of its prudence. In this case, it made a puppet of the arrogant Appius, and soon after, Machiavelli restates the principle itself in shocking or comic exaggeration. When the plebs had seceded, because of the incident of Virginia (Appius had forcible designs upon her, and her father had killed her "to free her"), they demanded that "the Ten" be surrendered so that they might burn them alive. The two ambassadors of the Senate condemned the cruelty of this intention, but also advised that it be concealed until the plebs recovered its authority. Then they would not lack means of satisfying themselves. Machiavelli generalizes: "For one should not show one's intent, but try to seek to attain one's desire in any mode. For it is enough to ask someone for his arms without saying, I want to kill you with them, since you can satisfy your appetite after you have the arms in hand" (D I 44). In fact, the plebs had to be satisfied with a trial of Appius under the law on accusation, since the Senate and a tribune prevented an illegal execution of Appius and a terror against the nobles. The arms were in the hands of the plebs, but the necessary prudence was in the head of the Senate, which did not show its authority because it did not show its mind or intent (*animo*) (D I 45). Machiavelli elegantly reflects the indirect government of the Senate in his own indirect instruction.

THE KINGLY ARM

Thus accusation, though not the most important "order" in the Roman regime, is characteristic of its indirect government. This regime used individual "princes" to attack and to acquire and the people to aid in acquisition and to reward and punish ambition. It was government by management, for the orders themselves were not individually vital to the whole; what mattered was the prudence of the management. A brief survey of the leading orders of the Roman regime will make clear how, in Machiavelli's view, they were interchangeable.

We have seen him praise accusation as necessary and useful to the republic because it seems to substitute ordinary means for extraordinary, while in fact it blends the two. He then presents the Roman dictator as a remedy for an emergency when it is not possible to appeal to the people "ordinarily"; the dictator is the extraordinary alternative to ordinary accusation (D I 49; cf. III 25). But he also praises the dictator as a legal means of avoiding extraordinary means, and immediately states that republics must take refuge "under a dictator or similar authority" (*D* I 34). As extraordinary means become ordinary and legal, which they should, they also become dispensable. Machiavelli specifies that the necessary authority similar to the dictator should have limited powers, which is to say that it should be an authority that has obtained power by ordinary means as opposed to magistrates "that are made and authorities that are given through extraordinary ways" (*D* I 34), such as the Decemvirs (*D* I 41). But in the discussion of the Decemvirs, this distinction disappears. The prudence of the Senate, once we have dismissed its "errors," consisted in electing those made "through extraordinary ways" and allowing them the authority they claimed, in particular Appius. Prudently accepting the inevitable, the Senate managed to make the extraordinary ordinary. Appius was used against the plebs as if he were a dictator, with powers more limited than he knew. He was deposed by a device similar to accusation, in which he convicted himself of ambition, and he would have been disposed of under the law on accusation if he had not, very fittingly, disposed of himself.

"Ordinarily," Dictators were substitutes for Consuls, though appointed by Consuls. But Consuls could become their own Dictators.[14] The Romans excelled in war because they gave full powers (or at least "very great" authority) to their "captains," that is, to "their Consuls, Dictators and other captains of the armies" (*D* II 33; cf. I 49). Tribunes were a check on the ambition of Consuls, but in a pinch, they could do the work of Consuls; on one occasion when the Consuls disagreed and then refused to set up a dictator to settle their disagreement, the Senate had recourse to the aid of the Tribunes, who, "with the authority of the Senate, forced the Consuls to obey."[15] It is no wonder, then, that the Senate was able to reconcile itself to the abolition of the Consuls when, as a result of the Terentillian law, Tribunes with consular power replaced them. The people were permitted to choose plebeians for these offices, but they were bamboozled by the Senate and chose only nobles. Either the Senate had the office asked for by the most reputable men in Rome, or they bribed some mean and most ignoble plebeians to ask for it together with plebeians of better quality who "ordinarily" asked for it (*D* I 39, 47, 48; III 11). This is how Machiavelli proves his contention that the people may be deceived about generalities but not about particulars. They were deceived about the general necessity of a nobility but not about the worth of particular nobles—except that when they were confused about the merits of particular plebeians, they could be induced to accept the general rule of the nobility. Revolving in this circle, we almost forget that the people are deceived one way or the other of necessity, according to Machiavelli, because they cannot be governed without being deceived by their government.

New necessities made it necessary to devise new laws, and so the Romans devised the Censors. At first they made the mistake of giving them too long a term, but this was corrected by a dictator. New as the Censors were, they can be understood, like the Tribunes and other such officers, as "orders" that restrained the insolence of ambitious men by forcing the republic to return to its beginning (*D* III 1). Ordinary means—that is, the orders of the regime—need to be inspired repeatedly by the extraordinary means that were necessary to found them. Rome began as a kingdom, when it was necessary for one man "to be alone," and in the third chapter of the *Discourses,* Machiavelli says that the Tribunes served the same function as the Tarquins (the kings) of damping the insolence of the nobles. In the chapter on returning to the beginnings (III 1), he refers to the case of Spurius Melius, a grain dealer who had sought to feed the plebeians at his own expense; and later he says that the "kingly arm" of a dictator punished him capitally (*D* II 28). The Roman republic was government by the Senate using its "kingly arm" under a number of disguises. It was necessary to find new disguises because the ordinary means of government were always in danger from the ambitious individuals in charge of them, and yet ambitious individuals could not be dispensed with. Therefore, the Senate had to find new orders, that is, extraordinary devices that become legalized remedies, to revive the degenerating old orders.

Ambition is the cause of degeneration in the orders of the regime, and yet ambition is also the remedy. Rome needed new orders to save itself from its former saviors, but the new orders were essentially devices to focus responsibility on a single individual. The Roman regime was, in Machiavelli's view, a succession of "countless, most virtuous princes" (*D* I 20, III 15), rather than a constitution of particular institutions in a fixed pattern of enduring relations. Yet it was not a regime in the classical sense, the rule of a succession of men who happened to be able.[16] It was an arrangement of institutions to place responsibility in individuals and then to limit them by placing responsibility in other individuals. In causing ambition to counteract ambition it was like a modern constitution, but it did not have the permanency, or aspiration to permanency, of a modern constitution. The only enduring relation was that between the Senate and its "kingly arm," the individual of the moment behind whom it concealed its indirect government. Machiavelli does not seriously claim that the Senate was as prudent as he usually makes it appear, and it certainly did not operate consciously on Machiavellian principles. The self-understanding of the Senate, we may suppose, is to be found in Livy, behind whom Machiavelli conceals himself, with a very different understanding.[17]

## PURGING AND DETERRENCE

In introducing accusation, Machiavelli said that it had two most useful effects, a deterrent effect on ambitious individuals and a purging effect on the people. Deterrence and purging are separable, for laws can deter crime without purging humors against the criminal, and conversely. Machiavelli connects them in his discussion of the two outstanding qualities of the Roman regime, its ordinary use of extraordinary means and the indirect government of the Senate. Extraordinary means, especially that of capital punishment, have the effect of purging malignant humors in the people, first concentrating their fear on the hatred of the individual and then releasing it by an extreme and notable deed or execution. Indirect government has the effect of deterrence, though not in the way that Machiavelli first indicates. It is not that fear of being accused keeps men from attempts against the state, since in the most virtuous princes, fear is overridden by (or extends to) the desire for glory (Cf. *D* I 7 and II 33). Attempts against the state cannot be prevented, but they can be converted into acquisitions for the state when ambitious citizens are allowed to compete for glory. And they compete not to check each other but to excel one another. Deterrence by indirect government works through management rather than mere prohibition, and thus brings acquisitions to the common good (*D* III 16).

Purging and deterrence are necessary to each other. Purging the people of their malignant humors makes it possible for the Senate to govern indirectly. If the Senate could not have provided release of popular animosities in the punishment of individuals, hatred would have built up against the nobility as an order. Partisan discords between the plebs and the Senate would have grown to become unmanageable by the latter, at last bursting in revolution. Rome would have become another Athens (or like modern Florence), a succession of partisan regimes, instead of acquiring an empire by means of a nonpartisan regime that adjusted internal partisan discords.

On the other hand, indirect government makes it possible to purge popular animosities. Only if the Senate stands out of the light, in the shadows of its ambitious individuals, can animosities be purged without harming—not only the Senate—but the republic. Common people do not understand or appreciate ambition; they do not feel it themselves and they do not see what it contributes to the common good. Their desire not to be dominated, though not unreasonable, is uninstructed. The people do not know that they can avoid domination only through a competition of individuals to dominate them. Consequently, if the Senate ruled them directly, they would eventually rebel against the nobility as an order, which is to say, against the necessity of ambition.[18] In this mood they could easily be captured by a prince like Appius, but more adaptable or less prudently opposed. By rebelling against ambition, they would become slaves of an ambitious man.

For Machiavelli, deterrence is associated with purging of malignant humors. It is not a narrow Benthamite calculation of how great a penalty must be attached to each crime so as to deter each kind of criminal. This does nothing either to satisfy popular vengeance or to satisfy the people about their security and hence about their government. Criminal justice must be considered as a whole, and this perspective is inevitably political. Machiavelli unabashedly mixes criminal and political justice, contrary to the Roman law and to the school of natural law that followed him. So, for example, accusation can be used against a noble because he is a noble, behaving as the few always behave (D I 7). His "private" conduct, arising from his dominating nature and reflecting his dominant situation, is political behavior. He cannot avoid committing his "crimes," and the common good would suffer if he could; neither can he be spared punishment, which is required by the nature of the people and also by the common good. What is crime, or at least which crimes are punished, varies with the regime (D III 1), and all regimes are alike chiefly in the need for dramatic punishment that may or may not coincide with justice and does not arise from it.

Accusation culminates in a punishment or execution (*esecuzione*). The chapter (*D* I 8) that ends with the statement that calumniators should be punished as Manlius was punished is followed by the chapter in which Machiavelli says that the founder of a republic must be alone. It includes his memorable excuse for Romulus's "homicide" (he does not quite call it execution) of his brother and also of his partner in rule, Titus Tatius. This is an instance of Machiavelli's impartiality. After showing how the nobility may through accusation focus general resentment against themselves on an individual and purge it by punishing him, he adopts the standpoint of the individual being focused on and shows that execution is again necessary both for his purpose and for the common good (*D* I 9, 18, 47, 52; *P* 7).

Both dictionary senses of *execution,* "carrying out" and "punishing capitally," converge in Machiavelli's long chapter on conspiracies (*D* III 6). To carry out a conspiracy is to punish the man or men conspired against. Machiavelli seems to define conspiracy merely as a firm determination to kill the prince held by more than one man. Since all regular orders of government can carry out their intentions only with punishment and the fear of punishment, and since punishment must be managed in private, public orders can be understood no less as conspiracies than private schemes. In this chapter, Machiavelli gives directions for conspiring against a prince and then for conspiring against one's native country; he also gives directions for conspirators and for those conspired against (*D* III 6; cf. I 55). By speaking to all openly and indiscriminately, he implies that conspiracy is nearer the ordinary business of government than it is taken to be. Management is a kind of conspiracy, not only because the policemen must know what the criminal knows but because he must do first what the criminal does.[19] The first execution by Romulus was illegal and extraordinary, so to speak a conspiracy by one man; and it was excused by the outcome. But every government needs to return to its beginning by means of fearful executions. These executions are as much in need of excuse as that by Romulus, and they receive the same excuse (*D* III 1). The ordinary rests on the extraordinary. The extreme defines the normal. The public is determined by the success of a private plan, by the execution of a conspiracy. Political science is essentially knowledge of the limits of politics, but not in the classical sense. In classical political science, politics can never attain the end it aims at; in Machiavelli's, ordinary politics originates from its limit, in the extraordinary and the fearful.

Machiavelli can be recorded as the author of the idea of constitutional dictatorship. The Roman dictator, he said in opposition to "some writers," was not the cause of tyranny but the means of preventing it. Tyranny came with the prolongation of commands in the later republic, which was caused by the very success of the republic in expanding itself. But in Machiavelli's argument, the idea of constitutional dictatorship is much wider than the office of the dictator by itself. It is the same as the idea of a constitution or republic. Machiavelli's constitution is composed of ordinary orders that permit, indeed encourage, extraordinary actions by an ambitious prince; and then they limit the consequences of these actions by encouraging other extraordinary actions from his rival princes. The constitution legalizes what would have been illegalities according to a stricter definition of the lawful. It separates the orders, which in the seventeenth century came to be known as "powers," to make them more effective. The individual who is elected to his office—or allowed to grasp its powers—is not hindered by traditional prescriptions or prohibitions, yet at the same time he can neither make himself tyrant nor leave his example as a precedent for future tyrants. In this system his selfish glory does more for the common good than could any amount of moral and political restriction on his desire for glory. Machiavelli did not conceive the separation of powers as a way of diminishing the power of government. Ambitious men would check each other, it is true, but for the purpose of increasing the good effects, by increasing the safety, of ambition.

Most men identify "lawful" with "ordinary means," failing to see things in the perspective of the founder (or preserver), who knows the need for extraordinary means. Aristotle endorsed this error (in Machiavelli's view) when he discussed the tension between the best men and the best laws, assuming that the best laws could never do justice to the best men. Machiavelli agrees (we have seen) that the best laws cannot do justice to the best men, but he argues that they cannot do justice to ordinary men, either. What is legal or political justice for Aristotle must be, for Machiavelli, security for the people and glory to the princes. Since he accepts the necessity of injustice with open arms, he does not mind including extraordinary means that might be very unjust. He resolves the tension between the best men and the best laws, between prudence and legality, by removing justice from both. The law can legitimize, and thus moderate, the disorder necessary to the maintenance of order; it makes extraordinary measures ordinary—or at least temporary—by treating them so.

To do this, Machiavelli had to suppose that the purpose of law is to secure order rather than justice. It was not enough to imply, with Aristotle, that a certain injustice to the best men is necessary to even the best regime, or that natural justice is not the same as political justice. For Machiavelli, the best regime can attain justice neither between its two ordinary orders nor within the princely order. Then, since neither natural nor political justice is attainable, the distinction between justice and injustice is not final. On the other hand, though disorder is inevitable, order is attainable by prudent princes who anticipate the inevitability of disorder. They provide for the inevitable not by accepting it merely as the chance imperfection of human things, but by making natural disorder the necessary foundation of humanly contrived order. Understanding the necessity of extraordinary measures, they can extend the limits of order beyond the confines of justice. This was the essential purpose of Machiavelli's new regime.

# ELEVEN

# MACHIAVELLI'S POLITICAL SCIENCE

Modern political science presents itself today as both narrowing and progressive. Despite certain misgivings arising from the encounter with the New Left in the late sixties, most political scientists still put their trust in the fact-value distinction[1] as the method designed to narrow their range of concern and thereby to bring social as well as scientific progress. To an observer, the narrowing might seem more evident than the progress. At least it must be admitted that scientific narrowing has lost its evident connection to progress, since the very meaning of the fact-value distinction is that any good that might come of it is strictly accidental. To understand modern political science, therefore, one should look back to a time when this connection was argued in comprehensive fashion. Before investigating, one cannot exclude the possibility that this comprehensive argument was conceived, not in gradual stages but *ad uno tratto* (with one stroke) in the thought of *uno solo* (one alone). To set forth this claim on behalf of Machiavelli, with a view to our own self-understanding, is the purpose of this chapter.

## MACHIAVELLI'S MODERNITY

We will not find the fact-value distinction in Machiavelli, for he passes value judgments right and left with unmethodical abandon. But we do find a realism that was ancestor or parent of the fact-value distinction in Machiavelli's famous call, in Chapter 15 of *The Prince*, not to depart from what is done for what ought to be done. As opposed to making a profession of good in all regards, one should

This chapter was originally published as "Machiavelli's Political Science," *American Political Science Review*, June 1981, 293–305.

align one's values with facts in the sense of deeds. So the distinction is between deeds and professions rather than between facts and values, and the lesson is for the good of men, not for a methodological purity that cannot be proved to be for the good of anybody. For the sake of one's preservation (which is good), even for the common benefit of each human being, one must learn how to be not good. With this promise of preservation, Machiavelli connects his political science to progress toward the human good.

What one's preservation requires, according to Machiavelli, will become clear only gradually, but it may be glimpsed behind the meaning today of "modern" as in the phrase "modern political science." "Modern" as we use it today is defined against "traditional" so that what is modern constitutes self-conscious progress beyond tradition. But when modernity is established and what is modern becomes traditional, modernity must define itself against what had once bravely claimed to be modern. Thus, modern is always in danger of being surpassed by more modern; defined as against the traditional—that is, in relation to the traditional—modern seems to have no definition. Nor does "tradition": "traditional" is or supports the status quo, and "modern" advances—or merely moves—beyond it. "Modern," then, has perhaps a moving definition; it is always ahead of itself, not to say self-destructive. Or one might say that modernity has a certain direction.

In politics, "more modern" means further left and more democratic, as we can see in the alleged progression of the great modern revolutions—American, French, Russian, Chinese—each more democratic, supposedly, than the preceding one. What is more democratic, it is assumed, disposes of barriers between men, both humanly created and otherwise, as far as possible. Such barriers are especially the forms or formalities that define distances between men, give society a structure, and keep it from dissolving into an undifferentiated mass. Thus, modern art and literature have shown an inherent tendency away from classicism in perfection of form toward romanticism or expressionism in concern for feeling that overrides form. Similarly, we have learned from Tocqueville that modern politics as a whole may be seen as the drive of extraconstitutional democratic forces to overcome the restraints of constitutional forms that were once modern themselves.[2] The liberalism that was to set men free has been attacked and pushed aside by movements let loose by those dissatisfied with liberal formalism, who desired a more radical freedom: for the decline in respect for forms and formalities is accompanied by a demand for more subjectivity and creativity.

Such, in brief, is the course of the modern world as it races toward perfect democracy and freedom. But this sort of perfection is indefinable; as soon as one defines the modern, it becomes the status quo and hence traditional, an easy target for the next progressive. To understand modernity, therefore, one cannot look to its *end*, as it seems to have none; one must look to its *beginning*, when progress was first set in motion. Especially since modernity now seems out of our control, and "progress" no longer seems progressive, we need to know what was intended and hoped for originally.

When one looks to the periods at which modern history is said to begin, however, they do not appear to suggest, much less to launch, the characteristic dynamism of modernity. Humanism puts man, rather than God, at the center of attention—which does not necessarily imply progress toward a new earthly future for men; and the Renaissance is a rebirth, perhaps a return to the ancients. Only Machiavelli, a single man soaked in the Renaissance and steeped in humanism, seems, of those in his times, to have declared himself for progress in terms we might begin to recognize.[3]

More precisely, Machiavelli is for novelty. In *The Prince* he praises the new prince over the hereditary prince because the new prince depends only on himself and thus gains more glory; the highest case is the new prince in a new principality who is also the prophet of a new religion (*P* 6, 24). And at the beginning of the *Discourses on Livy*, Machiavelli, comparing himself to those in his times who sought unknown seas and lands, says he is bringing "new modes and orders" to mankind. He appears to be the first political philosopher not merely to admit his own novelty (as for example Marsilius) but even to flaunt it; and he did this not merely to establish his new modes and orders but, in accordance with them, to give new reputation to those who seek out new acquisitions.[4] It is not that Machiavelli invented new political tricks. He admits to having borrowed techniques of government from the ancients and perhaps also from Christianity, and he was aware that before him there had always been half-hearted or untaught Machiavellians in need of instruction.[5] Rather, he believed that political men should be encouraged to make their own innovations so as to increase opportunities for glory and gain for themselves and their peoples, for "preservation" requires both glory and gain. The founder of a state does not legislate once in the hope that his forms will endure; instead, the healthy state must be made and remade, formed and reformed, or it will become corrupt.[6] Machiavelli is far from espousing a formless or stateless society, but he favors frequent reform and he is definitely no respecter of formalities.

Machiavelli's realism unites with his desire for innovation when one sees that learning how to be not good means especially learning how to introduce an innovation (P 8 [end], 17, 18, 19 [end]; D III 35). In the chapter of The Prince where he calls for learning how to be not good, he announces publicly that he departs in this "from the orders of others." Machiavelli thought he lived in times when men were weak and vile (at least in Italy); he spoke scornfully of modern politics and religion and by contrast appealed to "ancient virtue" (D I pr, 12, 55; II 2; III 1; P 3, 12, 26; AW pr). Such expressions might appear to put Machiavelli with the Renaissance and to demand a return to the ancients. But Machiavelli, we see, was very far from being reactionary. He rejects the authority of the ancients, for they, together with the Christians, were the "others" who based their political science on what should be done rather than on what is done, who elaborated the "profession of good" in all regards, and who therefore constructed imaginary republics and principalities such as Plato's Republic and Saint Augustine's City of God (P 15).

In regard to the teaching of politics, the strong ancients are at one with the weak moderns. So in the preface to the first book of the Discourses on Livy, Machiavelli indicates that he will honor ancient politics through ancient histories, not by imitating ancient political science. Moreover, the history he chooses is Roman, not Greek; and near the beginning of the Discourses on Livy, he reveals a definite preference for Rome over Sparta, the Greek city most favored by political philosophers. While making use of Polybius and Livy, he ignores Polybius's statement of indebtedness to Greek political science; and his use of Livy, of which much has been said, does not indicate acceptance of Livy's interpretations of events, to put it mildly.[7] Machiavelli puts his own interpretation on ancient virtue so that it becomes Machiavellian virtù. He values the large and imperialistic Roman republic above the Greek cities, and judges its virtue by its fortune in war, although that virtue was exercised in conquering the Greek cities among others (*D* I 9, 53, 59; II 1, 10; III 16; *P* 3). While bowing ironically to the authority of the ancients—so that he can use it against the authority of the moderns—Machiavelli in fact uses ancient examples to reproach ancient teachings. He returns to the ancients in order to improve on them.

Unless one dissolves Machiavelli's arguments into phrases and reduces his design to vulgar office-seeking, one cannot find another thinker or statesman in his times or before who reminds us so vividly and profoundly of the realism and dynamism of modernity. Today, many would perhaps agree with this judgment, if not this formulation. But there remains a great reluctance to admit, or even consider, that Machiavelli might be chiefly responsible for the spirit of modernity and thus is himself the origin of the modern world. Modernity now seems so powerful and all-encompassing that it appears to be unstoppable, and if unstoppable, apparently inevitable. Few are ready to believe that the modern world, which wishes to move in the direction of perfect freedom for men and to give men ever greater control over themselves and the world, could have been founded by the free act of a human being. Strangely, we find it more comfortable to believe in confused and contradictory "forces of history," relishing our fate since we cannot maintain our hopes.

Before estimating what Machiavelli's influence might have been, one must see what he intended and what influence he intended for himself. One may begin from a typical view of Machiavelli's realism, which is that he believed that morality can be one's guide in private affairs but not in politics. Such a view seems implied in a remark of Thomas Hobbes's, apparently directed at Machiavelli: "Successful wickedness hath obtained the name virtue . . . when it is for the getting of a kingdom" (*Leviathan,* chap. 15). It is supported in Machiavelli's *Discourses* I 9, where Romulus's killing of his brother is excused because it was necessary for him to rule alone to order a kingdom or a republic for the common good.[8]

Yet, returning to Chapter 15 of *The Prince,* we find that the title mentions "men and especially princes," while the principal advice is addressed to "whoever understands." Actual princes may be imprudent; indeed, according to Machiavelli, their sins are responsible for Italy's plight (*P* 12; *D* I 21; II 18; III 29). They must be replaced by prudent princes, who are now private men. But a private man must behave like a prince because a private man, if he is prudent, must become a prince—as Hobbes's remark suggests. Machiavelli's own suggestion, in his punning use of the word *privato,* is that a private man should regard himself as *deprived* of office.[9] Perhaps the rules of politics are not those of private morality, but when private men are compelled to become princes, they no more than princes can live by professions of good. Moreover, the prudent, private man who wants to become prince must not only be ready to make his way by such crimes as fratricide; he must also pave the way by making it easier for such crimes to be accepted as necessary. In *Discourses* I 10, just after providing an excuse for Romulus, Machiavelli shows how a founder is affected by his reputation, in particular how he can be hampered by an evil reputation as a tyrant. Machiavelli may have excused Romulus, but others—for example, Saint Augustine— have not.[10]

Thus, the prudent prince needs a whole new climate of political and moral opinion to facilitate his arrival and maintenance in power. This is what Machiavelli intends to supply. The prince, or founder-prince, "is alone" only if he alone sets the standards by which he is judged and his reputation is made. Only he who sets these standards is alone above ordinary moral persons who live by them and above princes who may share them and who must conform to them, or appear to conform, for the sake of reputation. The highest prince, who is in the fullest sense prince, is the moral or political philosopher who establishes the opinions in which lesser princes operate.[11] If, according to Machiavelli, public and private immorality must be controlled by the political necessity of acquiring and maintaining a state, then the highest prince is the political philosopher or scientist, Machiavelli himself—the one who brings "new modes and orders" for the common benefit not merely of Florentines or Italians but also of everyone.

PRUDENCE AND THE ART OF WAR

In this prospectus for "new modes and orders" establishing a new climate for prudent princes and private men, however, there is an evident difficulty. Is the end of the political scientist to pave the way for princes (thus also improving the lot of peoples), or, since the political scientist too is in a sense a prince, is his end to be prince himself? In the former case, Machiavelli's political science would be teachable to all and his status as teacher of all for the common benefit would be superior to his ambition of ruling as "one alone." He would indeed be teacher rather than prince, for his discoveries, like those of any scientist or philosopher, would not carry along to present and future beneficiaries the personal rule of their discoverer. The scientist, as teacher, is not strictly "one alone," and if he discovers "new modes and orders," his glory is merely to have been the first to see, and not now to be the first in rule, as prince.

Yet this formal truth regarding teaching in general seems overborne by the content of Machiavelli's particular teaching. When the teacher's lesson requires rising to sole rule, it seems unreasonable that the teacher should except himself and unlikely that he will. His status as teacher would be subordinate to his ambition as prince, and the prudence he exercises in his own interest would control the science or art that he claims to be in the common interest. How can one sincerely advise "successful wickedness"?[12] If wickedness succeeds for those advised, then why not also for the adviser? And if the advice is wicked, why should it help those advised? Although Machiavelli's difficulty can be sensed by anyone of ordinary moral experience, it is obscured by scholars who make excuses for Machiavelli, conceal the wickedness of his advice and thus blindly rob him of the glory he claimed for having begun the scholarly practice of making such excuses. To excuse Machiavelli is to dismiss not only every popular but also every interesting sense of the word "Machiavellian."

In the dedicatory letter to *The Prince,* which was written to be understood "in a very brief time" by an actual prince, this difficulty of Machiavelli's political science appears in the relation between art and prudence, and the word "science" does not occur. Indeed, for some reason Machiavelli does not speak at all of "political science." "Science" is discussed in the *Discourses* (III 39), which were addressed to potential princes with more time on their hands. In this summary treatment, we shall mainly consider *The Prince.*

Machiavelli's dedicatory letter offers to Lorenzo his "knowledge of the actions of great men," which is the gift of everything he knows. From this he dares to "discuss and give rules for the government of princes" and says he possesses knowledge of the nature of princes. What he knows of the government of princes seems to be practical, and what he knows of the nature of princes, theoretical. These two kinds of knowledge appear to combine in the third chapter, where "the Romans" are cited as the example for wise princes of overcoming the particular difficulties of acquiring and maintaining a new principality. The Romans knew the remedies for these difficulties because they knew them "at a distance" (*discosto*) or saw ahead.[13] Such knowledge is likened to that of physicians taking timely measures to cure consumption, but it is then limited to "a prudent one," as opposed to "the wise men of our times," and said to be "given" only to that one. The same foresight is recommended in the sixth chapter to "a prudent man"; he should imitate the great men who have not imitated anybody and have made altogether new principalities. He should behave like "prudent archers" who shoot at a mark above the target in order to hit the target. Where one would expect "skillful archers" one finds "prudent archers," as if prudence, understood as discounting ahead of time, were assimilated to art and art thereby given command over the future.[14] He who follows this procedure is said first to have "some odor" of the great men he imitates, and then, because archers know the virtue of their bows, and use the aid of the high mark, they are allowed to "succeed in their design." In a turn typical of Machiavelli's writing, the (singular) prudent man whose prudence is "given" to him becomes the (plural) prudent archers whose learned prudence supplies the lack of highest virtue. We are made aware of, but not directed to, the difference between the prudence of imitating great men and prudence that is similar to possessing an art. When imitating great men, one follows their beaten track and thus does not truly imitate their innovation; but each archer, as such, is as "prudent" as any.

Machiavelli alludes to this difference at the end of the ninth chapter when he remarks that "a wise prince" must think of a "mode" through which his citizens will always have need of him and thus will always be faithful to him. Can a wise prince do this with political science? At the end of the tenth chapter, Machiavelli says he has solved the problem of keeping citizens loyal, at least in part, for "a prudent prince." In the first part of *The Prince* (Chapters 1–11), on the kinds of principalities and how to acquire them, he joins theory and practice or wisdom and prudence, while leaving unclear whether they must be given as prudence or may be learned as an art.

The second part of *The Prince* (Chapters 12–14), on the necessity of using "one's own arms," heightens the difficulty. Machiavelli condemns the use of mercenary arms but praises a certain mercenary captain in the service of the Florentines, Paulo Vitelli, as *uomo prudentissimo* for having risen from private fortune to very great reputation. If he had taken Pisa for the Florentines, Machiavelli remarks, the Florentines either would have had no recourse had he left them or would have had to obey him. Machiavelli does not remark that in fact this "very prudent man" did not take Pisa and was thereupon killed by the Florentines. They spied the danger to them in Vitelli's prudence, since "mercenary arms" to them were "his own arms" to him. But they also did not know how to take advantage of his prudence, such as it was. In Chapter 13 Machiavelli deplores "the lack of prudence in men" by contrast to the wisdom that is given to the few, and he criticizes the Romans whose prudence he had praised in Chapter 3. Among the few wise who order their own arms, he names Philip of Macedon, whom he had cited in the preceding chapter as a mercenary captain who took away the liberty of his employers. Machiavelli says he gives himself over entirely to Philip's (and to others') orders. Does Machiavelli then admit that the few wise, perhaps including himself, hire out their wisdom and rob their employers in the manner of mercenary captains?

Machiavelli answers this question provisionally in the fourteenth chapter of *The Prince.* Although the chapter heading does not mention the art of war, Machiavelli suddenly announces that the art of war should "therefore" be a prince's only object and only thought.[15] Whence the "therefore"? If the dubious mercenary captain named at the end of Chapter 13, to whose orders Machiavelli gives himself over entirely, can be presented as teaching an *art,* then his wisdom can be made to appear as benefaction. Such is the virtue of this art that it not only maintains those born princes but also often causes men to rise from private fortune to the rank of prince. When princes have thought more of delicacies (*delicatezze*) than of arms, they have lost their states. Using a weighty phrase, Machiavelli says that the "first cause" of losing one's state is to neglect the art of war, and that the cause of gaining it is to be "professed" in the art.[16]

This is illustrated by Francesco Sforza, who through being armed became duke of Milan, and by his sons, who through avoiding arms became private men.[17] The example of the Sforzas does not in truth illustrate the principle because it fails to mention the art of war; besides, Francesco, however proficient in that art, did not "profess" it in the sense of teaching it. Nonetheless, as we have seen, a mercenary captain who fights on all sides for hire and gains his own personal "state" illustrates our problem of art and prudence. Is his art so powerful as to be the first cause of his rise or does he also need his prudence to attune his art to circumstances? In this statement, the art of war has swallowed up prudence. Machiavelli goes on to say that no proportion exists between one who is armed and one unarmed, and that it is not reasonable for the armed to obey willingly whoever is unarmed. Thus, Machiavelli concludes, a prince who understands nothing of militia, among all his other misfortunes, is not trusted by his soldiers. He seems clearly to deny here the fundamental principle of classical natural right, the rule of the wise: it is not reasonable for someone who is unwise but armed to obey one who is wise but unarmed. Yet if the art of war is understood in its full extent as the only object and thought of a prince, Machiavelli in truth affirms the classical principle, while improving on it. For to understand "militia" or to possess the art of war is sufficient to make one armed, and to be armed is sufficient to make oneself obeyed, at least by one's soldiers and perhaps also by one's subjects.[18] Contrary to the classical writers, Machiavelli argues that knowing leads to commanding, and so the art of war in the extended sense includes politics. Nowhere else does Machiavelli give the art of war such amplitude.[19]

Moreover, he says next that a prince (or one) must never lift his thoughts from the exercise of war, and in peace more than in war. Never?[20] Does this mean that thought (or at least a prince's thinking) should never be detached from advantage in war? Does "effectual truth" mean effectual in war, whether foreign or domestic, and is this the only truth one should seek? Machiavelli's elaboration of this startling "never" seems to take away from its naked force, but only at first. He says that the exercise of war in peace is done in two modes, with works (*opere*) and mind (*mente*). But apart from keeping one's own arms in order, he says that a prince should always be on the chase so that he can accustom his body to hardships and learn the nature of sites. Machiavelli then discusses this topographical knowledge, of which one should take "the greatest care." The "works" of exercising war in peace seem hardly distinct from "mind."

Knowledge of sites is useful because it enables one to understand what is required for self-defense and because the topographical features in one region have a "certain similitude" to those in other regions. Knowledge of one site thus enables one to comprehend any other site. Such knowledge, the "first part" of a captain, is accompanied by reasoning, as Machiavelli makes clear by the example of Philopoemen, a prince who used to ride in the country with his friends and pose hypothetical questions to them concerning all the chances (casi) an army might encounter. With these "continuous cogitations," no accident could ever arise for which Philopoemen did not have the remedy: again, a sweeping claim of efficacy for the art of war.[21]

This "first part" of a captain seems equivalent to the "firm science" Machiavelli discusses in Discourses III 39, also on the knowledge of sites, where he also praises hunting.[22] He says that Xenophon (in his work that Machiavelli mistitles "Life of Cyrus") makes it clear that hunting is "an image of a war"; and Machiavelli adds that for great men this exercise is honorable and necessary. It appears that particular knowledge of one country can be generalized and the familiar made applicable to the new by the use of images representing the similitudes mentioned in Chapter 14 of The Prince. By contrast to that chapter, Discourses III 39 speaks of both images and sciences so as to suggest that images (in addition to similitudes) are necessary to science (as beyond mere art). It was "firm science" that on one occasion enabled a Roman tribune to save the Roman army, despite the bafflement of the Consul in charge, by spying a summit above the enemy on which both he and that army could take refuge. An image, then, might be a similitude visible only to one person or to a few, for sometimes it takes a rare brain to see an invisible similitude in a visible one; and the use of images would make possible the "perfect possession" of a science and therewith the rapid comprehension of new things. Such a science might be teachable only in part to the soldiers of an army, that part being the art of war; but the art of war would imply a complete understanding and might therefore be said to encompass that understanding in a work addressed to actual princes in which Machiavelli does not advertise himself as the inventor of new modes and orders.[23] Even in *Discourses* III 39 Machiavelli speaks modestly of "general and particular knowledge" as knowledge of sites, and is far from claiming the glory of founding a new science in the comprehensive sense, as did Bacon and Descartes.

Machiavelli's "firm science," although making use of images, does not incur his own condemnation of the many (in *P* 15) who have imagined republics and principalities "that have never been seen or known to exist in truth." Those imaginary states are based on a "profession of good," whereas Machiavelli's imagination begins from "what is done." In *Discourses* III 39, where he reports Xenophon's use of hunting as an image of war, Machiavelli indicates by "hunting" that he means catching one's prey. One may suppose he was aware of the difference (and the similarity) between hunting as catching and hunting as dialectic in Plato's *Laws*.[24] If hunting is for catching, and hunting is an image of war, we can infer—because politics centers on acquisition—that in *The Prince* and the *Discourses* Machiavelli uses war as an image of politics. More attention might be given to the use of imagination in Machiavelli's behavioral political science.

Returning to Chapter 14 of *The Prince*, we see that Machiavelli recommends for the second part of the art of war, the exercise of the mind, that the prince read histories in which the actions of excellent men are considered.[25] He must above all do as some excellent man has done in the past who has taken someone before him to imitate who had been praised and glorified, as it is said Alexander the Great imitated Achilles; Caesar, Alexander; Scipio, Cyrus. Thus, contrary to the impression given at the beginning of the sixth chapter, even excellent men may imitate others. Those they imitate are found in "histories," and as in *Discourses* III 39, Machiavelli singles out the "life of Cyrus written by Xenophon" and asserts that in his chastity, affability, humanity, and liberality, Scipio conformed to what had been written about Cyrus by Xenophon. Those whom excellent men imitate, then, are men of whom authors such as Homer and especially Xenophon, the Socratic philosopher, have written. From whatever source princes learn the art of war, they imitate the virtues or qualities taught by authors, and, it is implied, their art is incomplete without these qualities. As with founders as Machiavelli describes them in *Discourses* I 9–10, princes possessing the art of war are not self-sufficient but dependent on the moral opinion of society. Accordingly, Machiavelli closes the chapter with a less promising remark about fortune; with this imitation a wise prince can *resist* fortune's adversities, not have a remedy for any accident.

With this modulation we are led to the fifteenth chapter of *The Prince,* entitled "On those things for which men and especially princes are praised or blamed." Here begins the second half of *The Prince,* in which the difficulties caused by the moral qualities are considered.[26] For apparently the art of war cannot teach one to surmount the moral expectations of one's subjects and friends that stand in the way of one's necessary acquisitions. Machiavelli's exaggeration of the art of war does put one in the right frame of mind; for in representing prudence as art, in contradiction to Aristotle, he makes prudence morally neutral (*NE* 1140b 25; 1144a 7–9, 23–37). We are thus prepared to be told that one must be prudent to know how to avoid the infamy of those vices that take away one's state (*P* 15), for example, "the name of stingy" (*P* 16), that a new prince must temper his cruelties with prudence and humanity (*P* 17), and that a prudent lord should not keep faith when keeping it works against him (*P* 18). Machiavelli offers a definition of prudence in Chapter 21 that sums up its morally neutral use of the moral qualities: "Prudence consists in knowing how to recognize the qualities of inconveniences and in picking the less bad as good."

After Chapter 14, meanwhile, the status of art is diminished as the arts are reduced to partial human activities such as the art of gaining reputation (*P* 19) or subordinated to the virtues (*P* 21) or contrasted with violence (*P* 25). Remarkably, the art of war, which was said to be the sole object and thought of a prince in Chapter 14 because it seemed to comprehend all human activities, is not even mentioned after that chapter. Instead, soldiers are said to love a prince of "military spirit" (*P* 19), Caracalla and Philip of Macedon are praised as "military men" (*P* 19, 24), and Lorenzo is exhorted to revive "military virtue" in Italy with a saying of Petrarch's predicting that virtue, not art, will take up arms there (*P* 26).

As art is reduced to activities that can be ordered but are still subject to chance (Aristotle, *NE* 1140a12–20), prudence is enlarged to include the governing of fortune. At the end of Chapter 23, Machiavelli says that a prince who is not wise himself cannot be well advised unless by chance he gives himself over[27] to "one alone" (*uno solo*) to govern him in everything, who would be *uomo prudentissimo*. This second occurrence of *prudentissimo* in *The Prince*, used to describe the adviser of a prince who indeed governs him in everything, reminds us of the "very prudent" Paulo Vitelli (*P* 12), who would have had the Florentines in a dilemma if he had taken Pisa. Machiavelli will show how to solve the problem of the adviser who governs the advised, thus benefiting the advised and, not incidentally, saving himself from the fate of Vitelli (cf. *D* I 21; II 33). As adviser of princes (or republics), Machiavelli both is and is not a prince himself. He cannot acquire a new principality for himself, but in teaching princes he gains some of their glory, leaving for them the obvious glory enjoyed by successful politicians and taking for himself the glory of having facilitated their glory, a glory evident only to the discerning. Thus, in the next chapter[28] Machiavelli speaks of the double glory of "having given a beginning to a new principality" (*avere dato principio a uno principato nuovo*), a phrase that both falls short of and exceeds "acquiring a new principality." It exceeds acquiring a new principality because this prince does not merely imitate the great men whose beaten paths a prudent man was previously required to follow (*P* 6). His advice gives a beginning to every principality by supplying the moral prerequisites and their theoretical foundation.[29]

The last part of *The Prince* (Chapters 24–26) concerns the problem of sustaining the prince's glory despite "the brevity of life" (*P* 25). Ordinary princes may not receive the glory they deserve or may receive more glory than they deserve, according to how ill or how well their habits and nature are suited to their times. But the prince who gave ordinary princes their beginning can afford to wait patiently while virtue and fortune are sorted out, since the opportunities for his virtue, and hence his glory, are not bound by the brevity of his life.[30] He alone has sure defenses against stormy times, as only for him do such defenses depend on himself and his virtue (*P* 24). Machiavelli's art has disappeared into his virtue, which is his alone. With his virtue he teaches the art of war or something like it to ordinary princes, but their opportunities for using his teaching depend on their fortune after all. Machiavelli will not allow "these princes of ours" to accuse fortune rather than admit their indolence; he demands, in the notorious sentence at the end of Chapter 25, that they proceed impetuously to manhandle lady fortune. Imitating the furious Pope Julius II, they should go beyond where "all human prudence" would have led them. This now limited and subdued prudence serves to distinguish virtue from caution for the generality of Machiavelli's readers as they rush from the necessities he describes toward the prizes he holds out for them. But only he is truly impetuous. Only he is not bound by the moral qualities because only he has learned how to be good and not good. His impetuosity is both impetuous and respectful: impetuous in theory by comparison to other writers, and respectful in practice to Lorenzo and other princes, both actual and potential, to whom he allows their subordinate glories. His position as adviser enables him to share in the natures of all whom he advises as he uses the diverse qualities of those who follow his advice. So by the use of the moral qualities of others, he is not bound by his times as are others, hence not bound by his nature.[31] Since he is not bound by his nature and knows how to be flexible (both *facile* and *duro*) in all times,[32] his fortune is assured. Others may absorb his teaching, and a few may perhaps equal or surpass him, but if his teaching is true, they follow his fortune. They follow the fortune of the man who first showed men how to become responsible for their fortune. His virtue depends on himself alone, his glory is unrepeatable and he is *uno solo,* not in contemplative isolation but governing for the common benefit of each. His government is established *ad uno tratto* in his books, but also over time as his influence or fortune advances.

Machiavelli could be said to have "ornamented and confirmed" his new principality "with good laws, good arms, good friends and good examples" (*P* 24) to be found in his books, but he did not write the handbook of an art of politics with rules for all occasions. Nor did he, like Thomas Hobbes, author a new political science or "civil philosophy" on the basis of a new method, and claim credit for it.[33] Even if Machiavelli had thought it possible for a political art to do the work of prudence, and even if the new scientific method had been available to him as it was to Hobbes, he would have had reason to decline the honor of founding a new political art or science. Such a founding would have given him too much glory because it would have subtracted from the glory of later princes—and not enough glory, because later princes applying an impersonal science would not have been subjects of his (see *D* III 13 end).


## THE CYCLE AND THE SOUL

Machiavelli presents his new political science in opposition to classical political science. But despite his statement in Chapter 15 of *The Prince* against the imaginary republics and principalities essential to classical political science, his opposition becomes clear only gradually. As can be seen from the preface to the first book of the *Discourses,* he found it convenient to condemn the weakness of his own age by contrast to the ancients, for in doing so he could appeal to opinion in his age favorable to the ancients. My account of his critique of classical political science, passing over the subtlety of his rhetoric, will consider two points of Machiavelli's attack, the cycle and the soul.

In the preface just mentioned, Machiavelli says that the ancients have been imitated in many things, though not in politics. Yet soon after, in *Discourses* I 2, he makes a significant departure from classical political science in regard to the cycle. Classical political science (here assembled from diverse sources) had supposed that regimes tend to change in a regular way—from good to less good to bad to worst; or alternating from good to bad and bad to good. These regular changes make a circle or cycle, coming back to their beginning and beginning again, with the consequence that the progress in human affairs that we moderns expect does not occur and should not be expected. Good times are followed by bad, and bad by good; so, as Isocrates once remarked, a reasonable man might wonder whether it is better to be born in good times that will worsen or bad times that will improve.[34] Civilization may progress as morality, arts, and sciences advance; but civilizations are subject to natural catastrophes that return them to their barbarous beginnings, from which they must recommence. The cycle of regimes assumes that the city is self-sufficient; that it becomes better or worse through the actions of its own ruling class, which deserves praise or blame for them; that domestic policy is therefore primary. The cycle of civilizations, however, reminds men of the power of extrahuman forces and of the fragility of human constructions. But this reminder of the limits to human choice actually promotes human choice because it

teaches men that in the end all merely human force will be overborne, hence that they need not judge their actions merely by their
consequences nor their governments by their durability. Moderation—not fearful, but responsible moderation—is the moral lesson
of the classical teaching on the cycle.

Machiavelli did not approve of this lesson. In *Discourses* I 2 he
almost copies an account of the cycle from Polybius, without naming
him as source. The closeness of his copying enables one to see the
significant differences, which center on his replacement of "nature"
in Polybius by "chance" or "necessity" to explain the origin of governments and of morality.[35] After concluding this account, Machiavelli abruptly adds that almost no republic could survive these ups
and downs without becoming subject to a neighboring state better
ordered than itself. Speaking for himself ("I say"), he says that all
these regimes are pestiferous, the good ones because of their "brevity
of life" and the bad ones because of their malignity. Then, having
introduced foreign policy as the decisive consideration and thus having denied the assumptions of the classical account of the cycle, he
loses interest in the cycle of regimes and never discusses or even
refers to it again.

Machiavelli offers, still in *Discourses* I 2, two kinds of legislated
beginnings for cities: *uno solo* may make all the laws *ad uno tratto*,
as Lycurgus in Sparta; or, as in Rome, the city may lack perfect
order but may have made a good beginning apt to become better,
and through the occurrence of accidents, may be capable of becoming perfect. At first the beginning that is legislated all at once—the
mixed regime of classical political science—seems superior, but
Machiavelli shows in *Discourses* I 3–8 that the way of perfection
through accidents is far better. Although subject to party discord
and "tumults" (in which men shout at each other instead of adjudi-
cating their claims),[36] Rome's way was more flexible in meeting "accidents," especially the accident that if someone wishes to conquer
you, you will have to conquer him first. Since every state must meet
this accident, it should have, like Rome's, a regime that enables it
to keep what it has got. Rome could expand successfully, converting
foreigners into Romans, while Sparta could not. Rome's regime of
accidental perfection, with its emergency solutions and individual
initiatives, was superior to Sparta's regime of planned perfection.
One should not infer from this that human planning is incompetent

in politics, however. We may suspect that Machiavelli, who had to overcome the prejudice against tumultuous republics (*D* I 4), arranged the accidents of the Roman republic as supplied by Livy to suit his plan of perfection. His plan, we have suggested, is legislated all at once in his books but allows for accidents, especially of foreign policy, as they arise over time. It thus combines the two kinds of legislated beginnings set forth in *Discourses* I 2.

One particular difficulty in the accidental perfection of Rome calls for Machiavelli's intervention. It appears in *Discourses* I 7, where he is considering why party government worked successfully in Rome and brought disaster in Florence. In Florence certain party politicians were able, when pressed, to appeal to "foreign forces," "outside forces," or "private forces." Machiavelli refers to Francesco Valori, a prince of the city as it were, a man who was judged to have wished "with his audacity and spiritedness [*animosità*] to rise above [*trascendere*] civil life," and who could be resisted only with a "sect" contrary to his. Valori's "sect" was the party of Savonarola, who is not mentioned. Soon after, in *Discourses* I 11, he refers to Savonarola himself, and says that Savonarola was able to persuade the people of Florence, who did not think themselves ignorant or rude, that he spoke with God. Clearly one who can persuade others that he speaks with God has a private advantage over other party politicians. He appeals to both a foreign (or outside) and a private source of power.

In the next chapter Machiavelli informs his readers that the Roman Church keeps Italy disunited, chiefly because the Church is not strong enough to seize Italy but strong enough to prevent anyone else from doing so. It prevents others from conquering—or should one say unifying?—Italy by appealing to outside powers such as the king of France to intervene on its behalf. But why can it do this? Because the pope can persuade not necessarily the king of France but the French people that he speaks with God. Thus Machiavelli speaks in this chapter of "Christian states and republics" and of the "Christian republic." Christian republics are divided from each other because of what unites them—a religion that gives opportunity, or makes it necessary, for priests to interfere in politics.

A wider view is therefore necessary. One must look not merely to the regime but also to the religion that controls the part of the world where the regime is, to the *sect*. "Sect" is an important Machi-

avellian term apparently borrowed from Marsilius—and Machiavelli follows Marsilius's impudent application of it to Christianity,
for example in the strange phrase "Catholic sect."[37] Machiavelli
takes up the cycle of sects in *Discourses* II 5, where he considers
what cause is responsible for their rise and fall—men, heaven, or
nature. He raises the possibility that men, or even a single man,
could control not the cycle of regimes but the cycle of sects. For
sect is a more comprehensive phenomenon than regime; it includes
language and customs, the moral climate of government, as well as
politics. Even names and dates are determined by sects. In the *Florentine Histories* (I 5), Machiavelli refers to the fact that after Christianity was established, people stopped naming their sons Caesar and
Pompey and began calling them Peter, John, and Matthew. And he
takes note of the manner in which we date events by ensuring that
all the dates given in the *Discourses*—twenty-six of them—occur in
his own lifetime.

From the viewpoint of sects, one must consider foreign or outside forces in the widest sense of things foreign to or outside of man.
One becomes aware that Machiavelli is not an unreflective humanist
who puts human concerns first but a philosopher reflecting on God
and nature who puts human necessities first. He does not behold
God and nature with wonder and discourse on what he understands
of them. Rather, he regards them with fear and sees this fear exem-
plified in fearful, wholesale changes of sect (*D* III 1; FH I 5, VII 1);
and so he discourses on the remedies he finds for the fears men must
have of their beginnings. Then, from the viewpoint of sects, one
could say that in modern times, that is, Machiavelli's times, the cycle
is stalled. The proximate cause of the stall is Christianity, which
does not esteem the honor of the world and keeps it weak (*D* II 2).
But the ultimate cause is in the principles of classical political science,
perhaps especially in the classical notion of soul. In reading through
*The Prince* and the *Discourses,* the only works of Machiavelli's in
which he says he puts everything he knows, one does not find the
word "soul" (*anima*).[38] What does this fact mean?

As conceived by Plato and Aristotle, the soul was intended to
give protection against "outside forces" in the extended sense. Having soul enables men to be different from their environment, to have
dignity above the rest of nature and to be free of (or within) the
forces of nature and gods outside them. In the classical definition of

soul, there were two essentials: the soul as beginning of motion and the soul as intellect. Having soul, men can begin an action on their own, not determined from outside; and because men have soul, this action can be intelligent. The problem of this definition was in connecting the two essentials. Whatever action one begins seems to be his own, and yet if the action is to be intelligent, one must be capable of detachment from one's own to achieve an impartial outlook that does not merely endorse one's prejudices. Yet while the two essentials are difficult to connect, it is also necessary to connect them. One's actions are not his own if they are determined by fancy or chance, that is, stupidly or by blindly following the authority of another.[39]

According to Machiavelli, and for a reason to be explained, there is terrible danger to mankind in the attempt to detach oneself from what is one's own. He therefore denied the possibility of detachment in the human soul. What was left in the classical definition was the soul as beginning of motion; but the soul cannot begin motion unless it can act intelligently. Other animals have instincts instead of intelligence and are incapable of truly voluntary or deliberate action. So, in denying the possibility of detached intelligence, Machiavelli had to pay the price of denying that men are capable of voluntary action.[40] But instead of having instincts, men are determined by necessity, or by the necessity that they have the prudence to recognize and foresee. Necessity well understood, not any fool's opinion, replaces deliberate choice in the soul as that which begins voluntary actions. Men may choose, but the only prudent choice is anticipation of necessity (*P* 3, 6, 9, 25; *D* I 1, 30, 32, 33, 52; III 5, 6). The human desire for glory, which seems to be opposed to necessity because it seems to seek what is in excess of necessary, is in truth comprised in necessity.[41] As we have seen, glory is redeemed from incaution by Machiavelli's plan for the common benefit of mankind, and at the same time it is required for the virtuous promotion of one's own.

It is notorious that Machiavelli once said in a letter that he loved his native country more than his own soul.[42] But which was his native country, Florence or Italy? Should he promote Florentine independence or Italian unity; and if one should get in the way of the other, which should he prefer? Machiavelli does not speak only to Florentines or to Italians but to all men. We may not be Florentines or Italians, but we can nonetheless be Machiavellians. Machiavelli shows his solicitude for foreigners by giving them advice in both *The Prince* (3) and the *Discourses* (I 23) on how to invade Italy. Much as he loved Florence and Italy, he is not fundamentally a city or national patriot. He is a patriot on behalf of humanity, seeking to protect men against outside forces, consequently a patriot of the home of human beings, the earth.

In *Discourses* III 2 Machiavelli praises a trick played by Junius Brutus, the father of Roman liberty. According to the oracle of Apollo (as reported by Livy), the first among a group of young men, including Brutus, who kissed his mother, would come to the "highest power in Rome." Brutus decided that his mother was the earth, and pretended to fall in order to kiss the earth. Machiavelli urges us to believe not only that Brutus was ambitious for himself but also that he wished to crush the kings and liberate his native country. Summing up the point in its highest case, Machiavelli says that a "man who is notable for his quality" cannot live quietly and untroubled out of politics. However insistently he forswears honor and profit, his excuses will be heard but not accepted. The attitude of philosophic detachment is impossible even for one who does not feel the attraction of honor and profit. You cannot stand so far from princes as not to arouse their suspicion, and if you attempt it, you will nonetheless be involved in their fall. This "middle way" of classical political science between partisanship and unconcern cannot be sustained because the extreme of unconcern is impossible. Even Plato and Aristotle can be described (though to a pope) as no less ambitious for glory than are princes.[43]

Necessity is always one's own necessity; that is why necessity overpowers any human capacity of detachment. What is necessary for me is especially what is necessary for me against you. Machiavelli says: "It is enough to ask someone for his weapon without saying, I wish to kill you with it; then after you have the weapon in your hand, you can satisfy your appetite" (*D* I 44). Since necessity is one's own as opposed to the necessity of others, one's designs prompted by necessity must be disguised. Like Brutus, the prudent man must use deceit. The most general mode of deception practiced by humans is by use of authority.[44] You say that some authority, for example the oracle of Apollo, supports or commands you, when in truth necessity requires it. When men use an authority, they put their own opinions in someone else's mouth—in the mouths of God or of their ancestors, or, like poets, in the mouths of their characters. Under necessity reason is translated into authority. Authority is reason in disguise, or better to say, authority is the effectual truth of detachment. Those who live a life of the mind, detached from politics, in effect elevate some authority in politics. This authority is not truly detached; it only pretends to be. It is their own necessity in disguise.

The greatest example of detachment become authority is the Christian God, which for Machiavelli, I will suggest, was the effectual truth of the classical notion of soul. The soul was intended to preserve human freedom and dignity, but the detachment of soul could be preserved only if one supposed that the soul is divine—that intelligence or soul is God, as Aristotle said. To prevent the divinity of soul from endangering human freedom, Aristotle may have conceived God as impersonal, but this reservation was unavailing. Any idea elevated above human beings is bound to be personified by them and made responsible for their good,[45] and the God of intelligence will be humanized and made providential. Aristotle's God was transformed into the personal Christian God that was used by priests to interfere with princes and tyrannize over peoples. The effectual truth of Aristotelianism was Christianity or that combination of Aristotle and Christianity which Thomas Hobbes was to call Aristotelity. Aristotle should have known that his detached intelligence in the soul would become a God that would be an outside force threatening the liberty of men.

Acting under necessity, then, Machiavelli substitutes what he calls *animo* ("spirit" or "spiritedness") for *anima* ("soul").[46] Whereas *anima* never occurs in *The Prince* and the *Discourses,* *animo* occurs frequently. *Animo* means a spirited defense of one's own, especially of one's own body; for *animo* defends a body and is satisfied with that body, but *anima* always attempts to transcend the body. *Animo* also means intent, as when Machiavelli urges the man notable for his quality to conceal his *animo* (*D* III 2); but the intent, even in this case, is never contemplative or detached from one's own concerns. *Animo* is responsible for *ostinazione,* the obstinacy characteristic of spirited infantry who have planted their feet on the ground.[47]

Machiavelli's principle of spirited selfishness offers something for everybody, not in a common good to which all may contribute different virtues, but (as he says so precisely) for the common benefit of everyone in the sense of each one (*ciascuno*). Each one in his separate body is encouraged by Machiavelli in the spirited defense of his own, because one's own body is the only common thing that can be benefited. Thus everyone can fight for his own glory and yet be one of the "good and faithful soldiers" to Machiavelli.[48] Machiavellism can advance without paying allegiance to Machiavelli. A new sect will emerge with an invisible leader that will offer princes more glory and people more security. Depending not on the virtue of rulers but only on virtue in the Machiavellian sense of imaginative aggrandizement, this sect will not be subject to the ups and downs of the cycle. States will rise and fall, but the whole will remain strong and mankind will progress in a condition Machiavelli calls "the perpetual republic."[49]

If Machiavelli's ambition seems grandiose, we should look carefully at the modern world we live in to see whether our ambition, which resembles his, is reasonable. Machiavelli, indeed, left a restraint on human aggrandizement, which has not proved durable. Since for him there is no soul or principle *above* one's own country, there could be no universal principle *beyond* one's country. The crucial political implication is that, for Machiavelli, no *patria* could ever regard itself as essential to the destiny of mankind. There could be no chosen people, race, or class. Machiavelli would have abhorred our twentieth-century tyrannies, but with our century in view he might have to admit that he had left no effectual alternative to dubious patriotism but a modern version of the "pious cruelty" (*P* 21) he had meant to destroy. Twentieth-century totalitarianism promises fantastic betterment in the human condition from the realization of universal principles, but it does not claim to improve the soul. It has, without reference to soul, proved to exceed the pious cruelty of any sect with which Machiavelli was acquainted.

Perhaps, then, not the asserted existence of soul but loss of moderation in the soul has been the cause of our troubles. But we shall never learn whether this is so if we hold to a political science that routinely excludes soul from what it calls "behavior" and flutters at the mention of virtue.

# TWELVE

# MACHIAVELLI'S *STATO* AND THE IMPERSONAL MODERN STATE

Nowadays when a person or party comes to power, it is said to take over *the* state or *the* government. It does not claim to advance *its* rule except through *the* state, as if to make it plain that the state does not belong, but is only delivered temporarily, in trust, to the winner of a struggle for power. The terms used may vary: in America one speaks of the Reagan administration, consisting of Reagan, his lieutenants, and an assortment of Republicans, as having taken over the (federal) government; in France, *le gouvernement* or *le régime Mitterrand* has acceded to *l'état*. But the impersonality of the modern state continues despite the variability of the terms used to express it. Even the Communists maintained the distinction, in theory, between their party and the state that the party established and yet existed to serve.

*The* state or *the* government is not constituted by the current holders of power; rather, it is there before they arrive, waiting to be claimed, and it will continue after they have departed, waiting with equanimity and impartial regard for the next claimant. The state may be thought to have no interest, like a neutral, or to have its own interest, in order to serve as an arbiter, but in either case the essential point is that it does not belong to any of the contending parties or groups. The state has an existence independent of such parties or groups. Indeed, its independence seems to be constituted not so much by self-subsistence, which would make it resemble those parties or groups, as by abstraction from them. Whenever the state gets "a life of its own," we may fear tyranny or hope for peace and

This chapter was originally published as "On the Impersonality of the Modern State: A Comment on Machiavelli's Use of *Stato*," *American Political Science Review*, December 1983, 849–57.

reason, but we do not understand that life to be the same as the lives of parties or groups from which the state is abstracted. If this discussion sounds abstract, it is partly because the modern state is an abstraction. We moderns find abstractions easier to denounce than to do without, and if we denounce the state as abstract, we mean, as Marx meant in denouncing Hegel, that it does not succeed in being abstract but remains a tool of the ruling party, group, or class. The ideal or standard of abstraction from personality is retained, or even heightened, in such denunciation.

Thus, when some modern person said *l'état, c'est moi,* this was already a paradox, stating a conjunction of the impersonal with his person.[1] He could not have said *c'est mon état,* implying that this state rather than some other or none was his. Our modern notions of legitimate power seem bound up with the impersonality of the modern state. Even the vaunted rationality of the modern state seems designed to ensure its impersonality. Hegel's rational state was to be ruled by a universal class of bureaucrats educated to remove the partialities of ordinary persons, and Max Weber's bureaucratic office is an ideal type of the modern attempt to deny that an office belongs to the officeholder.

Against this conception, one may set "the traditional idea of the prince maintaining his existing position and range of powers."[2] Such is Quentin Skinner's description of Machiavelli's usual or typical understanding of the relationship between prince and state. Skinner's impressive work, *The Foundations of Modern Political Thought,* aims to show how the modern state (or its foundations) evolved from this traditional idea of Machiavelli's to "the distinctively modern idea of the State as a form of public power separate from both the ruler and the ruled, and constituting the supreme political authority within a certain defined territory," which is to be found in Jean Bodin's thought at the end of the sixteenth century.[3] I shall question Skinner's description of Machiavelli's use of *stato* as traditional, but first I must endorse and elaborate his understanding of the traditional idea.

## ARISTOTLE'S PARTISAN REGIME

The traditional idea of the state comes from the notion of regime (*politeia*) in Plato and Aristotle, who do not make use of the term "state."[4] The regime, for them, means constitution in a fuller sense than the constitution of a modern state; it refers to the form or structure of the whole society and to its way of life as embodied in that structure. The offices or rules (*archai*) of the regime rule the society by giving that society its character; they are not separable from the society in such manner as to await impartially the winner of the power struggle within society. Only a democratic society, for example, consists with a democratic regime. A democratic regime, newly installed, proceeds as soon as it can to the democratizing of society and applies its principle of rule with partisan disregard for the neutrality of the "state" and the autonomy of "society."

Thus, says Aristotle, the city is chiefly the regime.[5] The city has territory and inhabitants, but these do not define it; one cannot make a city by constructing a wall around the Peloponnesus. Although a city must, of course, have a territory and a people, these are material for its *form,* which is its regime, and the city is defined chiefly by its form. It is not defined solely by its regime, because the regime is limited in what it can do by nature (for example, climate) and by human nature (the necessity to satisfy or to suppress human needs). It is also limited by custom, although custom, which consists anyway of practices established by the preceding regime or regimes, can sometimes change rapidly and utterly, to the amazement of all who rely on it. The regime of a city is not, moreover, some hidden essence lying behind its territory and people. Although the city is not defined by its inhabitants, the regime is *in* the inhabitants. It is publicly visible in its offices and in the characteristic behavior of its rulers as its ordering (*taxis*). A democratic regime, for example, *looks* democratic, for what is most visible is that which is public, and the public is what the rulers do not need or desire to conceal, their rule.

Far from being impersonal and impartial, like the modern state, the Aristotelian regime reflects—and advances—the characteristic claim of the persons who rule. Such persons do not merely claim to promote their own self-interest in a greater whole that is common to society, but they promote themselves in a partisan view of the whole that is typically theirs, and they advance that view against the opposing view of their typical opponents, democrats versus oligarchs, for example. As men cannot help preferring themselves, so regimes are necessarily partisan. In this view, *l'état, c'est moi* would apply to every regime, including a democratic one; in Aristotle's terms, the *politeia* is the *politeuma,* the body of rulers. They are the regime, and the regime is theirs.

If a mixed regime could be made, which is doubtful, it would advance the claim to rule of all parties or the whole. It would be impartial by combining all parties rather than by not promoting any party or by remaining indifferent to which party wins the struggle for power. This regime would be partisan to the common interest of all in virtue rather than impartial in the maintenance of liberty to facilitate the self-promotion of each person and all parties. By means of this mixed regime, one could judge the partisan claims of the lesser regimes and sort those regimes into good and bad. Such judgment is asked for, one could say, by the claims of the regimes. It requires an elevation above ordinary partisanship that begins from ordinary partisanship and that does not issue in neutrality.

We may suppose that the impersonality of the modern state, such as we find it in the full clarity of Hobbes's political science, may have been intended to correct the partisanship of the Aristotelian regime. For in the Aristotelian understanding as Hobbes saw it, the regime was left exposed to the capture of religious parties, who used it with tyrannical zeal and made it the prize of civil war. We may suppose, then, that the impersonality of the modern state was the chosen instrument of secularization. That hypothesis cannot be elaborated or tested here.[6] But it does seem necessary to have before us a more complete picture of the alternative to the modern state than is usually supplied in discussions of the usage of "state," so that we do not leave the impression that such usage evolved in mere response to changing circumstances or by naive, groping discovery of the only truly conceivable political unit, the modern state. Whatever may have been the causes that established the modern state, it had to be conceived against the authority of classical political science; and if it is to be argued that political necessities alone brought about the modern state, then it must be shown why those very necessities were newly conceived to require a new ordering and a new politics. In writing the history of the modern state, historians, it may be gently suggested, need clarification from political science.[7]

As far as I can see in the research of others, the classical understanding of the regime prevailed in medieval usage before Machiavelli. It is often not easy to see whether partisan regime or impersonal state is in question, because of the unhistorical habit, almost universal in medieval historians, of using the term "state" before it occurs or not as it was used in history.[8] This habit is a form of superiority that implies that the observer knows what is going on better than the participant, as, for example, when the observer knows that the participant lives in a "medieval" period whereas the participant knew or conceived no such thing. Many medieval historians are in truth scholars of the unnoticed beginnings of modernity. Sometimes they speak of "the state" as taking shape, implying that the state is essentially modern; sometimes they contrast the "medieval state" with the "modern state," implying that the state is essentially universal. Although Aristotle founded his political science on the distinction between *polis* and *politeia,* one can find both terms (in their Latin equivalents, *civitas* and *respublica* or *politia*) translated as "state."[9] This is not to say that "state" was from the first used impersonally (I shall argue that Machiavelli's use of *stato* was not impersonal), much less that words are always used with full awareness of their meaning or that meanings of words never change. But caution compels us to question whether the "state" is progressive or universal, as it may appear to us.

The word "state" does indeed occur in political contexts in the Middle Ages, but to name the regime, not a neutral, impersonal state. In this usage the Latin *status* does not stand alone, but requires some accompanying word or phrase to specify whose *status.*[10] The "state of the Church" (*status ecclesiae*) or "state of the realm" (*status regni*) has the general meaning of "state" as condition, still in use today, in which one must specify the condition of what. The condition implied is a condition of stability or a good condition, so that *status* could mean the welfare (of the realm) or the well-being (of the Church), which sets limits on the actions of the pope.[11] *Status* did not mean the extent of effective power, when power is abstracted from its particular ends and is generalized as the power to do anything. When *status* comes to mean abstract, general power, effective for any end, we see the connection between state as a general or universal condition and state as sovereign, and we recognize the modern state.

To illustrate the meaning of *status,* we may consider Thomas Aquinas's commentary on Aristotle's *Politics* (ca. 1260), an authoritative source because of its influence and because its object is political science, not legal argument. Neither Thomas in his commentary nor William of Moerbeke in his translation makes use of *status* for the discussion of the regime in the third book of the *Politics*. But *status* does enter the revision of Aquinas's commentary made by Ludovicus de Valentia in 1492 using Leonardo Bruni's translation of Aristotle from the early fifteenth century.[12] As instances of a general rejection of Moerbeke's Grecisms, *oligarchia* becomes *status paucorum,* and *democratia, status popularis*. This is done in a context where the *politia* (regime) is said to be nothing other than the *ordo dominantum* in the city.[13] The "state of the few," then, is their domination; but it is also their condition, order, or way of life, which is the condition of the city where they dominate. This thoroughly unmodern identification of the *power* in a society with the *condition* of that society, which makes its politics responsible for its way of life, seems characteristic of medieval usage, and of Florentine usage as well, before Machiavelli.[14]

## IMPERSONAL RULE

It is generally agreed that the modern state was constituted by an abstraction from personal to impersonal rule, but it is not generally appreciated how radical that abstraction was. To move from *status* with its concrete specification to *status* or state without such specification was not enough, if the state thus abstracted still refers to someone's or some group's personal rule, although it does not matter which. That state is no more abstract than Aristotle's regime, the term for which can stand alone but always signifies one or another form of personal rule. Skinner[15] finds the earliest impersonal use of "state" to be, perhaps, in Thomas Starkey's *A Dialogue between Reginald Pole and Thomas Lupset,* completed in 1535. There one finds "the whole state,"[16] "the perfect state,"[17] and "a mixed state."[18] But in these instances and in all others I could find,[19] "state" is used in the traditional Aristotelian sense of regime. For Starkey, the state was both the condition of being ruled and the rulers, with no hint of a distinction between state and society. Starkey used the term "state" impersonally, but he had by no means achieved the radical abstraction of an impersonal state.

Thus, to look for the rise of the modern state in the fashioning of sovereignty may be misleading, if it is done without attention to the peculiar character of sovereignty in the modern state. Modern sovereignty is impersonal, and the modern sovereign prescribes what he must (which may be much) only or mainly to keep the peace and his own power intact.[20] But if one is content to seek sovereignty in uncontested power, one will mistake the rediscovery of the regime in Aristotle's *Ethics* and *Politics,* which occurred in the thirteenth century, for the modern state.[21] The Aristotelian regime was not a way station toward the modern state but rather the greatest obstacle to its conception.

The rediscovery of the Aristotelian regime did undermine the legal character of medieval political thought. For according to Aristotle, the regime, or the human legislator, is the source of law, rather than law the source of the regime.[22] The reassertion of this truth could not fail to subvert the fundamental premises both of Roman law, the pretense by which an empire is presented as the choice of a republic, and of canon law, the claim that law has a divine source. Those who find the origin of the impersonal, modern state in the legal conceptions of medieval corporatism also underestimate the radical nature of the modern state. To realize the impersonality of the modern state, it is not enough merely to distinguish between person and office, since that separation is already accomplished in the offices of the Aristotelian regime. The modern state requires much more: that offices not be used for personal rule according to the opinions of the rulers. If this is to happen, the state as a corporation must be radically abstracted from the actual persons who govern through it. The medieval corporation, often called *universitas,* was the legal person of a preexisting group, for example the monks of a monastery. It conferred a legal immortality on their group, thus a certain impersonality, but it did not require the monks to abstract from their character as monks when constituting the *universitas.*

A greater abstraction occurred when *universitas* was used to describe the community that was the source of law beyond communities existing under the law.[23] But again, although a legal person, the *universitas* was a particular community, a particular people having an existence before its legal existence; the legality conferred by incorporation was a baptism, not a creation.[24] Hence, as Brian Tierney explains the principle of medieval corporatism, the people command as *universitas* but obey as individuals.[25] This is the precise opposite of the principle by which the modern state is incorporated: according to Hobbes and our present understanding, we are free as individuals and obey as citizens. The medieval individual is an individual *of* a certain multitude; the modern individual is abstracted from any multitude. The modern state is created by incorporation from the "state of nature" of abstract individuals or something like it. The modern state is not merely a legalized, incorporated version of a preexisting regime; it is artificial in order to abstract from any regime that might be lurking behind the medieval corporation.

## MACHIAVELLI'S PERSONAL STATE

With Machiavelli, however, we encounter a fundamental challenge to the classical regime, which is expressed in his use of *stato*. At first sight Machiavelli's use of *stato* appears quite traditional (as Skinner says) or Aristotelian, that is, quite foreign to us, for we are struck by the phrases *suo stato* and *loro stato,* which frequently inform us that the impersonal modern state is not in question.[26] At the same time we frequently encounter *lo stato* standing by itself, which might make us think that the impersonality of the modern state is under way. But such an impression would be misleading. With us *the* state signifies something impersonal, and we do not use a possessive pronoun. When Machiavelli uses *lo stato* without a possessive pronoun, however, he seems always to imply one. Merely because the word *stato* in the Italian of Machiavelli and of his contemporaries had acquired the ability to stand alone by contrast to the Latin *status,* it does not follow that *stato* meant "impersonal state" any more than did *politia* in Moerbeke's translation of Aristotle's *politeia,* which also stood by itself. The phrases Skinner cites[27] as possible counter-examples suggesting a tincture of impersonality in Machiavelli's *stato*—*la maestà dello stato, l'autorità dello stato, la mutazione dello stato*—prove on examination to refer to the majesty, authority, and change of *someone's* state. The someone may be collective, as in *stato di Firenze,* but that does not make Florence's state any less personal than Aristotle's *status popularis* (in Bruni's translation of Aquinas's commentary), which is a regime belonging to the people. If the *stato di Firenze* includes Pisa, that is because Pisa belongs to the Florentines.

When Machiavelli says at the end of the ninth chapter of *The Prince* that the wise prince should think of a way by which his citizens always have need *dello stato e di lui,* he distinguishes that prince from the state but hardly denies that the state is the prince's.[28] When he says in the same place that *lo stato* has need of the citizens, he obviously refers to that same prince's state. And in the eighteenth chapter of the *Discourses on Livy,* when he speaks of the difficulty of maintaining *lo stato libero* in a corrupt city, the difficulty is that of keeping free the state belonging to a corrupt people, not that of keeping an impersonal state free. For, as we learn in the sixteenth chapter, even the *libero stato* has partisan friends and enemies.

*Stato* can also appear in an objective genitive, as in *stato di Lombardia* and *stato di Asia* (*FH* I 37; *P* 4). These "states" did not belong to Lombardy and Asia, but they did belong to Filippo Visconti and Alexander, respectively. Machiavelli refers to *quello stato,* "which had ruled from 1381 to 1434" in Florence (*FH* III 29), meaning "that state" that was held by and passed through many hands in those years. But neither many hands at one time nor different hands over time make Machiavelli's *stato* any more impersonal than Aristotle's regime.[29] Nor does a personification of *stato,* which occurs rarely in Machiavelli, signify the presence of the modern impersonal state, because the state that is personified is still someone's, like the Aristotelian regime. *Ne creda mai alcuno stato* ("nor should any state ever believe," *P* 21) states clearly in the context what "the prince" should never believe, although "prince" here refers to the Venetians and the Florentines. And *il sospetto che lo stato aveva* ("the suspicion that the state had," *FH* III 23) refers to the "princes of the state" soon after. *Questi stati tengono il cuore disarmato e le mani e li piedi armati* ("these states keep their hearts unarmed and their hands and feet armed," *D* II 30) refers to a mistake of both princes and republics in regard to their states. *Stato* is not made impersonal with its own verb any more than with the impersonal article so long as someone's or some party's personal state is meant.[30] One person's *stato* can be exchanged for another's (*FH* VI 30); so *stato* is not as personal as an old shoe. As we shall see, *stato* is personal not because it suits you but because you have acquired it. The *arte dello stato* that Machiavelli said he had been studying for fifteen years (in the letter of December 10, 1513, in which he casually announces he has completed *The Prince;* cf. letter of April 9, 1513) is the universal or impersonal art of maintaining personal domination.[31] Without prolonging this discussion, I cannot say that I have found in any of Machiavelli's writings an instance of the impersonal modern state among his uses of *stato*.

This does not mean, however, that Machiavelli's *stato* is a regime in the traditional or classical sense. As J. H. Hexter has shown in his well-known study, *stato* in *The Prince* is used almost invariably in an exploitative sense: someone is almost always exploiting someone else by means of *lo stato*.[32] It might be better to say that *stato* is such exploitation,[33] and one might wish to avoid the anachronism "exploitation" and speak of domination (*dominio*) or mastery (*signoria*) or empire (*imperio*), as Machiavelli does. Machiavelli comes as close as he ever does to a definition of *stato* in the first sentence of *The Prince:* "All states, all dominions [*dominii*] that have had and have empire [*imperio*] over men have been and are either republics or principalities."[34] Here "states," either republics or principalities, are in apposition to "dominions" that have "empire" over men. A quick survey of some features of Machiavelli's political thought will show how far this empire over men is from the Aristotelian regime.[35]

Machiavelli's *stato* is someone's to acquire or to maintain. The state itself never acquires or maintains on its own account separate from the advantage of some person or group: this is the critical test that tells us Machiavelli's state is not impersonal.[36] But if *stato* is always the advantage of someone over someone else, acquiring and maintaining the state cannot be equally important. In the second chapter of *The Prince,* Machiavelli lets us think that the hereditary prince, who has not acquired his principality, is "the natural prince" because he maintains it more easily. But in the third chapter we are rudely informed of "the natural and ordinary desire to acquire," and in the sixth chapter we learn that those princes who acquire their states with difficulty and by virtue, in total contrast to hereditary princes, keep them with ease. Meanwhile, in the fifth chapter of the *Discourses,* Machiavelli says that those who want to maintain their possessions have the same wish as those who want to acquire, namely, the wish to acquire, since men do not think they possess anything securely unless they are acquiring something new. One cannot sit still to maintain what one has, we learn in the next chapter, because "all human things are in motion." Thus in both *The Prince* and the *Discourses,* for both princes and republics, acquisition comes first.

## MACHIAVELLI'S NEUTRALITY

This conclusion, so contrary to Aristotle's politics as well as his ethics, cannot but affect Machiavelli's notion of *stato*.[37] I shall mention three changes it produces by comparison to Aristotle's regime, in the ordering of the state, the claims it advances, and the neutrality it recommends.

First, whereas for Aristotle the regime is "some ordering of the inhabitants of the city" that remains visible in its form as long as the regime lasts, for Machiavelli the "order" or "orders" of the state must be subject to change.[38] Given the necessity to acquire and the consequent loosening of moral restraint, neither princes nor republics can afford to retain subordinates or maintain institutions that become inconvenient. Princes must be capable of using others as Cesare Borgia, himself the instrument of his father, Alexander VI, used Remirro de Orco (*P* 7); and in republics, "orders" must be manipulated with new "modes" and then changed into new orders when the "matter" of a city is becoming corrupted or when an emergency arises, for example the challenge to the Senate posed by ambitious leaders of the plebeians. In both cases the true ordering of the state is not what appears to the public, but what goes on behind the scenes; and this contrast is confirmed and expanded by the obvious importance of conspiracy in Machiavelli's political thought in comparison to Aristotle's.[39] What is visible in Machiavelli's state is not the character of power, but rather its effectual extent. With this difference we are on the way toward defining the state by its territory and people.[40]

Second, the necessity to acquire determines the characteristic claims of states. Since states must acquire, they must yield to, nay incite, the desire for glory in those men of a princely nature who most evince that desire. At the same time, the people must be conciliated and their desire for security satisfied when possible, if only to maintain the glory of princes and princely leaders in republics. If a common good is sought between princes and peoples, it must accommodate their diverse but complementary desires for glory and

security, whatever the claims of regimes may be. Although Machiavelli keeps the traditional Roman distinction between principalities
and republics, he does not stress the characteristically opposing
claims of those regimes; he throws cold water both on the typical
republican hatred for "the name of prince" and on princely disdain
for the fickleness of popular government (D I 58; II 2). He erodes
the traditional distinction with such phrases as "princes in the republic" and "civil principality" and with similar advice to both on how
to misbehave. Despite their contrasting claims to virtue, states are
to be judged by their "effectual truth" in acquiring glory and maintaining security. One hardly need add that, for Machiavelli, glory
and security are in this world. It was to prevent the appropriation
of the classical regime and its claims of justice by the city of God
and the "Christian republic" that he directed the attention of both
republics and principalities toward worldly gain.

Thus, on returning to the first sentence of *The Prince*, we can
see that Machiavelli's use of *stato* enables him to be neutral between
republics and principalities. Whereas for Aristotle the better regimes
are regimes in a truer sense than the worse ones,[41] for Machiavelli
principalities are as much states as are republics. His well-known
but not always well-examined preference for republics is carefully
qualified: the common good "is not observed if not in republics,"
but it consists in the oppression of the few by the many, and to be
conquered by a republic is the hardest slavery.[42] Nothing prevents
a prince in a "civil principality" (P 9) from benefiting the people as
much as they may be in a free republic, and in any case Machiavelli
sees quite clearly that *stato* won by collective selfishness has no
moral superiority over that acquired by individual selfishness. The
reason is that they hardly differ. Just as every prince needs a people,
so every people needs a head—an ambitious tribune, consul, dictator, or senate—to direct it as a people in its acquisitions.

Machiavelli's neutrality is evident in his use of the medieval term
for corporation, *università*, in Chapter 19 of *The Prince*. Although
in earlier chapters he had stressed the need for the prince to have
the favor, or at least to avoid the hatred, of the people in order to
maintain his state, he now suddenly changes his tune. Since the
prince cannot help being hated by someone, Machiavelli discloses
for the first time, he is at first compelled not to be hated by the
*università* (that is, the people or everyone); but when he cannot do

this, he must contrive to avoid the hatred of the most powerful *università* (in the plural), that is, the soldiers. Thus Machiavelli's preference for a democratic over an undemocratic policy is not absolute and is determined by necessity, not choice. In this statement of it, he uses the medieval term *università* in both senses of corporation within the law and community that is the source of law, but with brusque disregard for law and legality.

I conclude that the path to the modern state was not by way of Machiavelli's republicanism, as Pocock[43] has argued. Machiavelli's republicanism shows no more of the impersonality of the modern state than does his advice to princes. A republic is the *stato* of a certain group as a principality is the *stato* of the prince, in both cases an effectual acquisition. An effectual acquisition is one properly maintained, that is, continually refreshed with new acquisitions. Rather than in his republicanism, such as it was, Machiavelli's step toward the impersonality of the modern state can be seen in his impartial advice to all parties and persons to acquire when they can. The very universality of his advice to be partial to oneself requires that he be neutral between the parties he advises, for example between princes and republics.[44] Republicanism, therefore, is not a continuous tradition from ancient to modern times, for somewhere between ancient and modern republicanism, the concept of the impersonal modern state was introduced. Aristotle lacks it, and Rousseau has it.[45] This concept came not from within republicanism, but from an attitude of neutrality toward republics in the old sense of partisan regimes, which required a transformation of the republican spirit. To this consideration, one should add the impressive and obvious fact that everywhere in the West the modern state was, or was the work of, a monarchy.

Nonetheless, to say that the change from the personal state to the impersonal state was "the decisive shift," as Skinner does,[46] is somewhat misleading. Rather, the decisive shift was from the personal state in the Aristotelian sense to the *acquisitive* personal state of Machiavelli. For this change provided the impartiality that is fundamental to the modern state. Implicit in Machiavelli's general advice to acquire was an impartial regard for all who might be capable of applying it. After this it was but a step (although a step Machiavelli did not take) to a state that might acquire for all and facilitate the acquisitions of all impartially.[47] Thus the impersonal modern state was conceived not in, but out of, the thought of the most personal political philosopher that we know, in the sense of recommending self-aggrandizement. That is why finding medieval anticipations of impersonality does not suffice to explain the modern state, for the modern state expresses Machiavelli's impartial acquisitiveness in its formulations of impersonal legality.

The state of *ragione di stato* appeared in 1589, soon after Machiavelli, in a book of that name by Giovanni Botero, a seeming critic but actually a follower of Machiavelli. That state, as opposed to Machiavelli's, was said to be impartially acquisitive because the reasoning of its *ragione* was not the ruler's but the state's. Hence the state, unlike Machiavelli's, was not oppressive to the ruled.[48] But the full conception of the modern state had to await the political science of Hobbes.

What Skinner calls the "main elements" of the modern state gradually acquired between Machiavelli and Hobbes were mere materials assembled for Hobbes's construction on a foundation prepared by Machiavelli. It was Hobbes who distinguished state from society, thus allowing the state to represent society impartially; he who, to make this distinction, invented the concept of the state of nature yielding natural rights before natural duties and the right of self-preservation generalizing and legalizing Machiavelli's advice to acquire; and he it was who conceived the impersonal state as an artificial person whose words and deeds were "owned" by his subjects, not by himself. Only with a view to Hobbes could we know what the various anticipations of the modern state were anticipating, but the decision in the "decisive shift" to modernity was taken by Machiavelli.

# THIRTEEN

# MACHIAVELLI AND THE MODERN EXECUTIVE

The modern executive, whether in politics or business, feels a vague but uneasy kinship with Machiavelli that he rarely seeks to define or escape by reading the works of Machiavelli. Perhaps in his mind he delegates this task to the scholars of Machiavelli, most of whom assume that Machiavelli, despite his reputation as the philosopher of scheming evil, was neither a deep thinker nor a teacher of anything to make us uneasy. Whether out of complacency, pride, or fastidiousness, scholars have not accepted this commission and have not explored the instinctive kinship between Machiavelli and the modern executive. If they had done so, they might have found so precise a kinship as would compel them to consider whether Machiavelli might actually be the author of the modern executive. For not only do the two share an attitude and certain methods but also Machiavelli is the first writer on politics to use the word *execute* frequently and thematically in its modern sense.

What is that modern sense? An answer requires a brief consideration of Machiavelli's fundamental notions; then I connect these to Machiavelli's uses of *execute* and develop his notion of *esecuzioni* and the executive.

Machiavelli was not the first political philosopher to make a theme of execution. Marsilius of Padua in his *Defensor pacis* presents all government as executive of the will of the sovereign people. Marsilius was heir to the tradition of Aristotle, and although Aristotle made little or nothing of executive power, Marsilius remained true to him by subordinating executive power to natural law or

This chapter was originally published as "Machiavelli and the Modern Executive," in *Understanding the Political Spirit,* ed. Catherine H. Zuckert (New Haven: Yale University Press, 1988), 88–110.

natural right, so that executive power never escapes the supervision of law and morality. But Marsilius's and Aristotle's subordination or belittling of the executive in favor of law does not mean that they were blind to the problematic character of law.

That law cannot attain what it attempts is the problem to which the modern notion of executive power is a solution. Law is too universal to be rational, and it needs assistance from outside to specify what is reasonable in each case, which may be against the spirit as well as the letter of the law. Even if law were rational, it would need help in demonstrating its rationality against human beings' stubborn insistence on having things their own way. When law encounters this stubbornness, it resorts to universality and says: you are treated the same as everyone else. Thus the second difficulty feeds the first, and law introduces a problem it cannot resolve on its own.

Executive power is only one solution to the problem of law. Another solution is Aristotle's kingship, which is still to be found in Marsilius.[1] The kingship of the good man or the best man is above the law because of his virtue. This kingship is impossible or impracticable, but it reminds us that although law never attains virtue, it aims at virtue. If it could be shown—and Aristotle is doubtful about this—that virtue is man's perfection and that man's perfection makes a necessary contribution to nature as a whole, then the kingship of the good man would be according to nature. One would then have the ground on which to assert that departure from the law in the direction of this kingship is not tyrannical but is in accord with natural right, that the problem of law can be resolved, or at least can be treated, with regard to the virtue that our nature permits us. Machiavelli does not merely doubt this assertion, he denies it. Of his many and various statements by indirection, he says the most in his resounding silence on natural right or natural law, neither of which he ever mentions in any of his works. This is his most evident difference from Marsilius. Indeed, political science neither of his time nor of his tradition gives precedent or excuse for this silence, which cannot be inadvertent.[2]

With this silence Machiavelli calls forth, from the "context" into which he is often squeezed today, such as makes his thought appear derivative and harmless, to say something extraordinary and profoundly unsettling. He agrees with Aristotle that law is not enough but denies that departure from it can be justified by natural right; without a trace of squeamishness, indeed with evident relish, he swallows the conclusion that tyranny is necessary to good government. Since law cannot demonstrate its reasonableness, it needs force; since nature does not supply or justify this force, men must find or generate their own. In repeated, sensational acts of execution, men can compel obedience to the law by exercising force beyond the law. These acts, which Machiavelli calls *esecuzioni,* have, so to speak, nothing to do with either law or justice. Whereas in Aristotle what is beyond law is above it, in Machiavelli what is beyond law is below it. Aristotle always respects the law and requires that even the kingship of the best man adopt it. Machiavelli openly mocks the law; although he does not deny the need for good laws (see *D* I 33), he asserts that good arms are enough to ensure good laws (*P* 12).

While never referring to natural right, Machiavelli does mention nature and, as everyone knows, speaks frequently of virtue.[3] But his nature and virtue are not those of Aristotle or the tradition of classical political science. For Machiavelli, nature is understood as, or is replaced by, the necessity that forces us to gain nutriment, safety, and glory;[4] virtue becomes the habit or faculty or quality of anticipating that threefold necessity. The transformation of virtue required for its new function, in which it is no longer either an end in itself or devoted to human perfection, is indicated by the reluctance of Machiavelli's translators to render his *virtù* as virtue. They call it ingenuity or valor or vigor, thereby revealing that something new is intended while concealing the fact that Machiavelli calls it *virtue.*

In anticipating necessity, virtue for Machiavelli has a twofold character that is responsible for the peculiar ambivalence of the modern executive. The executive is strong but claims to be acting on behalf of a will or force that is stronger.[5] Virtue overcomes necessity and in this sense is understood in opposition to nature (by contrast to Aristotelian natural right), but to overcome necessity virtue makes use of necessity, and in this sense it is understood in obedience to nature (*D* II 3; III 1; also by contrast to Aristotle's natural right, which permits human choice). Thus, to anticipate necessity, you must get ahead of the other fellow; when you have succeeded in securing yourself (*assicurarsi*), you have defeated the other fellow but not the necessity of defeating him—and others after him. Your virtue is both strong and weak: strong because you have chosen to do what you would eventually have been forced to do; weak because you had no other choice. Accordingly, Machiavelli speaks of executors with ambivalence. At one point (*P* 6) he describes Moses as a "mere executor of the things that had been ordained by God," but later (*P* 26) he praises "the virtue of Moses" in taking advantage of an opportunity afforded him; and elsewhere he says that Moses was forced to kill countless men who out of envy were opposed to "his designs" (*D* III 30), that is, Moses' not God's. To balance the single mention in his writings of "mere executor" in *The Prince,* he refers once to the need for *uno ostinato esecutore* ("a determined executor") in the *Discourses on Livy* (III 1).

The Machiavellian executive is more usually known as the Machiavellian prince, and of course more usually called so by Machiavelli. But we shall find that the ways of the prince are essential elements of the modern executive; Machiavelli's frequent use of *executive,* perhaps in response to Marsilius, is far from incidental to his main conceptions. But *esecuzione* is fundamental for the modern executive. Seven elements of the modern executive originate in Machiavelli: the political use of punishment, which demands an outsized executive; the primacy of war and foreign affairs over peace and domestic affairs, which greatly increases the occasions for emergency powers; the use of indirect government, when ruling is perceived to be executing on behalf of someone or some group other than the ruler; the erosion of differences among regimes as wholes, through the discovery or development of techniques of governing applicable to all regimes; the need for decisiveness, for government is best done suddenly; the value of secrecy in order to gain surprise; and the necessity of the single executive, "one alone," to take on himself the glory and the blame. Each of these elements can be contrasted to Aristotle's notions to see how Machiavelli's executive is revolutionary, and all elements are illustrated in Machiavelli's use of the term *execute.*[6]

## POLITICAL PUNISHMENT

Among the many sensational statements with which Machiavelli takes delight in shocking his readers, few are more eye-catching than his pronouncement that "mixed bodies" such as sects, republics, and kingdoms need periodic "executions" to return them toward their beginnings in order to rid them of corruption (D III I). This is the most prominent of his remarks on executive power. The executions in question are both killings and punishments of lawbreakers— executions in both primary meanings of the word, which coincide in capital punishments. These executions do punish criminals, but they are praised for their "good effects" and not for their accuracy in retribution. It does not seem important that a formal law has been broken, still less that procedural regularity has been preserved. If a law has not been transgressed, then "orders" or institutions need to be revived when they have been used corruptly merely for self-advancement; indeed, it is human ambition and insolence that need to be restrained, rather than actual violations of the law punished. Machiavelli even promises that had Rome been able to schedule important executions every ten years, "it would follow of necessity that she would never have become corrupt" (D III I; see III 22). He does not entertain any doubts from the scrupulous as to whether deserving criminals would always keep to his schedule. What matters is that the executions be "excessive and notable." Soon after Machiavelli drops the reference to laws and orders as explicitly as only he can: "after a change of state, either from republic to tyranny or from tyranny to republic, a memorable execution against the enemies of the present conditions is necessary" (D III 3). The execution may as well be tyrannical as legal, provided that it be memorable. The good effects of such executions are to revive "that terror and that fear" (D III I) that has faded from vivid memory since the beginnings of the sect, republic, or kingdom.

Thus criminal justice is used—why not say perverted?—for political effect. The effect is not marginal: we would lose something significant by foregoing executions for the sake of legality; memorable executions are crucial to the salvation of the regime. Aristotle disposes his thought entirely to the contrary. In the *Ethics* he distinguishes criminal justice from distributive justice, and he connects distributive justice to politics and political justice. Criminal justice, hardly discussed, is categorized with the justice of contracts as a kind of transaction (NE 1131a2) and is left aside as neutral or inconsequential to the politics of a city. In the *Politics* little is said of punishment and nothing is made of the offices of punishment because Aristotle wants to remove politics from subservience to punitive gods. For Aristotle, the true beneficiaries of an enlarged execu-

tive power would be the priests; he wanted to keep them subordinate
to the offices of the regime in which human choice and deliberation
could prevail.[7] The sacral cities around him were not to be encouraged in their desire for revenge and punishment. Aristotle's anticlericalism has to be discerned through the delicate conciseness of his
rhetoric and through the moderation necessitated by his opposition
to philosophers. In the different circumstances that Marsilius faced,
with the papacy a "singular cause" of disunion, Aristotle's subdued
dislike came out into the open.

Machiavelli easily surpassed both Aristotle and Marsilius in
anticlericalism, and he wished to hold priests under political control,
but he thought it necessary to express or purge revenge and then
restrain it through fear rather than justice. The fear generated by
the return toward the beginnings substitutes for fear of God, which
Machiavelli remarks is used by priests but not felt by them: "They
do the worst they can, because they do not fear the punishment they
do not see and do not believe in" (D III 1). Memorable executions
not only restrain the ambition and insolence of those active in politics but also purge the people of the ill humors they feel against a
prominent citizen. The accusations Machiavelli says are necessary
to keeping republics in freedom definitively conclude with an "execution" that must be made without the "private" or "foreign" forces
that priests, especially, have at their call (D I 7). Similarly, in *The
Prince* Machiavelli explains that the Florentine people, through too
much mercy, once allowed disorders to spread that could have been
quelled with a very few examples of cruelty. Disorders, Machiavelli
points out, harm a whole people, but "the executions that come
from a prince hurt one particular individual" (P 17). Machiavelli's
lesson is that too much love leads to cruelty, but the economy of
single executions should not be mistaken for justice any more than
should their memorableness. In fact, when it comes to punishing a
multitude, Machiavelli does not hang back. He praises the greatness
of the Roman republic and "the power of its executions," among
which the decimation of a multitude was "terrible" (D III 49). For
when a whole multitude deserves punishment, and only a part receives it because there are too many to punish, one does wrong to
those punished and inspires the unpunished to err on another occasion. But when a tenth selected by chance are killed, and all deserve

it, the punished lament their bad luck and the unpunished are afraid to misbehave the next time.

This discussion could easily be interpreted (or misinterpreted if one wishes to preserve Machiavelli's innocence) as a political appropriation of the Christian doctrine of original sin, just as the memorable execution could be seen as a suggested use for the Christian doctrine of redemption. Machiavelli, it would appear, is not above reviving states through a notion of punishment taken from the very institution that he accuses of having "rendered the world weak and given it in prey to wicked men" (*D* II 2: see I pr). The modern doctrine of executive power begins in Machiavelli's appropriation, for worldly advantage and human use, of the power that men had been said to exercise in executing God's will. At the end of Machiavelli's dialogue *The Art of War,* the principal interlocutor Fabrizio laments that nature either should not have given him the knowledge of how to revive and expand states or should have given him the faculty of "executing" it (*AW* VII 367b). Since nature gives men knowledge without the faculty of execution, men must execute on their own, using (in Machiavelli's famous phrase) their own arms; they must not wait for help from God and nature. But they have at their disposal knowledge from nature, the knowledge of their own nature, including truths discerned and misapplied by Christian doctrine, now to be interpreted "according to virtue" (*D* II 2) by Machiavelli. Machiavelli attempted to make "the world," that is, mankind, strong again, but he did so by showing it how to submit to its own nature.

Because God or nature cannot be relied on to help execute men's laws, there being no natural law or natural right behind those laws, the power of execution must expand. Execution must lose the close subordination to law that it retains in Aristotle and Marsilius. Only once in Machiavelli's major writings, I believe, does "execute" occur with "law" in such a way that it is clear a law is being executed (*FH* VII 3). In other cases, the following are said to be executed: authority (*FH* I 16), undertaking (*FH* VI 29, VIII 4), office (*FH* V 21), thought (*FH* VII 34), conspiracy (*FH* VIII 4, 5; *D* III 6—of which more later), desire (*FH* VIII 26), public decisions (*FH* VIII 29, *D* I 33), important thing (*D* I 49), everything (*D* II 2), these things (*AW* V 331b), preparations (*AW* I 274b), practice (*AW* I 303b), policy (*AW* VII 362b), evil (*P* 19), command (*AW* VI 348a), and commission (*FH* IV 10, *D* III 6). Only the last two can be called weak uses of *execute*.[8] In many more cases, what is executed is left unstated—clearly a strong use (see *D* III 27, *FH* II 12, 25, 26, 34; III 14, 19; VII 6, 21, 32, 34; VIII 36). Nor must we forget the notable executions already discussed, from which law is conspicuously absent (*D* III 1, 3, see also *FH* II 34; III 19, 21; IV 30). In sum, these uses of *execute*[9] add up to an outsized executive who, because the function of punishment must be understood politically, is not confined to carrying out the law. Executions do indeed cause laws to be obeyed; in a general sense they are subordinate to law. But *legal* executions do not suffice, and law must accept the help of illegality to secure its enforcement.

### THE PRIMACY OF WAR AND FOREIGN AFFAIRS

Once execution is liberated from its clear subordination to law and its connection to justice, it becomes available as a remedy for emergencies generally, not merely for the exigencies of law enforcement. Such emergencies can arise from sudden foreign dangers as easily as from obstreperous ambition at home, and to be met they require a large delegation of power. One of Aristotle's five kinds of kingship is the general, with powers delegated for war; he is a regular official who ruled in accordance with law.[10] By contrast, Machiavelli praises the Roman practice of creating a dictator in emergencies "when an inconvenience has grown in a state or against a state" (*D* I 33). This gives "power to one man who could decide without any consultation and could execute his decisions without any appeal."[11] Machiavelli denies that dictatorial authority is harmful or that it brought tyranny to Rome, as had been alleged. The dictator was very useful not only when the Roman republic was threatened from without but also—now Machiavelli reverses the moral ground—"in the increase of its empire."[12]

Thus, just as with regard to punishment Machiavelli steps past the difficulties of law enforcement to embrace the necessity of injustice, so with foreign affairs he turns from dealing with emergencies that may arise from any state minding its own business to those that a state with imperial ambition necessarily seeks out or creates to serve as pretexts (see *D* III 16). Whereas Plato's *Republic* and Aristotle's *Politics* deal summarily with foreign affairs, Machiavelli's *Discourses on Livy,* according to its announced plan, is half devoted to foreign affairs, and *The Prince* at least as much. In the Middle Ages, the classical tradition had to be modified by Muslims and Jews to take account of their relations with gentiles. It had to be adapted by Christians to the broad sway of emperors and popes. These modifications introduced new matter for foreign policy yet did not affect the status of justice, hence the primacy of domestic affairs. But when fear replaces justice as the ground for politics, as in Machiavelli, acquisition is loosed from restraint, and political science assumes the task of explaining to princes how they must acquire and keep their states and to republics how they must overcome corruption and expand. Governments must be taught to treat their own peoples as they would treat foreign peoples subject to them—not necessarily badly but not with trust and justice. The notable executions that perpetuate states, together with the dictator's power to execute his own decisions, which expands states, indicate Machiavelli's new emphasis on survival in politics. Classical political science, assuming that all regimes moved through a cycle and were fated to die, judged regimes by how they behaved not by how long they survived. Machiavelli dismisses the cycle because states would surely become subject to better-ordered neighbors instead of suffering through their own ills in isolation (*D* I 2).[13] His new domestic policy justifies the primacy of foreign policy, and both are supported by expanded executive power.

## EXECUTION AS UNIVERSAL TECHNIQUE

The best regime, which is the theme of classical political science, does not exist according to Machiavelli. The natural right that would be required to elaborate the best regime, even if it could be done only in speech, does not exist according to him. He disdains such "imaginary republics and principalities" (*P* 15) and asserts that in all human affairs one inconvenience can never be canceled without giving rise to another (*D* I 6). His concern is with actual regimes and their deeds, not with the speeches in which they claim to be best, to be wholes, and to advance the common good. These claims give regimes their distinctive characters; they were seized on by classical political science as means of understanding capable of being refined to measures of judgment.[14]

Machiavelli, who rarely speaks of regimes, abandons the classical classification of six regimes (see *D* I 2) and adopts from Roman tradition the distinction between republics and principalities (*P* 1). But in making use of this distinction, he does not preserve the characteristic opposition between republics and principalities in what they claim against each other. He makes light both of the typical republican hatred for the "name of the prince" and the "name of king" and of princely disdain for the fickleness of popular government (*D* I 58, II 2). He also erodes the traditional distinction in such phrases as "princes in the republic" and "civil principality," which imply that republics are in need of princes and that principalities can be considered as republics. Republics and principalities converge in this way because both are to be judged not by their contrasting claims of virtue and justice but by a single standard, the "effectual truth" of those claims, their ability to acquire glory and maintain security. By this standard the boastful claims of regimes are reduced to their effect in producing benefits rather than taken seriously and even amplified as possible elements of the best regime. And the benefits of republics and principalities do not include the honor of living in a republic as opposed to under a prince, or the reverse; the form of government is not an end of government.

Accordingly, though Machiavelli speaks of virtue or goodness in republics, he does not speak of republican virtue, in which devotion to republicanism as a form or regime is identifiable apart from the benefits of republics. He does express a preference for republics over principalities, but it is carefully qualified: the common good "is not preserved if not in republics" (*D* II 2). But the common good of a republic does not extend to its neighbors, since to be conquered by a republic is the hardest slavery, and it is not really common, since it consists of oppression of the few by the many. Thus, when Machiavelli says that in republics everything "is executed to its purpose," whereas what helps a prince most often harms the city (*D* II 2), this must be balanced against his statement praising the "more merciful" prince Cesare Borgia because he knew how to confine his executions to a "very few examples" by contrast to the well-meaning republican Florentines, whose leniency harmed the whole people of Pistoia (*P* 17). More important than regimes are the two diverse humors or natures of princes and peoples to be found in both republics and principalities: the princes' desire to command and the peoples' desire not to be commanded (*P* ded.let, 9; *D* I 5). The success of government in either form requires prudent management of these two humors.

Or should one say that the advantage is to republics because, as Machiavelli asserts, "a republic has greater life and good fortune for a longer time than a principality" (*D* III 9)? Again, nothing is said about the greater lawfulness of a republic, nor indeed (by contrast to *D* II 2) about the common good. And why do republics live longer? Republics can be accommodated to diverse situations better than a principality because they have at their disposal a diversity of citizens instead of just one prince. But their institutions (or orders) would not permit them to make use of this diversity, given their notorious slowness to decide (*D* I 34, 59), if their institutions did not include the office of dictator, or something like it, which enables them to give responsibility to one person with the qualities needed at the moment. The dictator both is and is not an order. Machiavelli says that the executions of an accusation (which require a dictator or someone similar) are useful because they occur "ordinarily" without resort to private or foreign forces (*D* I 7). He then praises the Roman republic for instituting dictators for immediate executions in an "important thing," when the ordinary course would cause delay (*D* I 49) or when one man is needed to decide by himself without appeal (*D* I 33). Between these passages Machiavelli has shown that the orders of a republic become corrupt, and its authority goes stale, if ordinary means are not revived with "extraordinary means." So far from ruining republics (*D* I 7, 34), extraordinary means are necessary to them (*D* I 18; II 16), culminating in the aforementioned "notable and excessive" (*D* III 1) and "memorable" executions (*D* III 3). These require taking up an extraordinary authority (*D* III 3), "without depending on any law that stimulates you to any execution" (*D* III 1). The ordinary course of orders depends on occasional or periodic resort to the extraordinary for the renewal that gives a republic long life, indeed promises it perpetuity (*D* III 22).

Thus the distinction between lawful and unlawful, in which republics might have taken pride by contrast to the willfulness of princely rule, is transformed into a continuum from ordinary to extraordinary, which allows or requires republics to exchange lawfulness for long life. To do this, republics must incorporate the principality; the Roman republic was a succession of "countless most virtuous princes" (D I 20). Its longevity, in Machiavelli's interpretation, was due to its having combined with the princely state to secure the advantages of quick execution. But one could as easily say that a principality could combine with a republic in order to have, when necessary, a quick change of prince. Because of the need for executions, the inner workings of politics are not determined by its outward face.

## INDIRECTNESS

When government claims to be merely executive, like Moses, who was said to be a "mere executor of the things ordained by God" (P 6), its inner workings pretend to take direction from an outside authority. But as execution proves to require a "determined executor" (D III 1), the inner workings move on their own, producing memorable executions when necessary as surprises for the sake of greater effect. Machiavelli's executive government is not ordinarily visible, whereas in the Aristotelian regime the form or the look of politics shows the character of politics, so that political reality in general corresponds to political appearance. But Machiavelli's government is not simply invisible, either, because government cannot work without making an impression and thus cannot always hide itself behind authority. The inner workings of government must be revealed, on extraordinary occasions where government can be impressive because unexpected, in executions that recall to men both why they need government and what government can do to them if they disobey. Only on these occasions does political reality correspond to appearance. But precisely on these occasions, when primal fear is shown to be the first mover of politics—as well as in its ordinary course—government appears as necessity personified, returning men toward their own beginnings to a reawakening. Even at its strongest and most impressive, government acts for men in an executive role. Men do not govern according to principles they choose and profess, as in the classical regime, but they are governed by a prince or princes who remind them, periodically, that necessity is stronger than principle. Hence good effects are more useful than respect for forms. The indirectness of government lies in the fact that necessity must be brought home to each of us (see *AW* VI 348a), ordinarily complacent with partisan notions of how things should be run. Government is neither a choice by the rulers nor all imposition on the ruled but a revelation to each—and not from on high—of what is most powerful, not best, in him. To produce good effects, in the double sense of effects that make an effect, government must have the ambivalence to move on its own and ultimately on behalf of the people.

The popular humor is not the desire to rule but the desire not to be ruled; nonetheless, the people must be ruled. This difficulty sets the problem of government: to rule the people without their developing the intolerable sensation that they are being ruled. To accomplish this—for Machiavelli does not doubt he has a "remedy"—he adopts as his fundamental strategy a comical maxim of human perception: "Wounds and every other ill that man causes to himself spontaneously and through choice, hurt much less than those which are done to you by someone else" (*D* I 34). Why should kicking oneself hurt less than being kicked? And yet self-imposed taxes will be consented to more willingly than taxes imposed from above. Government should contrive, then, to let its exactions and especially its punishments seem to come from the people being mulcted and punished, at their behest or with their consent. Thus, although the people as such never rule and democracy strictly speaking is impossible, all government, whether republican or princely, must appeal to the people in the manner of the Roman method of accusation, which makes the people responsible for the attribution of guilt and execution (*D* I 7). Not only republics but also principalities are counseled by Machiavelli to adopt a generally democratic policy and to rely on the people rather than—or as opposed to—the few (*D* I 49, 55, 58; *P* 20). The contrast to Aristotle's generally aristocratic policy and his appeal to the kingship of the best man is impressive.

An appeal to the people, however, is not an appeal to their good nature or impartiality. It is the means of involving them in the necessities of government they would much rather ignore. Machiavelli praises the Swiss army's method of punishing soldiers "popularly by the other soldiers" (*AW* VI 345a), for if you want to prevent someone from defending or sympathizing with a criminal, get him to do the punishing. A person will look on punishment differently

if he is the executor of it. Another example of executions in an army
makes it clear that law and justice are not relevant to them. Rebels
from the Carthaginian army were incited by their leaders to kill
emissaries from that army together with prisoners they held. This
execution was intended to make them "cruel and determined"
against the Carthaginians (D III 32). Thus, common involvement in
a "crime" works as well as common involvement in the punishment
of a crime. Both are wounds that the army inflicts on itself, which
hurt much less than if executions were carried out by, or in the
name of, a prince. Machiavelli generalizes (as in D III 49) from the
decimations by which Roman armies were punished to the proper
way to punish a multitude: to make those who are guilty but unpunished watch themselves in the future. Though unpunished, indeed
through relief at being unpunished, they nearly punish themselves.

It is a mistake to give the power of executing punishment to a
foreigner in hope of finding an impartial judge (D I 7, 49; FH II
25). The foreigner will simply use executions to gain power for himself. Nor should one give it to the few, for "the few have always
been the ministers of the few" (D I 49). Rather, executions should
be used against the few to hold down their insolence and to dispel
envy (D III 1, 30; FH II 22). The few may be deterred, and the many
will be impressed. Executions are never the unprompted act of the
people, who would prefer to forget such necessities; to act, the people must be led or given a "head" (D I 57). But the people have a
love of the sensational that causes them to be easily impressed by
bold actions (D I 53), and the commission of great crimes is no bar
to their favor (P 8, 9). In every regime, the people are natural allies
of the strong executive who rules them in their name indirectly.[15]

## SUDDENNESS

To make an impression, execution must be sudden. In praising Giovanni and Lorenzo de' Medici, Machiavelli remarked that they were
quick to execute (FH VII 6; VIII 36). We today praise executives as
decisive and energetic in their initiatives, bearing witness to the effect
of suddenness as it seizes our attention by bringing regular (or ordinary) procedure to an abrupt halt. One of Machiavelli's favorite
phrases describes this event: *ad uno tratto* ("at a stroke"). At a
stroke the forceful executive can change a situation. People learn

that they cannot rely on the familiar (the terrible Roman execution of decimation was decided by lot [*D* III 49]); they must therefore look to the prince. By an impressive stroke the prince thus renews his authority and makes himself a new prince. His personal power, instead of disappearing into the regularity of his laws and ordinary methods, becomes visible; his actions, if sufficiently ambitious, can achieve "the greatness in themselves" that silences criticism (*FH* I pr). In dealing with hostile parties in Pistoia, the weak Florentines did not know how to follow the first and safest method of simply killing the leaders: "such executions have greatness and generosity" (*D* III 27).

In a paraphrase of Livy that Machiavelli notes should be chewed on by every prince and every republic, he says that in ambiguity and uncertainty over what others want to do, one cannot find words; but once one's mind is made up and one has decided what is to be "executed," it is easy to find the words for it (*D* II 15). One must accommodate words to deeds, not deeds to words; and one does this by acting first, so as to confront others with a new situation. Machiavelli writes of the Roman dictatorship that in time of necessity offered the advantage of immediate executions (*D* I 49). But here Machiavelli goes beyond responding to necessity, advising that one create necessity for others. He says that slow deliberations are always harmful (*D* II 15). This is especially true in conspiracies, where menaces are more dangerous than executions (*D* III 6). Dangers in executing conspiracies arise in part from those who lose heart (*FH* VII 34), but they can be avoided by stepping up the pace of the execution so that the faint-hearted have no time to suffer an attack of conscience (*FH* II 32; *D* III 6). Machiavelli gives two examples of conspiracies that were executed first on fellow conspirators before they were executed on the objects of the conspiracy. The conspirators were told they must join against a tyrant or be reported to him for treason (*D* III 6). In such cases, and in general, the executor makes use of "the necessity that does not allow time" (*D* III 6), that is, time to repent.

In no respect does Machiavelli's executive differ more obviously from Aristotle's regime than in his suddenness. For Aristotle, the central part of the regime was the deliberative; and while deliberate is not the same as slow, deliberate in the sense of slow is the beginning of deliberate in the sense of prudent. The deliberative part, therefore, was chosen and authorized to act through a variety of formalities whose general purpose was to slow the haste of human willfulness by compelling propriety and due process.[16] Machiavelli does the very contrary. He advances deliberation into decision (in the usage of his time *diliberazione* meant both deliberation and decision) so that a good deliberation becomes one that issues in a decision, and a good decision is decisive (D II 15). "Decisive" is a quality known and explained after the fact, and while sudden is not the same as prudent, it is a necessary addition to prudence, as that appearance of willfulness that gets prudence obeyed. Machiavelli's executive cuts through the formalities of which Aristotle was so careful. In so doing, he makes it possible for republics, such as the Roman republic according to his interpretation, to combine quick action with the slow motion of excess procedure.

SECRECY

When a committee of the United States Congress meets in executive session, it meets in secret. We have seen the connection between execution and secrecy in Machiavelli's discussion of the Roman office of dictator, who executes not only without appeal but also without consultation (D I 33). If execution requires surprise, secrecy is clearly necessary. The surprise is not a happy revelation, of course, but something more sinister. Just how sinister execution is may be gauged from the fact that the greatest density of *execute* in the *Discourses on Livy* occurs in the long chapter on conspiracies, III 6 (forty occurrences out of sixty in the entire work; forty-nine together with the related chapters, III 1 and III 3). Whereas Machiavelli speaks only once in his major works of executing a law (*FH* VII 3), he speaks several times of executing a conspiracy (D III 6; *FH* VIII 5; *Life of Castruccio Castracani,* 757b); he orders his entire discussion of conspiracies in that chapter around execution—before, during, and after the deed. As we have seen, the way to keep the secret of a conspiracy is to hasten its execution (D III 6; *FH* II 32). The execution of a conspiracy perfectly combines the two meanings of execute, "kill" and "carry out," since the conspiracy is executed when its object is executed. It is almost needless to add that conspiratorial execution takes place in utter illegality.

What is Machiavelli's reasoning for removing execution from

its subordination to law, where it had been firmly confined by Marsilius, and enlisting it in the management of conspiracies? Conspiracy itself must be much closer to the essence of government than
had hitherto been thought. Machiavelli implies this when he writes
that conspiracies are made not only against the prince but also
against the fatherland (*patria*) by the prince (*D* III 6). But even this,
like so many of his statements, is a mere introduction to his reasoning. Government, according to Machiavelli, is the agent of necessity
rather than the minister of justice, because we cannot afford justice.
But we like to think that we can afford justice, especially for ourselves, and we often see no need for actions that anticipate that we
will not be able to afford justice—actions that anticipate necessity.
This is the popular humor that does not desire to rule or command
or oppress but desires not to be ruled. The desire not to be ruled
constitutes a reluctance to face facts or necessity. Government has
the ambivalent task of bringing necessity home to the people, so that
they survive, while concealing it from them, so that they are happy
and innocent. Machiavelli's remedy is to make government seem to
come from the people and its wounds seem self-inflicted. This requires fraud (*P* 18; *D* II 13; III 2, 40) and conspiracy (*P* 19; *D* III
6), not merely as dangerous devices locked away in a cabinet for use
by trusted hands only in the worst emergencies but as instruments
available generally if not routinely, and to be used without hesitation
or scruple.

Conspiracies comprise, Machiavelli says, either one or more.
But, he continues, if it is one person, it cannot be said to be a
conspiracy; rather it is a "firm disposition arising in one man to kill
the prince" (*D* III 6). So conspiracies, properly speaking, involve
more than one person sharing a secret or knowledge together (*coscienza*). The relationship among conspirators is never that among
friends, because men usually deceive themselves in the love they
judge that another bears for them; you can never be sure of it unless
you test it, and this is most dangerous (*D* III 6). Consequently, at
least ordinarily the relationship among conspirators must be that of
principal and executives instead of equal friends. The executive or
secretary (the connection between secret and secretary should not
be forgotten) may be more capable than the principal, so that it
becomes unclear who is using whom (*P* 22), but the inequality of the
relationship remains. To the extent that for Machiavelli conspiracy

underlies all politics, we have again reached a fundamental difference from Aristotle, for whom friendship underlies justice and all
politics (*NE* 1155a23–33). Aristotle said that friends do not need
justice among themselves, as they are above it; Machiavelli thought
that, given the secrets they keep from each other and from themselves, they could not even attain justice.

## UNO SOLO

Machiavelli praised the Roman dictatorship that gave one man the
power to execute his own decisions in order to respond quickly to
"extraordinary accidents" (*D* I 33, 49). But Machiavelli also praised
(in *D* I 9) the original ordering of the Roman republic, attributed
by him to Romulus, because it had been accomplished in consequence of Romulus's fratricide by "one alone" (*uno solo*). Both the
original ordering and the departures from order necessary to maintain order—by the dictator and by memorable executions (*D* III 1,
3)—must be done by one person. Why must this be?

Machiavelli says that many are not adept at ordering a thing
"since they do not know what is good for it, which is caused by
the different opinions among them" (*D* I 9). Thus, it appears that
everything must depend on the mind of one man, not because he
necessarily knows better than the many, but because it is better to
have one opinion than many. The prudent orderer must, like Romulus, contrive to get all authority for himself even if he has to dispose
of a wiser brother, since Machiavelli says nothing to indicate that
Romulus knew more than Remus. It is better to have one opinion
and one authority because, with responsibility focused on one, ambition can be used to promote the common good. If the one succeeds,
he will have made a lasting state and deserve glory; if he fails, he
can be blamed and accused (*D* I 9), thus purging the hatred of the
multitude and, if he is sufficiently important, serving as a memorable
execution. Although Machiavelli in his popular humor allows himself to inveigh against ambition (*D* I 37; II pr), his politics make
use of ambition untempered, unabashed, and restrained only by the
ambition of others. Glory, like fear, individuates men, but also enables them to be enlisted for the common good more readily and
surely than through the social virtue of justice: "Those who fight

for their own glory are good and faithful soldiers" (*D* I 43; cf. III.30, 35, 40).

If ambition is to be loosed from moral restraint, however, can it be altogether separated from wisdom? It goes without saying that ambitious princes must be prudent, but then prudence for Machiavelli has ceased to be a moral virtue distinct from cleverness (*P* 15; cf. *NE* 1144a24). Must there not be some prudence beyond the ordinary that justifies Machiavelli's corruption of it in the service of ambition—his own *grandi prudenze* (*D* II 26)? If government culminates in conspiracy and conspirators cannot be equal, must there not be a brain behind the operation, a "rare brain" (*D* I 55), one that does not suffer from "confusion of the brain" (*D* III 6)? Machiavelli was aware of the problem that the one who knows politics cannot execute his knowledge by himself (*AW* VII 367b); he can be *uno solo* only in his knowledge. In fact, Machiavelli was preoccupied with the problem of the relationship between the teacher of politics and the politician. When he says in *The Prince* that Moses was a mere executor of the things ordained by God (*P* 6), he describes God not as all-powerful but as the "great preceptor." He devotes a chapter in the *Discourses on Livy* to the dangers of being alone against many in advising something (*D* III 35; cf. *P* 6, 22); and the thirty-ninth example in the chapter on conspiracies (*D* III 6) concerns an unsuccessful attempt by two disciples of Plato to kill two tyrants. In the *Florentine Histories* he describes a poet, inspired by Petrarch, who sought to be the "executor" of a glorious enterprise to free Rome from the popes (*FH* VI 29).

In his own glorious enterprise to bring "common benefit to each" (*D* I pr) with the reform of morality and politics, Machiavelli cannot do everything himself. He cannot be both teacher and prince. But he can put his knowledge into execution, not least with his doctrine of execution, so that princes who follow him become in the deepest sense his executives. This deepest sense of execution is perfectly compatible with the need of each prince to be *uno solo*, because Machiavelli has left space for princes to win their own glory. They can be determined executors instead of mere executors, and it is not necessary that they realize they are executing his knowledge; indeed, it is better that they do not. As Machiavelli shows, a conspiracy can be executed even when only one person fully knows its object (*D* III 6). But to be this person, the only true *uno solo*, he must erase the distinction between kingship and tyranny.

With our hindsight from liberal constitutionalism, Machiavelli seems to have gone too far. His statements ring true but his conclusions seem exaggerated, and we fail to take him seriously. We would like to believe that his insights can be retained and his extremism discarded, that his notion of *esecuzione* can be absorbed into the modern liberal constitution without the tyrannical requirement of *uno solo* that may give us a shiver or may merely seem quaint. Machiavelli may have founded the modern doctrine of executive power, but in his extremism he stopped short of developing doctrines of power and of separation of powers. The doctrine of power, in Hobbes's conception, was to make virtuous princes unnecessary by giving any sovereign, virtuous or not, all the power he could want; the separation of powers was developed by Locke and Montesquieu to check the prince by law and by formal institutions. Both doctrines, while accepting much of Machiavellian morality, were directed against the extreme political conclusion demanding space for *uno solo*. But it is not clear that the development of a doctrine improves it. With the same hindsight from constitutionalism, Machiavelli might have chosen not to retract. He could have noted that we have found no substitute for virtuous princes (in his sense) and that every successful organization in our self-congratulating democracy is run by a chief executive officer. He could declare that we obscure the reality with talk of executive power. After our experience of totalitarian tyranny, however, he might have shivered himself.

PREFACE

1. Girolamo Savonarola, *Prediche sopra Ezechiele,* ed. R. Ridolfi (Rome: Belardetti, 1955), 1:27; *Prediche sopra l'Esodo,* ed. P. G. Ricci (Rome: Belardetti, 1956) 1:127–28, 178; Saint Paul, 2 Corinthians 10:3–11.

ONE    MACHIAVELLI'S VIRTUE

1. Studies of the word *virtù* are Edward W. Mayer, *Machiavellis Geschichtsauffassung und sein Begriff virtù* (Munich: R. Oldenbourg, 1912); J. H. Whitfield, "The Anatomy of Virtue," chap. 6 in his *Machiavelli* (Oxford: Blackwell, 1966), 92–105; Neal Wood, "Machiavelli's Concept of *Virtù* Reconsidered," *Political Studies* 15 (1967): 159–72; John Plamenatz, "In Search of Machiavellian *Virtù,*" in *The Political Calculus: Essays on Machiavelli's Philosophy,* ed. Anthony Parel (Toronto: University of Toronto Press, 1972), 157–78; Russell Price, "The Senses of *Virtù* in Machiavelli," *European Studies Review* 3 (1973): 315–45. Of studies that comment on Machiavelli's *virtù,* the most outstanding are Friedrich Meinecke, *Die Idee der Staatsräson* (1924; Munich: R. Oldenbourg, 1957), chap. 1; Leo Strauss, *Thoughts on Machiavelli* (Glencoe, Ill.: Free Press, 1958); Sheldon S. Wolin, *Politics and Vision* (Boston: Little, Brown, 1960), 195–238; Jerrold Siegel, "*Virtù* in and since the Renaissance," in *Dictionary of the History of Ideas* (New York: Scribner, 1973–74), 4:476–86; Claude Lefort, *Le travail de l'oeuvre Machiavel* (Paris: Gallimard, 1972); J. H. Hexter, *The Vision of Politics on the Eve of the Reformation* (New York: Basic Books, 1973), 188–203; J. G. A. Pocock, *The Machiavellian Moment* (Princeton: Princeton University Press, 1975), chaps. 6, 7; Clifford Orwin, "Machiavelli's Unchristian Charity," *American Political Science Review* 72 (1978): 1217–28. Quentin Skinner, *The Foundations of Modern Political Thought* (Cambridge: Cambridge University Press, 1978), vol. 1, chaps. 5, 6; Quentin Skinner, *Machiavelli* (New York: Hill and Wang, 1981), chaps. 2, 3; Gennaro Sasso, *Niccolò Machiavelli,* rev. ed. (Bologna: Il Mulino, 1980), chap. 5; Isaiah Berlin, "The Originality of Machiavelli," in his *Against the Current* (New York: Penguin Books, 1982), 25–79; Arno Baruzzi, *Einführung in die Politische Philosophie der Neuzeit* (Darmstadt: Wissenschaftliche Buchgesellschaft, 1983), 17–34; Mark Hulliung, *Citizen Machiavelli*

(Princeton: Princeton University Press, 1983); Paolo Vincieri, *Natura umano e dominio: Machiavelli, Hobbes, Spinoza* (Ravenna: Lungo editore, 1984), 23–46; W. R. Newell, "How Original Is Machiavelli? A Consideration of Skinner's Interpretation of Virtue and Fortune," *Political Theory* 15 (1987): 612–34. Wolfgang Kersting, *Niccolò Machiavelli* (Munich: C. H. Beck, 1988), 112–25; Anthony J. Parel, *The Machiavellian Cosmos* (New Haven: Yale University Press, 1992), chap. 5.

2. *P* 8. NM goes on in this passage to distinguish between the most excellent captain, who might have to commit crimes, and the most excellent man, who would not. But later in *The Prince*, he praises the virtue of Hannibal (*P* 17) and Severus (*P* 19), who committed many crimes, without mentioning this distinction. On Agathocles, see Michael McCanles, *The Discourse of "Il principe"* (Malibu, Calif.: Undena, 1983), 59–65; and the fine discussion in Victoria Kahn, "*Virtù* and the Example of Agathocles in Machiavelli's *Prince*," in *Machiavelli and the Discourse of Literature*, ed. Albert Russell Ascoli and Victoria Kahn (Ithaca: Cornell University Press, 1993), 195–217.

3. As does Russell Price in "The Senses of *Virtù*," who omits the sense of evil, while struggling with the case of Agathocles, 331; Neal Wood, in "Machiavelli's Concept of *Virtù*," has the merit of seeking a unity of meaning for the word. See also Hanna F. Pitkin, *Fortune Is a Woman* (Berkeley: University of California Press, 1984), 80–81; Goffredo Quadri, *Niccolò Machiavelli e la costruzione politica della coscienza morale*, 2d ed. (Florence: La nuova Italia, 1971), 55–58; Gérard Colonna d'Istria and Roland Frapet, *L'art politique chez Machiavel* (Paris: Vrin, 1980), 57–58, 77; and the outstanding discussion in Lefort, *Le travail de l'oeuvre Machiavel*, 374–80, 422–23.

4. See especially NM's discussion of the rise and fall of *virtù* in various times and places, as opposed to a varying definition, in *D* II pr.

5. See NM's reference in *D* I 25 to "an absolute power which is called tyranny by the authors" in the light of his name for such power in the next chapter, the "new prince." On this point see Strauss, *Thoughts on Machiavelli*, 48–49, and Raymond Aron, "Le Machiavélisme de Machiavel," in his *Machiavel et les tyrannies modernes* (Paris: Fallois, 1993), 61. NM speaks of the "two diverse humors" of men, of which one "desires to command and oppress the people," *P* 9; see *D* I 4–6; *FH* II 12; III 1. And in *D* II 2, he makes it clear that even the common good in republics is achieved only with oppression and aggression. He promises to work for "the common good of everyone" only in his own name (*D* 1 pr) and does not allow it to be the goal of any actual prince or republic.

6. The six instances of *antica virtù* in *D* are I pr, 9; II 16, 17 (twice); III 22.

7. Strauss, *Thoughts on Machiavelli*, 20.

8. Note *antico valore*, equated with *virtù*, in the lines NM quotes from Petrarch to end *The Prince* (*P* 26).

9. NM calls the Ostrogoths superior in virtue to "all the other peoples,"

apparently to other barbarian peoples and of course to the Romans at that time; *FH* I 4.

10. Burckhardt's work begins from "The State as a Work of Art," of which he says: "Of all who thought it possible to construct a State, the greatest beyond all comparison was Machiavelli." Jacob Burckhardt, *The Civilization of the Renaissance in Italy,* trans. S. G. C. Middlemore (1860; London: Phaidon, 1950), 55–56. For testimony to Burckhardt's continuing dominance, see Denys Hay, "Storici e Rinascimento negli ultimi venticinque anni," in *Il Rinascimento negli ultimi venticinque anni* (Rome, 1979); and Dain A. Trafton, "The Permanence of Jacob Burckhardt," *Continuity* 7 (1983): 55–76. Gene A. Brucker and Felix Gilbert give Francesco Guicciardini equal credit with NM, to which anyone with a view either to depth of thought or to future influence must protest; see Gene A. Brucker, *Renaissance Florence* (Berkeley: University of California Press, 1969), 278–280; Felix Gilbert, *Machiavelli and Guicciardini* (Princeton: Princeton University Press, 1965).

11. "It is . . . in the state of moral feeling among the Italians of those times that we must seek for the real explanation of what seems most mysterious in the life and writings of this remarkable man." Thomas Babington Macaulay, *Miscellaneous Works* (New York: Putnam, n.d.), 1:73. "What determined the composition of *The Prince?* In the last resort, only one answer can be given: The general condition of Italy." Lord Acton, "Introduction to Niccolò Machiavelli," in *Il principe,* ed. L. Arthur Burd (Oxford: Clarendon Press, 1891), 22. See also Alfredo Bonadeo, *Corruption, Conflict and Power in the Works and Times of Niccolò Machiavelli* (Berkeley: University of California Press, 1973), 121.

12. You can be more evil than Giovampagolo Baglioni, the man who did not know how to be altogether bad: *D* I 27.

13. J. G. A. Pocock, "Custom & Grace, Form & Matter: An Approach to Machiavelli's Concept of Innovation," in *Machiavelli and the Nature of Political Thought,* ed. Martin Fleisher (New York: Atheneum, 1972), 169. Pocock, *Machiavellian Moment,* chap. 6; Roberto Esposito, *La politica e la storia: Machiavelli e Vico* (Naples: Liguori Editore, 1980), 119–26; Colonna d'Istria and Frapet, *L'art politique chez Machiavel,* 9–20.

14. See Leo Strauss, "Machiavelli and Classical Literature," *Review of National Literatures* 1 (1970): 12–13; W. R. Newell, "Machiavelli and Xenophon on Princely Rule: A Double-Edged Encounter," *Journal of Politics* 50 (1988): 108–30.

15. See chapter 2.

16. Wayne A. Rebhorn, *Foxes and Lions: Machiavelli's Confidence Men* (Ithaca: Cornell University Press, 1988), 193–98; Hulliung, *Citizen Machiavelli,* 206; Herfried Münkler, *Machiavelli: Die Begründung des politischen Denkens der Neuzeit aus der Krise der Republik Florenz* (Frankfurt: Europäische Verlaganstalt, 1982), 319–21.

17. In *D* II 19 NM speaks of "parsimony and . . . other most excellent

virtues": see also I 51. Cf. Aristotle, *Nichomachean Ethics* 1120a19–22; Lefort, *Le travail*, 407–8; Clifford Orwin, "Machiavelli's Unchristian Charity," 1222.

18. If men operate well under pressure of necessity, then necessity can be understood as a substitute for virtue. Accordingly, in *P* 18, *necessity* appears eleven times and *virtue* not at all; this is the central of the seven chapters in *The Prince* in which *virtue* does not appear.

19. See chapter 10.

20. Strauss, *Thoughts on Machiavelli*, 240–44.

21. Duvernoy says that since virtue is in effect the appearance of virtue, politics for NM is based not on science but on rhetoric. But it is wrong to think that the appearances are effects controllable by rhetoric rather than by deeds; it is rather the reverse. Jean-François Duvernoy, *La pensée de Machiavel* (Paris: Bordas, 1974), 66–67. The same difficulty is to be found in Lars Vissing, *Machiavel et la politique de l'apparence* (Paris: Presses Universitaires de France, 1986). See Luigi Zanzi, *I "segni" della natura e i "paradigmi" della storia: Il metodo di Machiavelli* (Manduria: Lacaita, 1981), 68–76.

22. So Shakespeare's Machiavellian Prince Hal in *King Henry IV*, Pt. I, I.2.213–15: "My reformation, glitt'ring o'er my fault, / Shall show more goodly and attract more eyes / Than that which hath no foil to set it off." Also see Plato, *Republic* 402c.

23. On virtue as impressive, see also *P* 6 (Theseus showing his virtue), 7, 8 (Cesare Borgia, Agathocles and Liverotto combining virtue with impressive criminality), 18 (the prince must appear virtuous), 19 (the prince is not known for moral virtue), 21 (the prince must reward virtue and make it recognized), 24 (new princes are known to be virtuous; the opposite of virtuous is cowardly [*vile*]); *D* I 30 (violence has something honorable in it), 46 (the people can be misled by the appearance of virtue); II 17 (using and showing virtue); III 21 (the captain's virtue makes him reputed), 22 (being held virtuous), 34 (virtue and the extraordinary).

24. Strauss, *Thoughts on Machiavelli*, 260–65; Orwin, "Machiavelli's Unchristian Charity," 1219; Plamenatz, "In Search of Machiavellian *Virtù*," 174–78; Vissing, *Machiavel et la politique de l'apparence*, 137. Speaking against Croce's notion of NM's "autonomy of politics," Hulliung says that NM would have preferred to say the "ubiquity of politics." Hulliung, *Citizen Machiavelli*, 103. In answer to Price's remark that NM does not speak of "political virtue" as does Plato—in contrast to true, philosophical virtue—one could say that the reason is that for NM *all* virtue is political; Price, "The Senses of *Virtù*," 325n.

25. Giacomo Leopardi, *Tutte le opere: Le poesie e le prose*, ed. F. Flora (Verona: Mondadori, 1968), 1:1052.

26. See esp. *D* III 2 on men of quality who would like to live quietly and without fuss; NM denies the possibility of satisfying that desire. Pierre Manent, *Naissances de la politique moderne: Machiavel, Hobbes, Rousseau* (Paris: Payot, 1977), 21; Harvey C. Mansfield, Jr., *Machiavelli's New Modes*

*and Orders* (Ithaca: Cornell University Press, 1979), 307–8. Gilbert misconstrues *D* I 26 on this point, supposing that what one ought to wish (namely, to live privately rather than be a king like Philip of Macedon, who uses the cruelest modes) is what necessity permits one to do. Gilbert, *Machiavelli and Guicciardini*, 196–97. See also Maurizio Viroli, "Machiavelli and the Republican Idea of Politics," in *Machiavelli and Republicanism*, ed. Gisela Bock, Quentin Skinner, and Maurizio Viroli (New York: Cambridge University Press, 1990), 152–53.

27. On *virtù* as quality or qualities, see *D* let ded; III 31; *P* 6, 15, 18, 19.

28. See Strauss, *Thoughts on Machiavelli*, 256: "The virtue which is truly virtue [for NM] can best be described as republican virtue." But this does not make NM a partisan of republican virtue, as Skinner claims: NM "is in fact a consistent and even a fervent partisan of popular government." Skinner, *Foundations*, 1:159.

29. Aristotle, *Politics* 1310a12–13; 1323b40–1324a1.

30. The main fault of the republican interpretation of NM by Pocock and Skinner is not to distinguish NM's republicanism from Aristotle's. The reason in Pocock's case is his indebtedness to Hannah Arendt, whose interpretation of Aristotle removes virtue as the end of republics and institutes the *vita activa* of republic citizens as an end in itself. Arendt thus erases the difference between Aristotle, for whom the common good is in part directed to virtue above it, and NM, for whom republican virtue is directed, with the necessary qualifications in my argument, to the common good. Skinner, in turn, allows that he builds in part on Pocock's work. See Hannah Arendt, *The Human Condition* (Chicago: University of Chicago Press, 1959), chap. 1. Pocock, *Machiavellian Moment*, 56, 64, 66–77, 201–3, 212, 329, 550, and chap. 3's title; on Pocock, see Stephen G. Salkever, *Finding the Mean: Theory and Practice in Aristotelian Political Philosophy* (Princeton: Princeton University Press, 1990), 72; and Vickie B. Sullivan, "Machiavelli's Momentary 'Machiavellian Moment'; A Reconsideration of Pocock's Treatment of the *Discourses*," *Political Theory* 20 (1992): 309–18. Skinner, *Foundations*, 1:173, 179, 184; and Skinner, *Machiavelli*, v–vii, 56 (but note the contrast with Cicero, 54).

31. See Strauss, *Thoughts on Machiavelli*, 339n151.

32. That is the key to understanding *D* I 58, where NM says that there is more virtue in the people than in the prince. See Mansfield, *Machiavelli's New Modes and Orders*, 168–74. For the relationship betwen *bontà* and *virtù*, see *P* 11, 15, 19, 22; *D* I 2, 9, 17, 55, 58; II 13, 23; III 1, 8, 13, 30; *FH* I 4; II 39; III 5, 13, 17, 23, 25; IV 1; VII 13, 23.

33. See Strauss, *Thoughts on Machiavelli*, 193–95.

34. Mayer, *Machiavellis Geschichtsauffassung*, 98; Strauss, *Thoughts on Machiavelli*, 225–32.

35. For virtue and religion, see also *P* 8 (Agathocles's virtue without faith), 13 (virtue with faith), 26 (the virtue of Moses compared with his being a mere executor of God in *P* 6); *D* I 15 (virtue and the use of religion);

III 33 (virtue must accompany the "little things" of religion). For virtue and success, see *P* 12 (virtue can have a bad end), 15 (well-being and virtue), 18 ("one looks to the end"); *D* I 4 (whoever examines the end well), 9 (the end excuses); III 3 (judge the intention from the end), 33 (the end of a thing shows the true virtue), 35 (men judge things from the end); *FH* VI 8 (a more virtuous than prosperous captain).

36. See De Grazia's nice formulation of the "ungolden rule"; Sebastian De Grazia, *Machiavelli in Hell* (Princeton: Princeton University Press, 1989), 299.

37. The "wise" and the "good" are contrasted in *D* III 30; *FH* IV 1; VII 13, but are together in the person of Cincinnatus, *D* III 24.

38. In *D* I 9 NM says: "Where the act accuses, the effect excuses." The effect excuses; it does not justify or legitimate (as we might say). An excuse requires an excuser; the prince who excuses must keep himself necessary in the situation. See Mansfield, *Machiavelli's New Modes and Orders*, 63–66.

39. See Harvey C. Mansfield Jr., *Taming the Prince* (New York: Free Press, 1989), 139–42.

40. Gilbert: "*virtù* . . . was an italianization of the Latin word *virtus* and denoted the fundamental quality of man which enables him to achieve great works and deeds"; *Machiavelli and Guicciardini*, 179. See also Pitkin, *Fortune Is a Woman*, 48. A more skeptical view can be found in Hulliung, *Citizen Machiavelli*, 5, 28–29; and a middle position in Skinner, *Foundations*, 1:88–89, 128–38. In *D* III 33 NM himself translates Livy's *virtus* as *virtù*. In the context, speaking of the importance of the virtue of "one's own soldiers," NM makes Livy say words he did not in fact say. The suggestion is that NM makes Livy into one of his own soldiers, or that NM's virtue is an appropriation of classical virtue. Mansfield, *Machiavelli's New Modes and Orders*, 407.

41. NM, letters of Apr. 16 and Dec. 10, 1513.

42. Francesco Petrarca, *Opere Latine*, ed. A. Bufano (Turin: UTET, 1975), 2:1046, 1106–12. Petrarch adds: "Si mirari autem Ciceronem, hoc est Ciceronianum esse, Ciceronianus sum" (II 1122). In the vicinity Petrarch calls Saint Augustine in support, despite being against Augustinian Christianity according to Skinner, *Foundations*, 1:91, 97, 99.

43. Petrarca, *Opere Latine*, 2:1108, 1122.

44. Paul O. Kristeller, *Renaissance Thought: The Classic, Scholastic, and Humanistic Strains* (New York: Harper, 1955), 18. Etienne Gilson spoke of humanism as the "aetas ciceroniana"; Gilson, "Le Message de l'humanisme," in *Culture et politique en France à l'époque de l'humanisme et de la Renaissance, Etudes reunies et presentées par F. Simone* (Turin: Accademia delle Scienze, 1974), 4. But this does not mean that the humanists put rhetoric over philosophy or considered it an "ideal"—which Cicero himself did not do. See Marc Fumaroli, *L'age de l'éloquence* (Geneva: Librarie Droz, 1980), 37–57, 77–81. See also Jerrold Siegel, "Civic Humanism or Ciceronian Rhetoric," *Past and Present* 34 (1966): 32–44.

45. Cicero, *Tusculan Disputations* I 2; *De Republica* II 10, 14.
46. Cicero, *Tusculan Disputations* I 3; II 1.
47. Ibid. II 4, 18; III 3.
48. Ibid. II 18. See Petrarca, *Le Familiari* XXI 13.1; XXII.2.28.
49. Plato, *Republic* 341b.
50. Eugenio Garin, *La cultura del Rinascimento* (Bari: Laterza, 1976), 20; De Grazia, *Machiavelli in Hell,* 152–54, 289.
51. Newell, "How Original Is Machiavelli?" 624.
52. Cf. *FH* I 31 on Cola di Rienzo, another enemy of the pope, but not said by NM to be inspired by Petrarch.
53. See Hulliung, *Citizen Machiavelli,* 132.
54. For the Medici as a theme in NM, see Mansfield, *Machiavelli's New Modes and Orders,* 154–55; and see chapter 6 below.
55. On NM and the humanists, see Nino Borsellino, *Machiavelli* (Rome-Bari: Laterza, 1973), 113–14; Paolo Marolda, "Le radici neoplatonische del 'savio' machiavelliano," *La ressegna della letteratura italiana* 7 (1979): 95–116; Skinner, *Machiavelli,* 37; Hexter, *Vision of Politics,* 192.
56. See Skinner, *Machiavelli,* 40.
57. Strauss, *Thoughts on Machiavelli,* 78. On Chiron, see also Ezio Raimondi, *Politica e commedia: Dal Beroaldo al Machiavelli* (Bologna: Mulino, 1972), 265–86; Giulio Ferroni, *Mutazione e riscontro nel teatro di Machiavelli* (Rome: Bulzoni, 1972), 88.
58. For an original version in NM's favorite, see Xenophon, *On Hunting* I; XII, 18; *Cyropaedia* IV.iii.17–22; also Ovid, *Metamorphoses* II 630, 676; VI 126. Francis Bacon, *Of the Advancement of Learning,* in *The Works of Francis Bacon,* ed. J. Spedding (London: Longman, 1859), 3:345; Raimondi, *Politica e commedia,* 278–80; Peter S. Donaldson, *Machiavelli and Mystery of State* (New York: Cambridge University Press, 1988), viii; Zanzi, *I "segni" della natura e i "paradigmi" della storia,* 36–38. On virtue and ferocity in NM, see *P* 7 (Cesare Borgia), 19 (Severus virtuous and a most ferocious lion); *D* II 2 (ancient peoples more ferocious); III 36 (natural ferocity of the French versus the ordered virtue of the Romans). Cf. Aristotle, *Politics* 1338b29–32.
59. NM would not have agreed with Mussolini when he said "meglio vivere un giorno da leone che cento anni da pecora [better live one day as a lion than a hundred years as a sheep]."
60. Lefort interprets the lion to be what disguises force as law, *Le travail de l'oeuvre Machiavel,* 411. See also Pitkin, *Fortune Is a Woman,* 34–39, 46, 104.
61. In considering NM's source for the passage on the lion and the fox in Cicero's *De Officiis,* Colish fails to appreciate that in appropriating the images, NM, as Hulliung says, turned Cicero upside down. Cicero, *De Officiis* I.11.34, 13.41; Marcia L. Colish, "Cicero's *De Officiis* and Machiavelli's *Prince*," *Sixteenth Century Journal* 9 (1978): 81–93; Hulliung, *Citizen Machiavelli,* 213. Raimondi goes so far as to suspect NM of a *calcolo malizioso* here; Raimondi, *Politica e commedia,* 266–68.

62. NM's virtue is thus not characterized by "instinctiveness," as Gilbert says, but, as we shall see, by *animo* that gives spirit to prudence; Gilbert, *Machiavelli and Guicciardini,* 197.

63. See *P* 9, in which NM speaks in the beginning of "a fortunate astuteness" (*una astuzia fortunata*) as distinct from virtue and at the end of a "wise prince" who does the same thing without depending on fortune and without NM's calling it "astuteness."

64. *Animo* is the source of the *énergie vitale* that Guillemain attributes to NM's *virtù;* Bernard Guillemain, *Machiavel: L'anthropologie politique* (Geneva: Droz, 1977), 256–58.

65. *Animo* occurs twenty-five times, *virtù* only twice, in *D* III 6.

66. Strauss, *Thoughts on Machiavelli,* 200, 333n59. Cf. Fleisher: "There is no reason why we cannot loosely translate [*animo*] as 'soul' "; Martin Fleisher, "A Passion for Politics: The Vital Core of the World of Machiavelli," in his *Machiavelli and the Nature of Political Thought,* 118–24. See Mansfield, *Machiavelli's New Modes and Orders,* 135, for the connection between *animo* and glory.

67. Kersting, *Niccolò Machiavelli,* 114. Pitkin says with this incident in view that "Machiavelli's writings never transcended the conventional misogyny of his time"; *Fortune Is a Woman,* 305. But Arlene Saxonhouse argues, and shows, that he did; *Women in the History of Political Thought, Ancient Greece to Machiavelli* (New York: Praeger, 1985), 151–73.

68. See Price, "The Senses of *Virtù,*" 335; Parel, *Machiavellian Cosmos,* 86–88; Leo Strauss, *What Is Political Philosophy?* (Glencoe, Ill.: Free Press, 1959), 289. See the exchange between Gilbert and MacKinney on the medicinal meaning of *virtù;* Felix Gilbert, "On Machiavelli's Idea of *virtù,*" *Renaissance News* 4 (1951): 53–55; L. C. MacKinney, "Discussion," *Renaissance News* 5 (1952): 21–23, 70–71.

69. The "virtue" of a tree trunk is useful to a "good cultivator" (*D* II 3). Note also the "natural virtue" of infantry in *AW* II (289a; cf. 299b). Parel cites a passage from NM's poem *Capitolo pastorale* that says that "heaven wanted to show its virtue" in order to support his thesis that NM's political thought depends on his cosmology. But heaven's virtue is presented there as a sum of the separate virtues of the Olympian gods, not of the planets; and it is notable that pagan gods, not the Christian God, serve as the models of human praise. "Heaven" so composed is the human or poetic rendering of "nature" as we would wish it. *Capitolo pastorale,* 866, lines 31, 39; Parel, *Machiavellian Cosmos,* 93.

70. Strauss, *Thoughts on Machiavelli,* 269. See NM's *L'asino d'oro,* VIII, lines 103–7, 839, where a pig says that nature dispenses her virtue more to animals than to humans.

71. Cf. the "hidden virtue [of heaven] that governs us" in NM's poem *Di Fortuna,* line 119, 847.

72. As a point of numerology one may note that the number of chapters in the *Discourses* in which *virtù* does not occur is seventy-one (together with seven in *The Prince*) and that there are twenty-six such chapters in the

third book, which is especially concerned with NM's own enterprise. In *P* 22 and 23, *virtù* does not occur, as the subjects of these chapters are too close to NM himself; note, too, that in *P* 25, the remedy for the brevity of life and the inability to change one's nature are taken up together. See also Mansfield, *Machiavelli's New Modes and Orders*, 292.

73. Sasso stresses NM's reliance on extraordinary will for his notion of virtue, but where is NM's *art* in this formulation? Sasso, *Niccolò Machiavelli*, 335–36, 375, 431–32.

74. See Giovanni Di Napoli, "Niccolò Machiavelli e l'Aristotelismo del Rinascimento," *Giornale di metafisica* 25 (1970): 248–64; Gioacchino Paparelli, "Virtù e fortuna nel medioevo, nel rinascimento e in Machiavelli," *Cultura e Scuola* 9 (1970): 76–89; Newell, "How Original Is Machiavelli?" 621–29.

75. Lefort, *Le travail de l'oeuvre Machiavel*, 439–44; Pocock, "Custom & Grace, Form & Matter," 174; Marolda, "Le radici neoplatoniche," 97; Vincieri, *Natura umano e dominio*, 41–46. Cf. Aristotle's statement that the virtues are the "mistresses" (*kuriai*) of happiness: no beating down. *NE* 1100b10.

76. NM, *D* I 60, II pr. See Lefort's excellent essay, "Machiavel et les jeunes," in Claude Lefort, *Les formes de l'histoire* (Paris: Gallimard, 1978), 153; Saxonhouse, *Women in the History of Political Thought*, 156–58, 162–65.

77. So Hulliung, *Citizen Machiavelli*, 194: "Machiavelli boldly substituted Machiavellianism for Stoicism as the inner meaning of Roman history." See also Guillemain, *Machiavel: L'anthropologie politique*, 352, 375; Kahn, "*Virtù* and the Example of Agathocles in Machiavelli's *Prince*," 207.

TWO    NECESSITY IN THE BEGINNINGS OF CITIES

1. Federico Chabod, "Sulla Composizione di "Il principe" di Niccolò Machiavelli," *Archivum Romanum* 11 (1927): 330–83.

2. Felix Gilbert, "The Structure and Composition of Machiavelli's *Discorsi*," in his *History, Choice and Commitment*, ed. Franklin Ford (Cambridge University Press, 1977), 118; L. J. Walker, ed., *The Discourses of Niccolò Machiavelli* (London: Routledge and Kegan Paul, 1950), 1:40–45.

3. Machiavelli has "composed a little work" but is sending it to his friends for comment; letter of Dec. 10, 1513.

4. The debate is well summarized by Sergio Bertelli in Niccolò Machiavelli, *Opere Complete* (Milan: Feltrinelli, 1960–67), 1:109–16.

5. Hans Baron, "The *Principe* and the Puzzle of the Date of the *Discorsi*," *Bibliothèque d'humanisme et Renaissance* 18 (1956): 405–28.

6. Felix Gilbert, "The Structure and Composition of Machiavelli's *Discorsi*."

7. J. H. Hexter, "Seyssel, Machiavelli and Polybius VI: The Mystery of the Missing Translation," *Studies in the Renaissance* 3 (1956): 75–96.

8. Baron, "The *Principe* and the Puzzle of the Date of the *Discorsi*," 406–8; Baron, "Machiavelli: The Republican Citizen and the Author of

'The Prince,' " *English Historical Review* 76 (1961): 217n; Hexter, "Seyssel, Machiavelli and Polybius VI," 95; Gilbert, "Structure and Composition of Machiavelli's *Discorsi*," 152; Gennaro Sasso, "Intorno alla composizione dei 'Discorsi' di Niccolò Machiavelli," *Giornale storico della letteratura italiana* 135 (1958): 257.

9. Gilbert, "Structure and Composition of Machiavelli's *Discorsi*," 127, 131; "loose structure" according to Baron, "*The Principe* and the Puzzle of the Date of the *Discorsi*," 406, 413, 419; J. H. Whitfield, "Discourses on Machiavelli VII, Gilbert, Hexter and Baron," *Italian Studies* 13 (1958): 43–46; Gennaro Sasso, *Studi sul Machiavelli* (Naples: Morano, 1967), 112–13.

10. Gilbert, "Structure and Composition of Machiavelli's *Discorsi*," 133.

11. Gilbert, *Machiavelli and Guicciardini*, 193. Ridolfi says Machiavelli was a poet, and "there can be no real wickedness [*tristizia*] where there is poetry." Roberto Ridolfi, *The Life of Niccolò Machiavelli*, trans. C. Grayson (Chicago: University of Chicago Press, 1963), 13, 107, 168, 252.

12. Ernst Cassirer, *The Myth of the State* (Garden City, N.Y.: Doubleday Anchor, 1955), 149.

13. On this chapter see Strauss, *Thoughts on Machiavelli*, 138–39.

14. *D* I pr; cf. I 9 on Agis and Cleomenes.

15. *P* 2; *D* II 1; III 19, 42; see Strauss, *Thoughts on Machiavelli*, chap. 1.

16. *FH* I 3, 29. Respect for the pope did not prevent Attila from killing Bleda, his brother, in order to be sole ruler; but since he left Italy, this respect did prevent him from founding an Italian city after the example of Romulus. *D* I 9, 18.

17. *D* I 1; cf. *FH* II 2, in which it appears that "the reputation of the Roman republic under the Roman empire" was responsible for the early security of the site of Florence and that Florence was laid waste later by Totila, king of the Ostrogoths.

18. Venice, the other Christian city mentioned here, needed the long repose of a safe site; *FH* I 29; II 1. Guicciardini's criticism that a colony need not be dependent on its mother country would be pertinent if NM were not thinking of man's dependence on God; Francesco Guicciardini, *Considerazioni intorno ai Discorsi del Machiavelli sopra la Prima Deca di Tito livio. Opere* (Milan: Riccardi, 1941), 2:430.

19. *Latori di leggi* occurs in a similar context in *D* I 42 and II 1, as opposed to *legislatori* in I 6, *ordinatore,* which first occurs in I 2, and *fondatore,* first appearing in I 9. To signify the human, conventional character of building, NM uses the word *build* in all its variants twenty-one times in I 1. Cf. II 24, the eighty-fourth chapter, on building fortresses, where *build* occurs thirteen times.

20. Plato, *Laws* 704d–705c; Aristotle, *Politics* 1326b27–1327b18, 1330a34–b18; Cicero, *De Republica* II 3.5–5.10; Thomas Aquinas, *De Regno* II 5. NM depreciates the importance of the site in *D* I 21; II 3.

21. Cf. *D* I pr, for NM's "natural desire that has been in me always for doing without any respect those things which I believe will bring common benefit to everyone."

22. Including Moses?

23. Lanfranco Mossini, *Necessità e legge nell'opera del Machiavelli* (Milan: Guiffre, 1962), 70, 260; Kurt Kluxen, *Der Begriff der Necessità im Denken Machiavellis* (Bensberg, 1949), 31, 68–71.

24. *D* I 1, first sentence; cf. the next to last sentence.

25. On Deinocrates, see esp. Lucian, *pro Imaginibus*, 9; Vitruvius, II 1–4; Thomas Aquinas, *De Regno* II 7. His name means "terrible ruler"; so Alexander was rejecting the advice of a "terrible ruler."

26. Alexandria and Florence are the two cities of unfree origin given in the first chapter, but NM tells no story about Florence. Cf. *D* I 49; *FH* II 1, 2 on Florence.

27. *D* I pr. For the understanding of this sentence, see Strauss, *Thoughts on Machiavelli*, 176–77.

28. In *D* I 20 Alexander serves as an exemplar of human acquisition in the widest sense, "acquiring the world."

29. Note "the one who has been the beginning," *D* I 1.

30. As Leo Strauss notes, NM begins thirteen chapters of the *Discourses* with the first person of the personal pronoun; the first of these is I 2, introducing the thought that the specifically human necessity is the necessity to acquire. Strauss, *Thoughts on Machiavelli*, 312n22. Kluxen's existentialist interpretation (positing *sein eigenes Ich absolut*) goes too far, not because it is bold but because it fails to consider the necessity of acquisition as taking *from,* and hence of religion and rhetoric. Nevertheless, its conventional radicalism is closer to NM's thought than is conventional blandness; Kluxen, *Der Begriff der Necessità,* 64, 96, 102.

31. See Strauss, *Thoughts on Machiavelli,* 97–106, 312–13, for the plan of the *Discourses.*

32. *D* I 11. NM's apology at the beginning of I 9 was made necessary by the distinction between ordinary and extraordinary, which he tried to sustain in I 2–8, for the founder overcomes it: he makes the ordinary by having recourse to the extraordinary.

33. Cf. *D* III 21: NM, on the way to persuading himself of the truth of Tacitus' maxim in III 19, suggests parallels between the native prince and the prince who makes himself loved and between the foreign prince and the prince who makes himself feared. But both Hannibal and Scipio were foreigners where they were, respectively, feared and loved; and besides, NM gives his preference to the methods of Hannibal, the feared enemy of Rome. If it is better for a prince to be feared than loved, it is better for him to be a foreigner or to behave like one. See *P* 17.

THREE    BURKE AND MACHIAVELLI ON PRINCIPLES IN POLITICS

1. See Harry V. Jaffa, *Crisis of the House Divided* (New York: Doubleday, 1959), chaps. 1, 2; and Harry V. Jaffa, *Equality and Liberty* (New York: Oxford, 1965), chap. 4.

2. *D* I 27, 55; II 15; III 6; *FH* III 13; VI 20; VII 23.

3. Edmund Burke, *Works* (London: Bohn Library, 1854), 1:377.

4. *D* ded let; *I* pr; cf. *P* ded let, 15. In the *Discourses* NM chooses to make the novelty of his doctrine first visible in regard to discord and party government. His first *advertised* difference with "all writers," which occurs near the end of Book I (I 58), is not this difference, but his high estimation of the character of the people.

5. Aristotle, *Politics* 1296a7–13, 1301a36–b4; *Eudemian Ethics* 1235a5–29, 1243a32–34; Cicero, *De Officiis* I.25; *De Republica* I.32.49, 55; II.23.42–43, 39.65–66, 42.69; III.13.23; Sallust *Bellum Iugurthinum* 5, 37, 41; Polybius, VI.10, 44; Plutarch, *Praecepta gerendae Reipublicae* 32; Dionysius of Halicarnassus, *Roman Antiquities* VI, VII, esp. VII, 65–66; Livy, II, 32, 44; III, 20, 65–66; Thomas Aquinas, *De Regno, Ad Regem Cypri* IV.33, V.39; Harvey C. Mansfield, Jr., "Whether Party Government Is Inevitable," *Political Science Quarterly* 80 (1965): 517–42.

6. Plato, *Republic* 421d1–423c1; *Laws* 704d5–705b6, 707d1–6, 737a5–b4, 744d1–8; Aristotle, *Politics* 1256b27–38, 1288b22–1289a25, 1291a8–19, 1295b39–1296a3, 1326b21–1327a32.

7. Polybius, VI.4. Polybius says that the regimes arise and degenerate according to nature, whereas NM says that they arise by chance and degenerate of necessity. The kinship between Polybius and NM has been much overestimated by the many commentators who neglect the movement of NM's rhetoric; see Strauss, *Thoughts on Machiavelli*, chap. 1; pp. 111, 134, 201–2, 222. See also Gennaro Sasso, *Niccolò Machiavelli: Storia del suo pensiero politico*, rev. ed. (Bologna: Mulino, 1980), 441–47; Sasso, *Studi su Machiavelli* (Naples: Morano, 1967), chaps. 4, 5; Guillemain, *Machiavel: L'anthropologie politique*, 266–67.

8. NM has now twice hinted that he prefers the threefold to the sixfold classification; *D* I, 16, 25, 26, 40, 52; II 13; III 6, 8; *P* 8, 9.

9. Cf. *D* I 9 and *FH* IV 1, with Polybius, VI.2, 9, 10.

10. *D* I, 2, 3; cf. the moderation in the Roman plebs caused by its experience under the Decemvirate, I 35, 40, 44.

11. See Gennaro Sasso, ed., *Il Principe* (Florence, 1963), 95n4. Compare the threefold appearance and twofold reality of Florence, *FH* pr; II 34, 36, 42; III 1; VII 1. On the middle part of Aristotle's mixed constitution, see *Politics* 1294a19–25, 1295b2–1296b2.

12. *D* I pr, 60; II pr; *FH* V 1. That is why he comments on an ancient historian whose "matter" can be reshaped, rather than on a political philosopher, whose thought would resist reshaping and would have to be refuted. To study NM with historical exactness, the reader must be no more "historical" than NM. For Livy's opinion of parties, see II 1, 30.2, 32 (the speech of Menenius).

13. *D* I 5; cf. I 4 and *P* 9, 19; *FH* III 1.

14. On Venice, see esp. *D* III 31; also I 35, 49, 50; II 30, 33; III 1; *P* 3.

15. *D* I 6; compare organizing a state anew to organizing it from the beginning, I 1, 26; *P* 6, 19, 20.

16. Note the density of *credo* here; see Strauss, *Thoughts on Machiavelli*,

117, 126, 321; cf. J. H. Whitfield, *Machiavelli* (Oxford: Blackwell, 1947), 119–22.

17. See *D* I 20; II 1; III 15. Compare the debate between democracy and oligarchy in Aristotle's *Politics,* which is not decided but left open to the possible influence of a persuasive appeal to justice, 1282b14–23, 1288b22–1289a8.

18. *D* I 6; cf. I pr, 1, 4, 16, 29, 37, 46; II 2, 3, 4, 19; *P* 3, 9, 12. In the corresponding passage of Polybius, VI.50, the choice between maintaining the city and expansion is left open. See NM, *Discorsus florentinarum rerum,* in *Tutte le opere,* ed. Mario Martelli (Florence: Sansoni, 1971), 30, on the instability of mixed governments.

19. *D* I 21, 23, 32, 58; II 26; III 49; *P* 20–22, 24.

20. *D* I 7, 20, 29, 30, 37, 43, 46, 50; II 2, 24, 33; III 15, 21, 23.

21. Cf. *D* I 2 and 9, from which it is clear that Sparta was neither peaceful nor devoted to the legislation of Lycurgus for anything like eight hundred years.

22. *D* I 1, 2, 4, 9, 11, 18, 21, 26; II pr, 1, 2, 5; III 1, 29, 43.

23. *D* I 15, 21; II 1, 2, 9; III 11; Strauss, *Thoughts on Machiavelli,* 120, 140, 154.

24. *D* I 8, 16, 17, 18, 37, 51, 52, 60; II 4, 19; III 8, 25, 49; *P* 14.

25. *D* I 30, 58; II 24, 33; III 31, 33; *P* 13.

26. NM calls attention to the change from chapter two by saying "as I said," referring to a previous statement in the same sixth chapter.

27. *D* I 9, 21; II 3, 4; III 6, 13; *P* 5. Athens rises as Sparta falls, in NM's argument: *D* I 9, 11, 40; II 3, 10.

28. *D* I 5, 7; Strauss, *Thoughts on Machiavelli,* 261.

29. *D* I 40. *P* 9 contains a statement that corresponds to the quotation from *Discourses* I 4; but in the *Prince,* which is addressed to a prince, "liberty" seems identical to "principality" in order to be distinct from "license" (*P* 9). The source of "license" is the factiousness of the barons and the cardinals or perhaps of the cardinals alone (*P* 11). Thus, party government, which must be a threat to the prince, is presented as a threat from the Church; and NM manages to attack the main obstacle to true party government even where he cannot praise party government (cf. *P* 20). *FH* II 12; III 1 contain an equivocation similar to the one discussed here, also complicated by the religious question.

30. NM implies the ambiguity of "people" by calling attention to the conventional character of "gentlemen," *D* I 6 (beg.); cf. "nobles" and "ignobles" in I 5; and see I 55.

31. *D* I 5. NM puts this policy into the Spartan argument, but when he says that one must "subtly examine the whole," he means that one must combine the Spartan and Roman arguments.

32. *D* I 58; III 34; *FH* III 15; IV 18; VI 24; Strauss, *Thoughts on Machiavelli,* 128–30.

33. On popular rule, Aristotle, *Politics* 1281b1–8, 1290a30–b4,

1291b31–38,    1317a40–b17;    on    demagogues,    *Politics*    1274a6–8,
1292a4–24, 1307b21–22.

34. *FH* IV 1; VII 13; *D* I 52, 55, 57, 58; III 3, 6, 7, 8, 30.

35. Aristotle, *Politics* 1297a17–22. For NM's view of Romulus on this
point, cf. *D* I 9, and I 18 (end); it cannot be excused as Whitfield believes,
*Machiavelli*, 82. See also *FH* V 8, 9; VII, 1.

36. Aristotle,    *Politics*    1283a23–29,    1290a7–11,    1294b13–18,
1295b19–24, 1297a4–13. Cf. *FH* II 12: "It is not possible for [the powerful
and the people] to understand each other."

37. Charles S. Singleton, "The Perspective of Art," *Kenyon Review* 15
(1953): 169–89; Strauss, *Thoughts on Machiavelli*, 18–19, 295–98.

38. Cf. *D* I 7 (beg.), with the example of Piero Soderini later in the
chapter, from which it appears that "the people" is the people properly
guided.

39. Note the parallel in *D* I 7 and I 8 of the sequence of the bad results
of calumny in Rome and in Florence: in the Florentine sequence, "hatred"
replaces "fear" and "sects" replaces "parties"; cf. *FH* VII 1.

40. *D* I 11, 12; II pr, 5, 25; III 1, 25; *P* 6, 8, 15, 20; *FH* II 3, 25; III 4;
VII, 1.

41. *D* I 11; cf. I 1, 14, 45, 49; *FH* I 9, 14, 15, 17, 26, 39; II 4, 10, 14,
21, 32; III 1, 15; IV 18; V 6; VI 29, 32, 34; VII 1; VIII 11, 17. Felix Gilbert
sees that a party is bad according to Machiavelli when it makes special
claims, but he does not apply this point to the Church: *Machiavelli and
Guicciardini*, 186–87.

42. Five references to NM can be found in Burke's works, *Works*, I 10,
20; II 196; V 249, 383.

43. Burke, *Letter to Sir Hercules Langrishe*, in *Works*, 3:340 (emphasis
in the original); Thomas Aquinas, *Summa Theologica*, Ia, IIae, 94.5.

44. Burke saw the danger of new men through the influence of Boling-
broke's theories, not from the direct influence of NM; on the relation of
Bolingbroke and NM, see Harvey C. Mansfield, Jr., *Statesmanship and Party
Government: A Study of Burke and Bolingbroke.* (Chicago: University of
Chicago Press, 1965).

45. Richard Pares, *King George III and the Politicians* (Oxford:
Clarendon Press, 1953), 13, 84n; John Brooke, *The Chatham Administra-
tion, 1766–68* (London: Macmillan, 1956), 84, 232, 281; L. B. Namier,
"The Character of Burke," *The Spectator*, 19 Dec. 1958, 895–96.

46. Burke, *An Appeal from the New to the Old Whigs*, in *Works*, 3:85–
86; Machiavelli, *P* 2, 6.

47. Burke, *Reflections on the Revolution in France*, in *Works*, 2:308–9.

48. Ibid., 2:359; Burke, *Appeal*, 3:112; on the connection between continuity and transcending self-interest, see C. P. Ives, "Edmund Burke and
the Legal Order," in *The Relevance of Edmund Burke*, ed. Peter J. Stanlis
(New York: P. J. Kenedy, 1964), 75–76.

49. Burke, *Reflections*, in *Works*, 2:422. For the best and most recent
study of prescription in Burke, see Francis Canavan, *Edmund Burke:*

*Prescription and Providence* (Durham, N.C.: Carolina Academic Press, 1987.

50. Burke, *Reflections*, in *Works*, 2:307; *Tracts on the Popery Laws*, in *Works*, 6:43.

51. Burke, *Reflections*, in *Works*, 2:368

52. Hobbes, *Leviathan*, chap. 15.

53. Burke, *Thoughts on the Cause of the Present Discontents*, in *Works*, 1:345.

54. Burke, *Letters on a Regicide Peace*, in *Works*, 5:236; cf. John C. Weston, Jr., "Edmund Burke's View of History," *Review of Politics* 23 (1961): 203–29.

55. Burke, *An Abridgment of English History*, in *Works*, 6:236; see Peter J. Stanlis, ed., *Edmund Burke: Selected Writings and Speeches* (Garden City, N.Y., 1963), 64–65; Peter Stanlis, *Edmund Burke and the Natural Law* (Ann Arbor: University of Michigan Press, 1958), 193.

56. See Burke, *Reflections*, in *Works*, 2:430.

57. See the end of his *Thoughts on French Affairs*, in *Works*, 3:393.

58. See Strauss, *Thoughts on Machiavelli*, 174–223, esp. 198–99.

59. Burke, *Reflections*, in *Works*, 2:284; 3:26–33. See Conor Cruise O'Brien, *The Great Melody* (Chicago: University of Chicago Press, 1993.)

FOUR    MACHIAVELLI AND THE IDEA OF PROGRESS

1. For a more detailed description, see Mansfield, *Machiavelli's New Modes and Orders*, ad loc.

2. The following is based on Harvey C. Mansfield, Jr., "The Unfinished Revolution," in *Three Beginnings: Revolution, Rights and the Liberal State*, ed. Stephen F. Englehart and John Allphin Moore, Jr. (New York: Peter Lang, 1994), 9–15.

3. Alexis de Tocqueville, *L'ancien régime et la révolution*, pt. 3, chaps. 1–8.

4. Burke, *Reflections*, in *Works*, 2:352; Burke, *Thoughts on French Affairs*, in *Works*, 3:350; Burke, *A Letter to William Elliot, Esq.*, in *Works*, 5:76; Burke, *A Letter to a Noble Lord*, 5:111.

5. See Mansfield, *Machiavelli's New Modes and Orders*, ad loc.

FIVE    AN INTRODUCTION TO MACHIAVELLI'S
        *FLORENTINE HISTORIES*

1. L. A. Ferrai, "Lettere inedite di Donato Giannotti," *Atti del R. Istituto Veneto di Scienze, Lettere ed Arti*, ser. 6, 3 (1884–85): 1582.

2. Felix Gilbert, *History, Choice and Commitment*, 139.

SIX    PARTY AND SECT IN MACHIAVELLI'S *FLORENTINE HISTORIES*

1. This is true even of the "two sects of armies" in V 2; see note 35 below. The word *sect* occurs forty times in the *Florentine Histories* in eighteen different locations, nineteen times in a sequence of seven chapters, III 3–9. The only book whose first chapter contains "sect" is the seventh. In

*The Prince* and the *Discourses* taken together, *sect* occurs twenty-one times, in seven locations in the *Discourses*, first in the seventh chapter where it refers to the "sects" of Savonarola and of his opponents, and seven times in the body of one chapter, II 5. It does not occur in *D* I 26 as one might expect from II 5. When *sect* means "party," it is never used to refer specifically to the ancient parties, and in the *Florentine Histories* NM uses the expression "Guelf sect" but never "Ghibelline sect," cf. *FH* II 4; *P* 20. It is some indication of the difference between the *Florentine Histories* and the *Discourses* that in the former he speaks of Catholic or heretical sects within Christianity, since the context is Christian, and in the latter of the "Christian sect" as opposed to the "Gentile sect."

2. Neither of these two historians, Leonardo Bruni and Poggio Bracciolini, in fact ended his history at 1434. They did not adequately discuss civil discords in the past, a mistake as we have seen in chapter 5. The mistake is indicated in Bruni's assertion that the Florentine people are a free people "not conquered in wars outside but oppressed by internal and civil discords." Bruni does not appreciate the connection between inside and outside things, "Rerum Italicarum Scriptores," in Book 12 of *Historiarum florentini populi*, ed. Emilio Santini and Carmine de Pierro (Città di Castello: S. Lapi, 1926), vol. 19, pt. 3, p. 22; E. Santini, "Leonardo Bruni Aretino e i suoi *Historiarum florentini populi libri XII*," *Annali della R. Scuola Normale Superiore di Pisa* 22 (1910): 121–22. See note 51 below. Cf. the writers discussed in *D* I 4 who "condemn the tumults between the Nobles and the Plebs."

3. *FH* let ded, pr, I 10. Of thirty-four quoted speeches in the *Florentine Histories*, twelve are introduced with the formula *in questa sentenza* and one, in III 11, of which NM says the words are true, with *in questa forma*. There are also seventeen indirect speeches.

4. Herodotus, I.1; Aristotle, *Rhetoric* 1360a37; Aristotle, *Poetics* 1451b3; Polybius, I.1.4; Cicero, *De Oratore* 2.12.52–14.58; Cicero, *De Legibus* I.2.5.

5. "1434" occurs eleven times in the *Florentine Histories*, and first appears as "the year of the Christian religion 1434" (*FH* pr). To show the power of sects in establishing the narrative of events, NM begins forty-nine chapters with parts of the verb *to be*, thirteen of them in Book I. There are 107 dates in the work in seventy-five locations; thirty-five dates are given with the formula "the year . . ." In the *Discourses* there are twenty-six dates (all in NM's lifetime) in twenty-three chapters.

6. The first four and the last four books have 143 (11 × 13) chapters; the first book has 39 (3 × 13) chapters, and the last seven books, 247 (19 × 13) chapters. NM's *The Prince* has 26 (2 × 13) chapters; and the *Art of War* has 182 (14 × 13) speeches. The *Discourses* has 142 chapters, but this is the same as the number of books in Livy's *History*. It would have been preternatural for Livy to have anticipated NM's need. Strauss, *Thoughts on Machiavelli*, 48–49, 52.

7. This was a mistake of the nobles; see *D* I 33; *FH* IV 3, 27. Niccolò

da Uzzano's foretelling, IV 19 (end), foretells Rinaldo's foretelling in IV 30 because it indicates the division of the Florentine nobility.

8. Just before Rinaldo died, he tried, NM says, "to earn a celestial fatherland for himself, since he had lost his earthly one"; *FH* V 34. His failure to see that one cannot have both—that all men are "exiles" from one or the other—was the source of his credulity. Cf. IV 22 and IV 26 for Rinaldo's naive request for protection against "false calumnies" and V 8 for his naive request for aid from the duke of Milan.

9. Lorenzo was able to claim, in 1478 after the failure of the Pazzi conspiracy, that Cosimo returned from exile "not with arms and by violence but with your consent and union." *FH* VIII 10. For another ludicrous triumph, see VIII 23.

10. *FH* IV 27. Niccolò da Uzzano, a noble who opposed the use of "extraordinary modes" against Cosimo, gives a discourse, accurate in its view of future events, that perfectly exposes the impotence of morality in its "ordinary ways." His discourse concludes in a prayer and with the advice to "live neutrally," as if men in need of God's help could forget the cause of their need, their natural partisanship and self-interestedness.

11. For the meaning of Cosimo's "restoration," see *FH* VII 5–6, where NM's "extraordinary" method of praising Cosimo is perhaps more effective for being seen once, and not always. Cf. *D* I 52; *P* 7; NM's letter of Aug. 30, 1524.

12. In *FH* VIII 36, Machiavelli says that the cardinalate received by Giovanni de' Medici at age thirteen "was a ladder enabling his house to rise to heaven, as happened in time following." After his son Giovanni died, Cosimo said: "This is too big a house for so small a family." NM almost omitted this "necessary" saying of Cosimo's; VII 6. Lorenzo, speaking to the *signori* and certain citizens, said "our house . . . has always been exalted [*esaltata*] by you"; VIII 10; see the untruth in note 9 above. Cosimo in his magnificence built churches and private houses for his family, but no public buildings, VII 4–5.

13. *D* I 11; *FH* V 1, VI 34; cf. III 16. See "external force" in *D* III 1. "Extraordinary" means "supernatural" in *P* 26.

14. One would expect them to be mentioned in *FH* II 2.

15. *FH* V 1. This consideration could never apply against NM himself, who teaches men to use or seize their own arms. Perhaps it takes an "extraordinary force" from this philosopher-captain to overcome the customary oscillation of virtue between quiet and glory and to rescue a people kept in ruin by means of another "extraordinary force."

16. Even Cosimo, who spent continually for the building of temples and in charity was never able "to spend as much for the honor of God as was said to be due him in his books"; *FH* VII 6. For the connection between magnificence and religion, see Aristotle, *NE* 1122b20. Florence is a city of beautiful buildings partly because Christianity turned its princes from magnanimity to magnificence.

17. *FH* I 5; in II 2 the first book is called "our universal treatise" to

indicate that Christianity, not nature, is the context of the *Florentine Histories*. See Strauss, *Thoughts on Machiavelli*, 307n22.

18. *FH* IV 33; VII 6. Of numerological interest are the facts that these two chapters are separated by seventy-eight chapters, when the two chapters out of narrative order are removed, V 2–3; that Cosimo is first mentioned in IV 11; and that he succeeds his father in IV 16. On *patria,* see note 8 above. On Lorenzo, see VIII 36.

19. See notes 1, 5, and 6 above.

20. *FH* let ded; cf. V 1; VIII 9, 29. Roberto Ridolfi, *Vita di Niccolò Machiavelli*, rev. ed. (Florence: Sansoni, 1978), 321–22, 331–32, 567n25.

21. *FH* VIII 36; V 15; VIII 5, 6; letter of Mar. 9, 1498.

22. *D* I 56. Roberto Ridolfi, *Vita di Girolamo Savonarola* (Rome: Belardetti, 1952), 1:73–74. Another sign of impending calamities was that the princes "through their spokesmen [*oratori*]" declared their sorrow to Florence at Lorenzo's death; *FH* VIII 36. Spokesmen for princes are like interpreters of signs. Cf. *FH* VII 28 for NM's prose version of a sign.

23. He does mention Lorenzo's patronage of a rival of Savonarola's; NM, *Istorie fiorentine*, ed. Gaeta, 575n14.

24. *FH* VIII 1. See references to the preceding or following books in I 39; III 1, 29; VI 38; VII 1, 34. NM treats of conspiracy in *D* III 6 and *P* 19, each the longest chapter in the work.

25. *Occultamente* and *secretamente* are used interchangeably. Opposition to the Medici in NM's day would still have to be secret; Gilbert, *Machiavelli and Guicciardini*, 239. See the letter of Donato Giannotti (1533) quoted in chapter 5 above.

26. NM is more explicit in *D* III 6.

27. The alternative of patience and conspiracy stated in VIII 1 is false. Both conspiracies related at length had master conspirators; see VII 31, 33; VIII 2; and cf. *D* I pr (end), 9 on Agis; III 6 on Alexamenus, Pelipodas; and the two cautions at the end of the chapter.

28. *D* II 13; *P* 7; *FH* III 13. In V 23 Niccolò Piccinino makes an escape from his enemies inside a sack carried on the back of his German servant. This adventure of Niccolò's—for NM keeps calling him Niccolò in this vicinity—occurs between accounts of two stratagems of war that worked because the enemy thought them impossible; and it must be compared with the mistake of another Niccolò in I 31, who tried to escape to the German emperor. Perhaps our Niccolò will escape from his enemies with an impossible trick, by hiding inside a sack carried not by the emperor but by the pope (who commissioned this work). At any rate *The Prince* and the *Discourses* were first published under papal authority together with the *Florentine Histories*. Cf. *D* II 33 and Strauss, *Thoughts on Machiavelli*, 106–7.

29. Note "industry" as opposed to "force" in *FH* VI 2; cf. the chapter preceding the first inquiry, I 39: the Florentines "had through many divisions destroyed its nobility and that republic was now in the hands of those brought up in trade." See *D* II 8.

30. See the contrary advice of good men and wise men in *FH* VII 13.

Rinato de' Pazzi was "considered a wise and good man" (for all the good it did him) because he was lacking in pride, that is, in the desire to make himself powerful. See note 32 below.

31. See *FH* II 29 on Ramando di Cardona; VI 6–7 on the murder of Baldaccio.

32. See *FH* III 17, 22 on Florence's ingratitude to Michele di Lando. Michele was both prudent and good. His goodness consisted in "never allowing a thought to enter his mind that was contrary to the general good"; his prudence "allowed him to conduct things in such a way that many of his party yielded to him and the others he could overcome with arms"; III 17. His partisan thoughts clearly were not contrary to the general good, in NM's view; cf. let ded. Giovanni de' Medici told Rinaldo degli Albizzi that because men are quicker for revenge than gratitude, "the duty of a wise and good citizen, he believed, was not to change the customary orders of the city"; IV 10. Then, knowing his man, he advised Rinaldo to follow the policy of his father and gain the gratitude of the people by benefiting them. Rinaldo never considered this, and shortly afterward Giovanni took his own advice, changing the orders of Florence to benefit the people and himself. Giovanni was a man "of very great prudence," and his prudence consisted in departures from his goodness and a seeming lack of ambition. Florence, that is, the Florentine people, showed more gratitude for his benevolence, done at the expense of the rich, than it would have shown for conquests taken from enemies; IV 14, 16. Cf. "the grace mixed with power" characteristic of Cosimo and Neri Capponi; VII 2.

33. Party conflict in Florence was for a time moderated by intermediaries using arguments to calm the zeal of both sides, but the arguments said nothing about justice or impartiality and the conflict began anew five years and two chapters later; *FH* II 14, 16.

34. "And it is more true than any other truth, that if where there are men there are not soldiers, this arises through a defect of the prince; and not through another defect of the site or of nature"; *D* I 21. Cf. II 29, sixty-eight chapters later; and Strauss, *Thoughts on Machiavelli*, 178.

35. *D* II 2. In *FH* V 2, where NM mentions the "two sects of armies," he relates an instance in which the pope preferred a dishonorable peace to a dangerous war against Francesco Sforza. Sforza, having seized some lands of the pope, sent him a letter with an insolent Machiavellian salutation punning on an ecclesiastical greeting, *invito Petro et Paulo*. At the invitation of, or despite, Peter and Paul: Christianity, despite its best wishes, needs worldly armies, and because of its best wishes, cannot profit from them. Its rootless priests give rise to rootless warriors.

36. *D* I 4. To be sure, the attack on parties in *FH* III 5 is deflated at the beginning of III 6; and Luigi Guicciardini's speech against vengeful discords in III 11 is diminished by the events related in III 12 and opposed by the speech of the plebeian leader in III 13. Note the different effect of Luigi's "true" words and the "persuasions" of the plebeian on the *animi* of their listeners, and the lack of effect of true words in III 27.

37. The distinction is explicitly abandoned in *FH* VII 2, where Cosimo is said to have used his "friends" instead of his "partisans" to oppose his "friends."

38. *FH* I 5, 26, 39. In I 26 NM mentions the wars of both the Visconti against the Guelfs and of Castruccio Castracani against the Florentines; he adds a digression on the Visconti but not on Castruccio. He also includes a discussion of Venice "in its place," I 3, 28, 29, but not of Florence.

39. *D* I 1 is entitled: "What have universally been the beginnings of any city whatever and what was that of Rome."

40. *FH* II 1 (end); cf. "whatever the cause of its origin," II 2.

41. *FH* I 9; on the affinity between Christianity and the East, see I 3 (end).

42. Invitations of popes to emperors were paralleled and preceded by concessions of eastern emperors to western barbarians; I 3, 4, 6. Cf NM's contrary invitation in the title of *P* 26: "An exhortation to seize Italy and set her free from the barbarians."

43. *FH* I 9, 15; cf. II 16 for the answer Henry IV could not give to the pope. Lorenzo's answer is in VIII 10. But with all his spiritual power, the pope could not prevent the death by diarrhea of his champion the Magnificent Robert, though he did give "the body" every kind of honor; VIII 23.

44. *FH* I 19. Note the discrepancy between the purpose of "the heavens" and that of the pope, I 25; and see VIII 11 for the Florentines' view that God can oppose his vicar.

45. *FH* I 19; cf. the extraordinary banquet of Frate Piero, VII 31.

46. *FH* I 14, 16, 18, 20, 25, 35; V 2; VI 29; VII 23, 27, 28; *D* I 12.

47. In *FH* V 7, a pope employs a cardinal to command his army, then loses the allegiance of the cardinal, who then loses the allegiance of his army back to the pope.

48. Having lost the war against Filippo Visconti, the Florentine nobles had neither booty to distribute nor glory to offer; they were unable to manage the ambition of Giovanni de' Medici; *FH* IV 3–7.

49. In *FH* V 11, "an older and wiser" noble of Lucca condemns the Florentine plebs with the purpose of keeping his own plebs loyal. Even the pope must understand "a universal peace" as confined to Italy for the purpose of war against the Turks; V 32, 37.

50. *FH* V 2; note that the beginning of VI 1 applies to the pope.

51. NM dwells on the relation of Florence to its colony Volterra in order to show the relation of the pope to Florence. See *FH* IV 17, where, by "God's aid" and contrary to the intention of certain noble Volterrans, Volterra was made a "vicarate" of Florence; and cf. VII 30 (end) and 31 (beg.). In *D* I 49 NM says that Florence began as a slave city, in direct contradiction to Bruni, who claimed that Florence had a free beginning under the Roman republic and who tried to trace the beginning of Florence beyond that of Rome to the Tuscans; Bruni, *Laudatio florentinae urbis*, in *From Petrarch to Leonardo Bruni*, ed. Hans Baron (Chicago: University of Chicago Press, 1968), 244–47. Baron has stressed the importance of this point in Bruni's

thought, in *The Crisis of the Early Italian Renaissance*, rev. ed. (Princeton: Princeton University Press, 1966), 62–75; cf. 465n1.

52. *FH* I 23, 25; cf. I 35 on Gregory XII, who renounced the papacy and was merely replaced, and VI 36 on Pius II, who abandoned his "private passions" but got his reward just the same.

53. *FH* I 39; cf. I 29; V 3. "Men nurtured [*nutricati*] in trade" might refer to spiritual merchants.

54. See *FH* V 8, where Rinaldo, by identifying the holy and the just, argues that the common good of Florence is to be found in justice to its exiles, not locally at home. In a lachrymose and enthusiastic response to Neri Capponi's speech, the Venetian senate exclaimed that their *patria* would always belong in common to the Florentines and themselves, V 21. Cf. the distinction between the celestial and the terrestrial fatherland in V 34, thirteen chapters later. See also the reply of the Pratesi to Bernardo Nardi, VII 26.

55. Consider the exile's argument of Rinaldo, asking the duke of Milan to be doctor to Florence's internal ills, *FH* V 8. But why should the duke of Milan wish to make Florence healthy? In politics the doctor must look to his own health. Cf. the parallel argument of a noble of Lucca, note 49 above.

56. *FH* I 15. Sixty-six Guelf and Ghibelline families are listed in II 4.

57. *FH* pr; II 5 (foreign judges), 32 (beg.); VI 8 (beg.); VII 25 (beg.). In VIII 10 Lorenzo asks: "Thus if we have honored strangers, how would we have injured our relatives?"

58. *FH* II 3; the temptation is in the first quoted speech of the work.

59. Aristotle, *Politics* 1303b18–19; cf. 1303b39–1304a4. See the "little changes" of *FH* II 5 and the "little things" of *D* III 33. Bruni merely adds the force of the Italian parties to this incident without attempting to see a connection, *Historiae florentini populi*, Bk. II, p. 49.

60. *Inferno* 28:103–10; cf. 13:144; *Paradiso* 16:136–44.

61. *D* I 7, 8; in *FH* see especially pr; I 11; II 12–14; III 3–11, 19, 20, 25; IV 19–22, 25–27; VI 30; VII 10.

62. This was not true, but NM wished to draw attention to the descendants of evil-doers and the descent of partisanship; see *Istorie Fiorentine*, ed. Gaeta, 215n3.

63. *FH* III 3; this chapter begins seven consecutive chapters in which *sect* occurs. Looking backward is of course unfavorable to the nobles, IV 14; VII 10; *D* I 37 (end).

64. *FH* VI 20; VII 4, 19, 21; VIII 10. On the connection between revenge and "inside and outside," see II 37.

65. The characteristic difference between the nobles and the people in regard to vengeance is portrayed in *FH* II 26–27. The nobles argued against a vengeful pursuit of Castruccio Castracani because it was unnecessary; then the people broke their promise to the exiles helping them against Castruccio because it was unnecessary to keep it, and turned their vengeance against the nobles.

66. See the speech of the Milanese to Count Francesco Sforza; *FH* VI 20. Though outwitted by the count, they tell him that God will punish him if—and they give the two conditions of divine retribution—faithlessness offends God and if God does not decide to befriend the wicked for some hidden good. Cf. III 11, 27.

67. On a Florentine embassy to Venice, Neri Capponi pretended that Florence was helping Venice out of liberality and not necessity, and he boasted to the Venetian Senate: "It is not possible that an old love or an old hate be easily cancelled by new merits or new offenses"; *FH* V 21. The next year he besieged and captured the territory of the count of Poppi, who seeing himself "abandoned by God and by men," surrendered. He begged Neri to leave him the state that his father had held for nine hundred years and from whom Neri's fathers had received "countless benefits." Neri replied that the count must be deprived of his state "necessarily" for the sake of "example," which was not the "eternal example of your clemency" that the count had spoken of in V 35. Neri here used necessity as an argument when none existed, and before, when necessity was present, he did not mention it. Besides, the "old hatred" of the Florentines for the duke of Milan was sustained by their present fear of the Florentine exiles; V 10. Book V tells of Florentine successes that came about because Florence understood its own necessity, though imperfectly, as is made clear in V 18, the central chapter of the central book of the Florentine section of the work. VI 29 contains a parody of the Last Supper to illustrate the necessity of infidelity. VI 30 contains a Machiavellian view of the same infidelity disguised in the infidelity of Gherardo Gambacorti, who despite his oath abandoned his son to his enemies; cf. *D* III 3–5.

68. After his father's death, Piero de' Medici received the insincere advice, under which "his ruin was hidden" to collect his father's old debts. Piero did this and fell into popular disfavor for failing to appreciate the difference between what was his own father's some time ago and what was recently and hence truly his own, *FH* VII 10; cf. VI 5, 17; VII 12, 16, 18. Note *Sogliono* at the beginning of *FH* V I, at the beginning of the speech in *VI* 20, and at the beginning of *The Prince*.

69. *FH* II 34, 36, 40; III 18.

70. *FH* II 32, 33, 37, 39. To expose the arrogance of the nobles was the unconscious role of the archbishop of Florence, who in accordance with his office and his natural goodness intervened to calm the party dispute and, still in accordance with both his office and his nature, exacerbated it.

71. *FH* II 39, 42; III 17, 18, 21. If the nobles are not arrogant, they are abject; there is no middle possibility of "modesty."

72. *FH* III 9; cf. III 4. On the "signs" of popular nobility, see II 34–37; III 1; IV 27.

73. *FH* II 12 (beg.) makes it clear that the modern parties are not the natural parties.

74. *FH* IV 7 offers an excellent example of this predicament. After a Florentine defeat, Rinaldo has to defend the party of disarmed nobles against the popular view that God justly willed their defeat to diminish their power. His advice is to consider God's will as fortune, to show fortune a bold face, to imitate their fathers, and not to lose their spirit (*animo*) against "any prince whatever." In effect, unknowingly and unsuccessfully, he advises the people to abandon Christianity.

SEVEN    AN INTRODUCTION TO *THE PRINCE*

1. See Mansfield, *Machiavelli's New Modes and Orders,* preface; and chapter 9 below.

EIGHT    AN INTRODUCTION TO MACHIAVELLI'S *ART OF WAR*

1. See Sasso, *Niccolò Machiavelli,* 581, 584; Neal Wood, *Introduction to Machiavelli's "The Art of War"* (Indianapolis: Bobbs-Merrill, 1965), 48, 59; Ridolfi, *Vita di Niccolò Machiavelli,* 277; Felix Gilbert, "Machiavelli: The Renaissance of the Art of War," in *Makers of Modern Strategy,* ed. Peter Paret (Princeton: Princeton University Press, 1986), 11.

2. *P* 1, 3, 4, 6, 7; *D* I 5, 20; III 12; *FH* III 13, VI 1. See *AW* VI 477, and especially the thirty-third deceit, VII 490, to be discussed below.

3. Francesco Sforza is mentioned three times, *AW* I 335–36, 348, and his political achievement is said to have enabled him "to live honorably in times of peace"—that is, not to have been an application of the art of war.

4. See chapter 1 above, and Mansfield, *Machiavelli's New Modes and Orders,* 375.

5. NM's only other dialogue is a *Discourse or Dialogue concerning our Language,* in which he appears arguing with Dante.

6. Felix Gilbert is an exception; see "Machiavelli: The Renaissance of the Art of War," 22.

7. Felix Gilbert, "Bernardo Rucellai and the Orti Oricellari: A Study on the Origin of Modern Political Thought," in his *History, Choice and Commitment,* 229–38. See also Rudolf von Albertini, *Die Florentinische Staatsbewusstsein im Übergang von der Republik zum Prinzipät* (Bern: Francke, 1955), 74–89.

8. Their docility should not be exaggerated, however, as by Pitkin, *Fortune Is a Woman,* 69; and Rebhorn, *Foxes and Lions,* 213–14.

9. Note *sotto l'ombra* three times in *AW* I 330–33.

10. Cf. other interpretations of the setting: Gennaro Sasso, *Machiavelli e gli antichi e altri saggi* (Milan: R. Ricciardi, 1987), 1:505; Pitkin, *Fortune Is a Woman,* 68; Rebhorn, *Foxes and Lions,* 203.

11. See especially Baron, *Crisis,* 457–60.

12. Aristotle, *NE* 1099a7, 1102a5, 1124b6.

13. Baron, *Crisis,* chap. 3.

14. In 1421 or, according to C. C. Bayley, 1422. See Bayley, *War and Society in Renaissance Florence* (Toronto: University of Toronto Press, 1961), 3, 362; cf. Baron, *Crisis,* 553, 560–61.

15. So, too, does Bruni's *Funeral Oration on Nanni degli Strozzi*, which stresses the outstanding patriotism of one who loves honor; Baron, *Crisis*, 419–20.

16. Aristotle, *Politics* 1267b23–31; Bruni, *De Militia*, in Bayley, *War and Society*, 371, 374.

17. Bayley, *War and Society*, 316–36.

18. Contrary to Baron, *Crisis*, 428–31.

19. Bayley, *War and Society*, 385.

20. Most recently, Piero Pieri, *Guerra e politica negli scrittori italiani* (Milan: R. Ricciardi, 1954), and J. R. Hale, *War and Society in Renaissance Europe, 1450–1620* (New York: St. Martin's, 1985).

21. Karl von Clausewitz, *Strategie*, ed. E. Kessel (Hamburg: Hanseatische Verlaganstalt, 1937), 41; Peter Paret, *Clausewitz and the State*, rev. ed. (Princeton: Princeton University Press, 1985), 169–79; Raymond Aron, *Penser la guerre Clausewitz* (Paris: Gallimard, 1976), 14–15, 20–25.

22. Clausewitz, *On War* II 3.

23. Quoted in Paret, *Clausewitz and the State*, 176.

24. In *D* I 11 NM makes Romulus's arts of war and Numa's arts of peace not only complementary but continuous. Livy had contrasted the two. Livy, I 21.5. See Mansfield, *Machiavelli's New Modes and Orders*, 70–71.

25. L. Arthur Burd, "Le fonti letterarie di Machiavelli nell' *Arte della querra*," *Atti della R. Accademia dei Lincei*, 5th ser., *Cl. di scienze morali, storiche e filologiche* 4 (1897): 187–261.

26. Plato, *Republic* 374b4; cf. 397e8, 422c6, 456a1.

27. Xenophon, *Memorabilia* III 1.

28. Xenophon, *Cyropaedia* VII 5.79.

29. Xenophon, *Memorabilia* III 9; cf. *Cyropaedia* I 6. 27, II 1.20.

30. On the importance of noticing *cose piccole* while reading NM's works, see Mansfield, *Machiavelli's New Modes and Orders*, 10; and Strauss, *Thoughts on Machiavelli*, chap. 1.

31. Pieri, *Guerra e Politica*, 56–62.

32. *D* I 5, 55, 58; III 20, 22; *P* 9; *FH* III 13.

33. The number of interventions by Cosimo—thirty-three in Book I, sixteen in Book II and three in Book III—gives an indication of Cosimo's importance in the dialogue. He is closer to NM than Fabrizio is.

34. *AW* I 333; see Sasso, *Niccolò Machiavelli*, 586.

35. Pocock, *Machiavellian Moment*, 199.

36. Pieri, *Guerra e politica*, 11–18.

37. On the "middle way" that Machiavelli says one must avoid in *D* II 23, see Strauss, *Thoughts on Machiavelli*, 156–57, 339n152, 340 n159.

38. *AW* I 346, 350; cf. Fabrizio's offhand reference to "my state" at II 373 when discussing the exercises of his troops.

39. See NM's explanation in *La cagione dell'ordinanza*, in Jean-Jacques Marchand, *Niccolò Machiavelli; i primi scritti politici* (Padua: Antenore, 1975), 120–43, 432–37. See also Sergio Bertelli, "Nota introduttiva," in

NM, *Arte della guerra,* ed. Sergio Bertelli (Milan: Feltrinelli, 1961), 79–89; Piero Pieri, *Il Rinascimento e la crisi militare italiana* (Turin: G. Einaudi, 1952), 436–43; Sasso, *Niccolò Machiavelli,* 157–80.

40. Only fourteen more times in the rest of the work.

41. In *P* 25 (end) trying one's fortune also goes with youth.

42. See the discussion in *D* II 16 and the commentary in Mansfield, *Machiavelli's New Modes and Orders,* 235–38.

43. This is the thirteenth caution and the fifth of nine speeches in Book IV.

44. Fabrizio's procedure recalls Aristotle's account of deliberation seeking its first cause, but in a context of choice, not necessity; *NE* 1112b16–20.

45. Polybius, *Histories* VI.42.

46. *AW* VI 478; cf. *D* III 22. See Maury D. Feld, "Machiavelli's Militia and Machiavelli's Mercenaries," in *The Military, Militarism and the Polity,* ed. M. L. Martin and E. S. McCrate (New York: Free Press, 1984), 85.

47. Burd, "Le fonti letterarie," 247–49.

48. *D* I 26; *P* 12, 13. Alexander the Great occurs eight times in *AW*, once mistakenly; Philip occurs three times.

NINE    STRAUSS'S MACHIAVELLI

1. Strauss's other writings on NM are "Walker's Machiavelli," *Review of Metaphysics* 6 (1953): 437–46; review of Olschki's *Machiavelli the Scientist* in *What Is Political Philosophy* (Glencoe, Ill.: Free Press, 1959), 286–90; "Machiavelli and Classical Literature," *Review of National Literatures* 1 (1970): 7–25; "Niccolò Machiavelli" in *History of Political Philosophy,* 3d ed., ed. Leo Strauss and Joseph Cropsey (Chicago: University of Chicago Press, 1987), 296–317.

2. Benedetto Croce, *Quaderni della "Critica"* 5, no. 14 (July 1949): 1–9.

3. Isaiah Berlin, "The Originality of Machiavelli," in Isaiah Berlin, *Against the Current* (New York: Penguin, 1982), 25–79.

4. Leo Strauss, *The Political Philosophy of Hobbes,* 2d ed. (Chicago: University of Chicago Press, 1952), xx.

5. Herbert Butterfield, book review, *Journal of Politics* 22 (1960): 729.

6. Felix Gilbert, book review, *Yale Review* 48 (1959): 466–69.

7. Gilbert, *Machiavelli and Guicciardini,* 158n19, 192.

8. Strauss, *Thoughts on Machiavelli,* 82.

9. John Hallowell, book review, *Midwest Journal of Political Science* 3 (1959): 300–303; Willmoore Kendall, book review, *Philosophical Review* 75 (1966): 247–54.

10. Arnaldo Momigliano, "Ermeneutica e pensiero politico classico in Leo Strauss," *Rivista storica italiana* 79 (1967): 1164–72.

11. Dante Germino, "Second Thoughts on Strauss's Machiavelli," *Journal of Politics* 28 (1966): 794–817.

12. Robert McShea, "Leo Strauss on Machiavelli," *Western Political Quarterly* 16 (1963): 782–97.

13. Lefort, *Le travail de l'oeuvre Machiavel*, 259–305.
14. Strauss, *Thoughts on Machiavelli*, 297.
15. Ibid., 30.
16. Gennaro Sasso, *Il principe e altri scritti* (Florence: La Nuova Italia Editrice, 1963), 128n20.
17. Gennaro Sasso, *In margine al V centenario de Machiavelli* (Naples: Guida editori, 1972), 34, 44n.
18. Kendall, 251.
19. Strauss, *Thoughts on Machiavelli*, 333, 259, 305.
20. Ibid., 134, 175, 201, 210, 292.
21. Ibid., 30.
22. L. J. Walker, *The Discourses of Niccolò Machiavelli*, 2:311–312; Strauss, *Thoughts on Machiavelli*, 35.
23. McShea, "Leo Strauss on Machiavelli," 792.
24. Walker, *The Discourses of Niccolò Machiavelli*, 2:39; Sergio Bertelli, ed., *Il principe e discorsi* (Milan: Feltrinelli 1960); Mario Puppo, ed., *Opere politiche di Machiavelli* (Florence: Le Monnier, 1969); Strauss, *Thoughts on Machiavelli*, 317n58.
25. Especially Lefort, *Le travail de l'oeuvre Machiavel*, 302.
26. Strauss, *Thoughts on Machiavelli*, 168; the passage is quoted correctly on p. 34. See also 203, 275.
27. Ibid., 34; Mansfield, *Machiavelli's New Modes and Orders*, 12.
28. Strauss, *Thoughts on Machiavelli*, 10.
29. "Teacher of Evil," *New Leader* 42 (October 12, 1959): 27–28.

TEN    MACHIAVELLI'S NEW REGIME

1. Plato, *Laws* 711c5–8; Aristotle, *Politics* 1276b10–12, 1278b11–13, 1288a23–24; Polybius, I.1.5, VI.2.9–10; Livy, III.32.
2. Aristotle, *Politics* 1253a4, 30–32.
3. *Livy* VI.15.
4. Note that only individuals should be punished; cf. the dictator's complaint against "calumnies put on him by the nobles," D I 5. Jeeves to Bertie Wooster: "It is a recognized fact, sir, that there is nothing that so satisfactorily unites individuals who have been so unfortunate as to quarrel amongst themselves as a strong mutual dislike for some definite person." P. G. Wodehouse, *Right Ho, Jeeves* (London: H. Jenkins, 1936), 309.
5. D I 24. Manlius was discharged from prison and executed later; Livy, VI.17–20.
6. Guicciardini, commenting on D I 26, says that Machiavelli "always took delight in extraordinary and violent remedies." Francesco Guicciardini, *Considerazioni intorno ai Discorsi*, 2:461.
7. See D I 50, where "ordinarily" is equivalent to "extraordinarily;" cf. *FH* VII 5, 6. It is a mistake to translate "ordinary" as "lawful" and "extraordinary" as "unlawful." When NM wished to say "lawful," he was capable of finding an expression for it, D I 58.

8. *Livy,* II.34–5.

9. This was alleged by the nobles when being accused themselves, *D* I 5; cf. I 60.

10. *D* III 38: "For titles do not give luster to men, but men to titles."

11. *Livy,* III.32.

12. Cf. *D* I 41; III 19, 46. Another, later Appius Claudius (the censor) was more prudent than this one, III 11, 33; or was the prudent device against the Tribunes, described in III 11, put into Appius's deeds by NM, as his prudent complaint against the irreligion of the Tribunes, described in III 33 was put in his mouth by Livy? Cf. *D* I 48; Livy, VI.40–41.

13. See the last sentence of *D* I 40.

14. *D* I 34. Camillus, a tribune with power, once served as his own dictator, III 30.

15. *D* I 50. In I 37 NM says that the Roman plebs "made sure of the nobles through the creation of the Tribunes," but he remarks in the next chapter that the Senate "always wished in every fortune to be the one who was prince of the deliberations that its subjects would make."

16. Cicero, *De Republica* II.1.2.

17. See *D* I 53, where NM distinguishes "the Senate" and the "wiser Romans." In the three examples of focusing responsibility on an individual, the two that turn out badly are blamed on the people and the one success is accorded to the Senate; but the Senate should have managed the people to avoid the defeat (in the central example) at Cannae. See also *D* II 21 for the "new way of ruling," that is, invisible government, which NM attributes to Livy, and of which Livy says nothing; Livy, IX.20.

18. In *D* I 5, note how the nobles used an accusation against the dictator "Menenius" to dissipate resentment against themselves as an order and to distract attention from their own ambition. On "Menenius" and "Fulvius" in I 5, see III 48 on the seeming mistake; in this case, the mistake is using the wrong name, but it is the princely nature of these plebeian princes that matters.

19. See *D* III 6, 204, on Nelematus, for the connection between accusation and conspiracy.

## ELEVEN   MACHIAVELLI'S POLITICAL SCIENCE

1. That science can establish facts but not values.

2. Alexis de Tocqueville, *Democracy in America,* ed. J. P. Mayer, trans. G. Lawrence (New York: Doubleday, 1969), 698. Consider the criticism of liberal formalism in Karl Marx, "On the Jewish Question," in *Early Writings,* trans. R. Livingstone and G. Benton (New York: Vintage, 1975), 219, 234.

3. See chapter 4 above. Two works emphasizing NM's republicanism have lost sight of his progressivism. In Pocock, *Machiavellian Moment,* 158–77, 218, NM's concern with innovation is given due emphasis with regard to *The Prince,* but denied with regard to the *Discourses;* and see Skinner, *Foundations of Modern Political Thought,* 1:xiv, 45, 179; cf. 1:

181. See also Karl-Heinz Gerschmann, "Uber Machiavellis Modernität," *Archiv für Begriffsgeschichte* 17 (1973): 175.

4. Although new acquisitions are useful to princes and peoples, they must mainly appear glorious in order to attract glory-seekers. NM would have found utilitarianism too staid to be useful. Compare what he says about *cose nuove* in *P* 6 with his remark on *cose presenti* in *P* 24; and note *innovare con nuovi modi li ordini antiqui* in *P* 7. Marsilius of Padua, *Defensor Pacis* I.I.3; I.XIX.3.

5. See especially *D* I 27 on *knowing* how to be altogether bad or good. On NM's borrowing from the ancients, see *P* 3 (praise of Romans), 6 (beg.), 19 (end); *D* I pr., 2, 4, 5, 21; II 16, 24, 33; III 2. On his borrowing from Christianity, consider *P* 7 (on "Remirro de Orco"); *D* I 52; II 16–18.

6. *D* I 6, 16–20; III 1, 3, 7. Note the progression from *P* 4 (end) to *P* 6 (on form and matter) to *P* 25 (end). But refounding "every day" would be offensive, *P* 8.

7. *D* I 5–6. Polybius VI.5.1; Livy IX.36.3; XXXIX.8.3. Strauss, *Thoughts on Machiavelli,* chap. 3; cf. Felix Gilbert, "The Composition and Structure of Machiavelli's *Discorsi,*" in his *History: Choice and Commitment,* 115–33.

8. Cf. *D* I 18 (end), where Romulus's killing is excused without reference to the common good. See *FH* I 3, regarding Attila, who also killed his brother in order to "be alone in the kingdom."

9. *P* 2, 6, 7, 8, 14; *D* III 2, 5. Note also the phrase *privata fortuna* in *P* 6, 7, 12, 14. The "private citizen" who must seek office must also have the princely "humor" (*P* 9) to be sure; but this fact does not justify the private lives of those who share the popular humor, who as such are deluded. See Russell Price, "The Theme of *Gloria* in Machiavelli," *Renaissance Quarterly* 30 (1977): 620.

10. Saint Augustine, *De Civitate Dei* XV.5.

11. One cannot create opinions altogether, since ordinary morality remains and will remain unaffected even by NM's instructions; see Mansfield, *Machiavelli's New Modes and Orders,* on *D* I 10. In *P* 15, "the orders of others" from which NM departs refer to qualities for which men are praised and blamed. See also *D* I pr; *FH* pr.

12. Or, how can one be a "teacher of evil"? Strauss, *Thoughts on Machiavelli,* 9. Claude Lefort, *Le travail de l'oeuvre Machiavel,* 260–62, has read past the first sentence in Strauss's book and has taken note of the *if* in that sentence.

13. See also *FH* VII 5.

14. Aristotle, *NE* 1139b7–8, 1140a18.

15. *Quella è sola arte che si espetta a chi comanda:* the article before *sola* is missing perhaps because NM is at a loss between the definite and the indefinite. Russo's suggestion, assigning *sola* to *chi comanda,* does not make sense; NM, *Il principe,* ed. Luigi Russo (Florence: Sansoni, 1963), 125n.

16. NM claims to be "professed" in the art of war in *AW* pr. See also *D* III 13. He does not claim to be a philosopher (*D* I 56) and characteristically uses weighty philosophical phrases only in political contexts.

17. Elsewhere Sforza is scolded by NM for having built a fortress that caused his heirs to lose their state; *P* 20; *D* II 24.

18. *P* 6 (on armed prophets); 19 (on Severus); *D* I ded (on the writers' praise of Hiero); I 21; III 13, 38.

19. Not in *AW* pr, I (beg.), where NM says that the art of war is necessary to defend the other arts and is useful for civil life; not in his exchange with the French cardinal in *P* 3, in which understanding war is distinct from understanding the state. See also the "arts of peace" in *D* I 11.

20. Cf. milder statements in *D* I 21 and III 31.

21. Livy merely says (XXXV.28.7) that Philopoemen did this so that "no consideration would be new to him in such a matter." NM has also suppressed Plutarch's remark that Philopoemen loved military affairs more than necessary; Plutarch, *Philopoemen* 4.6.

22. For a more complete interpretation, see *Machiavelli's New Modes and Orders*, 421–24.

23. In *D* III 39, Decius, the Roman tribune, puts on a cloak so that the enemy would not notice the leader.

24. Plato, *Laws* 823b; Xenophon makes a characteristically less obtrusive reference to "love of hunting" (*philotheria*), which Cyrus deprecates, *Cyropaedia* II.4.26.

25. Histories, not mirrors of princes; cf. *D* III 5.

26. *Resta ora*, *P* 15 begins; on the four parts of *The Prince*, see Strauss, *Thoughts on Machiavelli*, 56–60.

27. NM "gave himself over" to the orders of others (*P* 13, end), took that back (15), and now looks for a prince who will give himself over to his adviser (23).

28. *P* 24 begins: "The things written above, observed prudently . . ." On the glory of advising, see *D* III 3.

29. Cf. the double glory in *D* III 13 and *AW* VII.

30. On brevity of life, see also *P* 7, 11. And see *D* III 8, 34, 35.

31. "Nature" occurs twenty-six times in *The Prince* proper. The first occurrence is "the nature of government" (4); the ninth is "all other things in nature" (6); the eleventh is a "natural defect of spirit" (9), the thirteenth is "the nature of sites" (14); the fourteenth is "the nature of rivers and marshes" (14; cf. 25, beg.); the seventeenth is that a prince needs to know how to use "the one and the other nature" (18); and the nineteenth is "by nature or by art" (19). "Prudence" occurs twenty-eight times and "art" nine times. The sixth occurrence of "art" is with the nineteenth of "nature," the only association of "nature" and "art."

32. See especially *P* 24 and *D* I 41; on *facile* and *duro* see chapter 1 above.

33. Hobbes, *The English Works of Thomas Hobbes of Malmesbury*, ed. William Molesworth (London: Proto-Utilitarian, 1839–45), I viii–ix; VII

170–71). Cf. Dolf Sternberger, *Machiavellis "Principe" und der Begriff des Politischen* (Wiesbaden: Johann, 1974), 40–41.

34. Plato, *Laws* 676b–c; *Republic* 540e–541a; *Statesman* 271e–274e; Aristotle, *Physics* 223b24–31; *Politics* 1316a, 1522; *On Philosophy* 8; Polybius, VI.9.10; Isocrates, *Areopagiticus* 3–5.

35. See chapter 3 above.

36. Aristotle, *Politics* 1280a9–17.

37. *FH* I 5; V 1; Marsilius of Padua, *Defensor Pacis* I.X.3, 7; II.VIII.4; XVI.7; XX.I; Eugenio Garin, *Dal rinascimento all'illuminismo* (Pisa: Nistri-Lischi, 1970), 61.

38. Strauss, *Thoughts on Machiavelli*, 200, 333n59. *Anima* occurs occasionally in NM's other works.

39. Plato, *Laws* 896a–e; *Phaedrus* 245c–d, 247d; *Timaeus* 89a; *Republic* 353d; *Phaedo* 105c; Aristotle, *De Anima* 404b28–30, 432a15–18; *NE* 1139a5–12.

40. Men must make use of the beast, or beasts, in man; *P* 18.

41. Thus *uno prudente e virtuoso* has the task of introducing form into the matter, which will bring honor to him and good to the universality of men (*P* 26); such a one is perhaps not *prudentissimo* to show so much of his virtue. This is the second of three instances of "form" and "matter" together in *The Prince,* where "form" appears three times and "matter" thirteen times. See also *D* I 1, 36, 37, 43, 60; III 12.

42. Letter of Apr. 16, 1527, to Vettori. See NM, *Discursus florentinarum rerum post mortem iunioris Laurentii Medices,* in NM, *Tutte le opere,* ed. Mario Martelli (Florence: Sansoni, 1971), 30: "I believe that the greatest honor men can have is that which is voluntarily given to them by their fatherland; I believe that the greatest good that one may do, and the most pleasing to God, is that which is done for one's fatherland." Cf. Plato, *Laws* 731c. In his comments on NM's famous statement, Isaiah Berlin makes it uncertain whether NM "revealed his basic moral beliefs" or left open the possibility of choosing to save one's soul, "The Originality of Machiavelli," in his *Against the Current,* 50, 54, 64.

43. "And this glory [of reforming republics and kingdoms] has been so esteemed by men who have not attended to anything other than glory that, when they have been unable to make a republic in deed, they have made it in writing, like Aristotle, Plato and many others. They wished to show the world that if they were unable to found a civil association like Solon and Lycurgus, they did not fail because of their ignorance but because of their impotence. . . ." (NM, *Discursus florentinarum rerum,* 31–32). See also Manent, *Naissances de la politique moderne,* 21.

44. *P* 7; *D* I 7, 9, 34, 35, 53; II 12, 18; III 3, 5, 10, 30, 35, 38, 48.

45. As NM personifies *fortuna,* *P* 25; *D* II 29. See *D* I 53 for an instance of the people being deceived by a "false image of good"; also I 56, III 43. On the cause of making the Church powerful, see *P* 3 (end), 11.

46. As in the striking phrase, *virtù di corpo e di animo,* *P* 8; *D* III 8; *FH* VI 6; and in *grande virtù di animo,* *P* 19; *grandezza dello animo,* 8, 26.

See also the greater reliability of touching than seeing, *P* 18 (end), and the use of *umori* (humors of the body) in *P* 9, 19; *D* I 4.

47. There is republican obstinacy (*D* II.2), religious obstinacy (I 14, 15), obstinacy in the infantry (II 16, 17; III 12), and there are obstinate conspirators (III 6; *P* 19).

48. *D* I 43. See *P* 19 (end) on maintaining a state without having the respect of peoples.

49. A perpetual republic is denied in *D* III.17, but affirmed in III 22 after the remedy is found; and it is assumed possible in I 20; II 5; III 1, 3. See chapter 4 above.

TWELVE     MACHIAVELLI'S *STATO* AND THE IMPERSONAL
           MODERN STATE

1. Fritz Hartung, "L'état, c'est moi," *Historische Zeitschrift* 169 (1949): 1–30; Herbert H. Rowen, "L'état, c'est moi: Louis XIV and the State," *French Historical Studies* 2 (1961): 83–93.

2. Skinner, *Foundations of Modern Political Thought*, 2:354.

3. Ibid., 2:353; Skinner takes the definition of state from Max Weber, 1:x. See Nathan Tarcov, "Political Thought in Early Modern Europe," *Journal of Modern History* 54 (1982): 63–64.

4. Plato, *Republic* 473e, 501a, 544b–545d; *Statesman* 302b–303d; *Laws* 632c, 681d, 686c, 707d, 710d–e, 712e, 714b, 715b, 734e, 739e, 751a–c, 770e, 817b, 832c, 856b. Aristotle, *Politics* 1247b32–39, 1275a38–b4, 1276b1–12, 1279a26–b10, 1280a8–25, 1281a12, 1289a8–20, 1297a6.

5. Aristotle, *Politics* 1276b10–12.

6. See my attempts in chapter 11 and in "Hobbes and the Science of Indirect Government," *American Political Science Review* 65 (1971): 97–110.

7. One should immediately add that clarification is needed from political science that is aware of the classical regime; see Gaines Post, *Studies in Medieval Legal Thought* (Princeton: Princeton University Press, 1964): 7, 247.

8. Federico Chabod, "Alcuni questioni di terminologia: Stato, nazione, patria nel linguaggio del cinquecento," in his *Scritti sul Rinascimento* (Turin: Einaudi, 1967), 27.

9. Ernst H. Kantorowicz, *The King's Two Bodies: A Study in Medieval Political Theology* (Princeton: Princeton University Press, 1957), 214–16; Post, *Studies in Medieval Legal Thought*, viii, 39; Brian Tierney, *Religion, Law, and the Growth of Constitutional Thought, 1150–1650* (Cambridge: Cambridge University Press, 1982), 23, 39.

10. See Orazio Condorelli, "Per la storia del nome 'stato,'" *Archivo giuridico* 90 (1923): 80; H. C. Dowdall, "The Word 'State,'" *Law Quarterly Review* 39 (1923): 101; Post, *Studies in Medieval Legal Thought*, 270, 371n; see the exceptions in Brian Tierney "The Prince Is Not Bound by the Laws: Accursius and the Origins of the Modern State," in his *Church Law*

*and Constitutional Thought in the Middle Ages* (London: Variorum Reprints, 1963), 386; and Arnold O. Meyer, "Zur Geschichte des Wortes Staat," *Die Welt als Geschichte* 10 (1950), 230.

11. See Post, *Studies in Medieval Legal Thought*, 298–306; Kantorowicz, *The King's Two Bodies*, 271n; Tierney, *Religion, Law, and the Growth of Constitutional Thought*, 17, 64, 70; F. M. Powicke, "Reflections on the Medieval State," *Transactions of the Royal Historical Society* 19 (1936): 811.

12. On this humanist outrage upon Aquinas, see F. Edward Cranz, "The Publishing History of the Aristotle Commentaries of Thomas Aquinas," *Traditio* 34 (1978): 171–73; H.-F. Dondaine, "Le super politicam de Saint Thomas," *Revue des sciences philosophiques et théologiques* 48 (1964): 590–92; M. Grabmann, *Die Mittelalterlichen Kommentäre zur Politik des Aristoteles* (Munich: Sitzungsberichte der Bayerishen Akademie der Wissenschaften, 1941), 77; C. Martin, "The Vulgate Text of Aquinas' Commentary on Aristotle's Politics," *Dominican Studies* 5 (1952): 41–47; Thomas Aquinas, *Sententia libri politicorum,* in *Opera omnia,* ed. Leonine (Rome: Ad Sanctae Sabinae, 1971), 15–21.

13. Thomas Aquinas, *In libros politicorum aristotelis expositio,* ed. R. M. Spiazzi (Rome: Marietti, 1951), III.6, 385, 392–95.

14. See Nicolai Rubinstein, "Notes on the Word *Stato* in Florence before Machiavelli," in *Florilegium historiale,* ed. J. G. Rowe and W. H. Stockdale (Toronto: University of Toronto Press, 1971), 313–26. But I cannot follow Rubinstein when he says that Leonardo Bruni, clarifying Aquinas, "distinguishes clearly between government and the groups of individuals controlling it" (316). He seems to me clearly to equate the two, in accord with Aquinas and Aristotle.

15. Skinner, *Foundations of Modern Political Thought,* 2:356.

16. T. A. Starkey, *A Dialogue between Reginald Pole and Thomas Lupset,* ed. K. M. Burton (London: Chatto & Windus, 1948), 57.

17. Ibid., 69, 111.

18. Ibid., 165.

19. Ibid., see esp. 57, 64, 89, 99, 155, 164, 165, 167.

20. Francesco Calasso, *I glossatori e la teoria della sovranità* (Milan: Guiffre, 1957), 164.

21. See John B. Morrall, *Political Thought in Medieval Times,* 3d ed. (London: Hutchinson Universal Library, 1971), 80; Walter Ullmann, *Principles of Government and Politics in the Middle Ages* (New York: Barnes and Noble, 1961), 293; Ullmann, *Law and Politics in the Middle Ages* (Ithaca: Cornell University Press, 1975), 272.

22. Aristotle, *Politics* 1282b8–14, 1289a13–15.

23. See Tierney, *Religion, Law and the Growth of Constitutional Thought,* 22–26, 36, 42, 73; Sergio Mochi Onory, *Fonti canonistiche dell' idea moderna dello stato* (Milan: Vita e Pensiero, 1951), 259; Kantorowicz, *The King's Two Bodies,* 272; Pierre Michaud-Quantin, *Universitas: Expressions du mouvement communautaire dans le Moyen-Age Latin* (Paris: Vrin,

1970), 7, 40–41, 55, 57; J. P. Canning, "The Corporation in the Political Thought of the Italian Jurists of the Thirteenth and Fourteenth Centuries," *History of Political Theory* 1 (1980): 12–13, 31; M. H. Keen, "The Political Thought of the Fourteenth Century Civilians," in *Trends in Medieval Political Thought*, ed. B. Smalley (New York: Barnes and Noble, 1965), 110. See also John of Salisbury (*Policraticus* IV 2) for the expression *universitas rei politicae;* this is a *universitas* of the regime, which as such precedes the law but ought to live by the law. Understanding of the classical regime did not have to await the rediscovery of Aristotle's *Politics* a century later.

24. Michaud-Quantin, *Universitas*, 55.

25. Tierney, *Religion, Law, and the Growth of Constitutional Thought*, 57–58, 80.

26. Hans DeVries, "Essai sur la terminologie constitutionelle chez Machiavel" (doctoral thesis, University of Amsterdam, 1957), 58–59; F. Chiappelli, *Nuovi studi sul linguaggio del Machiavelli* (Florence: Le Monnier, 1969), 36n; cf. Fredi Chiappelli, *Studi sul linguaggio del Machiavelli* (Florence: Le Monnier, 1952), 59–73. See also *stato loro proprio*, "their own state," in *FH* VI 8, and "those to whom the state belonged," *FH* VII 2.

27. Skinner, *Foundations of Modern Political Thought*, 2:354.

28. Cf. DeVries, "Essai sur la Terminologie Constitutionelle Chez Machiavel," 61; *FH* VI 35.

29. Cf., DeVries, "Essai sur la terminologie constitutionelle chez Machiavel," 65, and Rubinstein, "Notes on the Word *Stato* in Florence before Machiavelli," 319. For Joseph R. Strayer, *On the Medieval Origins of the Modern State* (Princeton: Princeton University Press, 1970), 10, permanent, impersonal institutions, together with authority and loyalty, suffice to make a state; so he asserts, "certainly the Greek polis was a state." See Aristotle, *Politics* 1301b6–13.

30. DeVries, "Essai sur la terminologie constitutionelle chez Machiavel," 79; F. Ercole, *La politica di Machiavelli* (Rome: Anonima Romana, 1926), 77.

31. Chiappelli, *Nuovi studi sul linguaggio del Machiavelli*, 36n.

32. J. H. Hexter, "*Il principe* and *lo stato*," in *The Vision of Politics on the Eve of the Reformation*, ed. J. H. Hexter (New York: Basic Books, 1973); Ercole, *La politica di Machiavelli*, 107; Dolf Sternberger, *Machiavelli's "Principe" und der Begriff des Politischen* (Wiesbaden: Steiner, 1974), 42–43. Consider Machiavelli's famous joke: "For when the Cardinal of Rouen said to me that the Italians do not understand war, I replied to him that the French do not understand about the state" (*non si intendovano dello stato; P* 3). Note the rare instances of *reggimento* in *FH* II 11, 32.

33. Hexter, in "*Il principe* and *lo stato*," 171, speaks almost in successive sentences of Machiavelli's *stato* as an instrument and as the object of exploitation. As instrument of exploitation *stato* implies the existence of something like "the state" with which to exploit others. Hexter seems here to slip into the error of presupposing the modern state, for which he indicted Chiappelli (173–75). For more on Machiavelli's *stato*, see Chabod, "Alcuni

questioni di terminologia," 631–37; Gilbert, *Machiavelli and Guicciardini,* 326–30; and Whitfield, *Machiavelli,* 93–95.

34. See Dowdall, "The Word 'State,' " 110; Condorelli, "Per la storia del nome 'stato,' " 87. Note that nothing is said in Machiavelli's sentence about the future.

35. Cf. Sternberger, *Machiavelli's "Principe" und der Begriff des Politischen,* 38–39, 56–66.

36. Ercole, *La politica di Machiavelli,* 150–51.

37. Aristotle, *Politics* 1267a30–32 and *D* I 6 (end); see also *Politics* 1257b38–1258a1, 1323a34–b21, 1365a6–8; *NE* 1129b13.

38. Aristotle, *Politics* 1247b38; *D* I 18.

39. Mansfield, *Machiavelli's New Modes and Orders,* on *D* III 6.

40. J. H. Shennan, *The Origins of the Modern European State, 1450–1725* (London: Hutchinson University Library, 1974), 25.

41. Aristotle, *Politics* 1275b13; see Plato, *Laws* 712e; *Statesman* 303c.

42. *D* II 2; cf. *D* III 9, and see Mansfield, *Machiavelli's New Modes and Orders,* on *D* I, 55, 58–59; II 2, 19.

43. Pocock, *Machiavellian Moment,* vii–viii.

44. See chapter 11 above.

45. Rousseau, *Social Contract* I 6.

46. Skinner, *Foundations of Modern Political Thought,* 1:ix.

47. Orwin, "Machiavelli's Unchristian Charity," 1226–27.

48. Giovanni Botero, *Della ragion di stato* (Bologna: Capelli, 1930), 9, 26–33; see C. J. Friedrich, *Constitutional Reason of State* (Providence: Brown University Press, 1957), 4. *Ragione di stato* in Botero substitutes for fraud in Machiavelli, for when the *stato* becomes entitled to its own special reason, it no longer needs fraud. Cf. *per cagione dello stato* in *FH* VII 5, to describe a partisan consideration. The connection between reason of state and acquisition separates the former from medieval instances of *ratio status* discussed by Post, *Studies in Medieval Legal Thought,* 250–301.

THIRTEEN     MACHIAVELLI AND THE MODERN EXECUTIVE

1. Aristotle, *Politics* III 1284a3–17; Marsilius of Padua, *Defensor pacis* I.11, 6–7; 14.5, 8–9; II.12, 7–9. See Antonio Toscano, *Marsilio da Padova e Niccolò Machiavelli* (Ravenna: Longo, 1981), 112–13.

2. See *P* 15; *D* I 2. See also Strauss, *Thoughts on Machiavelli,* 13, 30, 59, 222, 236, 290; Lefort, *Le travail de l'oeuvre Machiavel,* 301; Sasso, *Studi su Machiavelli,* 50–65.

3. NM speaks of "natural virtues" in *D* I 56; these might perhaps belong to intelligences in the air that might come to the defense of mankind by issuing warnings and signs. See Mansfield, *Machiavelli's New Modes and Orders,* ad loc.

4. Cf. Harold D. Lasswell's three goals of "safety, income and deference" in *Politics: Who Gets What, When, How* (New York: Meridian, 1958), 13ff.

5. See Harvey C. Mansfield, Jr., "The Ambivalence of Executive Power,"

in *The Presidency in the Constitutional Order,* ed. J. Bessette and J. Tulis (Baton Rouge: Louisiana State University Press, 1981), 314–33.

6. So I call it, not to say that NM ever made scientific or academic use of terms that do not equivocate, but rather to suggest that his favorite phrases deserve study.

7. Aristotle wanted to keep the priests fifth, not first; *Politics* 1322b20–21; 1328b11.

8. But precisely on "commissions," see NM's praise for the Roman Senate's grant of "very great authority" to Fabius in the Ciminian forest affair; *D* II 33.

9. NM also uses *seguire* (e.g., *FH* II 20) and *mandare ad effetto* (*FH* I 24; II 10; VII 23; VIII 5, 23) in the sense of *execute.*

10. Aristotle, *Politics* 1285a4, 1286a3.

11. Cf. Aristotle, *Politics* 1285b1–4.

12. Contrast the beginning to the end of the first paragraph of *D* I 33.

13. See chapter 11 above.

14. Aristotle, *Politics* 1280a8–23, 1283a23–b35; Plato, *Laws* 690a–c.

15. Thus for NM to conceive the dictator as commissioned was not in contradiction to the prince as sovereign, as Carl Schmitt says; sovereign by commission is the essence of executive ambivalance. Schmitt cites *D* I 33 but not *D* III 1; Schmitt, *Die Diktatur* (Berlin: Duncker und Humblot, 1964), 6–9.

16. Cf. Plato, *Apology* 37a–b.

## WORKS BY NICCOLÒ MACHIAVELLI

*Arte della guerra.* Edited by Sergio Bertelli. Milan: Feltrinelli, 1961.

*Il principe.* Edited by Luigi Russo. Florence: Sansoni, 1963.

*Il principe e discorsi.*\Edited by Sergio Bertelli. Milan: Feltrinelli, 1960.

*I primi scritti politici.* Edited by Jean-Jaques Marchand. Padua: Antenore, 1975.

*Istorie fiorentine.* Edited by F. Gaeta. Milan: Feltrinelli, 1962.

*Opere complete.* 8 vols. Edited by Sergio Bertelli. Milan: Feltrinelli, 1960–67.

*Opere politiche.* Edited by Mario Puppo. Florence: Le Monnier, 1969.

*Tutte le opere.* Edited by Mario Casella. Florence: G. Barbera, 1969.

*Tutte le opere.* Edited by Mario Martelli. Florence: Sansoni, 1971.

## SECONDARY WORKS

Acton, Lord. "Introduction to Niccolò Machiavelli." In *Il principe,* edited by L. Arthur Burd. Oxford: Clarendon Press, 1891.

Arendt, Hannah. *The Human Condition.* Chicago: University of Chicago Press, 1959.

Aron, Raymond. "Le Machiavélisme de Machiavel." In his *Machiavel et les tyrannies modernes.* Paris: Fallois, 1993.

———. *Penser la guerre Clausewitz.* 2 vols. Paris: Gallimard, 1976.

Bacon, Francis. "Of the Advancement of Learning." In *The Works of Francis Bacon,* edited by J. Spedding, vol. 3. London: Longman, 1859.

Baron, Hans. *The Crisis of the Early Italian Renaissance.* Rev. ed. Princeton: Princeton University Press, 1966.

———. "The Principe and the Puzzle of the Date of the Discorsi." *Bibliothèque d'humanisme et Renaissance* 18 (1956): 405–28.

Baruzzi, Arno. *Einführung in die Politische Philosophie der Neuzeit.* Darmstadt: Wissenschaftliche Buchgesellschaft, 1983.

Bayley, C. C. *War and Society in Renaissance Florence.* Toronto: University of Toronto Press, 1961.

Berlin, Isaiah. "The Originality of Machiavelli." In his *Against the Current*. New York: Penguin Books, 1982.

Bonadeo, Alfredo. *Corruption, Conflict and Power in the Works and Times of Niccolò Machiavelli*. Berkeley: University of Callifornia Press, 1973.

Borsellino, Nino. *Machiavelli*. Rome-Bari: Laterza, 1973.

Botero, Giovanni. *Della ragion di stato*. Bologna: Capelli, 1930.

Brooke, John. *The Chatham Administration, 1766–68*. London: Macmillan, 1956.

Brucker, Gene A. *Renaissance Florence*. Berkeley: University of California Press, 1969.

Bruni, Leonardo. *Historiarum florentini populi*. Edited by Emilio Santini and Carmine di Pierro. Città di Castello: S. Lapi, 1926.

———. *Laudatio florentinae urbis*. In *From Petrarch to Leonardo Bruni*, edited by Hans Baron. Chicago: University of Chicago Press, 1968.

Burckhardt, Jacob. *The Civilization of the Renaissance in Italy*. Translated by S. G. C. Middlemore. London: Phaidon, 1950.

Burd, L. Arthur. "Le fonti letterarie di Machiavelli nell' *Arte della querra*." *Atti della R. Accademia dei Lincei*, 5th ser. *Cl. di scienze morali, storiche e filologiche* 4 (1897): 187–261.

Burke, Edmund. *Works*. 8 vols. London: Bohn Library, 1854.

Butterfield, Herbert. *The Statecraft of Machiavelli*. London: G. Bell, 1940.

Calasso, Francesco. *I glossatori e la teoria della sovranità*. Milan: Guiffre, 1957.

Canavan, Francis. *Edmund Burke: Prescription and Providence*. Durham, N.C.: Carolina Academic Press, 1987.

Canning, J. P. "The Corporation in the Political Thought of the Italian Jurists of the Thirteenth and Fourteenth Centuries." *History of Political Theory* 1 (1980):12–13, 31.

Cassirer, Ernst. *The Myth of the State*. Garden City, N.Y.: Doubleday Anchor, 1955.

Chabod, Federico. "Alcuni questioni di terminologia: Stato, nazione, patria nel linguaggio del cinquecento." In *Scritti sul Rinascimento*. Turin: Einaudi, 1967.

———. "Sulla composizione di 'Il principe' di Niccolò Machiavelli." *Archivum Romanum* 11 (1927): 330–83.

Chiappelli, Fredi. *Nuovi studi sul linguaggio del Machiavelli*. Florence: Le Monnier, 1969.

———. *Studi sul linguaggio del Machiavelli*. Florence: Le Monnier, 1952.

Colish, Marcia L. "Cicero's De Officis and Machiavelli's Prince." *Sixteenth Century Journal* 9 (1978): 81–93.

Colonna d'Istria, Gérard, and Roland Frapet. *L'art politique chez Machiavel*. Paris: J. Vrin, 1980.

Condorelli, Orazio. "Per la storia del nome 'stato.' " *Archivo giuridico* 90 (1923): 80.

Cranz, F. Edward. "The Publishing History of the Aristotle Commentaries of Thomas Aquinas." *Traditio* 34 (1978): 171–73.

Croce, Benedetto. *Quaderni della "Critica"* 5, no. 14 (July 1949): 1–9

De Grazia, Sebastian. *Machiavelli in Hell*. Princeton: Princeton University Press, 1989.

De Tocqueville, Alexis. *Democracy in America*. Edited by J. P. Mayer. Translated by G. Lawrence. New York: Doubleday, 1969.

DeVries, Hans. "Essai sur la terminologie constitutionelle chez Machiavel." Doctoral thesis, University of Amsterdam, 1957.

Di Napoli, Giovanni. "Niccolò Machiavelli e l'Aristotelismo del Rinascimento." *Giornale di metafisica* 25 (1970): 248–64.

Donaldson, Peter S. *Machiavelli and Mystery of State*. New York: Cambridge University Press, 1988.

Dondaine, H.-F. "Le super politicam de Saint Thomas." *Revue des sciences philosophiques et théologiques* 48 (1964): 590–92.

Dowdall, H. C. "The Word 'State.' " *Law Quarterly Review* 39 (1923): 101.

Duvernoy, Jean-François. *La pensée de Machiavel*. Paris: Bordas, 1974.

Ercole, F. *La politica di Machiavelli*. Rome: Anonima Romana, 1926.

Esposito, Roberto. *La politica e la storia: Machiavelli e Vico*. Naples: Liguori Editore, 1980.

Feld, Maury D. "Machiavelli's Militia and Machiavelli's Mercenaries." In *The Military, Militarism and the Polity*, edited by M. L. Martin and E. S. McCrate. New York: Free Press, 1984.

Ferrai, L. A. "Lettere inedite di Donato Giannotti." *Atti del R. Istituto Veneto di Scienze, Lettere ed Arti*, ser. 6, vol. 3 (1884–85): 1582.

Ferroni, Giulio. *Mutazione e riscontro nel teatro di Machiavelli*. Rome: Bulzoni, 1972.

Fleisher, Martin. "A Passion for Politics: The Vital Core of the World of Machiavelli." In his *Machiavelli and the Nature of Political Thought*. New York: Atheneum, 1972.

Friedrich, C. J. *Constitutional Reason of State*. Providence: Brown University Press, 1957.

Fumaroli, Marc. *L'age de l'éloquence*. Geneva: Librairie Droz, 1980.

Garin, Eugenio. *Dal Rinascimento all'Illuminismo*. Pisa: Nistri-Lischi, 1970.

———. *La cultura del Rinascimento*. Bari: Laterza, 1976.

Germino, Dante. "Second Thoughts on Leo Strauss's Machiavelli." *Journal of Politics* 28 (1966): 794–817.

Gilbert, Felix. "Bernardo Rucellai and the Orti Oricellari: A Study on the Origin of Modern Political Thought" and "The Composition and Structure of Machiavelli's *Discorsi*." In *History, Choice and Commitment*, edited by Franklin Ford. Cambridge: Harvard University Press, 1977.

———. *Machiavelli and Guicciardini*. Princeton: Princeton University Press, 1965.

———. "Machiavelli: The Renaissance of the Art of War." In *Makers of Modern Strategy*, edited by Peter Paret. Princeton: Princeton University Press, 1986.

———. "On Machiavelli's Idea of Virtù." *Renaissance News* 4 (1951): 53–55.

Gilmore, Myron P., ed. *Studies on Machiavelli*. Florence: Sansoni, 1972.

Grabmann, M. *Die Mittelalterlichen Kommentäre zur Politik des Aristoteles*. Munich: Sitzungsberichte der Bayerishen Akademie der Wissenschaften, 1941.

Guicciardini, Francesco. *Considerazioni intorno ai Discorsi del Machiavelli sopra la prima deca di Tito livio. Opere*. 2 vols. Milan: Riccardi, 1941.

Guillemain, Bernard. *Machiavel: L'anthropologie politique*. Geneva: Droz, 1977.

Hale, J. R. *War and Society in Renaissance Europe, 1450–1620*. New York: St. Martin's Press, 1985.

Hart, Jeffrey. *Viscount Bolingbroke, Tory Humanist*. London, 1966.

Hartung, Fritz. "L'état, c'est moi." *Historische Zeitschrift* 169 (1949): 1–30.

Hay, Denys. "Storici e Rinascimento negli ultimi venticinque anni." In *Il Rinascimento negli ultimi venticinque anni*. Rome, 1979.

Hexter, J. H. "Seyssel, Machiavelli and Polybius VI: The Mystery of the Missing Translation." *Studies in the Renaissance* 3 (1956): 75–96.

———. *The Vision of Politics on the Eve of the Reformation*. New York: Basic Books, 1973.

Hulliung, Mark. *Citizen Machiavelli*. Princeton: Princeton University Press, 1983.

Ives, C. P. "Edmund Burke and the Legal Order." In *The Relevance of Edmund Burke*, edited by Peter J. Stanlis. New York: P. J. Kenedy, 1964.

Jaffa, Harry V. *Crisis of the House Divided*. New York: Doubleday, 1959.

———. *Equality and Liberty*. New York: Oxford, 1965.

Kantorowicz, Ernst H. *The King's Two Bodies: A Study in Medieval Political Theology*. Princeton: Princeton University Press, 1957.

Keen, M. H. "The Political Thought of the Fourteenth Century Civilians." In *Trends in Medieval Political Thought,* edited by B. Smalley. New York: Barnes and Noble, 1965.

Kersting, Wolfgang. *Niccolò Machiavelli.* Munich: C. H. Beck, 1988.

Kluxen, Kurt. *Der Begriff der Necessità im Denken Machiavellis.* Cologne: Bensberg, 1949.

Kristeller, Paul O. *Renaissance Thought: The Classic, Scholastic, and Humanistic Strains.* New York: Harper, 1955.

Lasswell, Harold D. *Politics: Who Gets What, When, How.* New York: Meridian, 1958.

Lefort, Claude. *Le travail de l'oeuvre Machiavel.* Paris: Gallimard, 1972.

———. "Machiavel et les jeunes." In his *Les formes de l'histoire.* Paris: Gallimard, 1978.

Leopardi, Giacomo. *Tutte le opere: Le poesie e le prose.* 2 vols. Edited by F. Flora. Verona: Mondadori, 1968.

Macaulay, Thomas Babington. *Miscellaneous Works.* 10 vols. New York: Putnam, n.d.

MacKinney, L. C. "Discussion." *Renaissance News* 5 (1952): 21–23, 70–71.

Manent, Pierre. *Naissances de la politique moderne: Machiavel, Hobbes, Rousseau.* Paris: Payot, 1977.

Mansfield, Harvey C., Jr. "The Ambivalance of Executive Power." In *The Presidency in the Constitutional Order.* Edited by J. Bessette and J. Tulis. Baton Rouge: Louisiana State University Press, 1981.

———. "Hobbes and the Science of Indirect Government." *American Political Science Review* 65 (1971): 97–110.

———. *Machiavelli's New Modes and Orders.* Ithaca: Cornell University Press, 1979.

———. *Taming the Prince.* New York: Free Press, 1989.

———. "The Unfinished Revolution." In *Three Beginnings: Revolution, Rights and the Liberal State,* edited by Stephen F. Englehart and John Allphin Moore, Jr. New York: Peter Lang, 1994.

———. "Whether Party Government Is Inevitable." *Political Science Quarterly* 80 (1965): 517–42.

Marolda, Paolo. "Le radici neoplatoniche del 'savio' machiavelliano." *La rassegna della letteratura italiana* 7 (1979): 95–116.

Martin, C. "The Vulgate Text of Aquinas' Commentary on Aristotle's Politics." *Dominican Studies* 5 (1952): 41–47.

Mayer, Edward W. *Machiavellis Geschichtsauffassung und sein Begriff virtù.* Munich: R. Oldenbourg, 1912.

McShea, Robert. "Leo Strauss on Machiavelli." *Western Political Quarterly* 16 (1963): 782–97.

Meinecke, Friedrich. *Die Idee der Staatsräson*. 1924. Munich: R. Oldenbourg, 1957.

Meyer, Arnold O. "Zur Geschichte des Wortes Staat." *Die Welt als Geschichte* 10 (1950): 230.

Michaud-Quantin, Pierre. *Universitas: Expressions du mouvement communautaire dans le Moyen-Age Latin*. Paris: Vrin, 1970.

Mochi, Onory Sergio. *Fonti canonistiche dell' idea moreno dello stato*. Milan: Vita e Pensiero, 1951.

Momigliano, Arnaldo. "Ermeneutica e pensiero politico classico in Leo Strauss." *Rivista storica italiana* 79 (1967): 1164–72.

Morrall, John B. *Political Thought in Medieval Times*. 3d ed. London: Hutchinson University Library, 1971.

Mossini, Lanfranco. *Necessità e legge nell'opera del Machiavelli*. Milan: Giuffre, 1962.

Münkler, Herfried. *Machiavelli: Die Begründung des politischen Denkens der Neuzeit aus der Krise der Republik Florenz*. Frankfurt: Europaische Verlaganstalt, 1982.

Namier, L. B. "The Character of Burke." *Spectator,* 19 Dec. 1958, 895–96.

Newell, W. R. "How Original Is Machiavelli? A Consideration of Skinner's Interpretation of Virtue and Fortune." *Political Theory* 15 (1987): 612–34.

———. "Machiavelli and Xenophon on Princely Rule: A Double-Edged Encounter." *Journal of Politics* 50 (1988): 108–30.

Orwin, Clifford. "Machiavelli's Unchristian Charity." *American Political Science Review* 72 (1978): 1217–28.

Paparelli, Gioacchino. "Virtù e fortuna nel medioevo, nel Rinascimento e in Machiavelli." *Cultura e Scuola* 9 (1970): 76–89

Parel, Anthony J. *The Machiavellian Cosmos*. New Haven: Yale University Press, 1992.

Pares, Richard. *King George III and the Politicians*. Oxford: Clarendon Press, 1953.

Paret, Peter. *Clausewitz and the State,* rev. ed. Princeton: Princeton University Press, 1985.

Petrarca, Francesco. *Opere Latine*. 2 vols. Edited by A. Bufano. Turin: UTET, 1975.

Pieri, Piero. *Guerra e politica negli scrittori italiani*. Milan: R. Ricciardi, 1954.

———. *Il Rinascimento e la crisi militare italiana*. Turin: G. Einaudi, 1952.

Pitkin, Hanna F. *Fortune Is a Woman*. Berkeley: University of California Press, 1984.

Plamenatz, John. "In Search of Machiavellian *Virtù*." In *The Political Calculus: Essays on Machiavelli's Philosophy*, edited by Anthony Parel. Toronto: University of Toronto Press, 1972.

Pocock, J. G. A. "Custom & Grace, Form & Matter: An Approach to Machiavelli's Concept of Innovation." In *Machiavelli and the Nature of Political Thought*, edited by Martin Fleisher. New York: Atheneum, 1972.

————. *The Machiavellian Moment*. Princeton: Princeton University Press, 1975.

Post, Gaines. *Studies in Medieval Legal Thought*. Princeton: Princeton University Press, 1964.

Powicke, F. M. "Reflections on the Medieval State." *Transactions of the Royal Historical Society* 19 (1936): 8–11.

Price, Russell. "The Senses of *Virtù* in Machiavelli. *European Studies Review* 3 (1973): 315–45.

————. "The Theme of *Gloria* in Machiavelli." *Renaissance Quarterly* 30 (1977): 588–631.

Quadri, Goffredo. *Niccolò Machiavelli e la costruzione politica della coscienza morale*. 2d ed. Florence: La nuova Italia, 1971.

Raimondi, Ezio. *Politica e commedia: Dal Beroaldo al Machiavelli*. Bologna: Mulino, 1972.

Rebhorn, Wayne A. *Foxes and Lions: Machiavelli's Confidence Men*. Ithaca: Cornell University Press, 1988.

Ridolfi, Roberto. *The Life of Niccolò Machiavelli*. Translated by C. Grayson. Chicago: University of Chicago Press, 1963.

————. *Vita di Girolamo Savonarola*. 2 vols. Rome: Belardetti, 1952.

————. *Vita di Niccolò Machiavelli*. Rev. ed. Florence: Sansoni, 1978.

Rowen, Herbert H. "L'ètat, c'est moi: Louis XIV and the State." *French Historical Studies* 2 (1961): 83–93.

Rubinstein, Nicolai. "Notes on the Word *Stato* in Florence before Machiavelli." In *Florilegium historiale*, edited by J. G. Rowe and W. H. Stockdale. Toronto: University of Toronto Press, 1971.

Salkever, Stephen G. *Finding the Mean: Theory and Practice in Aristotelian Political Philosophy*. Princeton: Princeton University Press, 1990.

Santini, E. "Leonardo Bruni Aretino e suoi *Historiarum florentini populi libri XII*." *Annali della R. Scuola Normale Superiore di Pisa* 22 (1910).

Sasso, Gennaro. *Il principe e altri scritti*. Florence: La Nuova Italia Editrice, 1963.

———. *In margine al V centenario de Machiavelli.* Naples: Guida editori, 1972.

———. "Intorno alla composizione dei 'Discorsi' di Niccolò Machiavelli." *Giornale storico della letteratura italiana* 135 (1958): 257.

———. *Machiavelli e gli antichi e altri saggi.* 3 vols. Milan: R. Ricciardi, 1987.

———. *Niccolò Machiavelli: Storia del suo pensiero politico.* Rev. ed. Bologna: Mulino, 1980.

———. *Studi su Machiavelli.* Naples: Morano, 1967.

Savonarola, Girolamo. *Prediche sopra Esodo.* 2 vols. Edited by P. G. Ricci. Rome: Belardetti, 1956.

———. *Prediche sopra Ezechiele.* 2. vols. Edited by Roberto Ridolfi. Rome: Belardetti, 1956.

Saxonhouse, Arlene. *Women in the History of Political Thought: Ancient Greece to Machiavelli.* New York: Praeger, 1985.

Schmitt, Carl. *Die Diktatur.* Berlin: Duncker und Humblot, 1964.

Shennan, J. H. *The Origins of the Modern European State, 1450–1725.* London: Hutchinson University Library, 1974.

Siegel, Jerrold. "Civic Humanism or Ciceronian Rhetoric." *Past and Present* 34 (1966): 32–44.

———. "*Virtù* in and since the Renaissance." In *Dictionary of the History of Ideas,* 4:476–86. New York, 1968.

Singleton, Charles S. "The Perspective of Art." *Kenyon Review* 15 (1953): 169–89.

Skinner, Quentin. *The Foundations of Modern Political Thought,* 2 vols. Cambridge: Cambridge University Press, 1978.

———. *Machiavelli.* New York: Hill and Wang, 1981.

Stanlis, Peter. *Edmund Burke and the Natural Law.* Ann Arbor: University of Michigan Press, 1958.

Stanlis, Peter J., ed. *Edmund Burke: Selected Writings and Speeches.* Garden City, N.Y., 1963.

Starkey, T. A. *A Dialogue between Reginald Pole and Thomas Lupset.* Edited by K. M. Burton. London: Chatto & Windus, 1948.

Sternberger, Dolf. *Machiavelli's "Principe" und der Begriff des Politischen.* Wiesbaden: Steiner, 1974.

Strauss, Leo. "Machiavelli and Classical Literature." *Review of National Literatures* 1 (1970): 7–25.

———. "Niccolò Machiavelli." In *History of Political Philosophy,* edited by Leo Strauss and Joseph Cropsey. 3d ed. Chicago: University of Chicago Press, 1987.

————. *The Political Philosophy of Hobbes,* 2d ed. Chicago: University of Chicago Press, 1952.

————. *Thoughts on Machiavelli.* Glencoe, Ill.: Free Press, 1958.

————. "Walker's Machiavelli." *Review of Metaphysics* 6 (1953): 437–46.

————. *What Is Political Philosophy?* Glencoe, Ill.: Free Press, 1959.

Strayer, Joseph R. *On the Medieval Origins of the Modern State.* Princeton: Princeton University Press, 1970.

Sullivan, Vickie B. "Machiavelli's Momentary 'Machiavellian Moment': A Reconsideration of Pocock's Treatment of the Discourses." *Political Theory* 20 (1992): 309–19.

Tarcov, N. "Political Thought in Early Modern Europe." *Journal of Modern History* 54 (1982): 63–64.

Tierney, Brian. "The Prince Is Not Bound by the Laws: Accursius and the Origins of the Modern State." In his *Church Law and Constitutional Thought in the Middle Ages.* London: Variorum Reprints, 1963.

————. *Religion, Law, and the Growth of Constitutional Thought, 1150–1650.* Cambridge: Cambridge University Press, 1982.

Toscano, Antonio. *Marsilio da Padova e Niccolò Machiavelli.* Ravenna: Longo, 1981.

Ullmann, Walter. *Law and Politics in the Middle Ages.* Ithaca: Cornell University Press, 1975.

————. *Principles of Government and Politics in the Middle Ages.* New York: Barnes and Noble, 1961.

Viroli, Maurizio. "Machiavelli and the Republican Idea of Politics." In *Machiavelli and Republicanism,* edited by Gisela Bock, Quentin Skinner, and Maurizio Viroli. New York: Cambridge University Press, 1990.

Vissing, Lars. *Machiavel et la politique de l'apparence.* Paris: Presses Universitaires de France, 1986.

Von Albertini, Rudolf. *Die Florentinische Staatsbewusstsein im Übergang von der Republik zum Prinzipät.* Bern: Francke, 1955.

Von Clausewitz, Karl. *Strategie.* Edited by E. Kessel. Hamburg: Hanseatische Verlaganstalt, 1937.

Walker, L. J., ed. *The Discourses of Niccolò Machiavelli.* 2 vols. London: Routledge and Kegan Paul, 1950.

Weston, John C., Jr. "Edmund Burke's View of History." *Review of Politics* 23 (1961): 203–29.

Whitfield, J. H. "Discourses on Machiavelli VII, Gilbert, Hexter and Baron." *Italian Studies* 13 (1958): 43–46.

————. *Machiavelli.* Oxford: Blackwell, 1947.

Wodehouse, P. G. *Right Ho, Jeeves.* London: H. Jenkins, 1936.

Wolin, Sheldon S. *Politics and Vision*. Boston: Little, Brown, 1960.

Wood, Neal. *Introduction to Machiavelli's "The Art of War."* Indianapolis: Bobbs Merrill, 1965.

————. "Machiavelli's Concept of *Virtù* Reconsidered." *Political Studies* 15 (1967): 159–72.

Zanzi, Luigi. *I "segni" della natura e i "paradigmi" della storia: Il metodo di Machiavelli*. Manduria: Lacaita, 1981.

Acciaiuoli, Donato, 131
accusation: and calumny, 241–43,
246; and elections, 241–42;
and executive power, 300, 305,
307–8; and "extraordinary
means," 244–47, 250–51, 255;
and indirect government, 235;
and party government, 241–
42; in Rome, 247–50, 307;
and Savonarola, 98
Achilles, 269
acquisition, 13–16; in Aristotle,
13–14; and Burke's theory of
prescription, 104; in *Discourses,* 14; and foreign affairs,
303; and fortune, 47–48; and
indirect government, 238; and
inheritance, 13–16; and necessity, 14–15; in *The Prince,* 14,
181–83, 186–88; and republics, 23–24; and state, 290–91,
293–94
Acton, Lord, 10
Aeneas, 64–66, 69, 83
Agathocles the Sicilian, 6, 18, 40,
184, 187
Agis, king of Sparta, 9
Alamanni, Luigi, 194, 210
Albizzi, Piero degli, 166
Albizzi, Rinaldo degli, 141–42
Albizzi family, 166, 173
Alexander II, pope, 163
Alexander VI, 291

Alexander the Great, 64, 72–74,
76, 212, 217, 269, 289
Alexandria, 64, 72–73, 76
Ancus, king of Rome, 31, 77
*anima. See* soul
*animo. See* spirit
Antony, Mark, 35–36
Aquileia, 65
Aquinas, Thomas, 285–86
Aratus of Sicyon, 44
Aristotle, xiv, 30, 52, 55, 83, 117;
on ancient virtue, 3, 11–13,
14, 17–18, 20–22, 23, 42–43,
45, 48, 186; and acquisition,
13–14; and Burke, 100, 105;
and Christianity, 279; and civic
humanism, 197; in *Discourses,*
12; on domestic affairs, 91,
302–3; on executive power,
295–98, 312; on fortune, 48;
on justice, 21–22, 256–57,
299–300, 312; and party government, 165; on political science, 236–38; *The Prince* and,
12, 181; on prudence, 39, 270,
309–10; on rationality, 37; on
regimes, 71, 96, 112–13, 115,
282–84, 288–89, 291–93; on
republican virtue, 22–24; on
revolution, 112–15; on soul,
13, 276–78
*Art of War,* 46, 191–218; on authority, 211–13; on chance,

Hobbes, Thomas (*continued*)
39; political science of, 272; on
prudence, 43, 202; and Strauss,
220
Homer, 269
Horatius, 240
humanism, 11, 31–36, 194–98;
and *Art of War*, 126, 194–98,
203–5; and Christianity, 126.
*See also* history, humanist
human natures (humors): and acquisition, 75–76; in *Discourses*, 92–93, 95–97; and executive power, 304–5, 307,
311; in *Florentine Histories*,
150–53, 172–73; and indirect
government, 237–38; and modern state, 115; and morality,
24; and party government, 86,
92–93, 95; in *The Prince*, 186;
and virtue, 37–38
humors of men. *See* human natures

imperialism, 85–88, 91–92. *See
also* foreign affairs
indirect government, xiv, 235–38,
247–50, 306–8; and accusation, 235; and acquisition, 238;
and conspiracy, 255; and human natures, 237–38; Machiavelli's writing as, xvi; in Rome,
247–49, 250–53
*Inferno* (Dante), 166
inheritance, 13–16, 102, 104, 183
interpretation, 57–62; classical republican, xii, xiv-xv, 233; numerology and, xv–xvi; by
Strauss, 219–30
Isocrates, 273
*Italia mia* (Petrarch), 34
Italy, 35, 158; in *Florentine Histories*, 128, 140, 144, 147; and
Machiavelli's patriotism, 50,
109, 182; party government in,

161–64, 170–71; unification
of, x, 178, 183, 275, 277–78

Jesus Christ, xi, 4, 73
Joanna, queen of Naples, 162
Joan of Arc, 212
John, king of Bohemia, 164
Julius II, pope, 42, 51, 189, 272
*Julius Caesar* (Shakespeare), 52
justice, 239–40; Aristotle on,
21–22, 256–57, 299–300,
312; criminal, 254; and domestic affairs, 302–3; and executive power, 299–300; in *The
Prince*, 180–81; and virtue,
17–19

Kant, Immanuel, 42
Kendall, Willmoore, 222

Lamberti, Mosca, 165–68
Lando, Michele di, 27–28
*Laws* (Plato), 83, 269
Lefort, Claude, 223
Leopardi, Giacomo, 20
"Life of Cyrus, The" (Xenophon).
*See* "Education of Cyrus, The"
Livy, Titus, 11, 78, 83, 93, 117,
132, 246; on execution, 309;
fraud, use of, 61; and indirect
government, 248; and Machia-
velli's novelty, 261; and politi-
cal science, 85, 236; and
Strauss, 221, 225, 227, 229
Locke, John, 28, 39, 104–5, 114,
314
Lucretius, 42, 59
Ludovicus de Valentia, 286
Lycurgus, 84, 89, 91, 116, 274

Macaulay, Thomas Babington, 10
Machiavellism, xi, 27, 47, 193,
220, 225–26, 230. *See also*
evil; morality
management, 28–30, 237–38. *See
also* indirect government